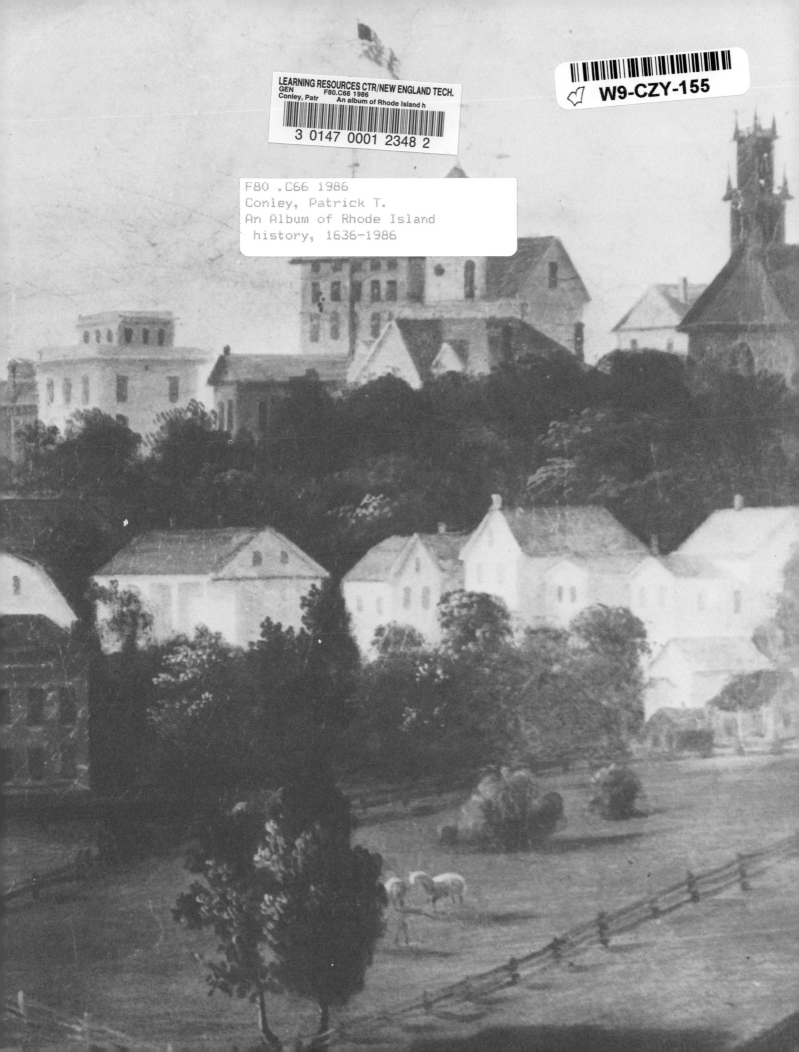

AN ALBUM OF
RHODE ISLAND
HISTORY
1636-1986

The Donning Company/Publishers
Norfolk/Virginia Beach

AN ALBUM OF
RHODE ISLAND
HISTORY, 1636-1986

By
Patrick T. Conley

Designed By Jamie Baccus Raynor

The Donning Company/Publishers
5659 Virginia Beach Boulevard
Norfolk, Virginia 23502

Library of Congress Cataloging-in-Publication Data

Conley, Patrick T.
    An album of Rhode Island history, 1636–1986.

    Bibliography: p.
    Includes index.
    1. Rhode Island—History—Pictorial works.
2. Rhode Island—Description and travel—Views. I. Title.
F80.C66   1986   974.5   86-29148
ISBN 0-89865-513-7

Contents

Foreword

As it has been since the tale began, this is a story about our lives told with pictures. It is a history of Rhode Island and its people on the occasion of Rhode Island's 350th anniversary as a state.

With our cameras, we at WLNE Television are in the business of recording history in the making, and so it seems fitting that we should sponsor the publication of this book, which was compiled for us by the noted Rhode Island historian Patrick T. Conley.

Among the pages which follow are the faces of many who have been here before us. Look into their eyes and you will see how very slightly changed we really are. The lives they led we are living now, the dreams they dreamed are ours. It is the tale of where we have been and where we are headed. It is our story, those of us who are here now, and those who will come in a while. . .we are one of a kind.

Preface

Having coauthored a pictorial history of Providence in 1982 on the occasion of the 150th anniversary of its incorporation as a city, I harbored the urge to produce a similar book as my contribution to the 350th anniversary of Rhode Island's founding as an English colony. After twenty years of teaching Rhode Island history at Providence College, I wanted to distill my lectures and random research into a coherent, interpretative essay directed at the general reader. The chapter introductions in this volume attempt such a synthesis, while the photos and captions are intended to highlight major themes, events, and personages in the state's history. The book's graphics were selected for their ability to convey a message of historical import rather than for their aesthetic quality or curiosity value.

When, despite persistent attempts, I could not secure public sponsorship for this effort, Dave Layman and his WLNE-TV6 colleagues salvaged the project with a generous grant to finance publication. This history is also their substantive contribution to the state's birthday celebration—a party at which substance has been noticeably lacking.

Because I intended this to be a companion volume to *Providence: A Pictorial History,* I encountered several problems, especially that of duplication, which were not completely overcome. In addition to being the first settlement, Providence has played the dominant role in Rhode Island history from the American Revolution to the present; at the dawn of this century four of every ten Rhode Islanders lived in the state's capital city. It is therefore necessary that Providence be given prominent treatment in any balanced history of the state, and I have worked herein to achieve that balance, even though it has meant the repetition of a few photos and captions from the earlier volume. But I have tried to make certain, too, that no area of the state has been slighted and that all major themes (of which I am aware) have received as much attention as a pictorial history of this scope and format will admit. Whether I have succeeded in that attempt is for the reader to judge.

As always, my debt to others is large. Joyce Botelho and Denise Bastien, graphics curators at the Rhode Island Historical Society, located and assembled the pictures that I had selected; Gail Cahalan expended long hours assisting me in that selection process; my oldest daughter, Kathleen Conley, prepared the manuscript for the publisher with seemingly endless copying and collating; and Phyllis Cardullo typed and retyped the entire volume. Dr. Hilliard Beller of the Rhode Island Publications Society copyedited and proofread the book with great patience and expertise, and Paul Campbell, coauthor of the Providence book, assisted me in writing the material on the Indians and the modern era.

Pictures and illustrations were derived from many repositories and private individuals, all of whom are acknowledged in the captions. Some contributors, however, were repeatedly and consistently helpful, especially Jeanne Richardson of the Providence Public Library, Jane Jackson of the Providence College Archives, and my good friend and longtime colleague in the book trade Mildred Santille Longo of Fortunate Finds Book Shop.

At times during the summer of '86, when most of this book was written, the repeated interruptions caused by my law practice and business pursuits made me question the wisdom of this undertaking, and perhaps the pressure to complete it during the 350th anniversary year has caused omissions or other flaws that greater care and sober reflection could have remedied. Hopefully I will be the book's severest critic; but if I am not, I take refuge in an observation of John Cardinal Newman: "Nothing would be done at all if a man waited till he could do it so well that no one could find fault with it."

Patrick T. Conley
Providence
September 11, 1986

This scene by artist Bob Selby authentically recreates the summer life-style of the Narragansett Indians (and that of surrounding coastal tribes). In spring each family raised a bark- or mat-covered wigwam near the coast, planted its corn, beans, squash, and pumpkins, and hunted and fished. In this graphic the woman at the right grinds corn into meal with mortar and pestle, a child sits in the corn-watch tower to frighten crows, and the men prepare to eat their dinner of fish and game. In winter the Indians abandoned the exposed shore to live in communal longhouses deep in the forest. Color illustration courtesy of the Providence Journal Company (PJC)

Primitive people of Asiatic origin, mistakenly named "Indians" by Columbus, were the first inhabitants of present-day Rhode Island. Archaeological evidence indicates their presence in this area more than eight thousand years ago.

European contacts with Rhode Island and its coastline have been claimed for several explorers, including medieval Irish adventurers sailing in skin-boats called currachs, Norsemen or Vikings (who were once thought to be the builders of the Newport Tower), and the daring Portuguese navigator Miguel Corte-Real, who allegedly carved his name and a series of symbols into Dighton Rock in the nearby Taunton River. None of these visitations has been substantiated beyond reasonable doubt, though each has its scholarly supporters. Therefore, the 1524 voyage of Italian navigator Giovanni Verrazzano stands as the first verifiable visit to Rhode Island by a European adventurer.

Verrazzano made his famous trip, searching for an all-water route through North America to China, in the employ of the French king Francis I and several Italian promoters. After landfall at Cape Fear, North Carolina, about March 1, 1524, he proceeded up the coast to the present site of New York City to anchor in the Narrows, now spanned by the giant bridge which bears his name. From there, according to his own account, he sailed in an easterly direction until he "discovered an island in the form of a triangle, distant from the mainland ten leagues, about the bigness of the Island of the Rhodes," which he named Luisa after the queen mother of France. This was Block Island, but Roger Williams and other early settlers mistakenly thought that Verrazzano had been referring to Aquidneck. Thus they changed that Indian name to Rhode Island, and Verrazzano inadvertently and indirectly gave the state its name.

Natives who paddled out to his ship off Point Judith were so friendly that Verrazzano sailed with their guidance into Narragansett Bay to a second anchorage in what is now Newport harbor. He remained for two weeks while his crew surveyed the bay and the surrounding mainland, noting the fertile soil, the woods of oak and walnut, and such game as lynx and deer. Their observations on the dress and customs of their hosts, probably the Wampanoags, were also most revealing. In early May 1524 Verrazzano departed to press on in a vain search for a northwesterly passage to the Orient.

For ninety years following Verrazzano's visit,

most European voyagers to North America unsuccessfully sought that elusive northwest passage or productively fished the Grand Banks off Newfoundland. In either case, their travels kept them far to the north of the Rhode Island coast. Not until 1614 were other significant visitations to Rhode Island made and recorded. In that year John Smith of Virginia fame explored and charted the New England coast and bestowed upon this region its name, while Dutch mariner Adriaen Block, en route to or from the Hudson River, visited Block Island and immodestly named it for himself.

From 1620 onward, the Dutch and settlers from nearby Plymouth Colony and the Massachusetts Bay Colony (established in 1628) ventured into the Narragansett region to trade with the Indian tribes. Finally, in 1635, the area that is now Rhode Island got its first permanent white settler—William Blackstone, an eccentric Anglican clergyman who built a home near Lonsdale on the east bank of the river which came to bear his name.

Blackstone and others who followed him found the area inhabited by several Indian tribes. The largest of these was the Narragansetts. These natives were part of the Algonquin family of Indian nations, a loose network of related peoples whose habitat stretched from what is now southern Canada to present-day North Carolina. Before the establishment of the permanent white settlements in New England, the Narragansetts occupied the area of Rhode Island from Warwick southward along Narragansett Bay to the present towns of South Kingstown and Exeter. The rest of Rhode Island was populated by other Algonquins, some friendly, some bitter enemies of the Narragansetts.

The Wampanoags were undoubtedly the Narragansett's principal rivals. Their sphere of influence extended throughout much of the eastern shore of Narragansett Bay and included Bristol Neck, portions of southeastern Massachusetts, Pawtucket, and parts of Lincoln and Cumberland. At the apex of their power the Wampanoags may have held many of the islands in the bay as well as territory within the present bounds of Providence and Warwick.

The Nipmucks, a weak tribe by comparison with the Narragansetts and the Wampanoags, maintained a tenuous foothold in what is now the northwesterly corner of the state. Initially tributaries of the Wampanoags, the Nipmucks by 1630 came under the yoke of the expanding Narragansetts, a fate that also befell two subtribes in the Warwick area, the Cowesetts and the Shawomets.

On the southern coast the Eastern Niantics populated much of the area now occupied by the towns of Charlestown and Westerly. It appears that they were driven out of Connecticut by the warlike Pequots sometime late in the sixteenth century. The Pequots—who took their name from an Algonquin word meaning destroyer—continued their expansion eastward, and in 1632 they engaged in a bitter war with the Narragansetts for control of the area just east of the Pawcatuck River in Westerly

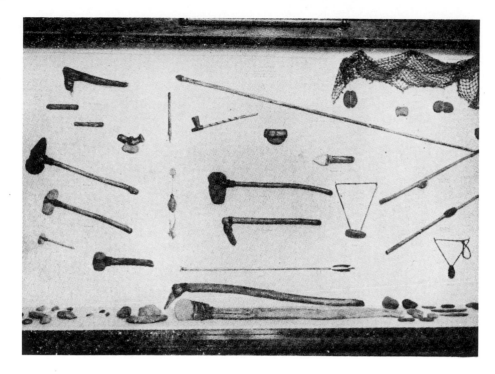

This exhibit of Indian artifacts (mostly Wampanoag) was collected by the Bronson Museum in Attleboro, Massachusetts. Photo from Milton A. Travers, The Wampanoag Indian Federation *(1961)*

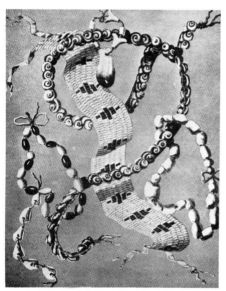

The Indians (and, later, Dutch, French, and English traders) used hard-shelled mollusks to fashion wampum as a medium of exchange. Roger Williams, in his Key into the Language of America *(1643), the first English-language dictionary of Indian words and customs, described two kinds of wampum: one white, made of periwinkles, six of which were equal in value to the English penny; and a second of black or blue quahog shells, three of which equaled the penny. Governor William Bradford of Plymouth noted that the Narragansett tribe, especially, had amassed large amounts of these valuable seashells, which made them "rich and potent." Wampum was made by grinding the thick section of a shell into a bead, which was then rubbed to a high polish and strung. Photo from Noble F. Hoggson,* Epochs in American Banking *(1929)*

and Hopkinton.

Informed anthropologists have estimated the Narragansett population at about seven thousand persons when the first white settlers arrived. This rough estimate also includes the Niantics, who were related to the Narragansetts by marriage and shared the same customs and language. These Indians subsisted on farming, fishing, and hunting. Roles were strictly defined in Algonquin society, and the women decidedly had the worst of it. Besides childbearing, females were responsible for planting, harvesting, toting of material possessions in their villages' seasonal relocations, preparation of food, shellfishing, utensil manufacture, and the erection of wigwams (the bark huts of the Indians). Men, on the other hand, performed the far less strenuous duties of fishing and hunting, and they spent a good deal of time in recreational activities.

The Narragansetts and Niantics lived in compact villages that were composed of families of shared kinship. Village leaders, sometimes called sub-sachems or petty sachems, answered to a higher authority. For the Narragansetts, the ultimate government leadership rested in the hands of two men, called chief sachems, who claimed an exalted status by virtue of royal blood. When Roger Williams founded the town of Providence, Canonicus and his young nephew Miantonomi reigned as the two chief sachems of the Narragansetts.

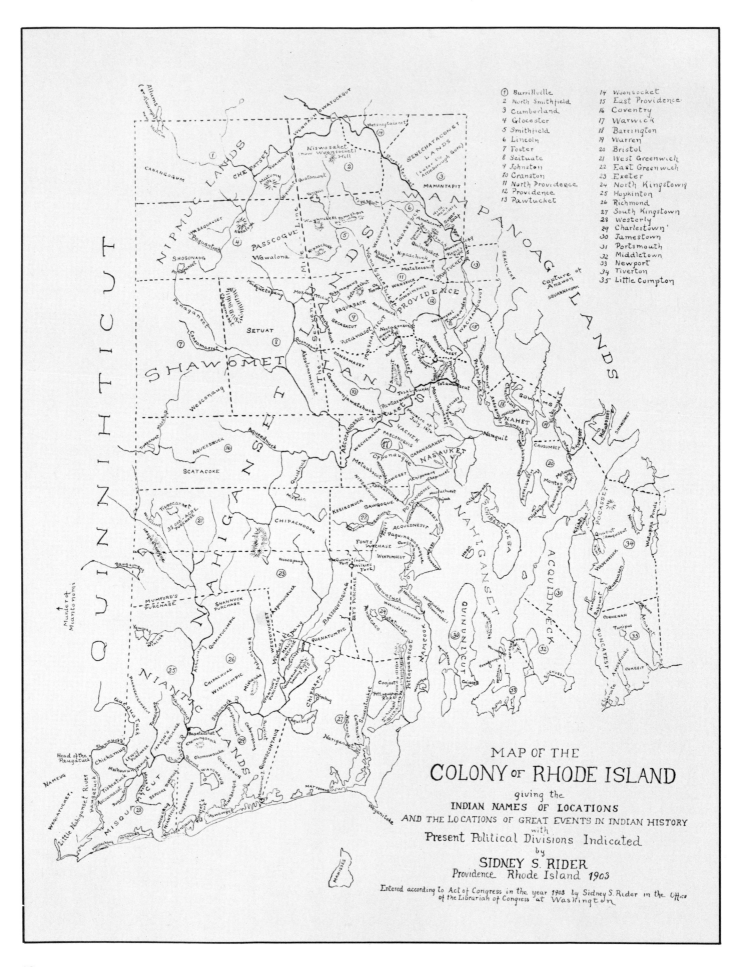

MAP OF THE
COLONY OF RHODE ISLAND
giving the
INDIAN NAMES OF LOCATIONS
AND THE LOCATIONS OF GREAT EVENTS IN INDIAN HISTORY
with
Present Political Divisions Indicated
by
SIDNEY S. RIDER
Providence Rhode Island 1903

Entered according to Act of Congress in the year 1903 by Sidney S. Rider in the Office
of the Librarian of Congress at Washington

1 Burrillville
2 North Smithfield
3 Cumberland
4 Glocester
5 Smithfield
6 Lincoln
7 Foster
8 Scituate
9 Johnston
10 Cranston
11 North Providence
12 Providence
13 Pawtucket
14 Woonsocket
15 East Providence
16 Coventry
17 Warwick
18 Barrington
19 Warren
20 Bristol
21 West Greenwich
22 East Greenwich
23 Exeter
24 North Kingstown
25 Hopkinton
26 Richmond
27 South Kingstown
28 Westerly
29 Charlestown
30 Jamestown
31 Portsmouth
32 Middletown
33 Newport
34 Tiverton
35 Little Compton

12

Once thought to be the handiwork of Norsemen (Vikings), Newport's old stone tower stands stolidly in Touro Park off Bellevue Avenue on land that once belonged to Benedict Arnold (1615-1677), Rhode Island's first governor under the charter of 1663 and the ancestor of the infamous Revolutionary War general. The structure was saved from demolition in the mid-nineteenth century by noted philanthropist Judah Touro (1775-1854), who bequeathed a fund to the city of Newport for the acquisition of grounds surrounding the mill to be laid out as a public park.

Thorough excavations of the foundations and surroundings of the tower in 1948-49 by Harvard archaeologist William S. Godfrey, Jr., have proved beyond any reasonable doubt that the structure was built around 1670 as a windmill that might possibly double as a fortress in the event of Indian attack. All artifacts uncovered, including coins, pieces of millstone, and clay pipes, were English colonial. However, the Viking name persists in Newport today, borne by a major hotel, the teams of Rogers High School, and several commercial enterprises. *Photo from Richard Alan Dow and E. Andrew Mowbray,* Newport *(1976)*

Although most leading authorities on the Age of Discovery reject the claim, some reputable scholars allege that Miguel Corte-Real of Portugal was the first European to explore Rhode Island's coastal areas. Typical of the hardy Portuguese adventurers who ushered in that era, this daring navigator left Lisbon in 1502 both to search for his brother's lost expedition and to explore the New World, but his own ill-fated expedition was never heard from again. Some historians theorize that he was shipwrecked along the New England coast, made his way to the Mount Hope Bay region, and lived for several years along local Wampanoag Indians. According to this hypothesis, Corte-Real inscribed his name, the Portuguese coat of arms, the Cruz de Cristo of the Portuguese Military Order of Christ, and the date 1511 on a large sandstone boulder at Assonet Neck in the Taunton River. This Dighton Writing-Rock is still preserved, but the existence and authenticity of Corte-Real's inscription is the source of considerable, though inconclusive, controversy. *Photo (1907) with preliminary chalking by Charles A. Hathaway from Patrick T. Conley and Matthew J. Smith,* Catholicism in Rhode Island: The Formative Era *(1976)*

In April 1524, while sailing in the employ of King Francis I of France in search of a route to China, Giovanni da Verrazzano (1485–1528) made the first verifiable exploration of Rhode Island by a European navigator. Four years later, on a voyage to the Caribbean, he became the victim of cannibals. This depiction of the Italian mariner is a late sixteenth-century copy of an earlier Florentine portrait; no likeness made in Verrazzano's own lifetime is known to exist. Portrait from Samuel Eliot Morison, The European Discovery of America: The Northern Voyages (1971)

Samuel Eliot Morison, the foremost authority on early American voyages of discovery, prepared this map of Verrazzano's 1524 visitation. The explorer called Block Island "Luisa" in honor of the queen mother of France and likened Aquidneck to the Mediterranean Isle of Rhodes. He named the Dumpling Rocks off Jamestown "Petra Viva" for the voluptuous wife of a banker who helped fund his expedition.

Verrazzano anchored in the harbor of present-day Newport and spent fifteen days exploring the entire Narragansett Bay region. He reported to his royal sponsor that he had observed fertile open fields, forests of oak and cypress, "many kinds of fruit," an "enormous number of animals—stags, deer, lynx, and other species"—and friendly natives. The Italian described the Indians (probably Wampanoags) glowingly: "These people are the most beautiful and have the most civil customs that we have found on this voyage. They are taller than we are; they are a bronze color, some tending more toward whiteness, others to a tawny color; the face is clear-cut; the hair is long and black, and they take great pains to decorate it; the eyes are black and alert, and their manner is sweet and gentle. . . ." Map from Morison, The European Discovery of America: The Northern Voyages (1971)

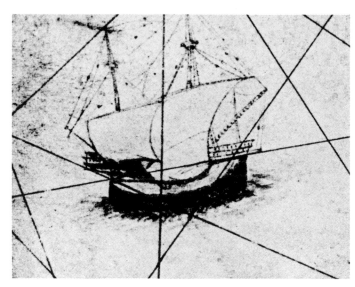

Sketched on a map prepared several years after the voyage, this caravel is probably La Dauphine, the vessel that Verrazzano commanded on his 1524 visit to Rhode Island. The caravel was a notable advance in ship design. It was a craft of fifty tons burden and upwards (La Dauphine was one hundred tons burden), measuring from twenty to thirty meters in length and from six to eight meters in breadth. It carried a crew of from twelve to fifty men (La Dauphine carried fifty). With a castle at the stern and two or three masts, it had lateen sails stretched on long poles suspended from the masthead. These sails allowed the caravel to sail to windward (toward the wind). Photo of a section of the Vatican Verrazzano Map from Morison, The European Discovery of America: The Northern Voyages (1971)

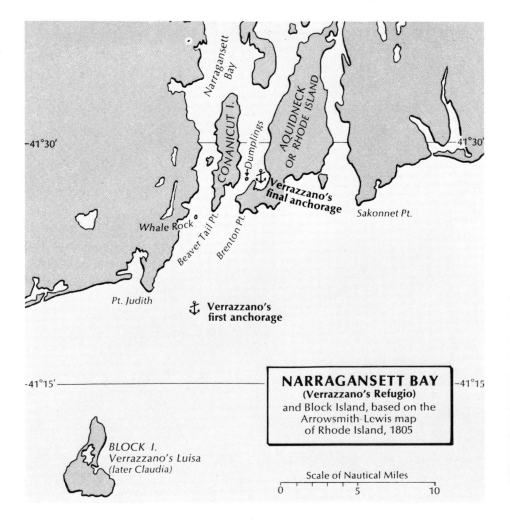

NARRAGANSETT BAY
(Verrazzano's Refugio)
and Block Island, based on the Arrowsmith-Lewis map of Rhode Island, 1805

Scale of Nautical Miles
0   5   10

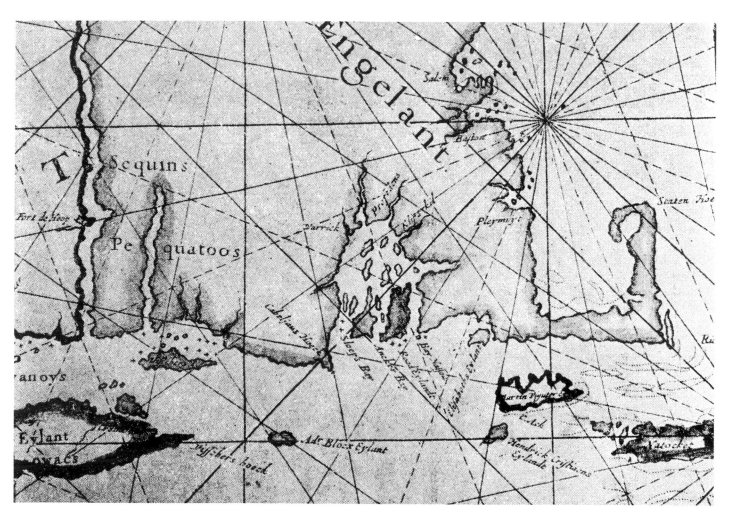

In 1614, on an expedition to establish the colony of New Netherland, the Dutch navigator Adriaen Block landed on Verrazzano's island of Luisa and named it for himself. For two decades thereafter, Dutch merchants visited not only Block Island but coastal Rhode Island as well. They established two trading posts, or forts, in Charlestown (one has been called Ninigret's Fort by those who believe it is of Indian construction) and lent their name to Dutch Island off Jamestown. On this 1648 Dutch map, the west passage of Narragansett Bay is called Sloop's Bay; the east passage, Anchor Bay; and the Sakonnet River, Nassau Bay. The Warren River, which the Dutch used to reach Massasoit's village of Sowams, they called Klips Kil. *Map photo from Sidney S. Rider,* The Lands of Rhode Island *(1903)*

Massasoit (ca. 1580–1661), chief sachem of the Wampanoags, greeted the Pilgrims in 1621 and sheltered Roger Williams in 1636 during the latter's winter exile. Father of Metacomet (or King Philip) and Wamsutta (Alexander), Massasoit was described in 1621 as a "very lusty man" with "an able body, grave of countenance and spare of speech." Though the strength of his tribe was greatly weakened by a devastating epidemic that raged from 1616 to 1619, he held sway over southeastern Massachusetts and eastern Rhode Island when the first English colonists arrived. His principal settlement was Sowams in present-day Barrington and Warren. Model of Massasoit's statue atop Cole's Hill in Plymouth, Massachusetts, sculpted by Cyrus O. Dallin, courtesy of the Pilgrim Society

The figure of the Indians fort or Palisado in NEW ENGLAND And the maner of the destroying It by Captayne Vnderhill And Captayne Mason

The Pequots were the first southern New England tribe to feel the wrath of the English colonists. Based in southeastern Connecticut, the warlike Pequots had extended their tribal domain into present-day Westerly and Hopkinton at the expense of the Narragansetts. In the early summer of 1636 they were erroneously blamed for the murder of an English trader on Block Island named John Oldham, prompting a declaration of war against them by the Puritans. In May 1637 a Connecticut army under John Mason and John Underhill, assisted by Mohegan and Narragansett Indians, surprised the Pequots in their town at Mystic.

As this contemporary drawing indicates, an outer ring of Indians and an inner circle of English rained arrows and musket balls into the palisaded Pequot stronghold, killing (according to conflicting eyewitness accounts) from four hundred to seven hundred men, women, and children. The remnants of the tribe in outlying areas were chased, caught, and either executed, enslaved by the Puritans, or integrated into the ranks of the Mohegans, Narragansetts, or Niantics. The tribe itself was disbanded. Illustration from John Underhill, Newes from America (1638), courtesy of the New York Public Library

17

William Blackstone (1595–1675) was the first Englishman to settle on the present site of Boston, and in 1635 he became the first to settle permanently within the present bounds of Rhode Island. This eccentric Anglican minister made his home at a site he called Study Hill, near Lonsdale on the east bank of the river that now bears his name. This area (actually acquired first by Plymouth Colony) was annexed by Rhode Island in 1746.

In 165_ Blackstone married a Boston widow who bore him one son. He some- *times visited Providence for supplies, books, and other necessities, traveling to and fro perched on the back of a large white bull. Blackstone died just before the outbreak of King Philip's War, a conflict that brought destruction to his house and extensive library. This monument to the recluse who gave his name to many sites and present-day business ventures in northeastern Rhode Island stands on Broad Street in Valley Falls. Photo from* Edward J. Hayden, Cumberland, Rhode Island: Historical Story (1976).

THE COLONIAL ERA, 1636-1763

Rhode Island's first permanent settlement was established at the head of Narragansett Bay in 1636 by English clergyman Roger Williams and a small band of followers who had left the repressive atmosphere of the Massachusetts Bay Colony to seek freedom of worship. Canonicus and Miantonomi granted Williams a sizable tract of land for his new village, which he named Providence. Other nonconformists followed Williams to the bay region, including Anne and William Hutchinson and William Coddington, all of whom founded Portsmouth in 1638 as a haven for Antinomians, a religious sect whose beliefs resembled those of Quakerism. A short-lived dispute sent Coddington to the southern tip of Aquidneck Island (also purchased from the Narragansetts), where he established Newport in 1639. The fourth original town, Warwick, was settled in 1642 by Samuel Gorton, another dissident from Portsmouth. During this initial decade two other outposts were established: Wickford (1637), by Richard Smith and Roger Williams, and Pawtuxet (1638), by William Harris and the Arnold family.

Because titles to the settlers' holdings rested only on Indian deeds, neighboring colonies began to covet these lands. To meet this threat, Roger Williams journeyed to England and secured a parliamentary patent in March 1644 uniting the four towns into a single colony and confirming his fellow settlers' land claims. This legislative document served adequately as the basic law until the Stuart Restoration of 1660 made it wise to seek a royal charter.

Dr. John Clarke was then commissioned to secure a document from the new king, Charles II, that would both be consistent with the religious principles upon which the tiny colony was founded and also safeguard Rhode Island lands from encroachment by speculators and greedy neighbors. He succeeded admirably. The royal charter of 1663 guaranteed complete religious liberty, established a self-governing colony with local autonomy, and strengthened Rhode Island's territorial claims. It was the most liberal charter to be issued by the mother country during the entire colonial era, a fact that enabled it to serve as Rhode Island's basic law until May 1843.

The religious freedom which prevailed in early Rhode Island made it a refuge for several persecuted sects. America's first Baptist church was formed in Providence in 1639; Quakers, who merged with the Antinomians, established a meetinghouse on Aquidneck in 1657 and soon became a powerful force in the

Roger Williams was banished from Massachusetts Bay Colony by its Puritan leaders because of his unorthodox views advocating the complete separation of church and state and his belief that the Indians should be paid for their land when whites settled on it. This mid-nineteenth century romantic painting by Peter F. Rothermel depicts Williams departing from Salem into a gloomy and forbidding winter wilderness, armed only with Bible and staff. Fortunately Williams was sheltered by Massasoit and the Wampanoags, whom he had befriended and visited while a minister at Plymouth.

Of Indian hospitality, Williams later wrote:

I've known them to leave their
house and mat
To lodge a friend or stranger
When Jews and Christians oft have sent
Christ Jesus to the Manger.

Painting in oil on canvas courtesy of the Rhode Island Historical Society (RIHS) (Rhi x3 3102)

colony's political and economic life; a Jewish congregation came to Newport in 1658; and French Huguenots (Calvinists) settled in East Greenwich in 1686 on a site still called Frenchtown.

The most important and traumatic event in seventeenth-century Rhode Island was King Philip's War (1675-76), the culmination of a four-decade decline in Indian-white relations. Roger Williams had won the grudging respect of his colonial neighbors for his diplomatic skill in keeping the powerful Narragansetts on friendly terms with local white settlers. In 1637 the Narragansetts were in fact persuaded to form an alliance with the English in carrying out a punitive expedition that extinguished the warlike Pequots. But by 1670 even the friendly tribes who had greeted Williams and the Pilgrims had become estranged from the white colonists, and the storm clouds of war began to darken the New England countryside.

Clashes in culture, the appropriation by whites of Indian land for their exclusive ownership, and a series of hostile incidents between the Wampanoag chief King Philip (Metacomet) and the aggressive

government of Plymouth Colony resulted in the terrible colonial conflict called King Philip's War. This futile struggle to rid New England of the white man consumed the lives of several thousand Indians and more than six hundred whites and resulted in enormous property damage.

The Narragansetts, at first neutral, joined forces with the Wampanoags after a Plymouth force staged a sneak attack on the Narragansetts' principal village in the Great Swamp (South Kingstown) in December 1675. The Great Swamp Fight cost the lives of three hundred braves and almost four hundred women and children. The Narragansetts regrouped and launched a vengeful offensive the following spring. On March 26 a large war party led by chief sachem Canonchet massacred a company of approximately sixty-five Englishmen and twenty friendly Indians led by Captain Michael Pierce on the banks of the Blackstone in present-day Central Falls. Three days later the victorious Narragansetts descended upon defenseless Providence, burning most of the buildings in that town. For Williams, who witnessed the event, it represented the destruction of four decades of hard-

20

This 1884 engraving by Rhode Island artist T. F. Hoppin is one of several attempts to depict the landing of Roger Williams at Slate Rock on the west bank of the Seekonk River in the spring of 1636. At that time the Seekonk was the western boundary of Plymouth Colony and also separated the tribal lands of the Wam-

panoags and the Narragansetts. The Indians who welcomed Williams on this auspicious spring day, and exchanged the salutation "What Cheer, Netop," were Narrangansetts.

The founders bypassed this rocky, hilly site and paddled around Fox Point and up the Great Salt River to a spacious cove.

There, on the east bank near a freshwater spring (where Roger Williams National Memorial has been recently established), they laid out their settlement. Having "a sense of God's merciful providence unto me in my distress," said Williams, I "called the place Providence." Engraving courtesy of RIHS (Rhi x3 2036)

earned progress.

But famine, disease, and wartime casualties soon decimated the ranks of the Narragansetts and their Wampanoag allies. The killing of King Philip in August 1676 by an Indian allied with the whites effectively ended the war. Remnants of the Narragansetts and Wampanoags sought refuge with the peaceful Niantics, who had remained neutral. This aggregate of remnant groups became the foundation of a new Indian community in Rhode Island that ultimately assumed the name Narragansett.

Other important seventeenth-century developments included the interruption in government caused by James II's abortive Dominion for New England (1686-1689), which was a vain effort to consolidate the northern colonies under royal governor Edmund Andros, and the beginning of the intermittent colonial wars between England and France (1689-1763), a seventy-five-year struggle for empire that frequently involved Rhode Island men, money, and ships. By the end of the seventeenth century, Newport—unscathed by King Philip's War—had emerged as a prosperous port and the

colony's dominant community, nine towns had been incorporated, and the population exceeded six thousand.

The first quarter of the eighteenth century was marked by the long and able governorship of Samuel Cranston (1698-1727), who established internal unity and brought his colony into a better working relationship with the imperial government in London.

The middle decades of this century were characterized by significant growth. Newport continued to prosper commercially, but Providence now began to challenge for supremacy. With this rivalry assuming political dimensions, by the 1740s a system of two-party politics developed. Opposing groups, one headed by Samuel Ward and the other by Stephen Hopkins, were organized with sectional overtones. Generally speaking (though there were notable exceptions), the merchants and farmers of Newport and South County (Ward's faction) battled with their counterparts from Providence and its environs (led by Hopkins) to secure control of the powerful legislature for the vast patronage at the disposal of that body.

A major boundary dispute with Connecticut was

This original deed to Roger Williams from the Narragansett Indian sachems Canonicus (who represented himself with a bow) and Miantonomi (who signed with an arrow) was executed on March 24, 1638. It confirmed earlier verbal grants. "Not a penny was demanded by either," wrote Williams, "It was not price nor money that could have purchased Rhode Island. Rhode Island was purchased by love."

The first town boundaries, established by this document (called the "town evidence"), extended from a point just above Pawtucket Falls on the north, southwesterly to Neutaconkanut Hill, thence southeasterly to the mouth of the Pawtuxet River. The Blackstone, Seekonk, and Providence rivers served as the eastern boundary. Photograph from Sidney S. Rider, The Lands of Rhode Island *(1903) from original in Providence City Archives*

resolved in 1727, and a very favorable settlement with Massachusetts in 1747 resulted in the annexation of Cumberland and the East Bay towns of Tiverton, Little Compton, Warren (which then included Barrington), and Bristol. The spread of agriculture on the mainland resulted in the subdivision of Providence and other early towns. By 1774 the colony had 59,707 residents, who lived in twenty-nine incorporated municipalities.

By the mid-eighteenth century the spacious farm plantations of South County, utilizing the labor of black and Indian slaves, reached the peak of their prosperity. Here and in the rolling fields of the island towns, colonial farmers raised livestock, especially sheep and a renowned carriage horse aptly named the Narragansett Pacer, and cultivated such commodities as apples, onions, flax, and dairy products. The virgin forests yielded lumber for boards, planks, timber, and barrels, and the sea provided whales and an abundance of fish for food and fertilizer. Most of these items soon became valuable exports for Rhode Island's ever-expanding trade network.

By the end of the colonial era, Rhode Island had developed a brisk commerce with the entire Atlantic community, including England, the Portuguese islands, Africa, South America, the West Indies, and other British mainland colonies. Though agriculture was far and away the dominant occupation, commercial activities flourished in Newport, Providence, and Bristol and in lesser ports like Pawtuxet, Wickford, East Greenwich, Warren, and Westerly. The most lucrative and nefarious aspect of this commerce was the slave trade, an enterprise in which Rhode Island merchants outdid those of any other mainland colony. Their traffic formed one leg of a triangular route which brought molasses from the West Indies to Rhode Island, whose distilleries transformed it to rum. This liquor was bartered along the African coast for slaves, who were carried in crowded, pest-ridden vessels to the West Indies, to the Southern colonies, or back to Rhode Island for domestic service in the mansions of the merchants or on the plantations of South County.

In the 1760s, when the tightening of the navigation system and the imposition of new administrative controls by the mother country threatened the colony's prosperity and autonomy, Rhode Island became a leader in the colonial resistance to these governmental innovations and took the first halting steps towards revolution and independence.

Anne Hutchinson, like Roger Williams, was banished from the Massachusetts Bay Colony because of her religious beliefs. Her sect was labeled "Antinomian," a word that meant against the law. This derisive name resulted from Hutchinson's belief that salvation came through faith and the indwelling of the Holy Spirit (a "covenant of grace") rather than through observing the formality of church rules or civil law. Her critics claimed that she advocated a religion which absolved its adherents from obedience to human law. Hutchinson's followers, foremost of whom was William Coddington, settled Portsmouth (1638) and Newport (1639). After the death of her husband William in 1642, the restless Anne, America's first significant white female leader, left Aquidneck for a site in present-day Westchester County, New York, where she and several members of her household were massacred by Indians in 1643. There are no contemporary portraits of the woman some called "the American Jezebel." This representation by sculptor Cyrus Dallin stands before the Massachusetts statehouse. Photo of sculpture from Helen Augur, An American Jezebel: The Life of Anne Hutchinson (1930)

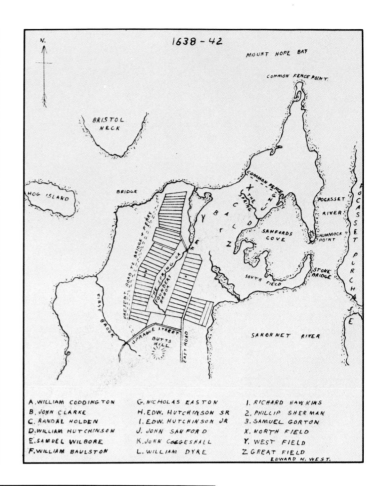

In 1642 religious dissenter Samuel Gorton—unwelcome in Plymouth, Portsmouth, and Providence—founded the town of Warwick on land just south of the Providence plantation. The early years of Gorton's settlement, originally named Shawomet, were marked by bitter controversy with the Massachusetts Bay Colony, which claimed this territory. Gorton was at one time seized and imprisoned by Massachusetts officials, and upon his release he went to England for vindication. There Robert Rich, earl of Warwick, head of the parliamentary commission on foreign plantations, upheld Gorton's right of colonization, whereupon Gorton renamed the town in honor of his protector. In this 1647 pamphlet, entitled Simplicities Defence Against the Seven-Headed Policy, *the radical Gorton denounced his Massachusetts antagonists. Photo of title page courtesy of RIHS (Rhi x3 5301)*

SIMPLICITIES DEFENCE
against
SEVEN-HEADED POLICY.
OR
A true complaint of a peaceable people, being part of the English in New England, made unto the state of Old England, against cruell perfecutors

United in Church-Government
in thofe parts.

Wherein is made manifeft the manifold out-rages cruelties, oppreffions, and taxations, by cruell and clofe imprifonments, fire and fword, deprivation of goods, Lands, and livelyhood, and fuch like barbarous inhumanities, exercifed upon the people of Providence plantations in the Nanhyganfet Bay by thofe of the Maffachufets, with the reft of the united Colonies, ftretching themfelves beyond the bounds of all their own Jurifdictions, perpetrated and acted in fuch an unreafonable and barbarous manner, as many thereby have loft their lives.

As it hath been faithfully declared to the Honourable Committee of Lords and Commons for Forrain Plantations, whereupon they gave prefent Order for Redrefs.

The fight and confideration whereof hath moved a great Country of the Indians and Natives in thofe parts, Princes and people to fubmit unto the Crown of England, and earneftly to fue to the State thereof for fafeguard and fhelter from like cruelties.

Imprimatur, Aug. 3ᵈ. 1646. Diligently perufed, approved, and Licenfed to the Preffe, according to Order by publike Authority.

LONDON,
Printed by *John Macock*, and are to be fold by *George Whittingfon* at the blue *Anchor* neer the *Royal Exchange* in *Cornhil.* 1647.

Portsmouth, Rhode Island's second town, was settled in 1638 on the northern end of Aquidneck Island shortly after its purchase from the Narragansett Indians by William Coddington. The settlement was established as a refuge for the Antinomian outcasts from the Massachusetts Bay Colony. Coddington, William Hutchinson (husband of Anne), John Clarke, Randall Holden, John Coggeshall, and eighteen others signed this initial compact of town government (far left).

The holdings of Portsmouth's original settlers are shown in this sketch (left) prepared by local historian Edward West after examination of the colonial records. Photo from Thomas W. Bicknell, The Story of Dr. John Clarke (1915), from the original in the Rhode Island State Archives (RISA); sketch of early Portsmouth courtesy of RIHS (Rhi x3 1650)

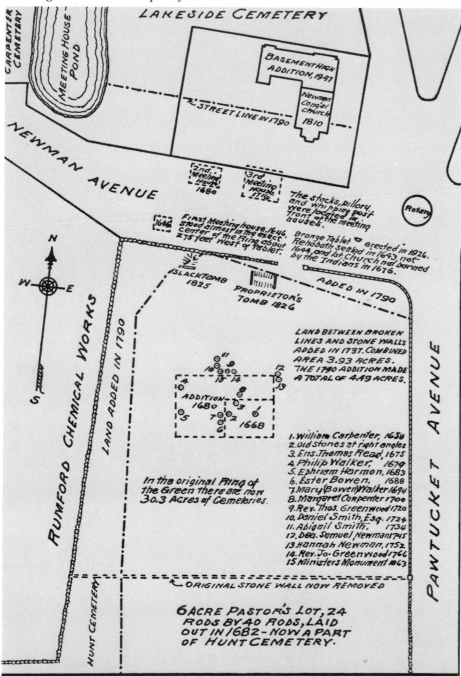

A 1949 PLAN OF THE OLD REHOBOTH TOWN SQUARE, NOW A PART OF NEWMAN AVENUE, RUMFORD, R.I., SHOWING THE LOCATIONS OF THE PRESENT NEWMAN CONGREGATIONAL CHURCH AND THREE EARLIER MEETING HOUSES; ALSO, THE ORIGINAL BURYING YARD AS ENCLOSED BY A STONE WALL IN 1668, ENLARGED IN 1680, 1737, AND 1790, THE WHOLE NOW CALLED NEWMAN CEMETERY.

One of Rhode Island's forgotten founding fathers is the Reverend Samuel Newman (1600–1663). This Congregational clergyman, famous in the mother country for compiling one of the earliest English-language concordances to the Bible, helped to establish the town of Rehoboth in 1643 and colonized it the following year. His original settlement was within the bounds of present-day Rhode Island in the Rumford section of East Providence. Richard LeBaron Bowen, the foremost historian of early Rehoboth, prepared this map of the original Rehoboth settlement and its subsequent development as a Plymouth Colony and a Massachusetts town. Newman Avenue and Newman Congregational Church are current reminders of this neglected pioneer. Map from Richard LeBaron Bowen, Early Rehoboth, IV (1950)

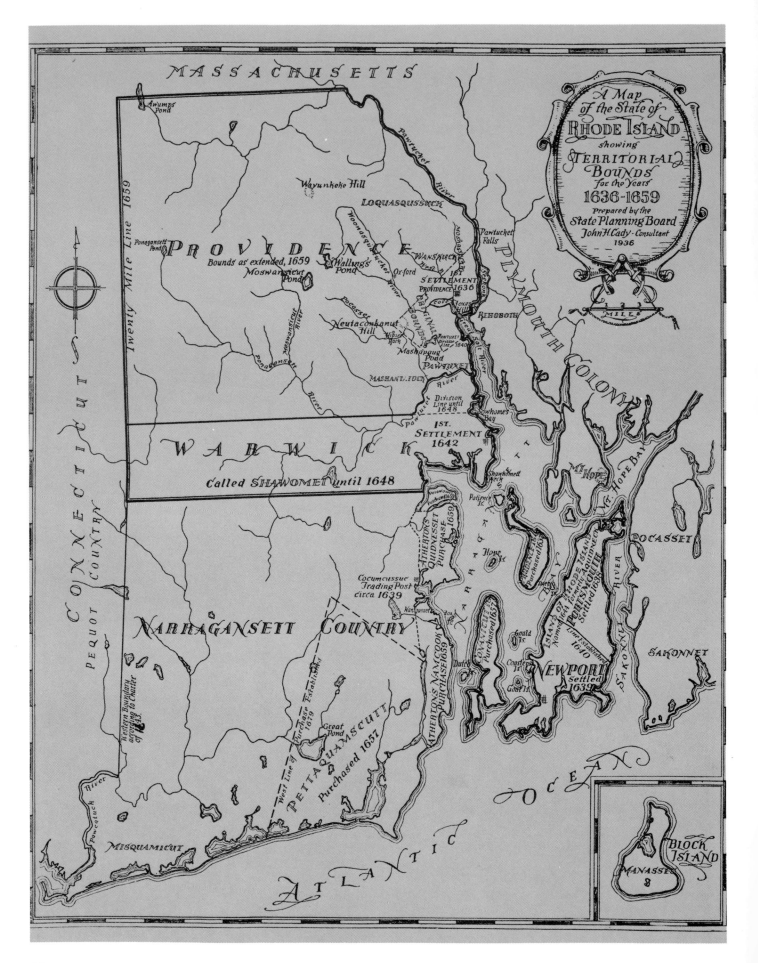

A Map of the State of RHODE ISLAND showing TERRITORIAL BOUNDS for the Years 1636-1659 Prepared by the State Planning Board John H. Cady · Consultant 1936

MASSACHUSETTS

CONNECTICUT

PEQUOT COUNTRY

Twenty Mile Line 1659

Awumps Pond

Wayunkeke Hill

LOQUASQUSSUCK

PROVIDENCE

Bounds as extended, 1659

Ponaganset Pond

Moswansicut Pond

Walling's Pond

Woonasquatucket River

Wanskuck

Orford

1st SETTLEMENT PROVIDENCE 1636

Neutaconkanut Hill

Pocasset River

Moswansicut River

Ponaganset River

Mashapaug Pond

PAWTUXET

MASHANTATUCK

Pawtuxet River

Division Line until 1648

WARWICK

Called SHAWOMET until 1648

NARRAGANSETT COUNTRY

Western Boundary according to Charter of 1663

West Line of Purchase Established 1679

Great Pond

PETTAQUAMSCUTT Purchased 1657

Pawcatuck River

MISQUAMICUT

PLYMOUTH COLONY

Pawtucket River

Pawtucket Falls

REHOBOTH

Sowhome's Bay

1st. SETTLEMENT 1642

Shawomett Neck

Patience I.

ATHERTON'S QUIDNESSET PURCHASE 1659

Cocumcussuc Trading Post circa 1639

Narragansett

ATHERTON'S NAMCOOK PURCHASE 1659

Hope I.

MT HOPE

Mt HOPE BAY

POCASSET

ISLAND OF RHODE ISLAND formerly Aquidneck

PORTSMOUTH Settled 1638

SAKONNET RIVER

SAKONNET

CONANICUT Purchased 1657

Dutch I.

Coaster's I.

Gould I.

Goat Is.

NEWPORT Settled 1639

ATLANTIC OCEAN

BLOCK ISLAND

MANASSES

MILES

From 1636 to 1659 Roger Williams made several land purchases from the Narragansett Indians which extended his Providence plantation westward twenty miles from Foxes Hill on present-day Fox Point. At that time the bounds of Providence plantation comprised all of present-day Providence County west of the Blackstone and Seekonk rivers—an expanse of about 380 square miles. This map by architectural historian John H. Cady shows the boundaries of the four original towns and the early purchases in the Narragansett Country, an area claimed by Rhode Island, Connecticut, and Massachusetts. Map from John H. Cady, Rhode Island Boundaries, 1636-1936 *(1936)*

In 1651 Dr. John Clarke (1609–1676), a versatile Newport physician and clergyman, journeyed to England with Roger Williams, where the two men were successful in thwarting William Coddington's attempt to separate Aquidneck and Conanicut from the mainland settlements and to preside over this island domain as its feudal proprietor. Clarke remained in England as Rhode Island's colonial agent, and in 1663 he skillfully secured the colony's famed charter from King Charles II. Although Clarke originally supported Anne Hutchinson, he later became Newport's foremost Baptist leader. Portrait attributed to Guilliam de Ville, courtesy of the Redwood Library.

King Charles II (1630–1685) returned from exile in France to assume the throne of England in 1660. In 1663 he granted the colony of Rhode Island and Providence Plantations a royal charter, which contained the famed guarantee of "full liberty in religious concernments." The original manuscript document contains its grantor's portrait. Photo of charter courtesy of RIHS (Rhi x3 2289)

Because Rhode Island had earned a reputation as a haven for dissenters (the Puritans described it as a "moral sewer"), members of the persecuted Quaker sect began migrating to the colony in 1657. Quakerism was similar in religious content to the Antinomian creed of Anne Hutchinson, and thus this persecuted sect won many local converts. When the English founder of Quakerism, George Fox, visited his Rhode Island followers in 1672, Roger Williams (then sixty-nine) paddled down Narragansett Bay from Providence to Newport to debate with him; although Williams defended the Quakers' right to practice their beliefs, he was sharply critical of the religious content of those doctrines. Williams discovered when he arrived in Newport that the English religious leader had departed, and so he had his confrontation with three of Fox's disciples instead. The course of that disputation was later sketched by Williams in his famous pamphlet George Fox Digg'd out of His Burrowes, published in 1676, a title that puns Fox and his Quaker associate, Edward Burroughes. Photo of title page courtesy of RIHS (Rhi x3 5779)

On December 19, 1675, six months after the outbreak of King Philip's War, English soldiers, mostly from Plymouth, staged a sneak attack on the winter village of the Narragansetts in South Kingstown's Great Swamp. This cruel massacre of the neutral Narragansetts took the lives of nearly three hundred warriors and three hundred to four hundred women and children. The raiders, led by Governor Josiah Winslow of Plymouth, suffered eighty dead.

In the following spring, the outraged Narragansetts under Chief Canonchet sought revenge. On March 26 a force of sixty-five Englishmen and twenty of their Indian allies, led by Captain Michael Pierce, was ambushed crossing the Blackstone near the present site of Macomber Stadium in Central Falls. The only ten English troops who escaped death at the river crossing were chased northward into Cumberland; and nine were caught, tortured, and killed at a site that eventually became a Cistercian monastery. This incident, the "Nine Men's Misery," was commemorated by the monks early in the twentieth century with a cairn of stones, and in 1928 a granite marker was placed by the Rhode Island Historical Society.

Fresh from his victory over Pierce, the youthful Canonchet burned Providence on March 29, but shortly thereafter he was captured by Connecticut soldiers and executed by their Indian allies. His body was quartered and burned and his head sent to Hartford as a trophy of war. Photo of cairn and tablet from Howard M. Chapin, Sachems of the Narragansetts (1931)

George Fox
Digg'd out of his
Burrovves,
Or an Offer of
DISPUTATION

On fourteen *Propofalls* made this laft Summer 1672 (fo call'd) unto *G. Fox* then prefent on *Rode-ifland* in *New-England*, by *R.w.*

As alfo how (*G. Fox* flily departing) the Difputation went on being managed three dayes at *Newport* on *Rode-Ifland*, and one day at *Providence*, between *John Stubs, John Burnet, and William Edmundfon* on the one part, and *R.W.* on the other.

In which many *Quotations* out of *G. Fox* & *Ed. Burrowes* Book in *Folio* are alleadged.

Eliska WITH AN *Coke*
APENDIX

Of fome fcores of *G. F.* his fimple lame Anfwers to his Oppofites in that Book, quoted and replyed to By R. W. of *Providence* in N.E.

B O S T O N
Printed by *John Fofter*, 1 6 7 6.

28

In the summer of 1676, a year after the outbreak of the bloody King Philip's War, a military mission was launched against the harried King Philip (Metacomet) by English colonists and their Indian allies. Philip was attacked in his stronghold at Mount Hope in present-day Bristol. While attempting to escape, he was shot by Alderman, an Indian warrior. The chief was then decapitated, his body dismembered, and his head placed above the stockade at Plymouth as a warning to other potential rebels.

Colonel Benjamin Church (1639–1718) of Little Compton (shown here) was a leader of the Mount Hope expedition. His memoirs provide us with much of the historical information concerning this final battle of a war which resulted in the deaths of six hundred English colonists and three thousand natives and broke the political and military power of the Indians of southern New England forever. Engraving of Benjamin Church courtesy of RIHS (Rhi x3 559); sketch of Philip's death by W. L. Greene, courtesy of RIHS (Rhi x3 5707)

This portrait of Ninigret II (son of Ninigret I, who was originally thought to have been the subject of this painting) is one of the few surviving depictions of a seventeenth- or early eighteenth-century Indian. After King Philip's War the remnants of the defeated Narragansetts (and perhaps some surviving Pequots) merged with the peaceful Eastern Niantics, who resided in present-day Charlestown, under the leadership of Ninigret II. Shortly thereafter, this amalgamated group assumed the once proud name of Narragansett. Ninigret II presided over the reconstituted tribe (but in subservience to Rhode Island colonial officials) until his death in 1723. Portrait of Ninigret II, oil on canvas, artist and exact date unknown; photograph courtesy of the Rhode Island School of Design, Museum of Art, gift of Robert Winthrop.

Cocumscussoc, or Smith's Castle, is the oldest plantation house in the Narraganstt Country of southern Rhode Island. At first this historic spot was the site of Indian trading posts which sprang up between 1637 and 1639 as a result of attempts by Roger Williams and his friend Richard Smith to establish commercial contact with the Indians. Sometime in the 1640s a large blockhouse was built, dubbed Smith's Castle because of its fortifications. Though it was destroyed in King Philip's War, the name was applied to the subsequent structure erected in 1678, which is still standing today and is open to visitors.

From this frontier enterprise there evolved a prosperous country estate that figured prominently in the affairs of the colony. According to Carl Woodward, late president of the University of Rhode Island and author of Plantation in Yankeeland, *Cocumscussoc's "broad acres and large herds set the pattern for other plantations which yielded shiploads of produce for the coastal and West Indian trade, and it was a center of social and religious life among the plantation families."*

The house and the land, which at its greatest extent comprised twenty-seven square miles, passed by marriage from the Smiths to the Updikes, a family of Dutch ancestry, who held it from 1692 through 1812. The plantation reached the pinnacle of its prosperity in the mid-eighteenth century, but the economic and social disruptions that attended the War for Independence sent it into a precipitous decline. Photo by Laurence Tilley, courtesy of the Cocumscussoc Association

The Eleazar Arnold House (1687) is regarded by architectural historians as the best-preserved seventeenth-century house in Rhode Island despite some alterations to the original design. This is high praise, because Rhode Island has a greater percentage of its structures on the National Register than any other state in the Union. This impressive stone-ender stands on Lincoln's Great Road, one of the most historic byways in the country still in daily use. Completed in 1683, the road provided a vital link between the Providence plantation and important inland markets centered around the seventeenth-century boomtown of Mendon, Massachusetts. Exterior photo courtesy of RIHS (Rhi x3 2335); interior photo from Henry Russell Hitchcock, Rhode Island Architecture (1939)

The Thomas Clemence House is a seventeenth-century stone-ender built by a farmer of modest means. It was constructed in 1680, just after King Philip's War, on land that was set off from Providence in 1759 to create the town of Johnston. Since nearly every structure in northern Rhode Island was destroyed in the devastating war of 1675–76, this house, located on George Waterman Road, ranks among the oldest in Providence County. Photo (ca. 1960) courtesy of the Providence Public Library (PPL)

Colonial historian Carl Bridenbaugh has written an interesting study of the agricultural-commercial society that emerged in seventeenth-century Rhode Island. In his book Fat Mutton and Liberty of Conscience, Bridenbaugh concluded as follows: "It was not, as has always been taught, that the failure of farming drove the men of the Narragansett region down to the sea; rather it was the prospect of marketing a lucrative agricultural surplus...that forced local merchants...to sail to faraway ports." Indeed, the grazing industry was "the prime source of wealth...that built the commercial republic of Rhode Island in the next century."

Although this painting by Worthington Whittredge of the Newport or Middletown coast was done in 1872, the house and the distant fields recapture the era that Bridenbaugh studied in his scholarly monograph. Painting, oil on canvas, from Robert G. Workman (ed.), The Eden of America (1986), courtesy of Phillips Academy, Andover

Members of the Society of Friends (Quakers) played a primary role in the political and commercial life of colonial Rhode Island. From its arrival in 1657, this persecuted sect infused vital energy into the Rhode Island economy. With one foot in the meetinghouse and the other in the countinghouse, shrewd, resourceful Quaker grandees established a far-flung trade network characterized by an extraordinary diversity of cargoes. This commercial empire extended along the coastal trade routes from Boston to New York, the Jerseys, the valley of the Delaware, the Chesapeake Bay region, Virginia, Carolina, the West Indies, Jamaica, Barbados, the Wine Islands, and Europe. The cargoes carried to these distant ports included livestock (especially horses and sheep), meats, and agricultural, forest, and marine produce. "Trade followed the meeting wherever the Friends went in the New World," observes historian Carl Bridenbaugh.

In 1699 Newport's Quakers began construction of a large meetinghouse at the corner of Farewell and Marlborough streets. This historic structure underwent many changes from that time until the 1850s, when this lithograph was done by John Collins. Photograph courtesy of RIHS (Rhi x3 1133)

Another famous Newport house of worship is Trinity Church. Its Anglican congregation, organized in 1698, was guided during its early development by the Reverend Samuel Honeyman, rector from 1704 to 1750. The first church, constructed in 1701, was replaced in 1726 by the present building, a magnificent spired edifice erected at the corner of Spring and Church streets. Built by Richard Munday from a design of English architect Sir Christopher Wren, the church is considered one of the finest of its type in America. Among its famous worshipers were George Washington, who occupied pew 83 when he visited Newport in 1781, and Queen Elizabeth II, who attended services there during her bicentennial visit in 1976. Trinity's famous churchyard holds the remains of many Newport leaders, and in one corner French admiral de Ternay lies buried in a special plot sanctified by the Roman Catholic Church after his death in 1781 during the French occupation of Newport. Today the church stands, facing the harbor, at the head of Queen Anne's Square, an impressive public park framed by historic buildings. Photo (1969) courtesy of Historic American Building Survey

Little Compton, like the entire East Bay region, was once part of Plymouth Colony. The first Plymouth settlers arrived there in the 1670s. They brought with them the Congregational religion and the custom of laying out their settlements around a central square or commons. Shown here, bordering on the commons, is the Little Compton Congregational Church, which dates from 1693, and its cemetery, where Betty (Alden) Pabodie, the daughter of Pilgrims John and Priscilla (Mullins) Alden, is buried. The nineteenth-century headstones in the foreground bear the name of Wilbur, a family that has been prominent in Little Compton for nearly three hundred years. Photo by Hartley Alley

This modern photo of the Silas Casey Farm on Boston Neck Road in the Saunderstown section of North Kingstown shows a well-preserved South County plantation house of the eighteenth century. Silas Casey inherited this farm from his father-in-law, Daniel Coggeshall. Casey and other owners of such estates—the Perrys, Potters, Champlins, Hazards, Stantons, and Robinsons—formed a local ruling gentry similar to that which prevailed in the colonial South. The Casey plantation remains a working farm today, open to visitors who wish a glimpse of colonial rural elegance. Photo by Hartley Alley

One of the spiritual and intellectual leaders of the Narragansett Country was the Irish-born Reverend James McSparran (1680-1757). For thirty-seven years McSparran was the distinguished rector of St. Paul's Church (Wickford), a far-flung parish that served the spiritual needs of South County Anglicans. In 1753 he gained renown by publishing America Dissected, a collection of letters to his friends in Ireland, which proved for its British audience a valuable source of information on the American colonies.

St. Paul's Church, which dates from 1707, was moved four miles northward in 1800 to its present site in Wickford, and it remains today as one of that historic village's most famous landmarks. Portrait of McSparran by John Smibert (1688-1751) from Wilkins Updike, A History of the Episcopal Church in Narragansett, ed. Daniel Goodwin (1907); photo of old St. Paul's Church from Carl Woodward, Plantation in Yankeeland (1971)

An Act for Declaring the Rights and Priviledges of His Majesties Subjects within this Colony.

BE IT EN-ACTED By the General Assembly of this Colony, And by the Authority of the same it is hereby Enacted, That no Free-man shall be Taken or Imprisoned, or be deprived of his Free-hold, or Liberty, or Free Customs, or Out-Lawed, or Exiled or otherways Destroyed, nor shall be passed upon, Judged or Condemned, but by the Lawful Judgement of his Peers, or by the Law of this Colony ; And that no Aid, Tax, Tailage, or Custom, Loan, Benevolence, Gift, Excise, Duty or Imposition whatsoever, shall be Laid, Assessed, Imposed, Levied or Required of or on any of His Majesties Subjects within this Colony, or upon their Estates, upon any manner of Pretence or Colour whatsoever, but by the Act and Assent of the General Assembly of this Colony.

AND that no Man, of what Estate and Condition soever, shall be put out of his Lands and Tenements, nor Taken, nor Imprisoned, nor Disinheretd, nor Banished, nor any ways Destroyed, nor Molested, without being for it brought to Answer by due course of Law ; And that all Rights and Priviledges Granted to this Colony by His Majesties Charter, be entirely kept and preserved to all His Majesties Subjects residing, in or belonging to the same ; And that all Men Professing Christianity, and of Competent Estates, and of Civil Conversation, who acknowledge, and are Obedient to the Civil Magistrate, though of different Judgmnts in Religious Affairs (Roman Catholicks only excepted) shall be admited Free-men, And shall have Liberty to Chuse and be Chosen Officers in the Colony both Millitary and Civil.

In 1719 the General Assembly enacted a digest (i.e., compilation) of Rhode Island laws that contained a statute directly contravening the theory and practice of Roger Williams and the letter of the royal charter. This measure—the only officially proclaimed discrimination against Rhode Island Catholics during the colonial period—provided that "all men professing Christianity and of competent estates, and of civil conversation, who acknowledge and are obedient to the civil magistrate, though of different judgments in religious affairs (Roman Catholics only excepted), shall be admitted freemen and shall have liberty to choose and be chosen officers in the colony, both military and civil." This curious language meant that Catholics (and Jews as well) could not be admitted to the status of freemen of the colony. Since freemanship included the right to vote, the right to hold political office, and such other civil rights as the ability to institute court suits and to sit on juries, Catholics and Jews, in effect, were relegated to second-class citizenship.

The discrimination against Catholics was removed in February 1783. The reform was influenced by the egalitarian spirit of the Revolution and was prompted in part by the benevolent occupation of Rhode Island by the troops of Catholic France. Photo of the Digest of 1719 courtesy of the Rhode Island State Archives (RISA)

Sailing ships abound in this 1730 painting of Newport harbor. At that time the town had emerged as the fifth most prosperous and populous commercial center in the original thirteen colonies, exceeded in size and importance only by Philadelphia, Boston, New York, and Charleston. Lithograph done in 1864 by J. P. Newell from a 1730 painting, courtesy of RIHS (Rhi x3 994)

THE

Rhode-Island Gazette.

WEDNESDAY, October 4. 1732.

FOREIGN AFFAIRS.

Edinburgh, July 8.

ESTERDAY died the Rev. Mr. John Gilerfon, one of the Miniflers of the Gofpel in this Place, after a long Indifpofition. He was a pious good Man, an excellent Preacher, and once Moderator to the General Affembly of this National Church.

Whitehall, July 11. This Day arrived an Exprefs from the Earl of Waldgrave, his Majefty's Embaffador Extraordinary and Plenipotentiary at the Court of France, with Letters from Mr. Keen, his Majefty's Minifter Plenipotentiary at Sevelle, dated July the 4th, N. S. giving an account, that on the 27th of laft Month, the Spanifh Gallies were got into the Bay of Oran, but the Fleet was at two Leagues Diftance, being detain'd by Calms; that they hop,d however to land the Troops the Day following, that the Moors had fir'd two Eight Pounders at the Gallies as they were Fifhing in the Bay; that about 37 were feen at a Diftance, judg'd to be capable of holding 200 Men each, but few Turks, and Provifions in proportion, to en the Spaniards all the Month of July before can make themfelves compleatly Mafters of

London, July 15. There are Letters in wifen fay the Spaniards were invited by Moors into B rrare, which is not unlike reafon they carried great Numbers of fpare with them. If it be fo, the Moors p to themfelves and their Pofterity more P Quierners, and lafting Happinefs than ever enjoy'd under their Turkifh Governors.

The following Promotions have lately been in the Flags of his Majefty's Navy, viz.
Sir Charles Wager, Vice Admiral of the made Admiral of the Blue.
Sir George Walton, Vice Admiral of the W made Vice Admiral of the Red.
Salmon Morris, Efq; Vice Admiral of the made Vice-Admiral of the White.
Philip Cavendith, Efq; Rear Admiral ol Red, made Vice-Admiral of the Blue.
John Balchan, Efq; Rear Admiral of the W made Rear-Admiral of the Red,
Charles Stewart, Efq; Rear Admiral of the mode Rear Admiral of the White.
Sir George Staunders, made Rear Admiral Blue Flag, in the Room of Charles Stuart Efq;
They were all fworn before the Lords o Admiralty laft Week, and have had their n ffions delivered to them.

This is page one of the second issue of the Rhode Island Gazette, *printed in Newport by James Franklin in 1732. The* Gazette, *the state's first newspaper, had a short life; it was discontinued on May 24, 1733, seven months after its initial appearance. Unfortunately, no known copy of the first issue has survived. Photo courtesy of RIHS (Rhi x3 5781)*

After constant disputes with Boston authorities, outspoken printer James Franklin brought this press to Newport in 1726. Younger brother Benjamin, who had been apprenticed on this machine, opted for Philadelphia. James began printing pamphlets in 1727, shortly after his arrival. These imprints were the first reading material published in Rhode Island. In 1735 James died, and the business was continued by his widow Ann until her son James Franklin, Jr., who had served his apprenticeship in Philadelphia under uncle Benjamin, returned to assume the management of the press in 1748. Photo courtesy of the Massachusetts Charitable Mechanics Association

A sign of eighteenth-century Newport's emergent cultural life is the Redwood Library, designed by architect Peter Harrison and built in 1748–49. This engraving shows the original structure, which has since been enlarged. As a private library society, the Redwood Library is the third oldest of its kind in North America and the oldest to survive in its original building. It derives its name from Quaker Abraham Redwood, its chief benefactor. Sketch by James Stevens, courtesy of RIHS (Rhi x3 319)

The Rhode Island Historical Society assembled this exhibition of eighteenth-century Rhode Island craftsmanship from its collections. The silver tankard (ca. 1725) bears the mark of Newport silversmith Samuel Vernon (1683–1737); Robert Feke painted the portrait of the Reverend John Callender, the first historian of Rhode Island, in 1745; and the great wing chair is attributed to the hand of John Goddard of Newport (ca. 1760). The handsome piecrust table was probably made in Charleston, South Carolina, but it has a history of early Rhode Island ownership. Photo by Coleman duPont and Paul Guertin, courtesy of RIHS Museum

For about a century—from 1740 to 1840—about twenty Newport craftsmen, sometimes called the Townsend-Goddard dynasty of cabinetmakers, made Rhode Island widely known for its fine furniture. These families, connected by marriage, were noted for their beautiful pieces constructed first of walnut and later of mahogany. The identifying characteristics of this school of artisans were the block front and the shell designs used on most of their creations. Examples of Townsend-Goddard furniture—hall clocks, desks, chests of drawers, secretaries, chairs, and tables—are now displayed in several local museums, including those of the Newport Historical Society, the Rhode Island Historical Society, and the Rhode Island School of Design. Newport's Whitehorne House contains these mahogany chairs made by John Townsend (ca. 1760) and a mahogany block-and-shell chest-on-chest also attributed to these famous craftsmen. Photo from Guinness and Sadler, Newport Preserv'd (1982), courtesy of Newport Restoration Foundation

Eighteenth-century Rhode Island's most famous scholar was Irish clergyman George Berkeley (pronounced Bar-clay), Anglican essayist and philosopher, who built and resided at the beautifully preserved Whitehall Farm in present-day Middletown during his eventful stay in America from 1729 to 1731. After the failure of his cherished but impractical project of establishing an Anglican college in Bermuda (with Rhode Island its source of food supply), Berkeley returned to Ireland, where he was rewarded with a bishopric. This contemporary portrait by John Smibert shows Berkeley with his family and some students. Smibert (who painted many prominent colonial Rhode Islanders) included himself in the scene and stands at the far left. Portrait courtesy of the Yale University Art Gallery

Built in 1739 from the designs of architect Richard Munday, the Colony House, or Old State House, stands at the head of Washington Square in Newport. It was the site of the General Assembly's annual organizational meeting until 1900, when Providence became the state's only capital. This Newport structure is the oldest of Rhode Island's "statehouses," as the old county courthouses were called. The General Assembly rotated its sessions among the five counties until 1854. A beautiful full-color, illustrated book detailing the history and architecture of the five historic county houses (and the present State House) has been published as part of Rhode Island's 350th anniversary celebration. Photo (ca. 1915) by John Rugen, courtesy of RIHS (Rhi x3 2177)

The town of Cumberland was originally part of the sprawling Plymouth Colony town of Rehoboth. In the early eighteenth century, Cumberland was referred to as Attleboro Gore. At that time the Ballou family of Providence moved to this area and helped organize a Baptist society in 1732. Shortly after Rhode Island acquired Cumberland in 1746, the Ballous, together with the Cooks and others, erected the area's first church, the Elder Ballou Meeting House. The structure stood until 1966, when it was destroyed by vandals. The section of Cumberland where this pioneer family settled was known as the Ballou neighborhood until the middle of the twentieth century. Eliza Ballou, one Cumberland-born member of this notable clan, was the mother of President James A. Garfield. Photo from Robert V. Simpson, North Cumberland: A History (1975)

Waterpowered gristmills for the grinding of corn and other grains were a common sight and a virtual necessity in colonial Rhode Island. The most famous local food derived from this grinding process was the Rhode Island johnnycake (or journey cake, as it was called by colonial travelers). The best corn for the meal is considered to be the hybrid Rhode Island Whitecap Flint, which has a high oil content and a unique nutty flavor. Recipe for the perfect batch of johnnycakes: Combine 7 tablespoons of meal, a level tablespoon of sugar, ½ teaspoon of salt, boiling water, and ½ cup of milk. When this mixture is of a smooth consistency, grease a heated griddle, drop the batter by spoonfuls on the griddle, and fry on each side until the cake is golden brown.

Here master miller Rowland Browning prepares to set in motion the waterpowered machinery at Carpenter's Mill on Moonstone Beach Road, South Kingstown. When this photo was taken in the late 1960s, only four gristmills were in operation statewide, and two of these used electrical energy. Photo (ca. 1967) by Laurence Tilley, courtesy of Rhode Island Yearbook Foundation

Stone walls, such as this North Smithfield fence, are still a common sight in suburban and rural Rhode Island and even run through densely wooded areas. Many of them date from the colonial era and were built by farmers as they cleared their fields for planting. The rocky terrain and short growing season in Rhode Island caused future generations of rural folk to abandon agriculture for factory employment or to migrate to more spacious farmland in the West. Photo by Walter Nebiker

In the period from 1689 to 1763, England, France, and Spain engaged in a great strug-gle for control of North America. During this contest the colony issued letters of marque authorizing privateering voyages against French and Spanish shipping. These voyages were a source of adventure and revenue for the seamen of colonial Rhode Island. Shown here is a letter of marque issued by Governor William Greene on the eve of King George's War (1744–1748). Also shown are two cannon from the Rhode Island sloop Tartar of Newport, a noted colonial privateer.

Doubling as a naval vessel, the Tartar *participated in the successful 1745 English campaign which captured the massive French fortress of Louisbourg on Cape Breton Island. The guns are now exhibited outside the Newport Historical Society head-quarters on Touro Street. Letter courtesy of RIHS (Rhi x3 1053); cannon photo from Richard Alan Dow and E. Andrew Mowbray, Newport (1976)*

41

The salient and most significant feature of Rhode Island government under the charter was that the crucial electoral arena was the colony—and later the state—as a unit. The governor and deputy governor, together with a secretary, an attorney general, and a treasurer, were elected annually in April on a colonywide or at-large basis, as were the ten "assistants" who composed the upper house. Only the deputies, elected semiannually in April and August, were chosen on a local basis. Thus there existed an obvious inducement to form colonywide parties in order to elect a full slate of general officers.

For these at-large contests, Rhode Islanders devised a peculiar system known as "proxing." A "prox" was a printed paper ballot upon which a party placed the names of its at-large candidates. On the third Wednesday in April, the elector in his town meeting took the prox of his choice, made any deletions or substitutions on it that he deemed desirable, and signed it on the reverse side in the presence of the town moderator, who then forwarded it to the town clerk to be recorded. When this ritual was concluded, the "proxies" were sealed in a packet and taken to Newport by one of the town's legislators for the start of the May session of the Assembly. On "election day," the first Wednesday in May, the ballots were opened and counted by the incumbent governor in the presence of the incumbent assistants and newly elected deputies sitting jointly in grand committee. The candidate having a majority of the total vote cast for his respective office was declared elected. Prox courtesy of RIHS (Rhi x3 4897)

In the generation preceding the American Revolution, politically precocious Rhode Islanders developed a system of two-party politics. The merchants and farmers of southern Rhode Island, led by Samuel Ward (shown here), battled with their counterparts from Providence and its environs, the more successful faction, led by Stephen Hopkins. The principal goal of these groups was to secure control of the legislature in order to obtain the host of public offices—from chief justice to inspector of tobacco—at the disposal of that powerful body. In these circumstances the governor, as party leader, acquired an informal influence far beyond his meager official power.

The semipermanent nature, relatively stable membership, and explicit sectional rivalry of the warring camps has led Jackson Turner Main, the leading authority on the early formation of American political parties, to state unequivocally that "Rhode Island produced the first two-party, or, more accurately, two-factional system in America." Ward, one of the founders of Rhode Island's two-party system, buried the hatchet when England threatened the

colony's autonomy and served with Hopkins in the Continental Congress. A leading member of that body, Ward was presiding over the Committee of the Whole in March 1776 when he was stricken by smallpox and died. Portrait of Ward by unknown artist, courtesy of RIHS (Rhi x3 628)

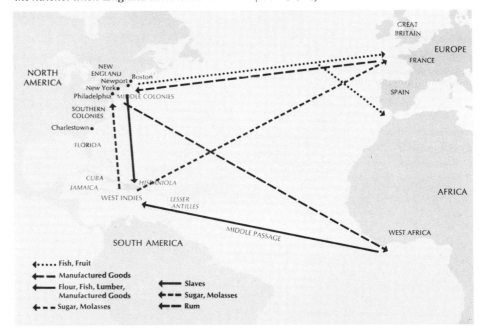

This diagram, from a standard American history textbook, shows the routes followed by eighteenth-century Rhode Island merchants in the infamous triangular trade. Recounting the history of the Rhode Island slave trade in his book The Notorious Triangle, *Jay Coughtry states that "Rhode Island was the principal American carrier"* of slaves from Africa's Guinea Coast to the New World. On a typical voyage, a Newport, Bristol, or Providence merchant (e.g., Aaron Lopez, James D'Wolf, John Brown) sent rum and other items to Africa, traded these commodities for blacks, who were transported along the brutal "middle passage" to the West Indies, and exchanged this human cargo for money, sugar, and

molasses to make more rum. Some select blacks were retained by these slave traders for domestic or agricultural service in Rhode Island. For the period from 1709 (the year of the first Rhode Island trip) to the end of 1807 (when Congress outlawed the traffic), Coughtry has documented 934 Rhode Island slaving voyages carrying 106,544 Africans to bondage in the New World—and his figures are admittedly incomplete. "The trade," says Coughtry, "was a staple of Rhode Island commerce." Diagram from T. Harry Williams, Richard N. Current, and Frank Freidel, The History of the United States to 1877 (1969)

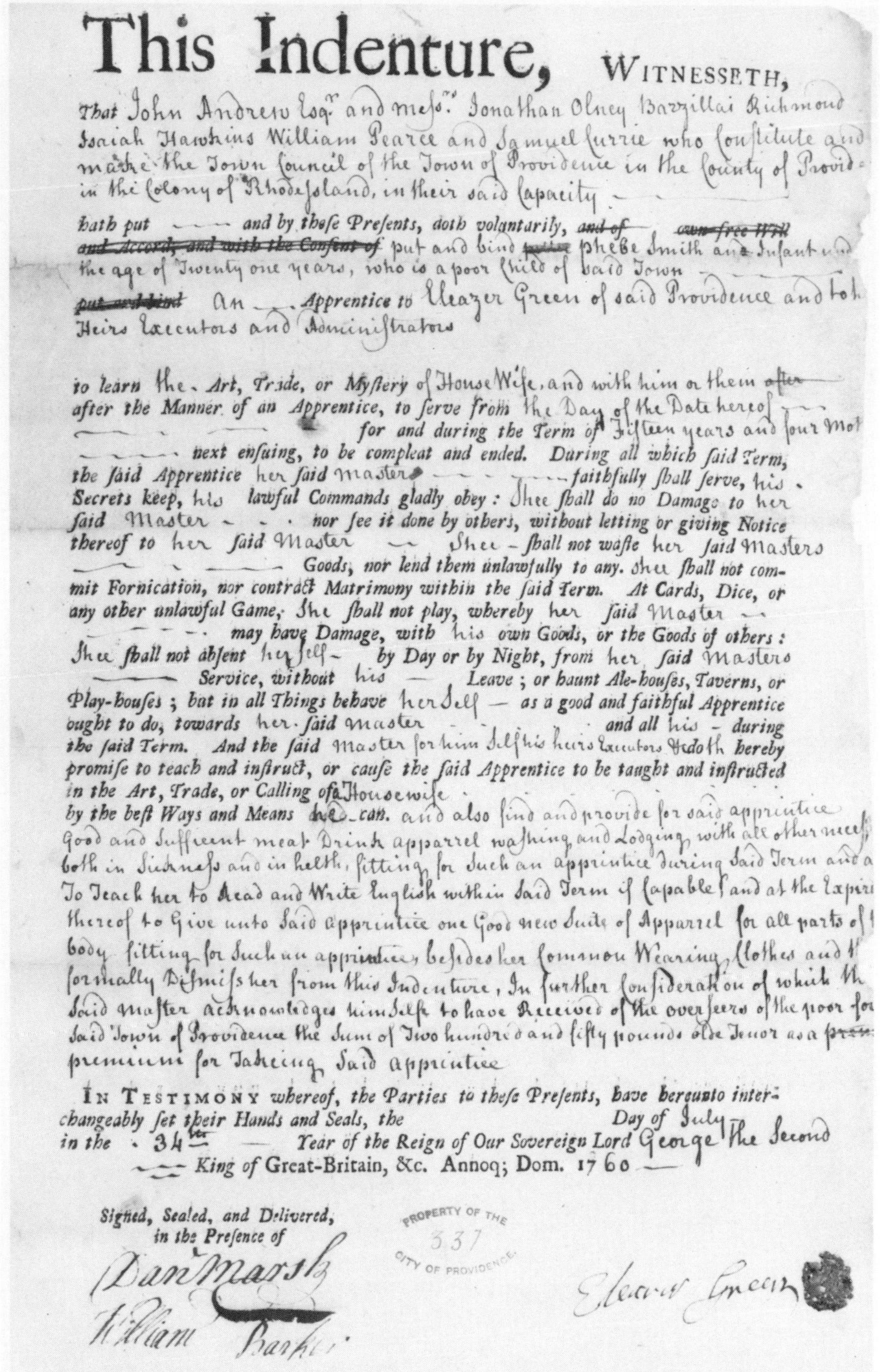

This Indenture, WITNESSETH,

That John Andrew Esqr. and Messrs. Jonathan Olney Barzillai Richmond Isaiah Hawkins William Pearce and Samuel Currie who constitute and make the Town Council of the Town of Providence in the County of Provid- in the Colony of Rhodeisland, in their said Capacity

hath put and by these Presents, doth voluntarily, ~~and of~~ ~~own free Will and Accord, and with the Consent of~~ put and bind ~~putter~~ Phebe Smith and Infant und the age of Twenty one years, who is a poor Child of said Town ~~put and bind~~ An Apprentice to Eleazer Green of said Providence and to h Heirs Executors and Administrators

to learn the Art, Trade, or Mystery of House Wife, and with him or them ~~after~~ after the Manner of an Apprentice, to serve from the Day of the Date hereof for and during the Term of Fifteen years and four Mo next ensuing, to be compleat and ended. During all which said Term, the said Apprentice her said Master faithfully shall serve, his Secrets keep, his lawful Commands gladly obey: Shee shall do no Damage to her said Master nor see it done by others, without letting or giving Notice thereof to her said Master Shee shall not waste her said Masters Goods, nor lend them unlawfully to any. Shee shall not commit Fornication, nor contract Matrimony within the said Term. At Cards, Dice, or any other unlawful Game, She shall not play, whereby her said Master may have Damage, with his own Goods, or the Goods of others: Shee shall not absent her Self by Day or by Night, from her said Masters Service, without his Leave; or haunt Ale-houses, Taverns, or Play-houses; but in all Things behave her Self as a good and faithful Apprentice ought to do, towards her said Master and all his during the said Term. And the said Master for him Self his heirs Executors &c doth hereby promise to teach and instruct, or cause the said Apprentice to be taught and instructed in the Art, Trade, or Calling of a Housewife by the best Ways and Means ~~he~~ can. and also find and provide for said apprintice Good and Suffecent meat Drink apparrel washing and Lodging, with all other neces both in Sickness and in helth, fitting for such an apprintice during said Term and a To Teach her to Read and Write English within said Term if Capable and at the Expir thereof to Give unto said apprintice one Good new Sute of Apparrel for all parts of t body fitting for such an apprintice, besides her Common Wearing Clothes and t formally Dismiss her from this Indenture, In further Consideration of which th said master acknowledges himself to have Received of the overseers of the poor fo said Town of Providence the Sum of Two hundred and fifty pounds olde Tenor as a ~~prem~~ premium for Takeing said apprintice

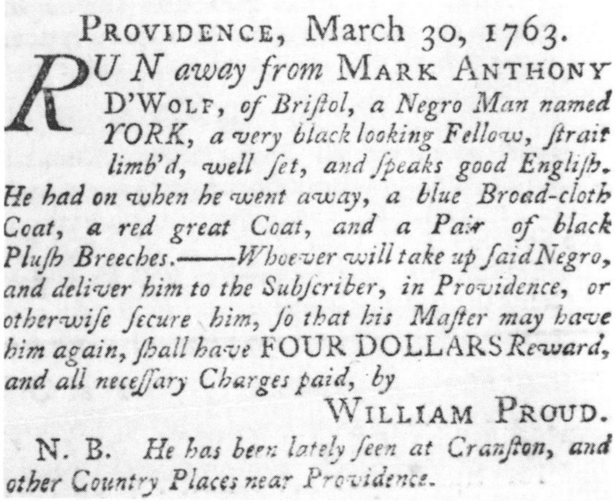

IN TESTIMONY whereof, the Parties to these Presents, have hereunto interchangeably set their Hands and Seals, the Day of July in the 34th Year of the Reign of Our Sovereign Lord George the Second King of Great-Britain, &c. Annoq; Dom. 1760

Signed, Sealed, and Delivered, in the Presence of

Dan Marsh
William Barker

Eleazer Green

PROVIDENCE, March 30, 1763.

RUN away from MARK ANTHONY D'WOLF, *of Bristol, a Negro Man named YORK, a very black looking Fellow, strait limb'd, well set, and speaks good English. He had on when he went away, a blue Broad-cloth Coat, a red great Coat, and a Pair of black Plush Breeches.——Whoever will take up said Negro, and deliver him to the Subscriber, in Providence, or otherwise secure him, so that his Master may have him again, shall have* FOUR DOLLARS *Reward, and all necessary Charges paid, by*

WILLIAM PROUD.

N. B. *He has been lately seen at Cranston, and other Country Places near Providence.*

A significant number of colonial Rhode Islanders were not free. Many blacks and Indians and their offspring of mixed blood were enslaved and labored on South County plantations or in the homes of wealthy merchants in Newport, Providence, and Bristol. Other colonists were indentured servants who were bound to work or apprenticeship for a fixed number of years. Shown here is a copy of a 1760 indenture issued by the Providence Town Council binding pauper Phebe Smith and her infant to the service of Eleazer Green for a term of fifteen years and four months. The other illustration is a Providence Gazette *advertisement for a runaway slave who escaped from the service of Mark Anthony D'Wolf of Bristol, a notorious slave trader. Indenture and advertisement courtesy of RIHS (Rhi x3 4098) and (Rhi x3 5780)*

During the colonial period Rhode Island established a brisk trade with the Caribbean, including the northeast coast of South America, where Surinam (Dutch Guiana) was located. Among the items supplied to the wealthy plantation owners of the Caribbean basin was a famous carriage horse bred in South County known as the Narragansett Pacer. Shown here is a rare contemporary painting of sea captains "carousing in Surinam" (as many Rhode Island mariners undoubtedly did). The picture belonged to the Jenckes family of Rhode Island, and according to tradition it depicts several prominent Rhode Island merchants, including Nicholas Cooke, Esek Hopkins, Godfrey Malbone, Nicholas Power, John Jenckes, and Daniel Jenckes. The woodcut of a Narragansett Pacer appeared in the Providence Gazette in January 1764. Nicholas Brown and Company advertised to obtain these horses to trade with the Dutch colony. Painting, oil on bed ticking, "Sea Captains Carousing in Surinam" by John Greenwood (ca. 1755) courtesy of the Saint Louis Museum of Art; advertisement courtesy of RIHS (Rhi x3 1740)

SHIPPING HORSES wanted.

NICHOLAS BROWN, and COMPANY, Want to buy immediately, a few likely SURINAM HORSES.

Newport's famous Brick Market, designed by architect Peter Harrison (1713-1775), was built in 1762 and stands at the west end of Washington Square. It was the center of trade for a bustling commercial town. The arches at the basement level, now windows, were once spacious enough so that farmers could drive their wagons inside and unload their produce in the stalls beneath the building. Photo from Desmond Guinness and Julius T. Sadler, Jr., Newport Preserv'd (1982)

This is an interior view of Newport's Touro Synagogue, the oldest Jewish house of worship in North America. It was constructed according to the plans of Peter Harrison in 1763 to serve the spiritual needs of the prosperous Newport Sephardic (Spanish and Portuguese) Jewish community, which dated from 1658. The Reverend Isaac Touro was this congregation's first spiritual leader. When the Revolution dealt a setback to Newport's economy, Jewish inhabitants moved to other port cities, and by 1791 the synagogue was virtually closed. A new Jewish migration during the Gilded Age prompted its reopening for regular services in 1883. Photo by Hartley Alley

Aaron Lopez was a Portuguese Jewish immigrant who came to Newport in 1752 at the age of twenty-one in search of religious freedom and economic opportunity. He found both. By the eve of the Revolution, Lopez was a distinguished member of a small but thriving Jewish community and one of Newport's most prosperous merchant princes, with a fleet of thirty ships, some of which were used in the slave trade. When hostilities broke out, however, the British occupation of vulnerable Newport and the vagaries of war had a disastrous impact on his far-flung commercial empire. In 1782, as his thoughts turned toward the reconstruction of his fortune, Lopez drowned in a bizarre accident.

The state legislature in 1762 had denied Lopez's petition for citizenship because he was a Jew. Although Rhode Island never interfered with the freedom of worship of any of its inhabitants, the Lopez case is a blemish on the state's famed liberality. According to Lopez biographer Stanley Chyet, it is probable that the Sephardic Jew's political associations with the Samuel Ward faction prejudiced the Hopkins-controlled legislature against him and that religion was "little more than a pretext in the denial" of his petition. Portrait by anonymous eighteenth-century artist, courtesy of the American Jewish Historical Society

John Brown (1736–1803), an extremely large and powerful man (over three hundred pounds in bulk), was a dominant figure in Revolutionary Providence. This merchant prince laid the cornerstone for University Hall in 1770, financed Stephen Hopkins's political ventures, organized the attack on the Gaspee, furnished the Katy for the U.S. Navy, and manufactured cannon at Hope Furnace in Cranston for the colonial cause. In the 1780s he engaged in the China trade and labored for the adoption of the Constitution. Late in life he served one term as a Federalist in the U.S. House of Representatives (1799–1801). On the debit side, Brown was a slave trader who continued in this unsavory practice despite state law forbidding it, defying also the protests of his brother Moses, a leading abolitionist. John, Moses, and their three equally enterprising brothers were the children of James Brown and Hope Power, daughter of Nicholas Power, an immigrant from Ireland. Miniature by Edward G. Malbone courtesy of the New York Historical Society

Chapter Three

THE REVOLUTIONARY ERA, 1763-1790

Rhode Island was a leader in the American Revolutionary movement. Having the greatest degree of self-rule, it had the most to lose from the efforts of England after 1763 to increase her supervision and control over the American colonies. In addition, Rhode Island had a long tradition of evading the poorly enforced navigation acts, and smuggling was commonplace.

Beginning with strong opposition in Newport to the Sugar Act (1764), with its restrictions on the molasses trade, the colony engaged in repeated measures of open defiance, such as the scuttling and torching of the British customs sloop *Liberty* in Newport harbor in July 1769, the burning of the British revenue schooner *Gaspee* on Warwick's Namquit Point in 1772, and Providence's own "Tea Party" in Market Square on March 2, 1775. Gradually the factions of Ward and Hopkins put aside their local differences and united by endorsing a series of political responses to alleged British injustices. On May 17, 1774, after parliamentary passage of the Coercive Acts (Americans called them "Intolerable"), the Providence Town Meeting became the first governmental assemblage to issue a call for a general congress of colonies to resist British policy. On June 15

the General Assembly made the colony the first to appoint delegates (Ward and Hopkins) to the anticipated Continental Congress.

In April 1775, a week after the skirmishes at Lexington and Concord, the colonial legislature authorized raising a fifteen–hundred-man "army of observation" with Nathanael Greene as its commander. Finally, on May 4, 1776, Rhode Island became the first colony to renounce allegiance to King George III. Ten weeks later, on July 18, the Assembly ratified the Declaration of Independence.

During the Revolutionary War itself, Rhode Island furnished its share of men, ships, and money to the cause of independence. Volunteers included a significant number of Negro and Indian slaves, who gained distinction as the "Black Regiment," a detachment of the First Rhode Island Regiment. Esek Hopkins (brother of Stephen, the signer of the Declaration of Independence) became the first commander in chief of the Continental navy—a force which Rhode Island helped create—and the able Nathanael Greene of the Kentish Guards became Washington's second-in-command and chief of the Continental army in the South.

The British occupied Newport in December 1776,

and a long siege to evict them culminated in August 1778 in the large but inconclusive Battle of Rhode Island, a contest which was the first combined effort of the Americans and their French allies. The British voluntarily evacuated Newport in October 1779, but in July 1780 the French army under Rochambeau landed there and made the port town its base of operations. It was from Newport, Bristol, Providence, and other Rhode Island encampments that the French began their march to Yorktown in 1781.

The Revolution did not alter Rhode Island's governmental structure (even the royal charter remained intact), but it did prompt some legal and political changes. For instance, the Revolution and sentiments it generated influenced legislation affecting Catholics and Negro slaves.

Whatever anti-Catholicism existed in Rhode Island was mollified by assistance rendered to the struggling colonials by Catholic France and by the benevolent presence of large numbers of French troops in Newport under General Rochambeau, some of whom remained when the struggle was over. Thus the General Assembly in February 1783 removed the arbitrarily imposed disability against Roman Catholics (dating from 1719) by giving members of that religion "all the rights and privileges of the Protestant citizens of this state."

Most significant of several statutes relating to blacks was the emancipation act of 1784. With a preface invoking sentiments of Locke, that "all men are entitled to life, liberty, and property," the manumission measure gave freedom to all children born to slave mothers after March 1, 1784. But the act, though an encouraging gesture, was not a complete abolition of slavery, for it failed to require the emancipation of those who were slaves at the time of its passage. A handful remained in bondage until May 1843, when a new constitution abolished slavery outright.

The emancipation act was followed by a concerted effort of Rhode Island reformers—particularly the influential Quaker community—to ban the slave trade. This agitation had a salutary result when the General Assembly enacted a measure in October 1787 which prohibited any Rhode Island citizen from engaging in this barbarous traffic. The legislature termed the trade inconsistent with "that more enlightened and civilized state of freedom which has of late prevailed."

A side effect of the Revolution to have important consequences for Rhode Island's political and constitutional development was the decline of Newport. Its exposed location, the incidence of loyalist sentiments among its townspeople, and its temporary occupation by the British combined to produce both a voluntary and at times a forced exodus of its inhabitants. In 1774 its population was 9,209; by 1782 that figure had dwindled to 5,532. The population of Providence—more sheltered at the head of the bay and a center of Revolutionary activity—remained stationary during these turbulent times.

The Revolution was a blow from which Newport never fully recovered. British occupation adversely affected both its population and its prosperity. From this period onward, numerical and economic ascendancy inexorably moved northward to Providence and the surrounding mainland communities.

In 1778 the state had quickly ratified the Articles of Confederation, with its weak central government, but when the movement to strengthen that government developed in the mid-1780s, Rhode Island balked. The state's individualism, its democratic localism, and its tradition of autonomy caused it to resist the centralizing tendencies of the federal Constitution. This opposition was intensified when an agrarian-debtor revolt in support of the issuance of paper money placed the parochial Country party in power from 1786 through 1790. This political faction, led by South Kingstown's Jonathan Hazard, was suspicious of the power and the cost of a government too far removed from the grass-roots level, and so it declined to dispatch delegates to the Philadelphia convention of 1787, which drafted the United States Constitution. Then, when that document was presented to the states for ratification, Hazard's faction delayed (and nearly prevented) Rhode Island's approval.

In the period between September 1787 and January 1790, the rural-dominated General Assembly rejected no fewer than eleven attempts by the representatives from the mercantile communities to convene a state ratifying convention. Instead, the Assembly defied the instructions of the Founding Fathers and conducted a popular referendum on the Constitution. That election, which was boycotted by the supporters of a stronger union (called Federalists), rejected the Constitution by a vote of 2,708 to 237.

Finally, in mid-January 1790, more than eight months after George Washington's inauguration as first president of the United States, the Country party reluctantly called the required convention, but it took two separate sessions—one in South Kingstown (March 1-6) and the second in Newport (May 24-29)—before approval was obtained. The ratification tally, thirty-four in favor and thirty-two opposed, was the narrowest of any state, and a favorable result was obtained only because four Antifederalists either absented themselves or abstained from voting.

Rhode Island's course during this turbulent era—first in war and last in peace—is attributable in part to its tradition of individualism, self-reliance, and dissent. Most of its residents feared the encroachment on local autonomy by any central government,

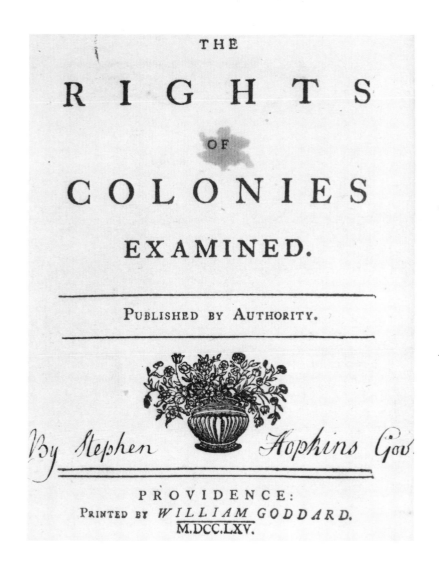

THE

RIGHTS

OF

COLONIES

EXAMINED.

PUBLISHED BY AUTHORITY.

By Stephen Hopkins Gov.

PROVIDENCE:
PRINTED BY *WILLIAM GODDARD.*
M.DCC.LXV.

whether located in London, Philadelphia, or Washington. This ideology, coupled with the economic concerns of the agrarian community, explains Rhode Island's wariness of the work of the "Grand Convention." Those economic worries consisted principally of a fear that the new central government would be financed by exorbitant taxes on land and that the new Constitution's ban on state emissions of paper money would terminate the inflationary financial scheme formulated by Hazard and the Country party to discharge public and private debts.

Because the Constitution three times gave implied assent to slavery, the influential Quaker community also denounced it. These factors explain the strength of Antifederalism. Small wonder that Rhode Island withheld ratification until May 29, 1790, making it the last of the original thirteen states to join the new federal union.

Fortunately, a number of equally influential factors turned the tide in favor of ratification. These included the desire of the holders of national securities and Continental Loan Office certificates to be paid by a strong, fiscally sound central government. Coastal towns desiring federal reparation for war-

time losses had a similar desire. The local press—Peter Edes's *Newport Herald,* John Carter's *Providence Gazette,* and Bennett Wheeler's *U.S. Chronicle* (Providence)—all urged ratification. Such a plea was aided by the prestige and integrity of the new national leaders, especially Washington, and by congressional passage of a Bill of Rights to safeguard individual liberties from federal invasion. The proposed federal assumption of state debts was a carrot, and the economic coercion exerted upon alien Rhode Island by the new central government (a tariff and a demand for debt payment) was a stick. Most bizarre was Providence's threatened secession from the state on the eve of the May convention if that body rejected or deferred ratification once more. In the end, a nearly immovable object yielded to an irresistible force; Rhode Island joined the union which had left it behind and embarked upon a new era of economic and political development.

Before examining that new age, however, it is worthwhile to note that the Revolutionary era was marked by more than battles, whether military or constitutional. Like any age, it had diversity and significant developments in many fields. Most

notable was the founding of Brown University (first situated in Warren and called Rhode Island College) by local Baptists in 1764. This institution, destined to emerge as one of America's foremost citadels of higher learning, was ably directed by the Reverend James Manning (1738-1791), its founder and first president.

In the economic realm, the famous Brown family of Providence rose to new financial, commercial, and industrial heights, surpassing in stature even the celebrated merchants Aaron Lopez, Joseph Wanton, and Christopher Champlin of Newport and James D'Wolf of Bristol. The resourceful Brown brothers—Nicholas (1729-1791), Joseph (1733-1785), John (1736-1803), and Moses (1738-1836)—guided by uncles Obadiah (1712-1762) and Elisha (1717-1802), laid the groundwork in this turbulent age for the remarkable commercial and industrial advances of the early national period.

In the years following 1763, when the mother country tightened up her administrative control over her American colonies and sought to raise revenue from them by taxation, Rhode Island, Massachusetts, and Virginia led the protests. The Sugar Act of 1764 interfered with Rhode Island's importation of sugar and molasses for its rum distilleries, and the Stamp Act of 1765, a novel "internal" tax, required that stamps (for which the colonists would pay) were to be placed on numerous items, including all decisions of civil courts, licenses, bonds, deeds, pamphlets, and newspapers. In Newport the Stamp Act was greeted by mob violence against stamp distributor Augustus Johnson and attorney Martin Howard, Jr., the latter of whom was deeply resented for alleged writings in support of the measure. In August 1765 Howard's home on Broadway (shown here) was ransacked. Howard fled to the harbor, boarded the British ship Cygnet, and returned to England to stay. The 1690 house, one of the oldest in Newport, passed through a succession of new owners. As the Wanton-Lyman-Hazard House, it is a National Historical Landmark now open to the public. Photo (1986) by Joyce M. Botelho

GEORGE R.

By the KING.
A PROCLAMATION:

FOR the difcovering and apprehending the Perfons who plundered and burnt the *Gafpee* Schooner ; and barbaroufly wounded and ill treated Lieutenant *William Dudingfton*, Commander of the faid Schooner.

WHEREAS We have received Information, that upon the 10th Day of June laft, between the Hours of Twelve and One in the Morning, in the Providence or Narrowganfet River, in Our Colony of Rhode-Ifland and Providence Plantations, a great Number of Perfons, armed with Guns and other offenfive Weapons, and led by Two Perfons, who were called the Captain and Head-Sheriff, in feveral armed Boats, attacked and Boarded Our Veffel called the Gafpee Schooner, then lying at fingle Anchor in the faid River, commanded by Our Lieutenant William Dudingfton, under the Orders of Our Rear-Admiral John Montagu, and having dangeroufly wounded and barbaroufly treated the faid William Dudingfton, took, plundered and burnt the faid Schooner :

WE, to the Intent that fuch outrageous and heinous Offenders may be difcovered, and brought to condign Punifhment, have thought fit, with the Advice of Our Privy Council, to iffue this Our Royal PROCLAMATION : And We are hereby gracioufly pleafed to promife, that if any Perfon or Perfons fhall difcover any other Perfon or Perfons concerned in the faid daring and heinous Offences, abovementioned, fo that he or they may be apprehended and brought to Juftice, fuch Difcoverer fhall have and receive, as a Reward for fuch Difcovery, upon Conviction of each of the faid Offenders, the Sum of *Five Hundred Pounds*: And if any Perfon or Perfons fhall difcover either of the faid Perfons who acted as, or called themfelves, or were called by their faid Accomplices, the Head-Sheriff or the Captain, fo that they, or either of them, may be apprehended and brought to Punifhment, fuch Difcoverer fhall have and receive, as a Reward for fuch Difcovery, upon Conviction of either of the faid Perfons, the further Sum of *Five Hundred Pounds*, over and above the Sum of *Five Hundred Pounds* herein before promifed, for the difcovery & apprehending any of the other common Offenders, abovementioned ; and if any Perfon or Perfons concerned therein, except the Two Perfons who were called the Head-Sheriff, and Captain, and the Perfon or Perfons who wounded Our faid Lieutenant *William Dudingfton*, fhall difcover any one or more of the faid Accomplices, fo that he or they may be apprehended and brought to Punifhment, fuch Difcoverer fhall have and receive the faid Reward or Rewards of *Five Hundred Pounds*, or *One Thoufand Pounds*, as the Cafe may be ; and alfo Our gracious Pardon for his faid Offence. And the Commiffioners for executing the Office of Treafurer of Our Exchequer, are hereby required to make Payment accordingly of the faid Rewards. And We do hereby ftrictly charge and command all Our Governors, Deputy-Governors, Magiftrates, Officers, and all other Our Loving Subjects, that they do ufe their utmoft Diligence in their feveral Places and Capacities, to find out, difcover and apprehend the faid Offenders, in Order to their being brought to Juftice, And We do hereby command that this Our Proclamation be printed and publifhed, in the ufual Form, and affixed in the principal Places of Our Town of Newport, and other Towns in Our faid Colony, that none may pretend Ignorance.

GIVEN at Our Court at St. James's, the Twenty-Sixth Day of Auguft, 1772, in the Twelfth Year of Our Reign.

GOD fave the KING.

Printed by SOLOMON SOUTHWICK, Printer to the Honorable the Governor and Company of the Colony of Rhode-Ifland and Providence Plantations, in New-England.

In June 1772 Providence citizens went from theory to action in expressing their opposition to British economic regulations. On June 9 the packet Hannah, *plying between New York and Providence under Captain Benjamin Lindsay, was chased up Narragansett Bay by the dreaded British customs sloop* Gaspee, *Lieutenant William Dudingston commanding. Attempting to evade capture, Lindsay sailed into shallow water off Warwick, and there, on Namquit (now Gaspee) Point, the recklessly pursuing Englishman ran his larger vessel aground.*

Lindsay docked in Providence, where news of the incident spread quickly. That evening the townsmen, led by merchant John Brown, assembled in Sabin's Tavern (which stood on the corner of Planet and South Main streets) to plot the destruction of the Gaspee. Discussions continued until 10 p.m. Then the rebels embarked from Fenner's wharf in eight five-oared longboats under the command of Abraham Whipple, a highly successful privateer captain in the French and Indian War. After midnight the attack party reached the stranded ship, and following an exchange of shouts, James Bucklin shot and wounded Lieutenant Dudingston in the groin. The Providence men thereupon boarded the Gaspee, overpowered the crew, and burned the sloop and its contents.

A royal investigation of the incident yielded insufficient evidence to indict the perpetrators, who were shielded by their fellow townsmen despite a reward of up to one thousand pounds offered by King George himself for information leading to the conviction of the Gaspee raiders. But the Gaspee inquiry led to the establishment by rebels of legislative committees of correspondence throughout the colonies—a major step on the road to the Revolution. Abraham Whipple, portrait by Edward Savage, courtesy of the United States Naval Academy; "Burning of the Gaspee," painting by Charles De Wolf Brownell, courtesy of RIHS (Rhi x3 3125); proclamation, broadside collection, RIHS (Rhi x3 727)

The H.M.S. Rose, *commanded by the domineering Commodore James Wallace, caused havoc in Narragansett Bay from the time of its arrival in December 1774 until its departure in June 1776. The* Rose *was the flagship of a small patrol squadron, whose five hundred sailors Wallace had to feed. When the Englishman cracked down on smugglers, the colonials refused to sell him food and provisions, so Wallace seized these stores in raids along the coast and then instituted a blockade against all shipping.*

Infuriated on one hand because Wallace enforced the law and on the other hand because he broke it, the colonial legislature authorized the creation of a Rhode Island navy to combat him. Two ships were commissioned to attack the British squadron: the sloop Katy, *with ten guns, and the* Washington, *with six. When Abraham Whipple, captain of the* Katy, *was threatened by Wallace with hanging, he replied with the following terse dispatch: "Sir—Always catch a man before you hang him."*

The H.M.S. Rose, *the ship that prompted the creation of Rhode Island's navy (the first of any colony), has been reproduced. In the 1970s John Millar, formerly of Newport, financed the construction of a replica of the* Rose *as a project for the bicentennial celebration. It is presently on exhibition in Bridgeport, Connecticut. Painting courtesy of the U.S. Naval Academy Museum*

In May 1775 the Rhode Island General Assembly refused to administer the oath of office to incumbent governor Joseph Wanton of Newport (left), who had been re-elected to the chief executive's post in the annual April ballotting. With Wanton deposed, Deputy Governor Nicholas Cooke (1717-1782) of Providence ascended to the governorship, where he espoused the rebel cause. In 1776 and 1777 this advocate of intercolonial *union was elected in his own right. Cooke spearheaded Rhode Island's ratification of the Articles of Confederation in February 1778. These portraits of the loyalist and the rebel suggest an intriguing contrast between the opposing sides. Portrait of Wanton by John Smibert, courtesy of the Redwood Library; portrait of Cooke by anonymous artist, courtesy of Brown University*

AN ACT repealing an Act, intitled, "An Act for the more effectually securing to his Majesty the Allegiance of his Subjects, in this his Colony and Dominion of Rhode-Island and Providence Plantations;" and altering the Forms of Commissions, of all Writs and Processes in the Courts, and of the Oaths prescribed by Law.

WHEREAS in all States, existing by Compact, Protection and Allegiance are reciprocal, the latter being only due in Consequence of the former: And whereas GEORGE the Third, King of Great-Britain, forgetting his Dignity, regardless of the Compact, most solemnly entered into, ratified and confirmed, to the Inhabitants of this Colony, by His illustrious Ancestors, and till of late fully recognized by Him—and entirely departing from the Duties and Character of a good King, instead of protecting, is endeavouring to destroy the good People of this Colony, and of all the United Colonies, by sending Fleets and Armies to *America*, to confiscate our Property, and spread Fire, Sword and Desolation, throughout our Country, in order to compel us to submit

This building deserves to be accorded the title "Rhode Island's Freedom Hall." In 1762 the Old State House in Providence was constructed with funds raised through lotteries or appropriated by the legislature. From that time to 1900, when the present State House was opened, it served as one of Rhode Island's five capitol buildings. Here, on May 4, 1776, Rhode Island became the first colony to renounce allegiance to King George III when the General Assembly passed a measure censuring the hapless monarch as a detestable tyrant who "is endeavoring to destroy the good people of this Colony, and of all the United Colonies, by sending fleets and armies to America to confiscate our property, and spread Fire, Sword, and Desolation." Although this act was not (contrary to popular opinion) a declaration of independence, it was nonetheless a major step in that direction.

Sitting here at the Old State House, in 1783 the General Assembly restored full civil rights to Roman Catholic citizens, and the following year it provided for the gradual abolition of slavery in Rhode Island. Photo of the Old State House, depicting a historical reenactment during the bicentennial year by the Artillery Company of Newport (established 1741), by Louis Notarianni, from the author's collection; photo of the Renunciation Act from Rhode Island Acts and Resolves, *RISA*

William Ellery, an ally of Sam Ward, replaced that deceased leader in May 1776 as Rhode Island's second delegate to the Continental Congress, and thus he gained the distinction (with Stephen Hopkins) of signing the Declaration of Independence. This Harvard-educated lawyer served in the national congress for nearly a decade, specializing in matters dealing with commerce and the navy. In the late 1780s Ellery became a leading supporter of the ratification of the Constitution. His advocacy of that successful cause earned him the lucrative collectorship of customs in Newport, a position he held for thirty years (1790-1820) until his death. Ellery had two illustrious grandchildren—writer and statesman Richard Henry Dana and Unitarian religious leader William Ellery Channing. Portrait of Ellery courtesy of RIHS (Rhi x3 786)

Commodore Esek Hopkins of Providence was the first commander in chief of the United States Navy. He owed his appointment not only to his experience as a mariner but also to the fact that his brother Stephen had been a principal legislative sponsor of an American fleet in the Second Continental Congress. Appointed on December 21, 1775, Hopkins sailed to Philadelphia to receive his orders. In February his fleet attacked a British base at Fort Nassau in the Bahamas, seized arms and munitions, and returned to Rhode Island waters. Ignoring the advice of naval colleagues, he took his ships up the bay to Providence, where the tiny, undermanned fleet was bottled up by the Royal Navy in December 1776. Thus incapacitated, Hopkins was attacked for incompetency by some important members of Congress, and he was dismissed from naval service on January 2, 1778, when he refused to appear before that body to explain his actions. He became a member of the state legislature and the Rhode Island Council of War for the duration of the conflict. Engraving by J. C. Buttre, courtesy of RIHS (Rhi x3 688)

The Continental sloop Providence (1774-1779) had a distinguished war record. Under the name Katy and the command of Captain Abraham Whipple, this twelve-gun vessel built by John Brown won the first official naval battle of the Revolution, capturing an armed tender of the H.M.S. Rose in June 1775. Renamed Providence in 1775, it became part of the original fleet of the United States Navy. It was the first ship to land U.S. Marines for combat (at New Providence in the Bahamas), and it became the first command of John Paul Jones. The Providence was scuttled by her crew in August 1779 after being trapped in Penobscot Bay, Maine, by a British fleet.

A replica of the ship was constructed as a bicentennial project by the Seaport '76 Foundation with a sizable grant from the state Bicentennial Commission. Berthed in Newport, the replica makes periodic visits to Providence and other East Coast ports. The warship and its exploits have been the subject of a book-length study by Hope Rider entitled Valour Fore & Aft. Painting by Kipp Soldwedel of Continental marines disembarking from the Providence during their amphibious assault on Fort Nassau in the Bahamas, March 3, 1776, from Florence Parker Simister, The Fire's Center (1978)

Newport, vulnerable to naval attack, suffered a severe setback to its growth and development when the British seized and occupied it during the Revolution. This contemporary painting by Robert Cleveley shows the December 8, 1776, landing of a large force under Sir Henry Clinton. Efforts to dislodge this force, including the August 1778 siege of Newport that culminated in the Battle of Rhode Island, were unavailing. The British left of their own accord in October 1779 when Clinton decided that the occupying troops could be more militarily useful in the South. Painting (1776) courtesy of the National Maritime Museum, Greenwich, England

One of the more daring exploits of the Revolution was performed by Colonel William Barton of Providence. The British had captured the island of Aquidneck in December 1776 and were occupying it with a force under the command of the overbearing Major General Richard Prescott. On the evening of July 9, 1777, Barton, with forty volunteers in five boats, crossed the bay from Warwick Neck to Portsmouth, where the English general was in temporary residence at an isolated farmhouse called the Overing House, at what is now Prescott Farm. Rumor persists that the general went there for a romantic rendezvous. Eluding British ships and sentries, Barton snatched the

partially clothed Prescott from his bed and returned with him to Providence. Later Prescott's freedom was purchased in an exchange for the captured American general Charles Lee.

Barton, a hatter by trade who owned the lot upon which the Fleet Bank Building now stands, invested in Vermont lands after the Revolution, lost money, and spent nearly fourteen years confined in the Green Mountain State as a debtor. When the Marquis de Lafayette visited America in 1824–25, he learned of his old ally's plight and paid Barton's obligation, thereby securing the aged soldier's release. Barton returned in honor to Providence, where he died in 1831.

The Newport Restoration Foundation, present owner of the Overing House, has recreated a typical early Rhode Island farm around it, using buildings it has restored and brought here from the surrounding area. The guard house, used by Prescott's troops, is now a museum displaying period furniture; an original windmill still grinds corn; and a country store, one of the early centers of social life as well as commerce, houses the medicines, fabrics, kitchen ware, and farm implements of the time. Portrait in oil on canvas (ca. 1780) courtesy of RIHS (Rhi x3 3018); photo of farm from Guinness and Sadler, Newport Preserv'd (1982), courtesy of the Newport Restoration Foundation

A year and a half into the British occupation of Newport, the Americans planned a siege to dislodge or capture the six-thousand-man British force there. In February 1778 France had entered into a treaty with the United States, and Rhode Island would be the testing ground of that new Franco-American alliance. By early August the rebels had assembled an army of ten thousand strong under General John Sullivan of New Hampshire while a newly arrived French fleet under Admiral Charles Hector, Comte D'Estaing, hovered off Newport.

Plans called for a combined attack—Sullivan from Tiverton and D'Estaing from the west passage—but these plans were scrapped when Sullivan, learning that the British had evacuated the northern end of the island, advanced prematurely. An angry D'Estaing then discovered that a large British fleet had appeared to reinforce the Newport garrison. On August 11, as the two fleets maneuvered, a hurricane descended upon Narragansett Bay, battering both sides. D'Estaing's flagship, the Languedoc, was dismasted. Ten days later, over Sullivan's strenuous objections, the French hauled anchor and sailed to Boston for repairs. This evacuation, depicted here by a French artist who accompanied the expedition, left England's Newport army open to reinforcement. According to Paul Dearden, the leading historian of the battle, this botched rehearsal for Yorktown marked a most "inauspicious dawn of alliance" with France. Sepia wash drawing by Pierre Ozanne (1778), courtesy of the Library of Congress

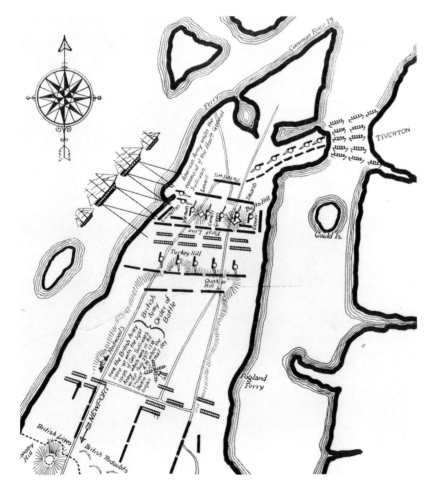

The Black Regiment. 1778   The Battle of Rhode Island

In addition to its own army, or home guard, and local militia units, Rhode Island furnished soldiers to the Continental army. The first troops—a fifteen-hundred-member "army of observation"—were sent to Boston in 1775 after Lexington and Concord and were taken into the Continental service as three distinct regiments. After that year the state supplied two regiments, which served mainly in New York and New Jersey and distinguished themselves especially in the defense of Fort Red Bank (October 1777) on the Delaware River opposite Philadelphia. In 1778, to recoup early losses, the First Regiment was restored to full strength by recruiting Rhode Island's free blacks and slaves (who were offered freedom for enlisting). Both regiments fought under General John Sullivan in the August 1778 Battle of Rhode Island. In 1781 the two regiments were consolidated and participated in the victory at Yorktown.

Shown here are renditions by military artists of the typical field dress of the Second Rhode Island Regiment (below left); the Rhode Island Train of Artillery, part of the home guard (below); and the black unit of the First Rhode Island Regiment (upper left). Sketch of the Second Regiment and the Train of Artillery by Charles M. Lefferts, Uniforms of the American, British, French, and German Armies in the War of the American Revolution (1926), courtesy of the New York Historical Society; commemorative plate of the Black Regiment (designed by Frank Quagan of the Gorham Division of Textron as a bicentennial tribute) from the author's collection

General Sullivan had advanced to the last ring of fortifications around Newport when D'Estaing departed. Realizing the siege was doomed, Sullivan withdrew northward to Portsmouth with British and Hessians in pursuit. On August 29 the Americans turned, and with their backs to the Sakonnet River, they repulsed three determined attacks. If the rebels had been overrun, Sullivan's entire army would have been captured. Conspicuous in fighting off the enemy offensive were the members of Colonel Christopher Greene's newly formed black regiment. Today a monument at the junction of Routes 114 and 24 in Portsmouth commemorates the heroism of this unit, which also saw much bloody action later in the war. The daring Warwick-born Christopher Greene (left), a veteran of the ill-fated Quebec expedition of 1775, met death when ambushed by Tories on May 14, 1781. Map of battle (far left), based on a contemporary sketch in the RISA, from Paul R. Dearden, The Rhode Island Campaign of 1778: Inauspicious Dawn of Alliance (1980); portrait of Colonel Christopher Greene by James Sullivan Lincoln from an unsigned original, courtesy of the Brown University Library

Ironically, Silas Talbot, an army man from Providence, was the only Rhode Island captain of a U.S. naval vessel who maintained an unsullied reputation during the Revolution (Hopkins and Whipple, for example, drew strong congressional criticism). Talbot occasionally got command of a ship, and when he did, sparks flew. In October 1778 he attacked the British schooner Pigot, *which was blocking the mouth of the Sakonnet River. Talbot plunged the jib boom of his sloop* Hawke *into the rigging of the British vessel to hold her tight while his men overran her. In July 1779, while in command of the* Argo, *Talbot captured a ten-gun British privateer and two other vessels of twelve and fourteen guns. Along with these prizes he recaptured three American ships which the British vessels had in tow. This feat by an army major prompted Congress in September 1779 to grant him the rank of captain in the Continental navy. Having moved to New York State after the war, Talbot resumed his naval career in the 1790s during the limited war with France. This daring and impulsive seaman died in 1813. Sketch from Welcome A. Greene,* The Providence Plantations for 250 Years *(1886)*

The swift-sailing Sloop HOPE.

On Thursday next will sail (compleatly fitted for a short Cruize of Fifty Days) the swift-sailing Privateer Sloop HOPE, mounting 10 Carriage Guns, CHRISTOPHER SMITH, Commander. All Gentlemen Seamen, and able-bodied Landsmen, who wish to try their Fortunes, may have an Opportunity, by applying at the Rendezvous, at Mr. Joshua Hacker's, or to the Commander on board, at Clark and Nightingale's Wharff.

Fortunately for British merchant shipping, Rhode Island's prospective privateers were bottled up in Narragansett Bay during most of the war because of the English occupation of Newport. Late in the conflict, however, some local mariners attempted to make up for lost time, as indicated by this August 1781 advertisement for crewmen "to try their fortunes." Courtesy of RIHS (Rhi x3 1052)

Landung einer Französischen Hülfs Armee in America, zu Rhode Island. am 11ten Julius 1780.

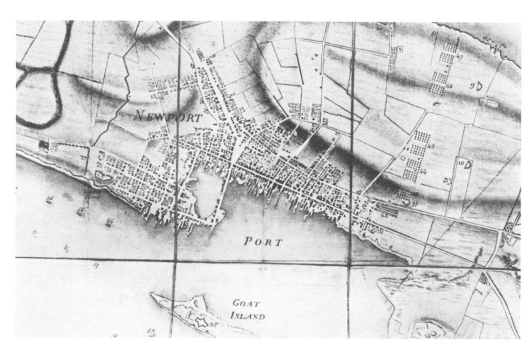

In July 1780 Newport experienced its second occupation of the Revolution when six thousand French troops under Count Rochambeau landed from ships commanded by Admiral de Ternay. Some of these soldiers were eventually quartered in Bristol and Providence. This French occupation was benevolent, and members of Rochambeau's army (which contained Irish and Polish units) developed amicable relations with their Rhode Island hosts and hostesses during their stay. The occupation continued until June 1781, when the troops began their fateful march to Yorktown.

Shown here is a contemporary artist's rendition of the Newport landing (above) and a map from Rochambeau's papers showing the positions taken by the French army and navy: at No. 43, artillery; at No. 44, the Bourbonnais regiment; at No. 45, the Royal Deux Ponts regiment; at No. 46, the Soissonnais regiment; at No. 47, the Saint Onge regiment; at No. 48, Lauzun's Hussars; and at Nos. 51, 52, 56, and 57, the positions of the French ships. En route to Yorktown in 1781 and returning in November 1782, the French army camped at Waterman's Tavern on Maple Valley Road in Coventry. Sketch of landing from Historisch-genealogischer calender oder Jahrbuch...fur 1784 *(Leipzig), courtesy of RIHS (Rhi x3 4317); map from the Rochambeau Papers, Library of Congress, reprinted in Allan Forbes and Paul F. Cadman,* France and New England, *I (1925); photo of Waterman Tavern (ca. 1923) by John R. Hess in Forbes and Cadman,* France and New England, *I (1925)*

Rhode Island's most notable contribution to the Revolutionary war effort was Nathanael Greene (1742-1786). Born in the Potowomut section of Warwick, Greene moved to Coventry at age twenty-eight to manage the family forge, and he represented that town in the General Assembly during the early 1770s. As the Revolution approached, this unorthodox Quaker helped organize a militia unit called the Kentish Guards. In May 1775 the legislature made him brigadier general of the state militia, and the following month he received the same rank in the Continental army. During the war Greene held numerous commands, including the post of quartermaster general (1778–1780), but his fame rests upon his brilliant Southern campaign of 1780-81 against Cornwallis. Military historians feel that Greene was America's most skillful practitioner of what we now call "guerrilla warfare," a distinction giving him new relevance as a military strategist. For his hit-and-run tactics, which debilitated Cornwallis's forces for the knockout blow at Yorktown, Greene has long been considered as second in ability only to Washington among the generals of the American Revolution. At present a multivolume edition of his papers is being published by the Rhode Island Historical Society. Portrait by Charles Willson Peale, courtesy of Independence National Historical Park

Rhode Island had some loyalists (or Tories, as the rebels called them), especially in Newport, where they formed a group called the Loyal Newport Associates. These defenders of the king paid for their opposition to the Revolutionary cause when the victorious "patriots" seized their lands and property. This Mount Hope home of a Bristol loyalist, appropriately named Isaac Royall, was confiscated and sold by the state to support the military effort. It was eventually bought by Deputy Governor William Bradford, a leading Federalist, who entertained George Washington here in 1793. Photo courtesy of RIHS (Rhi x3 5712)

University Hall was the first building constructed on the Brown University campus after the school's transfer from Warren, where it had been founded by Baptists in 1764. This structure, completed in 1771, was used during the Revolution as a barracks and hospital for American and French troops. Here George Washington received the honorary degree of doctor of laws in 1790.

To the left in the picture is the president's house, built for the Reverend James Manning, a Baptist clergyman who served as the first president of what was then called Rhode Island College. Manning (1738-1791) was very prominent in civic affairs. In addition to his educational duties, he was pastor of the First Baptist Church (where Brown commencements were held), a member of the Confederation Congress, and a leading campaigner for Rhode Island's ratification of the federal Constitution. Engravings from Reuben A. Guild, Early History of Brown University (1897)

61

The first settlers of Providence embraced a more radical brand of Calvinist theology than the Congregationalism of the Puritans. Because of their belief that baptism should be only for those who were apparently "elected" for salvation, they objected to the baptism of infants. In 1639 these Anabaptists, with Roger Williams among them, established the first Baptist congregation in America. The spiritually restless Williams soon left this group to become a Seeker—one who tried to live a humble and pious life while waiting for God to re-establish His Christian church—but despite this and other departures, and despite many doctrinal divisions within its ranks, the First Baptist Church prospered in colonial Providence.

In 1775 the church's members completed the construction of their splendid meetinghouse on a sizable lot bounded by North Main Street, Benefit Street, Angell's Lane (Thomas Street), and Waterman Street. Joseph Brown was the principal architect and his brother John the contractor. The church seated fourteen hundred people, and above its vestibule a wooden steeple rose 185 feet skyward. Still a major Providence landmark, the First Baptist Meeting House has been described as Providence's outstanding architectural work of the pre-Revolutionary period.

The church's bell, which doubled as the town alarm, bore this inscription:

> For freedom of conscience the town was
>   first planted.
> Persuasion, not force,
>   was used by the people.
> This church is the oldest, and
>   has not recanted
> Enjoying and granting bell, temple,
>   and steeple.

Print (1789) by Samuel Hill from Reuben A. Guild, Early History of Brown University (1897)

Ezra Stiles (1727-1795) was Rhode Island's most famous resident intellectual of the Revolutionary era. Stiles came from New Haven in 1755 at age twenty-nine to serve as minister of Newport's Second Congregational Church, a position he was to occupy for more than two decades. His interests and activities during this period were amazingly varied: he served as a librarian of the Redwood Library, mastered several languages, conducted numerous scientific experiments, and wrote a famous diary detailing his life in Newport, while he also performed his religious duties faithfully and often engaged in religious discourse with the Reverend Samuel Hopkins, a noted theologian and abolitionist who was his counterpart at Newport's First Congregational Church. An ardent patriot, Stiles left Newport in 1776 just before the British occupation. In 1778 he returned to New Haven as president and professor of ecclesiastical history at Yale, and he continued in these posts until his death. Portrait (1771), oil on canvas, by Samuel King, courtesy of Yale University Art Gallery

King's County (now Washington) was created in 1729. Three years later its first county house was built in the Tower Hill section of South Kingstown. Here, by law, the General Assembly held a session every other October. By 1752 the initial structure had fallen into disrepair, so an enterprising group who resided in neighboring Little Rest (Kingston) offered to build a new one to lure the county seat to their village. Their bid was accepted by the General Assembly, but this second edifice also became obsolete within two decades. In 1776 a third (and still surviving) structure was completed. It served as a meeting place for the legislature, and, therefore, one of the five state capitols, until 1854. The original design (shown here) was considerably altered in the 1860s, when the original gable roof with cupola and end chimneys was replaced by a French mansard roof and a projecting, towered stairway hall. Today the historic building houses the Kingston Free Library. Courtesy of RIHS (Rhi x3 853)

The fortune amassed by John Brown enabled him to construct a magnificent mansion on College Hill. Built between 1786 and 1788 from designs developed by his brother Joseph (who also designed his own house on South Main Street, University Hall, the Market House, and the First Baptist Church), this three-story brick structure was described by President John Quincy Adams as "the most magnificent and elegant private mansion I have ever seen on this continent."

In the mid-nineteenth century the house passed into the hands of the Gammell family, who in turn sold it in 1901 to financier and transportation magnate Marsden Perry. In 1936 John Nicholas Brown, great-great-grandnephew of the original owner, bought the house from the Perry estate and six years later donated it to the Rhode Island Historical Society. Today the well-preserved structure at 52 Power Street is maintained by the society as a museum of American decorative arts, furniture, and painting. It is open to the public. Photo courtesy of RIHS (Rhi x3 1803)

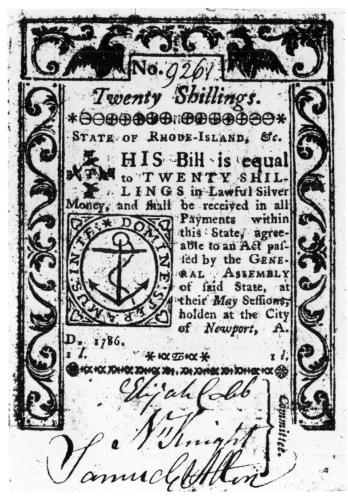

During the nationwide economic depression of the early 1780s, Rhode Island farmers groaned under the heavy land tax imposed upon them by the merchant-controlled General Assembly. Many lost their farms through tax foreclosure. Then, in 1786, a harried South Kingstown tax collector named Jonathan Hazard led a rural taxpayers' revolt, and his ad hoc Country party seized control of the state legislature. Immediately these farmers passed debtor relief measures, including the issuance of £100,000 of paper money that they could borrow from the state to pay their back taxes. Since the bills were legal tender and could also be used to discharge private debts, merchants and creditors howled. Rhode Island paper money, 1786 issue, author's collection

When many businessmen balked at accepting the paper money, the Assembly passed a "force act" imposing criminal penalties on anyone who refused this legal tender. This punishment was to be inflicted without benefit of trial by jury. When Revolutionary War marine hero John Trevett tendered a bill to his Newport butcher John Weeden, and Weeden declined it, the stage was set for Trevett v. Weeden, *the most important case in Rhode Island's judicial history. The case was heard before the highest court in the state, and it concluded with the court's refusing jurisdiction and dismissing Trevett's complaint.*

In the course of the trial, however, James

Mitchell Varnum, one of Weeden's defense attorneys, advanced a learned and eloquent argument urging the court to exercise its hitherto unused power to review

legislation and declare the force act unconstitutional. Although the court did not act on this plea, Varnum's printed brief was widely disseminated, and it probably influenced John Marshall in his famous formulation of the doctrine of judicial review.

Varnum, a distinguished Revolutionary War general and a founder of the Kentish Guards, left Rhode Island shortly after the trial to seek his fortune in the newly acquired Ohio Country, where his sudden death in 1789, at the age of forty, cut short a brilliant career. Courtesy of RIHS (Rhi x3 2018)

Associated with General Varnum as counsel in Trevett v. Weeden was Henry Marchant (1741-1796), a well-educated Newport intellectual and a protégé of Ezra Stiles. Marchant was an ardent Son of Liberty during the Stamp Act protest, and when war came, he served as a Rhode Island delegate to the Continental Congress (1777-1779). After the war he entered the General Assembly as a vigorous spokesman for the state's commercial interest (1784-1790).

In 1790, as a strong supporter of the new federal Constitution, Marchant introduced the successful bill for the call of a ratifying convention, at which he played a leading role. His efforts on behalf of Federalism were rewarded when George Washington appointed him Rhode Island's first federal judge, a post he held from July 1790 until his death in August 1796.

When the Revolution erupted, Marchant left Newport for this South County estate. Though he represented Newport in the General Assembly during the 1780s, he maintained this well-kept farm in South Kingstown. This pencil sketch (ca. 1790) by an unknown artist is a rare surviving eighteenth-century view of rural life in Rhode Island. Sketch courtesy of RIHS (Rhi x3 3019)

For numerous reasons—some petty, some commendable—Rhode Island delayed its ratification of the federal Constitution until May 29, 1790, thirteen months after George Washington's inauguration. Even then, the vote of approval was produced only by federal coercion and Providence's threatened secession from the state, and the 34-to-32-vote margin for ratification was the narrowest of any state. Rhode Island's dissenting tradition, its individualism, and its democratic localism contributed to its Anti-federalism. These traits were particularly strong in rural areas, and the Country party controlled the legislature during the era when the Constitution was framed and adopted. In addition, the Constitution's recognition of slavery alienated the state's large and influential Quaker community.

When the favorable vote finally came, the commercial towns rejoiced. This broadside by Providence Gazette editor John Carter announcing ratification speaks of "a discharge of thirteen cannon" and the "further demonstrations of joy" which were expected to take place. Broadside courtesy of RIHS (Rhi x3 1953)

RHODE-ISLAND and PROVIDENCE PLANTATIONS united to the Great *AMERICAN FAMILY.*

* * * * * * * * * *

PROVIDENCE, Monday, May 31, 1790.

SATURDAY Night, at Eleven o'Clock, an Express arrived in Town from Newport, with the important Intelligence, that the CONVENTION OF THIS STATE had ratified the CONSTITUTION OF THE UNITED STATES.

[The remainder of the broadside text continues in two columns, reproducing the ratification proceedings of the Convention of the State of Rhode-Island and Providence Plantations.]

[Printed by J. Carter.]

Samuel Slater (1768–1835) has been called the Father of American Manufactures. He began his industrial career in the British textile industry but migrated to the United States from Derbyshire in 1789, sensing a need for his talent here, since independence had removed the mercantile restrictions that Britain had imposed on American manufacturing. Shortly after his arrival he entered into an agreement with Moses Brown to construct waterpowered machinery for carding and spinning cotton yarn. For several months he labored with blacksmith David Wilkinson and woodworker Sylvanus Brown on this difficult project. Then, on December 20, 1790, spinning frames modeled on those of English inventor Richard Arkwright were activated by the force of Pawtucket Falls on the Blackstone River. This event marked the beginning of the textile-factory system in America. In 1793 the present Slater Mill was constructed on this advantageous site by the partnership of Slater, Brown, and William Almy.

In this modern scene the 1793 mill, as expanded and restored, is on the right, with David and Oziel Wilkinson's mill of 1810 at the left. Both structures are open to the public. Photo courtesy of Slater Mill Historic Site

RHODE ISLAND IN THE NEW REPUBLIC, 1790-1845

During the early years of the republic, the always romantic and sometimes lucrative China trade with the ports of the Orient flourished, then declined, and finally expired in 1841. In this age Rhode Island weathered a major hurricane (the Great Gale of 1815) and a locally unpopular confrontation with England (the War of 1812). Its major municipality, Providence, evolved from town to city (1832), and its political party system experienced two phases of opposition: Federalists vs. Democratic–Republicans (1794–1817) and National Republican-Whigs vs. Democrats (1828–1854). Its transportation system progressed from turnpikes utilizing horse-drawn wagons, carriages, and stages to railroads with steam-powered locomotives. From 1824 to 1828 a canal was constructed through the Blackstone Valley from Worcester to Providence in a vain attempt to capture the central Massachusetts market for Rhode Island entrepreneurs—an attempt which the Boston and Albany Railroad soon trumped and which the Providence and Worcester Railroad rendered obsolete in 1847.

With Providence civic leader John Howland in the vanguard, a system of free public education was established by the School Act of 1828 after a false start twenty-five years earlier. During the 1830s and 1840s that system grew and prospered, especially in Providence, owing to the exertions of Samuel Bridgham, Nathan Bishop, and Thomas Wilson Dorr. Henry Barnard was imported from 1843 to 1849 as the first state commissioner of education, with the aim of bringing the other towns to the high educational level achieved by Providence.

The large-scale immigration of foreigners of non-English stock also had its origins in this era. From the mid-1820s onward, Irish Catholics came to Rhode Island in ever-increasing numbers either to labor on such public works projects as Fort Adams in Newport (begun in 1824), the Blackstone Canal (begun 1824), and the railroads (begun 1833), or to work in the textile mills and metals factories that had begun to dot and to darken the local landscape.

The two most momentous developments in this formative era, however, were a transformation of the state's economy from an agrarian-commercial to an industrial base and a governmental transformation from colonial charter to written state constitution, accomplished after a long period of reform agitation and a serious political upheaval known as the Dorr Rebellion. The economic metamorphosis occurred

Moses Brown, the youngest of the five illustrious Brown brothers, was born in 1738. After his father's death in 1739 he was adopted by his wealthy uncle Obadiah and became his heir. He engaged primarily in mercantile activity from 1763 until the premature death of his wife ten years later; then the grief-stricken Moses embraced the Quaker faith and began a career of humanitarian service and philanthropy. His major effort was directed against slavery and the slave trade, and it was largely through his exertions that Rhode Island initiated the abandonment of the former in 1784 and outlawed the latter in 1787.

As the founder of the firm of Brown and Almy, Moses was the financial sponsor of Samuel Slater's venture in cotton manufacture and actually made his first move toward developing a textile mill in May 1787, almost two years before Slater's arrival at Pawtucket Falls. Among his many civic projects were Moses Brown School, the Rhode Island Bible Society, the Rhode Island Peace Society, and the Providence Athenaeum. Although plagued by attacks of vertigo, he lived a long and productive life, dying on September 7, 1836, two weeks short of his ninety-eighth birthday. Oil on canvas by Henry E. Kinney, courtesy of RIHS (Rhi x3 3128)

first and contributed to the constitutional crisis.

The impact of the American Revolution and the state's consequent release from the industrial restrictions of the British mercantile system were the first factors to effect a gradual shift in Rhode Island's economy. Newport, under military occupation during most of the war, declined and yielded its economic ascendancy to Providence, whose merchants and entrepreneurs (most notably the famous Brown family) began to experiment with manufacturing.

The year 1790 was marked by an event that served as the catalyst for the state's economic transition. That occurrence was the reconstruction of a cotton-spinning frame similar to those used in England and its employment in a mill at Pawtucket Falls on the Blackstone River. It was the first time cotton yarn was spun by water power in America. The men chiefly responsible for this promising venture were Providence merchants Moses Brown, Smith Brown, and William Almy; Samuel Slater, a young English immigrant with technical knowledge and managerial experience acquired in the cotton mills of his native land; and local craftsmen such as carpenter Sylvanus Brown and metalworker Oziel Wilkinson.

The Rhode Island cotton industry developed slowly, with Providence businessmen supplying most of its funds, managers, and expertise. The significant shift of commercial capital into cotton manufacturing began in 1804, prior to the Jeffersonian embargo and even before the peaking of the state's maritime operations (which now included the China trade). By the late 1820s the processing of cotton displaced commerce as the backbone of the Rhode Island economy, and the river valleys in the northeastern quadrant of the state hummed with activity.

In this era woolen production also flourished, especially in South County, and the need for textile machinery gave rise to a base-metals industry centered in Providence. Another early and important area of industrial endeavor was the manufacture of precious metals, especially gold and silver jewelry. For a century these four industries—cottons, woolens, base and precious metals—steadily expanded and dominated the state's economic life. But while these developments occurred, agriculture declined, many farms reverted to forest, and many rural towns experienced a substantial emigration.

Industrialization and its corollary, urbanization, combined by the 1840s to produce an episode known as the Dorr Rebellion—Rhode Island's crisis in constitutional government. The state's royal charter, then still in effect, gave disproportionate influence to the declining rural towns; it conferred almost unlimited

power on the General Assembly; and it contained no procedure for its own amendment. To retain their own power and influence, state legislators, regardless of party, insisted upon retaining the old real estate requirement for voting and officeholding, even though it had been abandoned in all other states. As Rhode Island grew more urbanized, this freehold qualification became more restrictive. By 1840 about 60 percent of the free adult males were disfranchised.

Because earlier moderate efforts at change (beginning as early as 1817) had been virtually ignored by the General Assembly, the reformers of 1840-1843 decided to bypass the legislature and convene a People's Convention, equitably apportioned and chosen by an enlarged electorate. Thomas Wilson Dorr of Providence, a patrician attorney, assumed the leadership of the movement in late 1841 and became the principal draftsman of the progressive People's Constitution, which was ratified in a popular referendum in December 1841. Dorr was elected governor under this document in April 1842. The reformers were resisted by a "Law and Order" coalition of Whigs and rural Democrats, who returned incumbent governor Samuel Ward King to office in a separate election and then used force and intimidation to prevent the implementation of the People's Constitution. When Dorr responded in kind by unsuccessfully attempting to seize the state arsenal in Providence on May 18, 1842, most of his followers deserted the cause, and Dorr fled into exile. When he returned in late June to reconvene his so-called People's Legislature in the village of Chepachet, a Law and Order army of twenty-five hundred marched to Glocester and sent the People's Governor into exile a second time.

The turmoil and popular agitation against the charter which produced the Dorr Rebellion forced the victors to consent to the drafting of a written state constitution. Arthur May Mowry, the first major historian of the Dorr War, calls this instrument "liberal and well-adapted to the needs of the state,"

In 1803 Robert Fulton made transportation history when his steamboat, the Clermont, *churned up the Hudson River. A decade before this heralded event, David French, one of Fulton's draftsmen, had visited Rhode Island to examine a boat aptly called* The Experiment. *This twelve-ton vessel had been built in 1792 by Elijah Ormsbee, a Providence carpenter, with a steam engine constructed by Pawtucket inventive genius David Wilkinson, Samuel Slater's associate and brother-in-law. The two young men printed tickets (shown here) for contemplated trips from Providence to Newport on their steamboat. With spectators lining the banks of the Seekonk, they navigated* The Experiment *from Providence to Pawtucket "between the bridges." According to Wilkinson's later reminiscences, the boat was propelled by a "goose-foot paddle" instead of a sidewheel.*

After the "frolic," as Wilkinson called it, the boat was "hauled up," and for some unexplained reason the promising venture was abandoned. Wilkinson's later exploits as an inventor and manufacturer of textile machinery won him national recognition, but Fulton got the credit for the steamboat. Facsimile of ticket (1792) from Edward Field, State of Rhode Island and Providence Plantations...A History, *II (1902)*

but his appraisal neglects one important item: the 1842 constitution established a $134 freehold suffrage qualification for naturalized citizens, and this anti-Irish Catholic restriction, not removed until 1888, was the most blatant instance of political nativism found in any state constitution in the land. The stranglehold on the state Senate which the 1842 document gave to the rural towns (there was one senator from each town regardless of its population) is also a fact of paramount importance and remained so at least until the "Bloodless Revolution" in 1935. Cumbersome amendment procedures made reform of the document a very difficult task.

This constitution, overwhelmingly ratified in November 1842 by a margin of 7,024 to 51, became effective in May 1843. Despite the margin of victory, the turnout was meager, for there were more than 23,000 adult male citizens in the state. That the opposition, in mute protest, refrained from voting

explains in part the constitution's apathetic reception and the lopsided vote.

A frustrated Dorr returned from his New Hampshire refuge in October 1843 to surrender to local authorities. Immediately arrested and jailed until February 1844, Dorr was prosecuted for treason against the state. In a trial of less than two weeks, he was found guilty by a jury composed entirely of political opponents and sentenced to hard labor in solitary confinement for life. He served one year before Governor Charles Jackson—elected on a "liberation" platform—authorized his release. A Democratic General Assembly restored Dorr's civil and political rights in 1851 and in 1854 reversed the treason conviction. But these gestures did little to cheer the vanquished reformer, whose spirit and health were broken. Disillusioned, he died in December 1854 in the midst of a local Know-Nothing campaign directed against immigrant Irish attempts to secure the vote.

The glamorous China and East India trade from the Port of Providence began in December 1787 when John Brown and his son-in-law John Francis sent the ship General Washington *to China with rum, cheese, spermaceti candles, and cannon from Hope Furnace. The ship returned on July 2, 1789, laden with tea (nearly eight hundred chests), gunpowder (which the Chinese invented), silk, flannel, chinaware, and a small fortune in profits for its sponsors. One of the most famous East Indiamen (as the ships in the oriental trade were called) was the Brown and Ives vessel* Ann and Hope, *named by the owners for their wives. (This name was also applied by the firm to its Lonsdale textile mill, and it was adopted by the local department store chain that began at the mill site when manufacturing operations ceased.) The 550-ton ship sank off Block Island during a storm in January 1806. Rhode Island's romantic and lucrative China trade ended in the early 1840s, when the Port of New York came to dominate American shipping and local merchants increasingly transferred their capital to industrial ventures. Painting of the* Ann and Hope *by Charles Torrey, courtesy of Robert Hale Ives Goddard*

Edward Carrington of Providence (1775–1843) was Rhode Island's leading China merchant. Many of the prized oriental items he acquired he retained for his personal use. The Rhode Island Historical Society was bequeathed many of Carrington's artifacts and now exhibits them at its John Brown House museum. Photo courtesy of PJC

Captain Robert Gray (1755–1806), a Tiverton native, was another oriental pioneer. From 1789 to 1793 he commanded the Columbia, *a vessel that carried him to the Oregon Country in search of furs and pelts to trade in China for that nation's silks, spices, porcelains, and other luxury items. In July 1789 Gray left the northwest coast for China and returned to his home port of Boston by sailing through the Indian Ocean and around Africa's Cape of Good Hope, thus completing the first American circumnavigation of the globe. Shortly after his triumphant return he set sail again for*

Oregon, and on this voyage he entered and explored the mouth of the great river of that region, the Columbia, which he named for his ship (shown here). This visitation established an American claim to the Pacific Northwest. Loaded with furs, Gray again sailed for China and then home, completing a second forty-two-thousand-mile world-encircling voyage. Painting of Gray courtesy of the Oregon Historical Society; etching of the Columbia *by C. J. A. Wilson from Francis E. Cross and Charles M. Pakin, Jr.,* Sea Venture: Captain Gray's Voyages of Discovery, 1787-1793 *(1981)*

At the turn of the nineteenth century the China trade was new and promising, but an older traffic still appealed to the greed of some Rhode Islanders. A Quaker-inspired state statue of 1787 had prohibited Rhode Islanders from engaging in the slave trade, but one could choose to operate beyond the state's borders (e.g., in South Carolina) and thus escape penalty. In addition, the foreign slave trade was protected by a provision in the federal Constitution that prevented Congress from outlawing that traffic prior to 1808.

James De Wolf (1764–1837), a prominent merchant, shipowner, and manufacturer from Bristol, preferred Africa to China. Prior to 1808 he brought hundreds of slaves from Africa to Charleston, and after 1808 he carried his black cargo to his sugar plantations in Cuba. When the War of 1812 interrupted his usual activity, De Wolf outfitted a privateer that reputedly captured over three million dollars of British property. In 1821 the Rhode Island General Assembly, undisturbed by his unsavory past, chose De Wolf to be United States senator. In 1837, after a full life as lawbreaker and lawmaker, he died on his elegant one-thousand-acre Bristol estate. Portrait, watercolor on ivory, artist unknown, courtesy of RIHS (Rhi x3 3070)

The British-oriented foreign policy of the Federalist party produced an American confrontation with its former ally, France. From June 1798 until September 1800, the two countries engaged in a limited naval war that prompted the United States to recreate a navy and erect coastal defenses. While Revolutionary War mariners such as Silas Talbot and Christopher Perry were activated, Fort Brown (popularly called Fort Dumpling) was built in Jamestown on an outcropping of rocks once noted by Verrazzano. The fort survived the French crisis and the War of 1812 without incident and then fell into disuse.

According to an 1872 guidebook, the Old Fort (as it was then called) afforded "one of the finest marine views of the whole coast." The site was described in William Cullen Bryant's Picturesque America (1878) as one of the garden spots of the Northeast. "We trust," said poet Bryant, "that it will be left undisturbed for ages, as it is one of the few memorials of our early history." The fort was nonetheless demolished in 1898 for a modern facility during the Spanish-American War craze. Steel engraving by Fenner, Sears, and Company from a drawing by W. G. Wall in 1831, courtesy of RIHS (Rhi x3 5682)

In Gilbert Stuart (1755-1828), Rhode Island produced one of America's most noted portrait painters. Stuart was born to a native Rhode Island mother and a Scots immigrant father who operated a snuff mill at their homestead in North Kingstown (this well-preserved structure, the Gilbert Stuart Birthplace, is now open to the public). When their manufacturing venture failed, the family moved to Newport, where the teenaged Stuart began his artistic career. In 1775 he left to continue his studies in London. From then onward, he had few connections with Rhode Island and his references to his humble boyhood were tinged with sarcasm.

During nearly two decades in London and Dublin, Stuart developed his skills and gained an imposing reputation. He returned to America in 1793, residing first in Philadelphia, next in Germantown, and then in Washington, D.C. His portraits of Presidents Washington, Jefferson, Madison, and Monroe are among the most notable in the annals of American portraiture. Especially noteworthy is his second rendering of Washington, done in 1796—a life-size standing depiction showing the left side of the president's face, his eyes gazing right and his right hand outstretched as if he is

addressing an audience.

Sometime in the summer of 1805 Stuart moved to Boston, where he lived for the remainder of his life, adding many more canvasses to his huge artistic production. He had a total of twelve children, four of whom survived him. Self-portrait of Stuart as a young man in Charles Merrill Mount, Gilbert Stuart: A Biography (1964), from an original in the Tate Gallery, London

The Kent (later called Greenwich) Academy was, perhaps, the town of East Greenwich's greatest claim to regional fame during the nineteenth century. Chartered in 1802, the Academy (as it was simply called) distinguished itself for 141 years in training the young of both sexes for careers in such varied fields as teaching, music, business, and missionary work. Its most notable graduates were Eben Tourjee, founder of the New England Conservatory of Music, and U. S. Senator Nelson Aldrich. Throughout the nineteenth century the Academy attracted a majority of its enrollees from other towns and cities; in 1865, for example, 257 of its 325 students were nonresidents. The school, says one local history, "was an object of pride among townspeople and the name Greenwich became synonymous with educational excellence."

In 1841 this private school was sold to the Providence Conference of the Methodist Episcopal Church. A new main structure was built in 1858 and demolished in the late 1950s. The Methodists conducted the school on a nondenominational basis, though Protestant teachings were made important components of the students' well-regimented curriculum. The organization ran the Academy or leased out its operation until 1943, when the town of East Greenwich bought the facility to house its public high school. Lithograph (ca. 1845) showing the Academy's original buildings. Courtesy of RIHS (Rhi x3 5686)

Dr. Solomon Drowne (1753–1834) and Theodore Foster (1752–1828), friends from their student days at Brown (class of 1773), collaborated in a fascinating way to shape the early history of the town of Foster. Set off from Scituate in 1781 and named for Theodore Foster, an influential lawyer and Providence town clerk, this western Rhode Island community became the home of both men when physician Drowne (shown right) returned to Rhode Island from his far-flung travels in 1801 and Foster left the United States Senate in 1803. Both men had long talked of establishing themselves in a setting conducive to contemplation and pursuing their respective professional interests in an idyllic rural retreat.

Their impact upon the town's development would require pages to relate, but Drowne's experiment at his estate, called Mount Hygeia after the Greek goddess of health, is most worthy of note. Combining his physician's belief that natural remedies were best with a botanist's curiosity in discovering new kinds and qualities of plant life, Drowne cultivated extensive botanical gardens around his north Foster home, growing medicinal plants and herbs and ornamental plants, both native and imported. In addition, he planted many varieties of trees, including the mulberry, which could be used to host silkworms. While carrying on this work, Drowne also served for more than two decades as profes-

sor of medicine and botany at Brown University's first medical school.

For many years after Drowne's death in 1834, Mount Hygeia was carefully maintained by his descendants. In this photo (ca. 1900) it still had a museumlike

appearance. From 1941 to 1963, however, with the death of Drowne's last direct descendant and ownership disputes among absentee heirs, the estate became vacant and vandal-prone. Fortunately the ownership problem has been resolved and this historic house has now been rescued and restored. Photo of Mount Hygeia from Foster, 1781-1981: a Bicentennial Celebration (1981); steel engraving of Drowne from a portrait by Eliza Hall Ward, courtesy of RIHS (Rhi x3 1276)

In 1752, eleven decades after the death of Anne Hutchinson, Rhode Island's second great prophetess was born, the eighth child of twelve in a well-to-do Cumberland farm family. By her early twenties, Jemima Wilkinson, a tall and graceful young woman, came under the spell of several evangelists, including a group of "New Light" Baptists which had just formed in Rhode Island. Soon afterward, during the course of a high fever, she fell into a prolonged trance, from which she emerged with the conviction that her body was now inhabited by the "Spirit of Life" which had come from God "to warn a lost and guilty, gossiping, dying world to flee from the wrath... to come." Taking the name of "Publick Universal Friend," she began to hold open-air meetings, which attracted large audiences. Her power, however, lay more in her charismatic personality than in her traditional calls for repentance. Gathering about twenty of her most devoted followers into a special band, she led a series of processions on horseback

through Rhode Island and Connecticut clad in a long, flowing robe. Between 1777 and 1782 she preached with great success in Providence and established churches in East Greenwich and South Kingstown.

The claim of her disciples that she was Jesus Christ come again scandalized orthodox churches and aroused much local resentment against her. Faced with this hostility, Jemima transferred her headquarters first to Philadelphia and then to the wilderness of western New York, where in 1790 she started a colony near Seneca Lake called Jerusalem. For several years this religious outpost prospered, but eventually dissension became rampant. Some disillusioned followers accused her of fraud and greed because of her habit of demanding personal gifts with the phrase "The Friend hath need of these things." She nonetheless built an elaborate house, in which she dwelt luxuriously. In her later years an affliction of dropsy destroyed her beauty and transformed her into an embittered old woman. She died in 1819, and her society dissolved soon after. *Portrait by John L. D. Mathies (1816) from Herbert A. Wisbey, Jr.,* Pioneer Prophetess: Jemima Wilkinson, the Publick Universal Friend *(1964)*

This rare panorama of an early nineteenth-century town was painted by English landscape artist John Worrall between 1808 and 1812. The subject is, of course, Providence's College Hill. The First Baptist Church (left), University Hall (left center), and the twin-spired First Congregational Church (right center), which burned down in 1814, dominate the skyline. This twelve-by-twenty-four-foot canvas was used as a drop curtain at the old Providence Theater. In 1832 Grace Church acquired the theater building as its congregation's first home, and it donated the painting to the ten-year-old Rhode Island Historical Society. Even more gratifying than the survival of this monumental artwork is the fact that most of the major structures depicted thereon have also been preserved. Courtesy of RIHS (Rhi x3 2570)

Christopher Perry, a Rhode Island sailor, was captured by the British during the Revolution and taken to a prison camp in Ireland. While there, he met Sarah Wallace Alexander and fell in love. After the conflict and Perry's release, he sailed back to Ireland to claim his bride. The union of this South County Yankee and his Irish immigrant wife produced several children, including Oliver Hazard Perry (shown here), born in 1785, and Matthew Calbraith Perry, his younger brother.

Appointed midshipman on his father's vessel, the General Greene, Oliver saw combat service in the West Indies during the 1798–1800 limited naval war with France (the Newport-based ship unfortunately brought back a plague of yellow fever that ravaged its home port in 1799). After Mediterranean duty against the

Barbary pirates, he was employed by the navy in building defensive gunboats along the southern Rhode Island coast. When the War of 1812 erupted, Perry volunteered for more challenging duty and received

command of American naval forces on Lake Erie, a fleet he had to build and man from scratch. On September 10, 1813, his ten-ship squadron decisively defeated a comparable British force, thereby giving America control of that strategic waterway. Since the capture of an English fleet by the American navy was unprecedented, the feat made Perry an instantaneous national hero, and his terse note to General William Henry Harrison—"We have met the enemy and they are ours"—has become an oft-quoted classic.

Perry remained in naval service after the war. While on a delicate diplomatic mission in Venezuela in 1819, he was stricken with yellow fever and died at the age of thirty-four. Engraving by W. G. Jackman from a painting by John Wesley Jarvis, courtesy of RIHS (Rhi x3 4077)

In June 1812, Congress declared war on England because of her repeated violations of American neutral rights on the high seas. The agrarian-based Democratic-Republican party of Madison and Jefferson reluctantly supported the war to vindicate the national honor, while the commercially oriented Federalist party opposed a declaration of war against England because of the destruction hostilities would bring to American maritime trade. With commercial centers and exposed coastal areas especially alarmed by the prospect of war with the "Mistress of the Seas," the Federalist party came to dominate Rhode Island politics in this turbulent era.

Despite her opposition to the war, Rhode Island participated actively in one phase of the conflict—privateering. Eighteen privately owned Rhode Island vessels secured commissions (letters of marque) from the federal government to prey on British commerce. Five of these ships sailed from Providence, four from Newport, and nine from Bristol. James De Wolf owned six of the nine Bristol privateers, in whole or in part, including the brigantine Yankee. This twelve-gun ship—by far the most successful American privateer of the War of 1812—made six cruises, seizing forty-one prizes valued at more than three million dollars. This booty depleted England's resources and greatly enriched De Wolf and members of the Yankee's crew, most of whom were Bristolians.

During the conflict English subjects were required to register with the U.S. marshal, and those who had no intention of becoming naturalized could be subject to deportation under the federal Alien Enemies Act. This Providence ship, appropriately called The Rising States, transported prisoners of war and other foreign nationals to British territory under a flag of truce. Drawing by Charles Simmons (1812), courtesy of RIHS (Rhi x3 1011)

Despite its disapproval of the War of 1812, Rhode Island produced the foremost naval hero of that conflict (Perry) and one of its most persuasive legal defenders, Henry Wheaton (1785-1848). This jurist, diplomat, and expounder of international law graduated from Brown (1802) and practiced law in Providence until 1812, when his legal defense of the policies of Jefferson and Madison prompted Democratic Republicans in New York City to offer him the editorship of the National Advocate, *their local party newspaper. During his three-year wartime tenure, Wheaton wrote forcefully and with learning on the questions of international law growing out of the War of 1812 and was considered the mouthpiece of the Madison administration. Rewarded with the post of U.S. Supreme Court reporter in 1816, he performed that job with ability and with praise, from jurists and lawyers alike, until 1827, when he embarked upon a long and successful diplomatic career. In 1847 Harvard offered him a distinguished lectureship in civil and international law, but he died before he could embark upon this new venture.*

Notable as Wheaton's career was, his most enduring achievement was his work as an expounder and historian of international law. His classic study, Elements of International Law *(1836), went through numerous editions and transla-*

tions. Its excellence has prompted historians to rank Wheaton with Marshall, Kent, and Story as a major architect of the American legal system. Portrait by George Peter Alexander Healy, courtesy of RIHS (Rhi x3 3099)

Though Rhode Island's coastal communities escaped the torch of the British, they received a much more devastating visitor in the early autumn of 1815—the Great Gale. On September 22-23 a violent hurricane swept in from the Caribbean and inundated the coastal towns. In Newport two dwelling houses and nine stores and workshops on Long Wharf were swept away. In one of the houses five people perished. In addition, church steeples were toppled, wharves destroyed, and ships driven ashore. In Providence the Great Bridge was washed away, thirty-five ships in the harbor were hurled against buildings or each other, wharves were demolished, about five hundred homes and smaller structures were flattened, and the streets were strewn with wreckage. "Chimneys, trees and fences were prostrated in every direction," according to one newspaper account, but most major public buildings were spared extensive damage, though the bowsprit of the Indiaman Ganges *pierced the third story of the Market House. Miraculously, only two townsmen perished, both at India Point. Painting by John Russell Bartlett, courtesy of RIHS (Rhi x3 3078)*

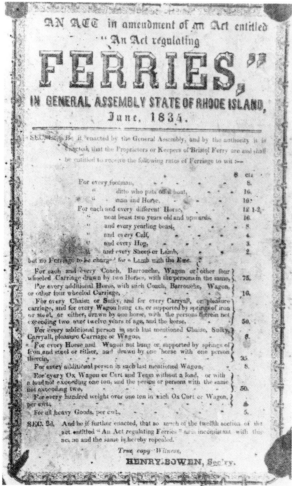

The state's best-known and most durable ferry plied the waters between Jamestown and Newport. Service was begun by the Carr family even before Jamestown earned its designation as Rhode Island's eighth town in 1678. The General Assembly granted its first license to operate this ferry route in 1695 to Caleb Carr, later governor of the colony. From time to time competing boatmen also gained this right of passage. In 1873, after some two hundred years of sailboat ferries operating at the mercy of wind and tide, the newly incorporated Jamestown and Newport Ferry Company placed a steamer in service on this route. The Carr family continued their involvement even after this reorganization, serving as officers of the corporation. Not until the completion of the Newport Bridge in 1969 did the ferry become obsolete. This early nineteenth-century painting shows Carr's sailboat ferry with old Fort Dumpling in the background, while the 1834 signboard displays the legislatively prescribed ferry rates. Painting and schedule from W. L. Watson, A Short History of Jamestown *(1933)*

In the years from 1794 to 1842, the Rhode Island General Assembly granted charters to approximately forty-six toll-road corporations. Generally these privately financed ventures used their publicly granted transportation monopolies to build new turnpikes or upgrade existing roads. The first of these corporations, the Glocester West Turnpike Company, received its charter in February 1794 to rebuild and maintain the road from Chepachet Bridge to the Connecticut line at Putnam. A decade later the pike was extended southeastward to Providence. This toll sign was posted at Harmony, the first village east of Chepachet on this so-called Putnam Pike.

In October 1794 Providence merchants secured approval to maintain a toll road through Johnston, Scituate, Foster, and Coventry to Norwich, Connecticut, via Plainfield (Plainfield Pike). A decade later entrepreneurs laid out a road from Providence to Douglas, Massachusetts (Douglas Pike), one from Providence to the mill villages at Woonsocket Falls (Louisquisset Pike), and another from Providence to Hartford (Hartford Pike).

Providence was the chief promoter and the beneficiary of toll-road construction. Eighteen companies proposed to give direct access to the city, twenty to construct through adjacent parts of Providence County, and still others to intersect the city routes in Kent and Washington counties (perhaps half these corporations actually went into operation). The roads constructed passed through the northern and western rather than the southern and eastern segments of the state. Thus the major routes radiated northeastward from Providence to Pawtucket to join the Boston turnpike; northward through Cumberland and Smithfield into western Massachusetts; and westward and southward across the breadth of Rhode Island into eastern Connecticut. In addition to freight, thousands of passengers were carried annually over the Boston and Providence turnpike to connect with New York packets or, after 1820, across the state via Providence and Westerly to make ferry connections at Stonington or New London.

Eventually the turnpike companies succumbed to railroad competition or to the political campaign in the 1830s directed against these government-granted private monopolies. Toll sign photo courtesy of RIHS Museum

RATES OF TOLL.

	Cts
For a Waggon, Cart or ox Sled not exceeding 4 Cattle	10
A Team of more than 4 Cattle	15
A Sley with more than 1 Horse	12½
A Sley with 1 Horse	6
A Coach Chariot, or Phaeton	40
A Chaise Chair or Sulkey	20
A Horse and Waggon	6
A Person and Horse	5
Horses and Mules in drovs per head	2
Neat Ccattle in droves per head	1
Swine in droves for every fifteen	10
For any number less than fifteen each	1
Sheep and Store shoats	½

During the first quarter of the nineteenth century, the Blackstone Canal was Rhode Island's most grandiose transportation scheme. Conceived by John Brown in 1796 to tap the economic resources of central Massachusetts and divert them from the Port of Boston, the project was not begun until 1822, when Benjamin Wright, of Erie Canal fame, conducted a survey for Edward Carrington and other Providence investors in the Blackstone Canal Company. The dig commenced in 1824, and on October 7, 1828, the Lady Carrington arrived in Worcester with much fanfare, becoming the first barge to traverse the entire length of the waterway.

The Blackstone Canal extended for forty-five miles. Thirty-two feet wide at the top, with a minimum depth of 3½ feet, it descended 451½ feet via sixty-two canal locks from its high point in Worcester to its outlet in Providence. The route adhered to the Blackstone River for most of its length, except for a divergence into the Moshassuck at Saylesville to connect more directly with the port facilities in the Providence harbor at the end of Canal Street (formerly known as North Water Street).

A product of the transportation revolution, the Blackstone Canal was also its victim. On October 25, 1847, the completion of the Providence-Worcester Railroad made the ditch archaic. As exuberant railroaders exclaimed: "The two unions between Worcester and Providence—the first was weak as water; the last is strong as iron." Today plans have been developed to create a linear park along the old canal route from Providence to Woonsocket.

This oil painting of the canal shows a horse-towed barge typical of those used on the waterway. Oil painting, artist unknown, courtesy of RIHS (Rhi x3 3307)

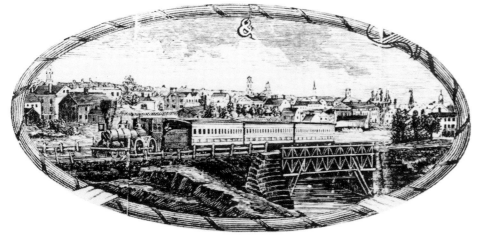

The state's first railroad was the Boston and Providence, whose tracks extended from Boston via Attleboro and Rumford, followed the east shore of the Seekonk River (then Massachusetts territory), and crossed the Seekonk to a terminus at India Point. The first run over this entire route occurred on June 2, 1835.

In 1832 the Rhode Island General Assembly issued a charter to the New York, Providence, and Boston Railroad Company to build a Providence-to-Westerly line. This grant was followed by a Connecticut charter allowing the extension of the proposed route to Stonington, providing a deep-water terminus and allowing passengers from Boston and Providence to board Long Island steamers bound for New York City. On November 10, 1837, the Providence-to-Stonington line was opened for traffic. Its rails approached Providence from the south along the present Harbor Junction spur and then proceeded northerly, paralleling the east bank of the Providence River to a terminus on a wharf near the present hurricane barrier, from which passengers were ferried to the Boston and Providence depot at India Point. The two terminals and the connecting ferry operated until a through railroad line (using the tracks of the Providence and Worcester Railroad) was opened in 1848 with a centrally located depot on the Cove in what is now downtown Providence. Shown here is an early passenger train on the Providence-Stonington route crossing the Pawcatuck River at Westerly. Lithograph from Ralph Bolton Cooney, Westerly's Oldest Witness (1950)

Although Newport's Brenton Point was fortified in colonial times and prior to the War of 1812, no early structure compared with the massive stone-and-earthwork fortress constructed on this strategic site between 1824 and 1842. Fort Adams, as it was named, was built to prevent a recurrence of the successful coastal invasions perpetrated by England during the War of 1812, when the British had captured and burned Washington. After the war President James Monroe prevailed upon a responsive Congress to establish a system of seacoast defenses, of which the Newport bastion was a major component. Fort Adams involved two basic types of military architecture—one to destroy ships entering the bay, the other to defend against siege by an army. In principle of design, it conformed to the French system of fortification developed by the eminent Vauban and improved by his successors, one of whom, Simon Bernard, aide-de-camp to Napoleon, helped to develop the fort's original plans.

The importance of Narragansett Bay to national defense was reflected in the magnitude of Fort Adams. It was one of the largest forts in the new defense system, with a five-sided perimeter of 1,739 yards and emplacements to mount 468 cannons. In time of war (which never came), it required twenty-four hundred troops to man it, although its peacetime garrison was set at only two hundred. Its fortifications

were built with scarp, parade walls and supports with Maine granite, vaults with bricks from nearby kilns, structural walls with shale from the immediate vicinity, and lime obtained from present-day Lincoln. Construction was directed by the noted American military engineer Colonel Joseph Totten, while much of the bullwork was performed by Irish immigrant laborers attracted to Newport in the 1820s by this huge public works project. The formidable granite walls shown here are mute but enduring monuments to Newport's early Irish workmen. Photo courtesy of PJC

The first significant influx of Irish Catholics to Rhode Island occurred in the mid-1820s, prompting Bishop Benedict Fenwick of Boston to dispatch Father Robert Woodley to Newport in 1828 as the state's first resident priest. There, in April 1828, the young cleric founded St. Mary's, the state's oldest parish. In 1829 the busy Woodley—whose mission territory included the states of Rhode Island and Connecticut in their entirety, plus southeastern Massachusetts—built the state's first Catholic church specifically constructed for that purpose at St. Mary's, Pawtucket.

When Woodley came to Rhode Island to establish a Catholic presence, Roman Catholics numbered about six hundred out of a total state population of ninety-seven thousand, a mere six-tenths of 1 percent. The six hundred faithful served by Woodley in 1828 were concentrated in Newport, where they worked as laborers on Fort Adams; in Portsmouth, where they were employed as miners at the coal pits; and in Providence, Cranston, Pawtucket, and

Woonsocket, where they served the needs of the growing factory system or were employed in such public works projects as the construction of the Blackstone Canal. Nearly all of them were Irish. The Irish migration continued in the 1830s as the railroad came to Rhode Island, and in the 1840s and 1850s it reached impressive proportions in the wake of Ireland's disastrous famine. By 1865 three out of every eight Rhode Islanders were of Irish stock, the state's Irish Catholic community numbered nearly fifty thousand, and pioneer missionary priests like the Reverend James Fitton (shown left) had established twenty widely scattered parishes. The energetic and seemingly ubiquitous Fitton, a founder of Holy Cross College (1843), was a driving force in the development of Rhode Island Catholicism, serving in every major area of Irish settlement, including Newport, Providence, Pawtucket, Woonsocket, and the Pawtuxet Valley. Photo of Fitton courtesy of St. Mary's Church, Newport

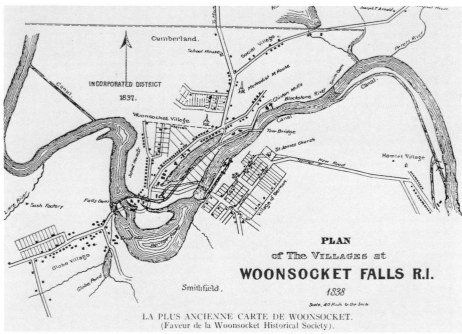

By the decade of the 1830s the Blackstone River was perhaps the most heavily industrialized waterway in the nation. Just before its southward course transformed it into the placid Seekonk, the river plunged over Valley Falls, Central Falls, and Pawtucket Falls, generating power with each sharp descent. This 1830s print shows Pleasant Street (left) and the town landing (right) from below the Pawtucket Falls, with the mills in the background whirring with activity. At this time the west side of the river was a mill village in the town of North Providence, while the east side was the Massachusetts town of Pawtucket, which had been incorporated in 1828. Engraving by J. S. Lincoln, courtesy of RIHS (Rhi x3 4664)

Further north on the Blackstone, near the Massachusetts border, Woonsocket Falls energized the early cotton mills. This 1838 map shows six villages clustered near the river. At this time the city of Woonsocket did not exist. South and west of the river was old Smithfield, with its mill villages of Globe, Bernon, and Hamlet; north and east was Cumberland, with its enclaves of Social, Clinton, and Woonsocket Village.

Not until 1867 was this section of Cumberland detached to form Woonsocket. Four years later Smithfield's three northern villages were added to the newly created industrial town to round out its present boundaries. Map from Marie Louise Bonier, Débuts de la Colonie Franco-Américaine de Woonsocket, R.I. *(1920)*

Zachariah Allen's impact on Rhode Island's economic development was comparable to that of Slater's. Allen (1795–1882) was an author, lawyer, medical doctor, town councilman, historian, and social reformer, as well as a first-rate scientist and inventor. In 1822 he introduced Providence's original fire engine and hose equipment to replace the hand-buckets previously used. Then he became a principal developer of the Providence waterworks. Among his many industrial patents were a central furnace system for heating houses by hot air, a method of transmitting power by leather

belting in place of the gear or "cogwheel" connections previously employed, a cloth-napping machine, a dressing and finishing machine for cotton textiles, a machine for spooling wool, and the automatic steam-

engine cutoff valve.

Allen also originated a system of mutual fire insurance for manufacturing property—a system that required underwriters to study methods for fire prevention and to calculate premiums on the adequacy of the safety equipment installed. To implement this approach, in 1835 he founded the Manufacturers' Mutual Fire Insurance Company, the forerunner of the Allendale Insurance Company. The incredibly versatile Allen richly deserves a full-length biography. *Engraving courtesy of RIHS (Rhi x3 5082)*

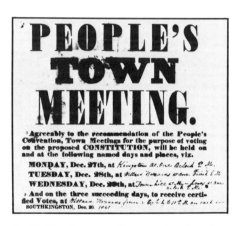

In 1840, after more than two decades of agitation had failed to convince the General Assembly that governmental reform and a written state constitution were necessities, a large, militant, and frustrated group of voteless men created the Rhode Island Suffrage Association, launching the so-called Dorr Rebellion. Adopting the ominous motto "Peaceably if we can, forcibly if we must," the association decided to bypass the conservative legislature and call a "People's Convention." Their belief that the state's basic law could be altered without approval from the existing government has been labeled "the doctrine of popular constituent sovereignty." It became the fundamental constitutional issue of the Dorr Rebellion.

On May 5, 1841, the association staged a mass meeting in Newport (simultaneous with the General Assembly's organizational session), where it scheduled town elections for delegates to the unauthorized reform convention set to convene on October 4. This poster announces the call for the August 28 election of such delegates in

South Kingstown. Ironically, both Newport and South County proved to be strongholds of the conservative opposition to this bold movement, whereas the mill villages of the north, such as Pawtucket, Valley Falls, Lonsdale, Manville, and Slatersville, were hotbeds of reform. *Broadside courtesy of RIHS (Rhi x3 600); banner from Walter Nebiker,* The History of North Smithfield *(1976)*

The tragic hero of the people's uprising was Thomas Wilson Dorr (1806–1854), a nephew of Zachariah Allen and the eldest son of Sullivan Dorr, a prominent Providence merchant and businessman. Harvard-educated and a lawyer, Dorr was recruited by the Suffrage Association in the spring of 1841 when these militant reformers decided to ignore both the legislature and existing voting requirements by holding their own constitutional convention. As an elected delegate from Providence, Dorr became the principal draftsman of the very progressive People's Constitution, a basic law committed to the doctrine of equal rights. This document was overwhelmingly ratified by the enlarged electorate in December 1841. Dorr was chosen governor under the authority of the new constitution in 1842, and when the charter adherents, led by Governor Samuel Ward King, refused to yield, there occurred an armed but bloodless confrontation. Engraving by W. Warner from a daguerreotype (ca. 1845) courtesy of RIHS (Rhi x3 2013)

After the election of rival governments in April 1842, Samuel Ward King's "Law and Order" faction began to arrest those elected under the provisions of the People's Constitution. After a futile visit with President John Tyler, Governor Dorr decided to take control of the state by force if necessary. Upon his return from the nation's capital, Dorr formulated a plan to seize the state arsenal next to the Dexter Training Grounds in Providence, using two antiquated cannon from a local armory as his principal weapons. Hearing of this plan, Johnston's Governor King (shown above) and Mayor Thomas Burgess of Providence placarded the walls of the city with a summons to arms. Ironically, among the many Law and Order supporters responding to the call to defend the arsenal were Dorr's father, his younger brother, and two uncles.

The asault on the arsenal was a fiasco. Fortunately Dorr's cannon misfired during this nighttime attack, but his decision to use force caused the defection of many respectable citizens from his ranks. On May 18, the day following the incident, Dorr went into exile for the first time. He returned to the state in late June to reconvene the People's General Assembly in the village of Chepachet, but when his legislators ignored his call and the King government raised a force of thirty-five hundred against him, he again fled the state, this time for New Hampshire, where he was given political asylum.

On October 31, 1843, after the forces of Law and Order had drawn up and secured the ratification of a new but conservative constitution to replace the royal charter, Dorr returned to Rhode Island and voluntarily surrendered to state authorities. He was charged with high treason against the state, tried in the spring of 1844 before a jury composed entirely of acknowledged political opponents, and condemned by Chief Justice Job Durfee to life imprisonment.

Many exaggerated statements have been made about the "battle" at Acote's Hill in Chepachet. Dorr returned in June not to fight but to reconvene the People's Legislature in a safe place, convenient to the Connecticut border. Dorr had no army, nor was there ever a real prospect of battle, except in the war stories of the thirty-five hundred citizen soldiers of the Law and Order faction. These contemporary illustrations (above) show the "capture" of the empty Acote's Hill and the deployment of the army of the charter regime. Portrait of King courtesy of RIHS Museum; map from Arthur May Mowry, The Dorr War (1901); lithograph of Acote's Hill from a drawing by H. Lord, courtesy of RIHS (Rhi x3 107)

The Four Traitors,*

Who most infamously sold themselves to the Dorrites, for Office and Political Power.

Let us not reward Traitors, but with just indignation abandon them as "Scape-Goats," to their destiny—forever.

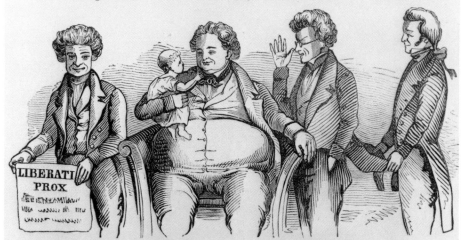

Charles Jackson.   **Samuel F. Man.**   **James F. Simmons.**   **Lemuel H. Arnold.**
Providence.   Cumberland.   Johnston.   South Kingston.

> "O, heaven, that such companions thou'dst unfold;
> And put in every honest hand a whip
> To lash the rascals naked through the world"

APOLOGETIC NOTE. At the present, dark, dismal and degenerate period of our history—when a man regardless of himself and his God, will sell his birthright for a mess of pottage—when an obscure individual like Polk, is elected to the Presidency, and a pompous, self-conceited man like Jackson, to the Gubernatorial chair—and other Dorrites, too contemptible to mention among men, are appointed to fill different offices under the general government—when Foreigners, ignorant, barbarous and uncivilised, as the wild ass of the wilderness, pour in upon us like the plagues of Egypt, scourging and desolating the land—when the murderer, with brazen front and seared conscience, his hands still dropping with human blood, stalks abroad, at noonday, unpunished—when there seems to manifest itself (among a certain, ignorant, low-bred Class of radicals, disorganisers, abolitionists assuming to be jurists, conscientiously afraid of the gallows, and vile, illiterate and decayed priests, a nuisance in society,) such a criminal and unhallowed sympathy for felons of every description, when we would do something for the public good, and attempt to stay the torrent of moral and political profligacy, which sapping the foundation, seems to threaten the overthrow of our most valuable institutions—when the law is trampled under foot with impunity—and every thing around is anarchy and confusion—to those who are disposed to cavil or criticise, and it is very easy to do so, we would say, that as the Originals could not be induced to sit for their portraits, without large sums of gold or pledges of high political trust, they were necessarily, with much difficulty, sketched from recollection; it cannot therefore be reasonably supposed, that their features are precisely exact; but if they had sat to the artist, the expression of their faces, being as variable as their characters, what might seem a good likeness to day, would cease to be so to-morrow; and this we deem a full and sufficient apology.

*The conduct of these men; two of them in particular, towards Governor Fenner, who fearlessly and nobly, sustained the State, through all its recent difficulties, is so treacherous, base and execrable, and is so well understood by the intelligent part of the community, that it needs no comment.

The harshness of Dorr's sentence prompted a national outcry. Liberation societies sprang up, and the national Democrats exploited the issue with their 1844 campaign slogan—"Polk, Dallas, and Dorr." In 1845 the Law and Order party split over the wisdom of Dorr's continued imprisonment. One faction, led by Charles Jackson and aided by Dorr Democrats, captured the governorship, whereupon Dorr was liberated by the newly elected governor on June 27, 1845.

Counting the time he spent in the county jail awaiting trial, Dorr had served nearly twenty months in prison, an ordeal that shattered his fragile health and contributed to his political and physical demise. This cartoon, prepared by the ultraconservative wing of the Law and Order party, denounces Jackson and his associates as "four traitors" for their 1845 stand in support of Dorr's liberation. Courtesy of RIHS (Rhi x3 5683)

The Dorr Rebellion kindled a martial spirit among Rhode Islanders. During the contest many dormant militia units were activated and new ones created. Jefferson Plain on Smith's Hill, the site of the present statehouse, was a well-used training ground. Here the charterites assembled their thirty-five-hundred-man force for the march on Chepachet in June 1842. Two summers later the site served as the encampment grounds of the New England Guards, shown in this contemporary lithograph. To the left, across the Cove, is the commercial center of Providence. On the north shore of the Cove, just below the brow of Smith's Hill, was the state prison where Thomas Dorr was then languishing for his "treasonable" efforts at reform. Lithograph (1844) courtesy of RIHS (Rhi x3 2174)

Although his stay in Rhode Island was of less than seven years' duration, Henry Barnard (1811–1900) had a profound impact on the state's educational system. After an impressive start in his native Connecticut, Barnard came to Rhode Island in 1843 as "agent" of the state, charged with preparing a plan to improve the public school system. Thanks to Thomas Dorr's innovations as school committee president in Providence, Barnard's stated objective was to raise the other local systems to the standards of that city. In his brief tenure Barnard succeeded admirably. Two years of investigation led to the drafting of his encyclopedic Report on the Condition and Improvement of the Public Schools of Rhode Island, *a study which prompted the passage of the School Law of 1845. This statute, drafted by the legally trained Barnard himself, was praised by the great educator Horace Mann as a measure that would give Rhode Island "one of the best systems of public instruction in the world."*

Barnard served as the state's first commissioner of education from 1845 until 1849, when a temporary break in health forced his resignation. After his recovery he labored in his chosen field for another half-century, writing voluminously and serving as the nation's first commissioner of education from 1867 to 1870. A selective elementary school on the campus of Rhode Island College in Providence is named in his honor. Portrait (1857), oil on canvas, by James Sullivan Lincoln, courtesy of RIHS (Rhi x3 3110)

CHANGE, CONTROVERSY AND WAR, 1846-1866

The twenty-year period from 1846 to 1866 was characterized by modernization, political and social friction, and conflict. The Mexican War, which a majority of Rhode Islanders opposed as an act of aggression, began the era, and the Civil War, which a majority of Rhode Islanders tried vigorously to avert, brought this turbulent age to a close.

The theme of modernization is apparent in the extent of technological and institutional change. Several major public works projects were instituted to meet the demands of rapid demographic and economic growth. The most important of these was railroad construction. In 1847 the first train ran over the Providence and Worcester line. The following year the Providence and Worcester Railroad (which is still a major factor in the state's economy) built a massive Providence terminal, the Union Passenger Depot, to service its operations.

In the 1850s other railroads traversed the state. The Hartford, Providence, and Fishkill line was completed in 1854, connecting Rhode Island with the Hudson River. In the following year the Providence, Warren, and Bristol line provided transportation for the East Bay region, an area whose dimensions were altered in 1862 when the Massachusetts towns of Pawtucket (east of the Blackstone) and East Providence (formerly part of Seekonk) were acquired in exchange for the Rhode Island town of Fall River (north of Tiverton).

Internal routes of travel were also improved. As its initial project, the Providence Gas Company, incorporated in 1847, undertook the lighting of city streets. Mains were laid first in the principal downtown thoroughfares, and gradually gas replaced whale oil in lighting highways throughout Providence and in other urban areas of Rhode Island.

Waterborne transport also improved when the United States Army Corps of Engineers surveyed the Providence River in 1853 prior to dredging a channel south of Fox Point to a depth of ten and a width of one hundred feet. This improvement allowed the Port of Providence to accommodate most of the new and larger vessels used in the coastal trade.

Apart from transportation and public works, another development that loomed large in this era was the establishment of institutions for the care or treatment of the unfortunate. For the mentally ill, the innovative Butler Hospital was opened in a pastoral setting overlooking the Seekonk River in 1847, and the General Assembly in 1851 offered a blueprint for reform by promulgating a report by Thomas R. Hazard on the status and treatment of the poor and insane.

In 1853 the Greater Providence Young Men's Christian Association was established. The YMCA, as it came to be called, was designed to build character and to provide wholesome recreational activities for its members.

For wayward children, the Providence Reform School, organized in 1850, was housed in spacious Tockwotton Mansion near India Point. It became the forerunner of the state reform school for juvenile offenders. Orphaned and neglected children also became an important social concern.

To supplement the work of the Children's Friend Society (established in 1835), the Association for the Benefit of Colored Children (organized in 1838) constructed a Providence facility, called The Shelter, in 1849. Two years later the Roman Catholic Sisters of Mercy established St. Aloysius Home in their convent on Claverick Street near the Cathedral of Saints Peter and Paul. By 1862 this orphanage—the oldest continuous social welfare agency in the diocese—occupied a spacious, modern building on Prairie Avenue. Providence Catholics also established a local branch of the St. Vincent de Paul Society, a lay organization dedicated to aiding the destitute. The cathedral unit, founded in 1853, was the first of many parish chapters throughout the state.

To care for the elderly, the Providence Home for Aged Women was organized in 1856. Its present building at Front and East streets, overlooking the harbor, was opened in 1864. Elderly men waited ten years longer for a comparable facility.

These activities were humanitarian responses to the increasingly impersonal nature of an emerging urban-industrial society. They were commendable attempts by civic-minded reformers to deal with victims of the rapid change, growth, and modernization that affected what had become the nation's most urbanized, industrial state.

One notable departure from contemporary humanitarian sentiment was the incidence of nativism in the 1850s. Prejudice toward Irish Catholic immigrants was fanned by the *Providence Journal* and its bigoted editor, Henry Bowen Anthony. Some more zealous nativists even planned a raid on St. Xavier's Convent, home of the "female Jesuits" (the Sisters of Mercy), but the angry mob dispersed when confronted by Bishop Bernard O'Reilly and an equally militant crowd of armed Irishmen.

Fortunately, this virulent strain of nativism subsided as quickly as it had reared its evil head. By 1860 bigotry again became subtle rather than overt as Rhode Island and the nation braced for yet another challenge—the specter of disunion. By the time that challenge came, the state had experienced a significant political realignment, one which might be called the development of the third (and present) party system. By 1854 the Whig party—split nationally over the issue of slavery into Cotton Whigs and Conscience Whigs—disintegrated locally. Those who considered the spread of slavery the greatest evil threatening the country embraced the newly formed Republican party, while those who saw Catholic immigration as the main menace joined the American (Know-Nothing) party, a secret organization that swept town, city, and state elections in the mid-fifties.

Rhode Island Democrats also divided. Reform-oriented followers of Thomas Dorr and his uncle and ally Governor Philip Allen (1851–1854) maintained their party allegiance, but many rural Democrats who had supported the cause of Law and Order during the Dorr Rebellion affiliated with the Know-Nothings. When that one-issue party also declined after 1856, both these rural Democrats and nativist Whigs gravitated toward the rapidly growing Republican party, bringing with them their anti-Irish Catholic attitudes. From this decade until the 1930s, the Democrats were Rhode Island's minority party.

Like every state in America, Rhode Island keenly felt the impact of the Civil War. This was a conflict many Rhode Islanders had hoped to avoid. Yankee businessmen, especially those producing cotton textiles, had economic ties with the South, ties which war would (and did) disrupt. As some critics remarked, there seemed to be an unholy alliance between the "lords of the loom" (the cotton textile manufacturers) and the "lords of the lash" (the slaveholders). In addition, many foreign-born Irishmen, resentful that they needed land to vote while blacks were subjected to no such discrimination, had little sympathy for freeing those who could become their rivals for jobs on the lower rungs of the economic ladder.

Consequently, when in 1860 the Rhode Island Republican party chose Seth Padelford—a man whose antislavery views were extreme—as its candidate for governor, a split occurred in the party ranks. Supporters of other Republican aspirants and Republican moderates of the Abe Lincoln variety joined with Democrats (who were softer on slavery) to nominate and elect a fusion candidate on the "Conservative" ticket. Their choice was twenty-nine-year-old William Sprague of Cranston, the heir to a vast cotton textile empire and a martial man who had attained the rank of colonel in the Providence Marine Corps of Artillery. Sprague outpolled Padelford 12,278 to 10,740. The victory was celebrated as a rebuke to abolitionism by the citizens of faraway Savannah, Georgia, who fired a one-hundred-gun salute in Sprague's honor.

But if Rhode Island and Sprague were soft on slavery, they were strong on Union. After the Confederate attack of April 12, 1861, on Fort Sumter, the local citizenry rallied behind their once conciliatory governor and rushed to the defense of Washington. President Lincoln issued his call for volunteers on April 15. Just three days later the "Flying Artillery" left Providence for the front, and on April 20 Colonel Ambrose Burnside of Bristol and Sprague himself led 530 men of the First Regiment, Rhode Island Detached Militia, from Exchange Place to their fateful encounter with the rebels at Bull Run.

During the war there were eight calls for troops, with Rhode Island exceeding its requisition in all but one. Though the state's total quota was only 18,898, it furnished 23,236 fighting men, of whom 1,685 died of wounds or disease and 16 earned the Medal of Honor. During the conflict Melville in Portsmouth became the site of a military hospital, and nearby Newport became the home of the United States Naval Academy. Relocated from Annapolis for security reasons, the academy occupied the Atlantic House hotel at the corner of Bellevue Avenue and Pelham Street and also had training ships and instructional facilities on Goat Island.

The state's contribution to the Union victory went beyond mere military and naval manpower. Some historians have claimed that the productive capacity of Northern industry was the decisive element in the outcome of the Civil War. Here again Rhode Island was prominent. Its woolen mills, especially Atlantic and Wanskuck, supplied federal troops with thousands of uniforms, overcoats, and blankets, fashioned on sewing machines made by Brown and Sharpe, while metal factories such as Providence Tool, Nicholson and Brownell, and the Burnside Rifle Company provided guns, sabers, and musket parts. Builders Iron Foundry (established in 1822 and still operating in West Warwick) manufactured large numbers of cannon; the Providence Steam Engine Company built the engines for

two Union sloops of war; and Congdon and Carpenter (established in 1792) supplied the military with such hardware as iron bars, bands, hoops, and horseshoes.

On the home front, the Civil War decade was a time of continued growth and modernization, especially for Providence. The city's most important and dynamic mayor, Thomas A. Doyle, began a nineteen-year reign in 1864. He promptly reorganized the police department into an efficient, modern force and converted the historic Market House into a municipal office building. City health and sanitation programs, under the capable direction of Dr. Edwin M. Snow, were models for other municipalities to emulate.

In education, business and commercial schools such as Scholfield's and Bryant and Stratton flourished as they provided a growing white-collar work force with the office skills needed to administer the affairs of Rhode Island's burgeoning industries. And in the public schools a momentous event, inspired by the outcome of the war, occurred in 1866: racial segregation was abolished throughout the state.

It was during the Civil War decade that urban mass transit came to Providence. Its vehicle was the horsecar, a mode of travel over the streets of the city that combined the old (actual horsepower) and the new (iron rails). The horsecar lines, extending from the Union Depot in Market Square over the surface of every major thoroughfare, were essential factors in the growth and settlement of the city's "streetcar suburbs"—the outlying neighborhoods of Providence. With the war a partial stimulus, industrial Rhode Island began to scale its greatest heights, pulled from above by its wealthy Yankee entrepreneurs and investors, pushed from below by a growing immigrant work force that now began to include migrants from Germany, Sweden, England, and, especially, French Canada. As the war clouds lifted, the state's Golden Age of economic and social prominence was about to begin.

William A. Mowry (1829-1917) ranks among Rhode Island's foremost educators. Besides writing a score of books (especially texts on history and civics), Mowry founded a highly regarded private high school in Providence, pioneered in the establishment of teachers' institutes, and served as superintendent of schools in Cranston and Salem, Massachusetts. His second teaching assignment, during 1848 in a Burrillville one-room school, always remained vivid in his memory. Mowry's recollection of that facility (shown here) gives us an excellent description of the nineteenth-century Rhode Island rural school:

> *The schoolroom was about twenty feet wide and thirty feet long. It had a seat made of chestnut plank along three sides of the room, under the windows. Before this seat was a long desk on each of the three sides, with a low seat in front. The stove stood in the middle of the room. On the fourth side, at one corner, was an entry through which the scholars must pass, in coming to and going from the schoolroom. In the opposite corner, leading from the room, was a large closet with shelves for the caps, bonnets, wraps and dinner pails. Between the entry and the closet was a large, old-fashioned stone fireplace, which had been closed when it was supplanted by the stove.*
>
> *Here I had pupils of all ages, as was common in the rural schools in those days, from the A-B-C class to grown men and women of twenty years old and more. The school was kept for four months, and an additional term of perhaps ten weeks was the custom in the summer. Here my pay was $15 a month, and I "boarded around." This "boarding around," fifty years ago, was the common custom in many places. If the term was to be sixteen weeks and there were sixteen scholars in the school, the teacher would board one week at the home of each scholar. If there were thirty-two scholars, each family would board the teacher half a week for each pupil sent to school.*

Photo from William A. Mowry, Recollections of a New England Educator, 1838-1908 *(1908)*

Institutional reform—in particular, the creation or improvement of facilities for the insane and the handicapped—was a major concern of humanitarians during this period of American history. For the mentally disturbed, "asylums" were established, an innovation primarily associated with Massachusetts crusader Dorothea Dix. Providence's response to this trend was Butler Hospital, a private facility endowed primarily with gifts from Nicholas Brown (thirty thousand dollars) and Cyrus Butler (forty thousand dollars), for whom the asylum is named. Butler (shown here), a Providence businessman and textile magnate, also financed the Arcade. The Butler Exchange, the city's first major office building, was named in his honor.

In 1847 Butler Hospital opened as a 108-bed facility in a tranquil, pastoral setting on the west bank of the Seekonk River. From the outset Butler was under the able direction of Dr. Isaac Ray (1807-1881), former head of the Maine Insane Hospital and one of the country's foremost psychiatrists. During Ray's tenure at Butler he decisively shaped not only the hospital's development but also the future of mental health treatment in Rhode Island.

At first Ray promoted a vision of universal hospital care for all of the deranged and made Butler a model of private philanthropy. Because of his nativistic distaste for lowly foreigners, however, by the time of his departure in 1869 he was encouraging a segregated system of institutional care in which wealthy or curable patients would be beneficiaries of institutions such as Butler, while the poor and incurable would be relegated to large public facilities such as the state hospital established in 1870 at Howard. In 1978 Butler again began accepting public patients through an agreement with the Providence Mental Health Center. Photo of Butler Hospital (ca. 1860) courtesy of RIHS (Rhi x3 4121); portrait by unknown artist, courtesy of Butler Hospital

The egalitarian spirit of the pre-Civil War age of reform, so well characterized in the 1830s and 1840s by the diverse efforts of Thomas Dorr, gained another influential exponent after Dorr fell from grace. Thomas Robinson Hazard (1797-1886)— agriculturalist, manufacturer, author, and social reformer—was a seventh-generation descendant of Thomas Hazard, the progenitor of the famous Hazard clan of Rhode Island and one of the nine founders of Newport; the grandson of Thomas Hazard (1720-1798), an eighteenth-century South County Quaker abolitionist called "College Tom" because of his advanced study at Yale; and the older brother of Rowland Gibson Hazard (1801-1888), a noted Peace Dale woolen maufacturer, railroad promoter, and writer on philosophical subjects.

Thomas Robinson Hazard grew wealthy as a South County sheepraiser and woolen goods magnate—a career that earned him the nickname "Shepherd Tom." By his forty-third birthday he had amassed a fortune sufficient to retire to Vaucluse, an estate in Middletown. His leisure and money also enabled him to promote various reform causes and pursue a religious passion called "modern spiritualism."

Shepherd Tom served as vice president of the American Colonization Society, an organization to relocate freed blacks; wrote an influential state-sponsored report on the poor and insane in 1851 that prompted several institutional reforms; led the successful 1852 fight for the abolition of capital punishment in Rhode Island; espoused women's suffrage; worked to upgrade the public schools; undertook relief efforts to aid the Irish victims of the Great Famine; and wrote in opposition to slavery and war. In his early eighties he penned Recollections of Olden Times, a work that casts a rich afterglow on nineteenth-century life in South County while also providing genealogies of the fascinating Hazard family. The Jonny-Cake Letters, a collection of his discourses, appeared in 1882. Photo of Hazard and his family (left to right: Gertrude, Barclay, Fannie, Anna, and Esther), courtesy of RIHS (Rhi x3 5426)

While "Shepherd Tom" promoted domestic reform, "Old Bruin" changed the course of our foreign policy. Newport-born Matthew Calbraith Perry (1794-1858), younger brother of Oliver, forged a distinguished naval career that extended from pre-War of 1812 skirmishes with the British as a young subaltern to commanding the American naval forces in the siege and capture of Vera Cruz during the Mexican War. Perry was a major promoter of naval education and training programs and a technological innovator who is sometimes referred to as "the Father of the American Steam Navy."

His 1853-54 mission to Japan, however, was his greatest exploit and one of the most important diplomatic missions ever entrusted to an American naval officer. His instructions were to procure from a backward, feudal country, closed to intercourse with Western nations, a treaty guaranteeing the safety of American seamen in Japanese waters and opening one or more ports to American merchant vessels. A display of firmness and a show of force on his first brief visit in July 1853 prompted a cooperative response from Japanese officials when Perry returned in February 1854 (as shown here), at which time he negotiated the historic treaty that opened Japan to the

West and served as a catalyst for its modernization.

The brisk, blunt, square-built Perry supervised the compilation of a massive three-volume report of his momentous expedition upon returning to America in 1855. Three years after his voyage Perry died in New York City and was buried at Island Cemetery in Newport. On the tenth anniversary of his death, a statue to his memory was erected in Touro Park by millionaire August Belmont and his wife Caroline, one of Perry's ten children. Lithograph of Perry greeting the commissioners at Yokohama from Francis L. Hawks (comp.), Narrative of the Expedition of an American Squadron to the China Seas and Japan (1856)

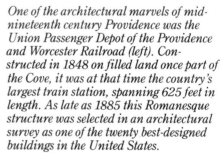

One of the architectural marvels of mid-nineteenth century Providence was the Union Passenger Depot of the Providence and Worcester Railroad (left). Constructed in 1848 on filled land once part of the Cove, it was at that time the country's largest train station, spanning 625 feet in length. As late as 1885 this Romanesque structure was selected in an architectural survey as one of the twenty best-designed buildings in the United States.

Equally remarkable was the genius of its twenty-two-year-old architect, Thomas A. Tefft (1826-1859), who prepared the plans for the massive terminal while still a student at Brown. Before his untimely death in Florence, Italy, at age thirty-three, Tefft was responsible for the designs of renovations at the Old State House (1851), of structures at Swan Point Cemetery, and of Central Congregational Church on Benefit Street (now Memorial Hall of RISD).

By late in the century the depot had become obsolete. On February 20, 1896, while the new Union Railroad Station was still under construction, the Tefft terminal burned in a spectacular fire. Engraving (ca. 1850) courtesy of RIHS (Rhi x3 1200)

While new train routes and facilities were being created to move Rhode Islanders to various points around the state and beyond (by 1856 the state had chartered seventeen railroad corporations), the era also witnessed the development of an urban mass transit system—the horsecar lines. The first route, the Providence and Pawtucket, was built in 1863. During the following year private investors constructed similar lines in Providence along Broadway, Elmwood Avenue, and South Main Street and laid their iron rails on Broad Street from downtown to the village of Pawtuxet.

With the new streetcar lines radiating like spokes into the outer reaches of Providence from the hub of Market Square, the original competing horsecar companies sometimes found it necessary to run for several blocks over the same route as competitors. Such a condition created confusion and antagonism. To avoid duplication and to achieve greater coor-

dination of the city's infant mass transit system, the Union Railroad Company was formed in 1865. Eventually it acquired control of all lines and established a monopoly over this mode of travel. In 1867 the company constructed the Union Railroad Depot at Market Square. This depot served as the center of the city's horsecar system for many years before being demolished in 1897.

The building of these lines gave rise to a phenomenon historians call "streetcar suburbs." These were outlying neighborhoods, remote from the factories of the central city, that could now be easily reached and settled by the more prosperous members of the work force. In Providence, Newport, and Pawtucket, the "horse railroad" companies were catalysts for neighborhood growth and development. Photo of the Providence-Cranston horsecar (ca. 1866), courtesy of D. Scott Molloy.

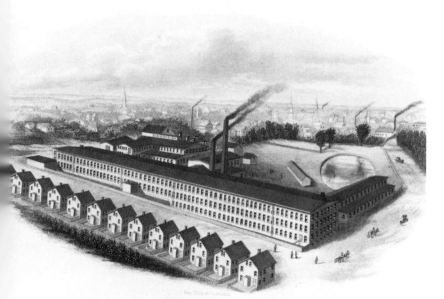

By mid-century, with the development of a railroad network and the widespread use of steam power, the pace of industrialization quickened. The single, wood-frame mill building of the previous generation gave way to an industrial complex of several large brick structures surrounded by a factory-spawned village. These industrial communities, where workers often lived in monotonous rows of factory-furnished housing, dotted the Rhode Island landscape, but they were particularly numerous in the valleys of the Blackstone and the Pawtuxet. Shown here are the Lonsdale Mills on the Blackstone (upper left); the A & W Sprague cotton mills in Arctic on the south branch of the Pawtuxet (upper right); and the Fales and Jenks Machine Shop, ca. 1850s, in the North Providence village of Pawtucket (lower left), an illustration that shows the spatial relationship between the mill and its housing. More elegant, though depressingly uniform, were the accommodations built in 1849 for the workers in Westerly's White Rock Mill (lower right). Engraving of Lonsdale Mills from H. F. Walling's map of Providence County (1851), courtesy of RIHS (Rhi x3 1529); cloth label depicting A & W Sprague mills (ca. 1850), courtesy of RIHS (Rhi x3 187); engraving of Fales and Jenks Machine Shop from J. D. Van Slyck, Representatives of New England: Manufacturers (1879); photo of White Rock Mill housing (ca. 1939) by Joseph McCarthy from Henry Russell Hitchcock, Rhode Island Architecture (1939)

This painting of Slatersville (ca. 1860) depicts a model Rhode Island mill village. Founded in 1806 by John Slater (brother and agent of Samuel) on the Branch River, Slatersville was built in a previously unsettled area around a broad road and central square to accommodate a new cotton textile mill. This view to the north from Tabor Hill shows the second mill (1826), the spired Slatersville Congregational Church (1838), and a row of mill houses spread out mainly to the east and west of the town center. Painting, oil on canvas, artist unknown, courtesy of the Slatersville Congregational Church

Clayville, on the Foster-Scituate boundary, is another picturesque Rhode Island village. In the 1850s, when this painting was made, the village contained a blend of agricultural and industrial activity. The earliest known factory in Clayville was the comb company owned by Josiah Whitaker in 1831. By 1853 Whitaker was operating a cotton mill on the same site (perhaps the large building in the right foreground). Painting, oil on canvas, artist unknown, courtesy of RIHS (Rhi x3 3104)

When this painting was done in 1860, East Greenwich (population 2,882) was a prosperous town of many faces—commerce, fishing, manufacturing, farming, and education. This scene captures some of that diversity. The imposing structure high on the hill is the newly constructed (1858) main building of the famed East Greenwich (formerly Kent) Academy. Painting (ca. 1860), oil on canvas, by Daniel Howland Greene, courtesy of Varnum Continental Ladies

The village of Narragansett at South Ferry was another small but diverse bayside community when J. P. Newell prepared this 1860 lithograph. This area, just north of Bonnet Shores, was part of South Kingstown until that municipality's easterly sector was set off and incorporated as the district of Narragansett in March 1888. Lithograph by J. P. Newell, courtesy of RIHS (Rhi x3 254)

Bristol harbor bustles with activity in this 1850s scene. At this time Bristol and neighboring Warren were modestly involved in the whale fishery. The view is east from Poppasquash Point. Lithograph by J. P. Newell, courtesy of RIHS (Rhi x3 5704)

Whaling was an important part of Rhode Island's early nineteenth-century maritime economy, and Warren was that industry's leading local practitioner. From 1840 to 1844 nearly one-half (twenty of forty four) of all Rhode Island whalers were registered in Warren; from 1855 to 1859 (just before the fishery declined), three-quarters (fifteen of twenty) of the state's whaleship fleet were of Warren registry, including the 806-ton Sea-Shell, then reputed to be the largest whaleship in the world.

During this era many businesses associated with whaling dotted the Warren waterfront, including cooperages, blacksmith shops, soap and candle factories, and

oil works. Shipbuilding also boomed in Warren during these years.

From 1840 to 1860, Warren craftsmen constructed boats totaling 19,492 tons—far more than any other Rhode Island port during this twenty-year span. This late nineteenth-century view of the Warren

waterfront shows a ship and many buildings constructed during Warren's pre-Civil War era of maritime prominence. Postcard view (ca. 1890s) from Rhode Island Historical Preservation Commission, Warren (1975)

This is Newport's Bellevue Avenue about 1860, as the City by the Sea was developing into a mecca for America's new leisure class. At this time there were only a small number of nonresident house owners, and most of the summer colonists preferred to patronize the luxury hotels—the Ocean, Atlantic, Bellevue, Fillmore, and Aquidneck—most of which were located on this prestigious thoroughfare. Engraving by Thomas Nelson and Sons, courtesy of RIHS (Rhi x3 5700)

An excellent view of mid-nineteenth century Providence from the south is furnished by this 1848 lithograph. The causeway across Hawkins Cove (center) approximates the route of present-day Allens Avenue. It carried the original tracks of the Providence and Stonington Railroad to its station at the foot of Crary Street. This train route was altered in 1848 when Union Passenger Depot became the line's new terminus. In this panoramic lithograph by Fitz Hugh Lane, Tockwotton House (site of the present Fox Point Elementary School) is at the extreme right and Beneficent (Round Top) Congregational Church is at the left. From Robert G. Workman (ed.), The Eden of America: Rhode Island Landscapes, 1820–1920 *(1986), courtesy of the Boston Athenaeum*

Less idyllic or luxurious than the preceding scenes is the one shown in this 1850 photo of Depot Square, then located in the Cumberland village of Clinton near the Providence and Worcester train station and the Clinton textile mills. In 1867 this site became the hub of the newly created town of Woonsocket. Photo from Marie-Louise Bonier, Débuts de la Colonie Franco–Américaine de Woonsocket, R.I. *(1920)*

That part of present-day Pawtucket east of the Blackstone-Seekonk River had been within the Massachusetts towns of Rehoboth (until 1812) and Seekonk (1812–1828) before it was incorporated in 1828 as a separate Massachusetts municipality. In 1848 town officials ordered this survey showing all its structures and their owners. In 1862 Rhode Island annexed most of this town along with a 13.85-square-mile section of west Seekonk that the General Assembly promptly incorporated as the town of East Providence. In 1874 the North Providence village of Pawtucket was joined to the east bank town to form modern Pawtucket, a municipality consisting of 8.68 square miles. Map from Robert Grieve, An Illustrated History of Pawtucket, Central Falls, and Vicinity *(1897)*

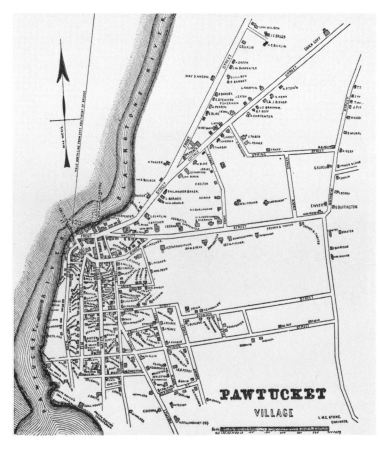

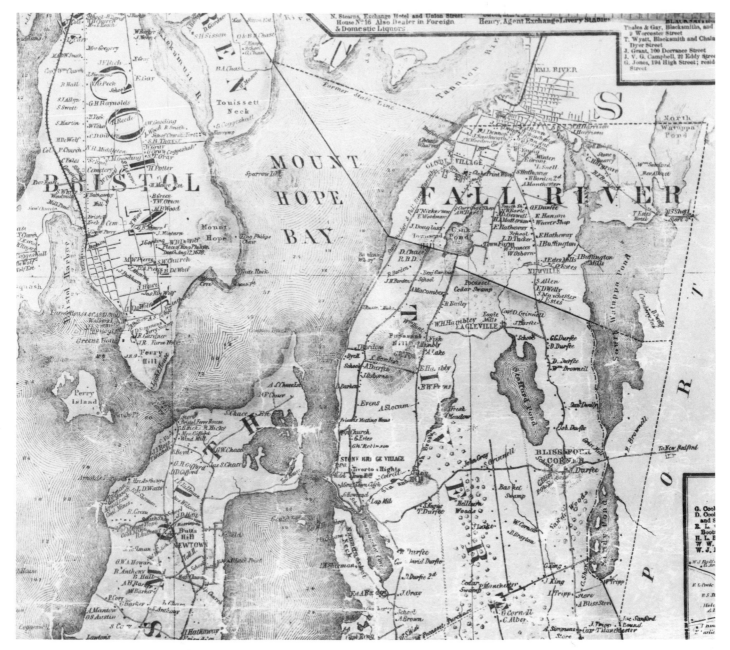

The 1862 boundary adjustment by which Rhode Island acquired eastern Pawtucket and East Providence resulted in the transfer of the state's newest town to Massachusetts. In 1856 the state legislature set off the industrialized northern portion of the town of Tiverton to form the separate municipality of Fall River located on a stream by that name. It did so in the midst of litigation between Massachusetts and Rhode Island concerning the proper boundary between Tiverton and the Massachusetts community of Freetown to its north. That dispute, stemming from a faulty survey done when the East Bay region was ceded to Rhode Island in 1746, was resolved by the U.S. Supreme Court in favor of Massachusetts. Thus, on March 1, 1862, Fall River, Rhode Island (two miles from north to south, with over three thousand inhabitants) was merged with Freetown to form modern-day Fall River, Massachusetts. Detail from H. F. Walling map of 1862, courtesy of RIHS (Rhi x3 5702)

In 1854 William Tripp, a Little Compton farmer, began an important development in the American poultry industry. Tripp marketed much of his produce in New Bedford, a major port that carried on trade with Southeast Asia. From a sailor returning from an Asian voyage, Tripp obtained a red cock that was said to be a Malay or a Chittagong. When he took the fowl home and let it run with his scrub hens, he observed that the new chicks grew into a stock that improved upon his nondescript natives: the hybrids were meatier and laid more and bigger eggs.

Another farmer, John Macomber of Westport, Massachusetts, became interested in Tripp's experiments, so the two men collaborated in further crossbreeding efforts. Eventually two professors at the United States Agricultural Experiment Station in Kingston also became involved, as did Isaac Champlin Wilbour of Little Compton, a well-to-do farmer. By 1896 Wilbour and the professors had given this new breed of "Tripp fowls" the name Rhode Island Red.

In the early twentieth century this hen

became a mainstay of the American commercial poultry industry, prompting the erection of a monument in 1925 near the village of Adamsville—allegedly the world's only memorial to a chicken. The Rhode Island Red has also been designated as the official state bird. Photo of monument courtesy of RIHS (Rhi x3 5703)

The Irish Catholic migration to Rhode Island, a trickle in the 1820s, became a flood in the wake of the Great Famine of 1846. The federal census of 1850, the first national survey to record the nativity of the population, revealed that the state had 23,111 foreign-born out of a total population of 147,545. At this point natives of Ireland totaled 15,944, or 69 percent of the foreign-born. By the time of the first state census in 1865, the foreign-born population had climbed to 39,703; of this figure the Irish-born accounted for 27,030, or 68 percent. When first- and second-generation Irish were counted, three of every eight Rhode Islanders were of recent Irish ancestry.

This inundation by poverty-stricken Celtic peasants, most of them Roman Catholic, prompted a militant native Protestant reaction called the Know-Nothing movement. Its political expression was the American party, which briefly captured control of city and state government in the mid-fifties with a limited and platitudinous platform (far right)

AMERICAN REPUBLICAN MEETING

····AT····

LESTERS' HALL

FRIDAY EVE'G, APR. 1, 1859,

Commencing at 7 1-2 o'clock.   To be addressed by

Hon. CHRISTOPHER ROBINSON,

OF CUMBERLAND, and the

Hon. CHARLES C. VAN ZANDT,

OF NEWPORT.

Let there be a Grand Rally!

Knowles, Anthony & Co's Steam Press.

demanding "a radical revision and modifi-cation" of immigration laws; "unquali-fiedly condemning the transmission to our shores of felons and paupers"; denying the vote to naturalized citizens until they resided in the United States for twenty-one years; and prohibiting "the traffic in all alcoholic liquors." In 1855 the American party backed the successful gubernatorial campaign of William W. Hoppin, while their candidate James Y. Smith (far left) won the Providence mayoralty. In the late 1850s the newly formed Republican party absorbed the personnel and the anti-Irish attitudes of the Know-Nothings. The merger of these two groups, as evidenced by this 1859 political poster (above), brought Hoppin to the governorship as a Republican in 1857 and Smith to the state's top post from 1863 to 1866 as the standard-bearer of the GOP. Engraving of Smith from Welcome A. Greene, The Providence Plantations for 250 Years (1886); broadside of platform, courtesy of RIHS (Rhi x3 5705); American-Republican poster courtesy of RIHS (Rhi x3 4405)

PLATFORM
Of the American Party of R. I.
Adopted by State Council, June 19, 1855.

Whereas, by a resolution this day adopt-ed by the State Council of Rhode Island, approving the action of our delegates in signing the platform based on the Minority Report to the Grand National Council at Philadelphia, this State Council has virtu-ally seceded from the Order as a National Party; and

Whereas, it is proper that we still labor together for the promotion of individual and National prosperity, therefore

Resolved, That we pledge ourselves to the following

PRINCIPLES.

1. The acknowledgment of that Almigh-ty Being who rules over the Universe, who presides over the Councils of Nations, who conducts the affairs of men, and who, in every step by which we have advanced to the character of an independent nation has distinguished us by some token of providential agency.

2. The cultivation and developement of a sentiment of profoundly intense American feeling; of passionate attachment to our country, its history and its institutions; of admiration for the purer days of our Nation-al existence; of veneration for the heroism that precipitated our Revolution; and of emulation of the virtue, wisdom and patri-otism that framed our Constitution, and first successfully applied its provisions.

3. The unconditional restoration of that time-honored Agreement known as the Mis-souri Compromise, which was destroyed in utter disregard of the popular will; a wrong which no lapse of time can palliate, and no plea for its continuance can justify. And that we will use all constitutional means to maintain the positive guarantee of that compact, until the object for which it was enacted has been consummated by the ad-mission of Kansas and Nebraska as Free States.

4. The rights of settlers in Territories to the free and undisturbed exercise of the elective franchise guaranteed to them by the laws under which they are organized, should be promptly protected by the Nation-al Executive whenever violated or threaten-ed.

5. Obedience under God to the Constitu-tion of these United States, as the supreme law of the land, sacredly obligatory upon all its parts and members; and stedfast re-sistance to the spirit of innovations upon its principles, however specious the pretexts.—Avowing that in all doubtful or disputed points it may only be legally ascertained and expounded by the judicial power of the United States. A habit of reverential obe-dience to the laws, whether National, State or Municipal, until they are either repealed, or declared unconstitutional, by the proper authority.

6. A radical revision and modification of the laws regulating immigration, and the settlement of immigrants. Offering to the honest immigrant, who from the love of liberty or hatred of oppression seeks an asylum in the United States, a friendly re-ception and protection. But unqualifiedly condemning the transmission to our shores of felons and paupers.

7. The essential modification of the nat-uralization laws—the repeal by the Legis-latures of the respective States, of all State laws allowing unnaturalized foreigners to vote. The repeal, without retroactive ope-ration of all the acts of Congress making grants of land to unnaturalized foreigners. The refusal to extend the right of suffrage to all foreigners until they shall have resid-ed in the United States twenty-one (21) years, and complied with the naturalization laws.

8. Hostility to the corrupt means, by which the leaders of parties have hitherto forced upon us, our rulers, and our political creeds. Implacable enmity against the present demoralizing system of rewards for political subserviency, and punishment for political independence. Disgust for the wild hunt after office which characterizes the age.

These on the one hand, on the other—

imitation of the practice of the purer days of the Republic; and admiration of the maxim "that office should seek the man and not man the office," and of the rule that the just mode of ascertaining fitness for of-fice is the capability, the faithfulness, and the honesty of the incumbent or candidate.

9. Resistance to the aggressive policy and corrupting tendencies of the Roman Catholic Church in our country by the ad-vancement to all political stations—execu-tive, legislative, judicial or diplomatic—of those only who do not hold civil allegiance, directly or indirectly to any foreign power whither civil or ecclesiastical, and who are Americans by birth, education and training, thus fulfilling the maxim—*Americans only shall govern America.* The protection of all citizens in the legal and proper exercise of their civil and religious rights and privi-leges; the maintenance of the right of eve-ry man to the full unrestricted and peace-ful enjoyment of his own religious opinions and worship, and a jealous resistance of all attempt by any sect, denomination or church to obtain an ascendency over any other in the State, by means of any special privileges or exemption, by any political combination of its members, or by a divis-ion of their civil allegiance with any for-eign power, potentate or ecclesiastic.

10. The reformation of the character of our National Legislature, by elevating to that dignified and responsible position, men of sober habits, of higher qualifications, pu-er morals, and more unselfish patriotism.

11. The restriction of executive patron-age—especially in the matter of appoint-ments to office so far as it may be permitted by the Constitution, and consistent with the public good.

12. The education of the youth of our country in schools provided by the State;—which schools shall be common to all, with-out distinction of creed or party, and free from any influence or direction of a denom-inational or partizan character. And inas-much as Christianity by the Constitutions of nearly all the States; by the decisions of most eminent judicial authorities; and by the consent of the people of America is considered an element of our political sys-tem, and as the Holy Bible is at once the source of Christianity, and the depository and fountain of all civil and religious free-dom, we oppose every attempt to exclude it from the schools, thus established in the States.

13. We advocate protection to American industry and genius, against the adverse policy of foreign nations; also facilities to internal and external commerce, by the im-provement of rivers and harbors.

14. The policy of the Government of the United States, in its relations with foreign Governments, is to exact justice from the strongest, and do justice to the weakest;—restraining, by all the power of the Govern-ment, all its citizens from interference with the internal concerns of nations with whom we are at peace.

15. The Union of these States should be made perpetual by a faithful adherence to the principles embodied in the Declaration of Independence, and confirmed by the Con-stitution.

16. We believe that neither nature nor the Constitution of our country, recognize the right of man to property in man.

17. We believe that the stability of our institutions depends upon the virtue and intelligence of the people, and whereas in-temperance surely tends to undermine and destroy that virtue, therefore,

Resolved, We are in favor of a legal con-stitutional prohibition of the traffic in all alcoholic liquors.

18. All the principles of the Order to be henceforth everywhere openly avowed; each member shall be at liberty to make known the existence of the Order, and the fact that he himself is a member; and there need be no concealment of the places of meeting of the Subordinate Councils.

E. J. NIGHTINGALE,
Pres't of State Council of R. I.
H. N. CLEMONS, Secretary.

In 1855, at the height of Know-Nothing-ism, a crisis occurred at the Sisters of Mercy Convent at Broad and Claverick streets in Providence, where the nuns had established an orphanage and a school for girls (St. Xavier's Academy). In March a false rumor circulated that a Protestant girl, Rebecca Newell, was being held captive in the convent of these "female Jesuits," and a nativist mob formed to liberate her. This Know-Nothing handbill (right), which the Providence Journal obligingly reprinted, summoned native Americans to the rescue on the evening of March 22. The Irish Catholic community thereupon armed itself to defend the sisters against the threatened attack. Bloodshed was fortunately averted when Bishop O'Reilly (called by some "Paddy the Priest") confronted the riotous crowd of over two thousand and caused it to disperse. This was the high-water mark of Know-Nothingism, for within months the Irish "menace" gave way to the slavery issue as Rhode Island's prime concern. Less than a year later, while returning from a clerical recruiting mission in Europe, O'Reilly was lost at sea on the ill-fated steamer Pacific, which sank without a trace. Photograph of broadside from the author's collection

The Irish influx of the post-Famine years created a demand for Catholic social services and schools. This need prompted Irish-born Bishop Bernard O'Reilly (1850–1856) to invite the Sisters of Mercy to Rhode Island. Led by Mother Mary Francis Xavier Warde, the American foundress of the order, the sisters enthusiastically accepted the challenge. Mother Warde (shown here) and four other sisters arrived in Providence on March 11, 1851, beginning a social and educational apostolate that has endured to the present time.

Bishop O'Reilly's motives in recruiting the Mercy order were clear. Faced with a public school system with strong Protestant overtones, he sought an alternative that would provide a Catholic value-oriented education. In addition, he had a special desire to aid the orphans of the diocese, who, through the untimely death of their parents or as a result of abandonment, were sometimes placed in Protestant homes.

Mother Warde immediately addressed both these needs in 1851 by starting St. Aloysius Orphanage at the Mercy Convent and by founding St. Xavier's Academy, the first Catholic secondary school in the state (and still in operation in Coventry). A boarding and a day school combined, St. Xavier's served as a novitiate and as a finishing school for girls of families with sufficient means. It was first housed in a cottage on High (Westminster) Street and then in the Stead mansion nearby. In 1856 it moved into a newly built brick building on Claverick Street (above), the capacity of which was doubled nine years later. After this highly successful beginning in the most trying of times, Mother Warde left Rhode Island in 1858 for missionary work in northern New England. Photo of Mother Warde and sketch of the 1856 St. Xavier's building from Seventy-Five Years in the Passing (1926)

The educational efforts of Bishop O'Reilly and Mother Warde prompted members of the local Irish Catholic laity to request public aid for their newly created school system, igniting a controversy that still simmers. Another major educational dispute of the 1850s, however, has long since become moot. It concerned Bible reading in the public schools, an issue created when school districts insisted that only the Protestant, or King James, version of the Bible be read at periods of public prayer.

Questions of Bible reading in the public schools and government aid to Catholic schools became burning issues when volatile Archbishop John Hughes of New York demanded separate Bibles for Catholic students in public schools and financial aid to church institutions. The spin-off from this New York affair was felt in Rhode Island when a Providence Catholic who taught at St. Patrick's, John Coyle, advanced these demands locally in 1853. The question of financial aid, of course, received no hearing, but Elisha R. Potter,

Jr., state commissioner of education, and the influential Providence Journal agreed that it would be inconsistent with the state's religious heritage not to allow Catholic school children the use of their own version of the Scriptures. Potter contended that "the reading of the Bible or conducting other devotional exercises at the opening or closing of schools is neither forbidden nor commanded by law, and

rests with the teacher, who should respect his own conscience and the consciences of his pupils and their parents." This enlightened view was not held by many, and the intolerant majority continued to demand that the Protestant Bible be exclusively retained. Potter, the scion of a leading South Kingstown family, was remarkable for much more than this balanced decision issued at the height of the Know-Nothing movement. Although an opponent of the Dorrite movement in 1842, he was moderate and reasoned in his opposition. Later, as a state senator in 1861, Potter sponsored a bill to give equal voting rights to naturalized citizens who fought for the Union cause. This able civil servant and historian was also (like his father) a United States congressman (1843-1845), and from 1868 to 1882 he served as an associate justice of the Rhode Island Supreme Court. Portrait, oil on canvas, by Edward Dalton Marchant, courtesy of RIHS Museum (Rhi x3 5715)

Although Lincoln called for troops in April 1861 to preserve the integrity of the Union, most American historians believe that the crusade against slavery was the basic, underlying cause of the Civil War. Arnold Buffum (1782–1859) of old Smithfield (above) was one of Rhode Island's leading prewar abolitionists. He joined with William Lloyd Garrison and others to form the New England Anti-Slavery Society in 1832 and served as the first

president of that strident organization. Buffum traveled throughout the north eloquently lecturing for the antislavery cause, although as a Quaker he was more moderate in his proposed solutions to the evils of slavery than his colleague Garrison.

The son of an abolitionist, Buffum was the father of one also. His daughter, Elizabeth Buffum Chace, more radical in the cause than her father, became a staunch supporter of Garrison and Wendell Phillips. When Elizabeth married a successful industrialist, she made her

Valley Falls home (shown here) a station on the Underground Railroad—an informal route used by some escaped slaves to reach freedom in Canada. From this house (directly opposite the Cumberland Town Hall), blacks would board a train to Worcester, transfer to one for Vermont, and then go overland across the border to safety. Portrait of Arnold Buffum from North Smithfield Centennial (1971); photo of Chace House from Tanya R. Saunders (ed.), Black and Indian Heritage in Rhode Island (1976)

No Compromise with Slavery!
ANTI-SLAVERY
Tea Party.

THE LADIES' ANTI-SLAVERY SOCIETY,
Will give a Social Tea Party, at

HOWARD UPPER HALL.

On Wednesday Eve'g Jan. 5, 1853.

The usual attractions presented on such occasions, will be fully displayed.

Friends of the Slave, Lovers of your country's freedom, come and help us!

ADMITTANCE 12 1-2 CENTS.
Tickets for Supper 37 1-2 Cents.

A. C. Greene, Printer, Providence.

Women were very active in the reform crusades of the pre–Civil War years, especially for temperance, free public education, communitarianism, peace, institutional reform, and antislavery (as this local broadside suggests). With conditions ripe for the formation of a moderate antislavery party by the mid-1850s, less than two years after this Providence gathering the Republican party came to Rhode Island, dedicated to the nonextension of slavery into the territories of the United States. Broadside (1853) courtesy of RIHS Museum (Rhi x3 4506)

Among the many well-educated and well-to-do Newporters, including summer colonists, who spoke and wrote against the continuance of slavery was this contingent of the city's literati, shown in an 1850s daguerreotype taken at the Cliff House. Standing (left to right) are publisher Thomas G. Appleton, reformer and writer Julia Ward Howe, and poet Henry W. Longfellow; seated are G. W. Coster, Mrs. Longfellow, and Mrs. Edward Freeman.

Mrs. Howe (1819–1910) was descended from two Rhode Island colonial governors, Richard and Samuel Ward, and though a resident of Boston, she summered regularly

in Newport. Shortly after the outbreak of the Civil War, while visiting an army camp outside Washington, she composed a poem to the rhythm of the folk song "John Brown's Body," which she entitled "The Battle Hymn of the Republic." This emotional effort immediately became the anthem of the Union cause. In later life Mrs. Howe (wife of noted reformer Samuel Gridley Howe) led the fight for women's suffrage, both in Rhode Island and nationally. Photo from Maude Howe Elliott, This Was My Newport *(1944), courtesy of the Boston Athenaeum*

Youthful William Sprague (1830–1915), heir to the Cranston-based textile empire, was the successful fusionist candidate for governor in 1860. His victory over abolitionist Republican Seth Padelford was made possible by the votes of moderate Republicans and Democrats. Sprague was inaugurated several months before his

thirtieth birthday, making him the state's youngest chief executive ever.

After Sumter, Governor Sprague—who had been colonel of the Providence Marine Corps of Artillery—promptly offered President Lincoln both political and military support. He even dipped deeply into his personal fortune to equip the state volunteer units which he accompanied to Washington in 1861. Acting as an aide to Colonel Ambrose Burnside (then commanding the Second Brigade, Second Division, Army of the Potomac), Sprague had his horse shot from under him during the disastrous Union defeat at First Bull Run. Later he

offered the rank of brigadier general of volunteers by Lincoln, but he prudently declined.

Reelected governor twice, Sprague relinquished that office to become Republican U.S. senator in March 1863. After he had served two undistinguished terms, his mental health and his finances failed. His final years were spent in Paris. When he died as the last of the nation's surviving war governors, his body was returned to Providence for burial in Swan Point Cemetery. Steel engraving by A. H. Ritchie, courtesy of RIHS (Rhi x3 5701)

This April 24, 1861, photo (top) depicts the departure from Providence's Exchange Place of the second wave—510 men—of the First Rhode Island Regiment of Detached Militia, Lieutenant Colonel Joseph T. Pitman commanding. The initial wave of 530 men had left with Governor Sprague four days earlier. The entire unit fought under Burnside at Bull Run, and 47 offi- cers and men were killed, wounded, or taken prisoner before the unit was dis- charged in early August.

Two other Rhode Island outfits in this ill-fated encounter also incurred signifi- cant casualties. The Second Regiment, Rhode Island Volunteers, suffered 28 killed (including its commander, Colonel John S. Slocum), 56 wounded, and 30 missing, and Battery A of the First Light Artillery (shown boarding ship at the Port of Providence) lost a total of 16. Photo (1861) courtesy of RIHS (Rhi x3 1380); sketch (April 1861) by J. H. Schell, cour- tesy of Mildred Santille Longo

As the bloody war progressed and expanded, the federal government and the governments of the states issued repeated calls for recruits. These typical posters appealed both to the patriotism and adventurous spirit of Rhode Islanders and to their pocketbooks, with generous bounties offered for enlistment. Photo of posters in the collection of the Providence Marine Corps of Artillery from Harold R. Barker, History of Rhode Island Combat Units in the Civil War *(1964)*

Ambrose E. Burnside (right), reading a newspaper and wearing the "burnsides" or "sideburns" that gave a new word to the language, sits opposite the famed Civil War photographer Mathew Brady in this unusual photo from Burnside's own collection.

By March 1862 Burnside, an Indiana native, had become a major general of volunteers. That October, Lincoln made the personable West Pointer commander of the Army of the Potomac. His major engagement in that capacity was the debacle at Fredericksburg. After demotion, followed by some successes on the western front, Burnside came east, where he again blundered—this time at Petersburg's Battle of the Crater.

He was a much better businessman (founding the Burnside Rifle Works in Bristol and the Rhode Island Locomotive Works) and politician (serving as governor from 1866 to 1869 and U.S. senator from 1875 to 1881) than he was a general. Burnside Park in downtown Providence, complete with a thirteen-and-a-half-foot bronze equestrian statue, is dedicated to his memory. Bristol, where Burnside lived and worked before the war, also has several memorials in his honor. Photo by an assistant to Mathew Brady, courtesy of RIHS (Rhi x3 1835)

These officers of the Second Regiment, Infantry, Rhode Island Volunteers, pose in the lines before Petersburg in the winter of 1864-65. Seated in the chair left of center is Colonel Elisha H. Rhodes of Pawtuxet, who compiled an interesting and comprehensive diary detailing the unit's activities from First Bull Run to Appomattox. In 1986 that diary was edited by Robert Hunt Rhodes and published as All for the Union: A History of the 2nd Rhode Island Volunteer Infantry.

Of the twenty-two Rhode Island batteries and regiments that served in the war, this unit had the most battle deaths (120), while the Fourteenth Rhode Island (Colored) Regiment suffered the most deaths from both battle and disease (329).

During the conflict 489 members of Rhode Island units were killed in action or died of wounds and another 1,206 succumbed to disease, producing a death toll of 1,685.

Sixteen Rhode Islanders won the newly created Congressional Medal of Honor. Photo from the E. H. Rhodes collection, courtesy of Andrew Mowbray Publishers

This scene depicts Battery A, Rhode Island Light Artillery, helping to repulse the famous and desperate fifteen-thousand-man charge of Confederate general George E. Pickett on the third day of battle at Gettysburg. Battery A is shown supporting the right center of the Union line by firing its cannon across a stone wall towards Pickett's left flank. This view looks toward the town of Gettysburg to the north. Battery A, commanded here by Captain William A. Arnold, suffered casualties at Gettysburg of four men killed and twenty-eight wounded. Photo from Harold R. Barker, History of Rhode Island Combat Units in the Civil War (1964), courtesy of the Gettysburg Cyclorama

War is made by the old and fought by the young. In this all-out brothers' war, each side used thousands of boys in their early teens. This is Hiram Joseph Eddy, age fourteen, drummer boy, Company C, Twelfth Rhode Island Regiment, Infantry. Photo from North Smithfield Centennial *(1971)*

In May 1861, less than a month after the bombardment of Fort Sumter, Commandant George S. Blake moved the United States Naval Academy from vulnerable Annapolis in the border slave state of Maryland to the relative safety of Newport. For the duration of the conflict, midshipmen were quartered at Fort Adams or in an old hotel called the Atlantic House (shown here), which once stood at the corner of Pelham and Touro streets facing the public park in which the Newport Tower stands. During its four-year sojourn the navy held infantry and artillery drills in a pasture near Ochre Point—now the site of mansions—and seamanship drills on the practice ships anchored in the harbor. For target-firing, the plebes used a battery of thirty-two-pounders in a shed on Goat Island. The three school ships on which the midshipmen trained while in Newport were the Santee, *the* Macedonian, *and the famous* Constitution *("Old Ironsides"), shown here with Fort Adams in the background. Despite repeated efforts by the Newport City Council to induce the naval academy to locate permanently on Coasters Harbor Island, the institution returned to Annapolis in the summer of 1865. Photo of plebes with Atlantic House in the background, courtesy of Newport Historical Society; lithograph of "Old Ironsides" and Fort Adams by J. P. Newell, courtesy of the Redwood Library*

Although the war was fought, in part, to free the slaves, Rhode Island's blacks enjoyed few advantages from the outcome of the conflict. Black males had already been given the right to vote without the need to own real estate because of the support given by the black community to the Law and Order faction during the Dorr Rebellion, and slavery had been formally abolished in the state constitution of 1843. But the war did inspire one significant advance for local blacks: the elimination of segregated public schools.

Here black businessman George T. Downing (1819–1903), a New York native and Hamilton College graduate, played a major role. In 1846 Downing moved to Newport, bought a house, and opened a restaurant. Four years later he acquired a catering business and a residence in Providence, and in the summer of 1855, with capital borrowed from his father, Downing built a luxury hotel in Newport called Sea Girt House, which attracted a distinguished and rich white clientele.

In the 1850s Downing's efforts turned not only towards abolitionism but also towards civil rights for freed blacks. Massachusetts legislation against segregated public schools in 1855 was the catalyst for Downing's unrelenting efforts to secure a similar law in Rhode Island that would prevent local school districts from racially segregating their schools. For the next decade Downing appeared before school committees in the offending communities, repeatedly petitioned the General Assembly, testified before legislative committees, wrote and published addresses, and tried to mobilize the black vote on behalf of his great cause, but to no avail. Then, in 1866, the legislature finally heeded Downing's plea: prompted by a temporary spurt of war-born idealism, it passed a statute outlawing racial segregation in public schools throughout the state of Rhode Island. Photo of Downing (seated, center) and his family, courtesy of the Rhode Island Black Heritage Society

In the aftermath of the Civil War—which left 360,000 Union and 258,000 Confederate troops dead—a reverence developed both for those who had died in the conflict and for those who had survived. In the North the Union veterans (called the Grand Army of the Republic, or the GAR) were feted, memorialized, and awarded generous pensions for their wartime service. Nearly every Rhode Island community has its Civil War monument.

Then, between 1889 and 1891, as the young men of the 1860s grew enfeebled with age, a grateful state established the Rhode Island Soldiers' Home on Bristol's Davis Wilson farm. This facility, designed to provide "a home for those men who served in the army or navy of the United States in the war of the rebellion, and were honorably discharged therefrom, who, by reason of wounds, disease, old age, or other infirmities, are unable to earn their living and have no adequate means of support," opened with elaborate public ceremonies in May 1891, forty years after Sprague and Burnside had rushed to the defense of Washington. In this early photo the surgeon's residence is on the left and the veterans' hospital on the right. Photo courtesy of PPL

113

Cotton textile production remained the backbone of Rhode Island's industrial economy during the late nineteenth century. The Blackstone and the Pawtuxet valleys were particularly noted for this line of activity. According to the state census of 1895, Rhode Island had eighty-eight cotton-manufacturing firms employing 25,086 workers, who produced an annual product of $24,392,788.

The most famous of the state's cotton textile companies was the Providence-based empire formed by Benjamin B. and Robert Knight. The Knight brothers, sons of a Cranston farmer, began their illustrious careers as lowly operatives in the Sprague (now Cranston) Print Works, one of the many firms they came to own. In 1852 they formed their fateful partnership as co-owners of the Pontiac Mill in Warwick (above). By 1895, under their still famous trademark Fruit of the Loom, they owned twenty-one cotton mills (including some out-of-state facilities) with an aggregate capacity of 11,000 looms and over 400,000 spindles, and employing nearly 7,000 operatives.

In addition to his textile ventures, Benjamin Knight (1813–1898) was also a Providence alderman and a representative in the General Assembly. Robert Knight (1826-1912) was active in Providence banking circles. Both built splendid Providence residences—Benjamin on Broad Street, Robert on Elmwood Avenue. The headquarters of their mammoth firm, allegedly the largest of its kind in the world, was at 3 Washington Row, the present site of the old Hospital Trust Bank Building. Though the company went bankrupt in 1924, its famous label lives on, having been bought in 1938 by the Union Underwear Company. Composite photograph from Fruit of the Loom Muslin and Other High Quality Fabrics, courtesy of RIHS (Rhi x3 4294 and 4295); lithograph of Pontiac Mills courtesy of RIHS (Rhi x3 5102)

Chapter Six

B. B. KNIGHT

FRUIT OF THE LOOM

ROBERT KNIGHT

THE GILDED AGE, 1867-1899

Industrialization, urbanization, and cultural pluralism are among twentieth-century America's most salient characteristics. During the last three decades of the nineteenth century (the so-called Gilded Age), Rhode Island came to exhibit these traits more markedly than any other state.

Rhode Island's four big industries continued to boom. Cotton textiles evidenced a trend towards consolidation—bigger mills, more employees, and more spindles. This enterprise dominated the economy of the Blackstone and Pawtuxet valleys, and the Providence-based cotton textile empire formed by Benjamin B. and Robert Knight was allegedly the largest in the world. In 1900 this industry had ninety establishments and an average yearly work force of 24,192.

Woolen production experienced a wartime expansion in the 1860s and continued to flourish at century's end. With entrepreneurs like Charles Fletcher leading the way, Providence ranked first among the cities of the nation by 1900 in the production of woolen and worsted goods, and Rhode Island, with fifty-four establishments employing 16,738, ranked third among the states in this area of manufacture.

In the base-metals trade the state was also prominent. Brown and Sharpe (located in Providence until its relocation to North Kingstown in 1964) was the largest producer of machine tools in the nation, and its managers, Joseph Brown and Lucien Sharpe, became renowned for such inventions as the micrometer and the vernier caliper.

The state also boasted the country's largest steam-engine factory, founded and run by George Corliss of Providence. The crowning achievement of this noted inventor and his firm was the construction of the gigantic steam engine used to power the machinery displayed at the mammoth Philadelphia Centennial Exposition of 1876.

Other giants of the base-metals industry included the file company of William T. Nicholson, the world's largest producer of metal files and rasps, and William G. Angell's American Screw Company, whose three large Providence plants turned out more wood and machine screws during this era than any other company in the world. By 1900 Rhode Island had 144 machine shops and foundries that employed 8,799 workers.

The precious-metals industry also enjoyed phenomenal growth. The Gorham Manufacturing

Company in Providence was the country's largest producer of silverware, and its statues, memorials, and architectural bronze work were famous nationwide. Among the best known of Gorham's creations is its statue of the Independent Man, which has stood atop the State House since 1899. While Gorham was the giant, many smaller jewelry and silverware firms also flourished—enough of them to make Providence and its environs the world's leading costume jewelry manufacturing center. By 1900 this industry claimed 249 establishments employing 8,767 people throughout the state.

During the Gilded Age these "big four" industries were joined by a fifth major area of manufacturing endeavor—rubber goods, especially footwear. Woonsocket, Providence, Bristol, and Warren contained this industry's principal plants, while entrepreneurs Joseph Banigan, Joseph Davol, Samuel P. Colt, and Governor Augustus O. Bourn provided this fledgling industry with either inventive genius or managerial expertise. Most interesting of these rubber tycoons was Banigan, an Irish Catholic immigrant who became a founder and president of the United States Rubber Company. In addition to his diverse business ventures, Banigan devoted much of his time and fortune to humanitarian causes and became the greatest single benefactor of the social programs of the Diocese of Providence.

Banigan was certainly not the average nineteenth-century Rhode Island entrepreneur. Horatio Alger stories like his were far from common. Collectively portrayed, the state's business elite would look, rather, like this: Neither an immigrant nor the son of one, the typical Rhode Island businessman was born in the northeastern United States, usually Rhode Island, and could trace his ancestry back to English forebears who settled here in the seventeenth and eighteenth centuries. He was raised in an urban environment, in a middle- or upper-class household, completed at least a secondary school education, and sometimes attended college. He was a Protestant, probably Episcopal or Congregational. He did not start to work until he was past nineteen years of age, and then it was usually in a business that was operated by a member of his family. By middle age he had reached a position of prominence within the state. He was usually connected with more than one business; a Republican, he participated in the running of his community through elected and appointed positions; he belonged to several clubs and took an active part in community affairs; he lived in the East Side–College Hill section of Providence and sometimes owned a summer house at the shore.

The industrial ventures of such men accelerated the urbanization of Rhode Island. Providence, which annexed nearly thirteen square miles of territory

from adjacent parts of Cranston, Johnston, and North Providence, grew from a population of 54,595 in 1865 to a thriving metropolis of 175,597 in 1900, ranking twentieth in size among the cities of the United States.

During this era the city of Woonsocket was created, first by consolidating the Cumberland mill villages of Woonsocket Falls, Clinton, and Social on the northeast bank of the Blackstone in 1867 and then by adding to them the Smithfield villages of Globe, Bernon, and Hamlet on the southwest bank in 1871. The densely populated mill town became a city in 1888.

Pawtucket also experienced a metamorphosis from a cluster of villages to a city. The Massachusetts town of Pawtucket was annexed in 1862, and in 1874 it was joined to the North Providence village of the same name. This 8.68-square-mile municipality became the state's second most populous city in 1885.

Another political cell division took place in the Blackstone Valley when "old" Smithfield was divided in 1871. In addition to the mill villages annexed by Woonsocket, the towns of Lincoln and North Smithfield were also set off. Eventually the densely populated manufacturing area of Central Falls was detached from Lincoln in 1895 and made the state's fifth city. Its small size—an area of 1.32 square miles—was its most unusual feature.

Closely related to industrialization and urbanization was immigration, with jobs the magnet that drew foreigners to Gilded Age Rhode Island. It was in this period that the state began to acquire its remarkable ethnic diversity.

From the 1860s through the 1880s, Franco-Americans from Quebec migrated in impressive numbers. During the Civil War, textile manufacturers recruited the Quebec *habitant* to relieve the manpower shortage in Rhode Island's mills. That move opened the floodgates, and by 1890 more French Canadians were migrating to Rhode Island annually than any other ethnic group. Most settled in the Blackstone Valley towns, especially Woonsocket, but large numbers went to the Pawtuxet Valley, especially to the village of Arctic. Providence, North Providence, and Warren also attracted a significant number of Franco-American residents. By the state census of 1895, there were 40,231 Rhode Islanders who had both parents born in French Canada.

The early Gilded Age also witnessed migrations from Germany and Sweden. In 1865 there were 1,626 Rhode Islanders of German parentage; by 1895 that figure had increased to 7,027. Most of these immigrants were Protestant, especially Lutheran, but one in every five was a Roman Catholic. Germans settled mainly in Pawtucket and Providence, particularly in the capital city's West End—Olneyville, Manton, Broadway, Elmwood, and West Elmwood. Many were

CORLISS STEAM ENGINE CO.

PROVIDENCE, R.I.

1 Machine Shop.
2 Ware Room.
3 Iron Foundry.
4 Pattern Shop.
5 Erecting Shop.
6 Boiler Shop.
7 Machine Shop.
8 Forge Shop.
9 Offices.

George H. Corliss was to Rhode Island industry in its maturity what Samuel Slater and Zachariah Allen had been during its infancy. Born in Easton, New York, in 1817, Corliss came to Providence in 1844 after several relatively unproductive years operating a general store. By 1849 he had patented a stationary steam engine with an automatic cutoff valve, one of sixty patents eventually registered in his name. This and other major innovations in engine design earned Corliss international honor and fame, including a first prize at the Paris Exposition in 1867 (in competition with over a hundred engine builders) and the Grand Diploma of Honor at the Vienna Exposition of 1873. In the technical world he is ranked with James Watt as a developer of steam power.

The Corliss Steam Engine Company (established with E. J. Nightingale in 1848 and incorporated eight years later) eventually occupied five acres and nine brick buildings at Charles and West River streets and employed more than a thousand workmen in the production of engines and boilers. Corliss (who was also a major Providence landowner and a state legislator) died in 1888. His nationally renowned company did not long survive him, failing in the depression of the 1890s. Composite photo: steel engraving of Corliss, courtesy of RIHS (Rhi x3 4097); steel engraving of Corliss Steam Engine Company, courtesy of RIHS (Rhi x3 5630)

117

skilled workmen who gained employment in the jewelry industry and such other trades as shoe manufacture, cabinetmaking, baking, and brewing.

Sweden, which suffered a famine in 1868 and a decline in the agricultural sector of its economy, sent many migrants to the United States in the late nineteenth century. Most went to the Midwest, but some made Rhode Island their New World destination. Those of Swedish parentage rose from fewer than 100 in 1865 to 6,915 in 1895. Providence accounted for approximately 40 percent of that total, most of them on the city's South Side. The Auburn, Eden Park, and Pontiac sections of Cranston also attracted large numbers of these migrants from Scandinavia. They sought work in textiles, base metals, and jewelry, but some engaged in gardening and other agricultural pursuits. The Swedes were devout Lutherans and became staunch Republicans.

A much overlooked element in early Gilded Age immigration was the British Americans. As late as 1885, migrants to Rhode Island from England and British Canada ranked third and fourth respectively behind the Irish and the Franco-Americans in the annual number of new arrivals. These British immigrants, many of whom brought industrial skills, settled mainly in Pawtucket, North Providence, and Providence. Most were Protestant in religion and Republican in politics, and they readily assimilated. By 1895 there were 30,380 Rhode Islanders with both parents born in England, plus another 7,671 with parents born in either Scotland or Wales.

The European arrivals discussed thus far—Irish, English, Swedes, and Germans—were from the northern and western sectors of the continent. Towards the end of the Gilded Age, a movement called by historians the "New Immigration" brought a great wave of refugees from southern and eastern Europe. Rhode Island received a generous share of this outpouring. From the south and the Mediterranean came significant numbers of Portuguese, Greeks, Armenians, Syrian-Lebanese, and, especially, Italians. From the east, Poles, Lithuanians, Jews, and Ukrainians began their exodus.

At century's end the streets of Rhode Island's major cities sounded with the babel of new tongues; inner-city neighborhoods and blocks took on old-world characteristics; parishes, ethnic congregations, and synagogues sprang up; and factories flourished with the cheap and abundant labor which these newcomers provided.

Worlds apart from industrial, urban, and ethnic Rhode Island were the life-styles of South County and Newport. The former area was still basically rural and agrarian, but farming was in a steady state of decline. Most South County towns continued to lose population as their inhabitants were lured by the city or the new cheap lands in the West. Two bright spots in their otherwise bleak economy were the nationally renowned granite industry of Westerly, which supplied more than one-third of the memorials on the Gettysburg battlefield, and the equally famous and flourishing coastal resort of Narragansett Pier, whose oceanfront hotels and fabulous Casino attracted wealthy summer residents from throughout the country.

Even more posh and prestigious as a summer resort was Newport, and the late nineteenth century was Newport's Golden Age. "The City by the Sea" had been a mecca for well-to-do vacationers since colonial times, and from the 1840s its popularity as a rich man's resort steadily grew. Several large hotels had been built in the three decades before the Civil War, but by the 1870s more and more summer colonists were choosing to build "cottages" with ocean vistas closer to the beaches. Favored sites for the very wealthy—the Astors, Vanderbilts, Wetmores—were along Cliff Walk and the newly extended Bellevue Avenue. From their exclusive haunts at the Casino (1880), the Newport Country Club (1894), and Bailey's Beach Club (1897), the magnates of late nineteenth-century America engaged in such leisure activities as yachting, fox hunting, polo, golf, and tennis. With such an auspicious debut, Newport later became the site of the America's Cup races and the International Tennis Hall of Fame.

During this splendid and extravagant era, the city of Newport (incorporated in 1853) also strengthened its ties with the United States Navy. In 1884 the prestigious U.S. Naval War College opened its doors. Alfred Thayer Mahan arrived soon thereafter to begin his distinguished career as a professor and the nation's foremost exponent and historian of seapower.

While the Newport "Four Hundred" engaged in luxurious leisure, other Rhode Islanders took their recreation in more popular and common ways. For the participant, cycling was the current rage, while rowing or canoeing on the Seekonk, the Pawtuxet, or the artificial lakes of the newly created Roger Williams Park was also a relaxing exercise. The more sedate could attend a concert by David Wallis Reeves's American Band, have a traditional clambake along the shore, or take a steamboat excursion on the bay to such popular amusement centers as Rocky Point, Oakland Beach, and Crescent Park.

A new form of entertainment was baseball, and Providence boasted its own major league team, the Grays. In 1879 and again in 1884 this talented squad won the National League title, equivalent to the championship of professional baseball. In the latter year the Grays' star pitcher, Charles "Old Hoss" Radbourn, registered sixty victories, still a major league record.

The crowning achievement of George Corliss and his company was the construction of this gigantic steam engine, which was used to power the machinery displayed at the great Philadelphia Centennial Exposition of 1876. Built at a cost of more than $100,000, the 1,400-horsepower Centennial Engine was one of the marvels in this spectacular display of American ingenuity. When it was set in motion by President Grant and Emperor Dom Pedro II of Brazil (shown right), a French observer described it as a work of art: "The lines were so grand and beautiful, the play of the movements was so skillfully and simply arranged, and the whole machine was so harmoniously constructed, that it had the beauty, and almost the grace, of the human form."

When the engine was stopped after six months of flawless operation, an Austrian engineer exclaimed: "Ehre dem jungen Lande! Ehre dem grossen Corliss!" ("Honor to the young land! Honor to the great Corliss!"). Engraving courtesy of RIHS (Rhi x3 4184)

The production of rubber goods was a new business that emerged as Rhode Island's fifth most significant industrial enterprise by the end of the nineteenth century. According to the manufacturing census of 1895, the rubber industry employed 3,211 workers and generated a product valued at $4,578,056. Pioneers in this new area of economic endeavor were Joseph Banigan and Joseph Duvol of Providence and Augustus O. Bourn and Samuel P. Colt of Bristol.

Banigan (right) was born in Ireland in 1839 and came to Providence with his family at the age of eight. After one year of schooling he began work in the New England Screw Company. While still in his twenties, he founded his own business, the Goodyear India Rubber Bottle Stopper Company—his first venture into the infant rubber-goods field. By 1866 he formed a company in Woonsocket for the manufacture of rubber footwear, and in 1889 he built the imposing Alice Mill, named in honor of his mother. Banigan, who became the country's leading importer of Brazilian crude rubber, eventually expanded his business to Millville, Massachusetts, and then to Providence, where in 1896 he built a footwear plant on Valley Street that gave employment to a thousand workers.

During the industrial consolidation movement of the 1890s, Banigan became a founder of the United States Rubber Company and served as that mammoth

combine's president from 1893 to 1896. Included among his diverse business interests were woolens, banking, publishing, and cable tramways. Banigan also served as president of the Providence Board of Trade; in 1898 he built the city's first "skyscraper," the ten-story Banigan Building (since 1954 called the AMICA Building); and he contributed heavily to the Catholic University of America and to the Mormon Church.

Influenced by his humble origins, Banigan was Rhode Island Catholicism's greatest benefactor, though his generosity is but dimly remembered. Among his many local endowments are the Home for Aged Poor in Pawtucket; St. Maria's Home for Working Girls, St. Joseph's Hospital, and St. Vincent de Paul Infant Asylum (originally on Regent Avenue), all in Providence; and St. Bernard Mortuary Chapel in St. Francis Cemetery, Pawtucket, where this self-made Irish immigrant was laid to rest in July 1898. Engraving by F. G. Kernan from Richard Bayles's History of Providence County (1891)

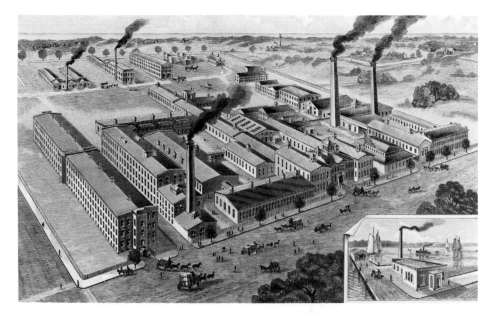

By century's end Bristol's National India Rubber Company was one of the giants of the rubber industry. Founded in 1864 by Augustus O. Bourn, it first manufactured rubber boots and shoes, but by the 1890s, with some fourteen hundred workers, it had expanded its production to include a wide array of rubber goods. Its catalog listed, for example, "hose of all kinds, for garden or steam purposes, belting, packing, spittoons, fire buckets, curry combs, perforated and pressed door mats, carriage cloth, mackintoshes, and a great variety of wearing apparel, carriage aprons, horse covers, water bottles and fountain syringes, carriage and chair cushions, bed pans, operating cushions, inflatable bath tubs, bed sheets, life preservers, tubing, and numerous other specialties in the line of druggists' sundries."

In 1883 Augustus Bourn was elected governor of Rhode Island, in which office he served until 1885. Later, as a state senator, he sponsored a constitutional amendment (Article VII) that removed the real estate voting requirement for naturalized citizens but limited the vote in city council elections to property owners, a restriction designed to keep the working class from controlling the government of the cities in which most of them resided.

Bourn was succeeded as CEO of National Rubber by Samuel Pomeroy Colt, a man with a distinguished lineage and career. The nephew of Samuel Colt, inventor of the famed revolving pistol, the brother of U.S. Senator LeBaron Colt, and the descendant through his maternal line of the Bristol De Wolfs, Colt, like Banigan, was a president of the U.S. Rubber Company. In addition, he founded Industrial Trust Bank, served the state in several official posts, including that of attorney

general, and made numerous charitable donations, particularly in Bristol. Colt gave a memorial school to the town in honor of his mother and later endowed an adjoining museum of fine arts. He is best remembered for his bequest to the public of his beautifully maintained four-hundred-acre retreat on Narragansett Bay, Colt Farm, which is now the Colt State Park. Steel engraving from Robert Grieve and John P. Fernald, The Cotton Centennial, 1790–1890 *(1891)*

In higher education Rhode Island made notable advances. In addition to the establishment of the Naval War College, this period witnessed the founding of the Rhode Island School of Design (1877), a nationally renowned industrial design institute. RISD was the centennial project of a group of Rhode Island women. Two decades later many of these same feminists broke the sex barrier at Brown and established Pembroke College (1897) as a department of that prestigious university.

In the area of public education, the defunct state normal school—the forerunner of Rhode Island College—was reopened in Providence in 1871 and furnished with an impressive modern building in 1898. Also, a land-grant state college for instruction in agriculture and the mechanic arts—the forerunner of the University of Rhode Island—was opened at Kingston in 1892.

Other important public service institutions had their origins during the Gilded Age, most notably Rhode Island Hospital (1868); Providence Public Library (1878); Roger Williams General Hospital (1878); Lying-In Hospital, now Women and Infants (1884); and St. Joseph's Hospital (1892).

In politics the last four decades of the century marked an era of Republican dominance. On national issues the GOP championed a high tariff and sound money. When native-born Irish grew numerous enough to challenge Republican ascendancy, the majority party (led after the death of U.S. Senator Henry Anthony in 1884 by U.S. Senator Nelson Aldrich and Charles R. "Boss" Brayton) removed the real estate requirement for voting in order to recruit and enfranchise certain sociocultural foes of the Irish—immigrants from French Canada, England, British Canada, and Sweden. By the end of the century the political battle lines between WASP Republicans and Irish Catholic Democrats were sharply drawn, with the newer immigrants holding the balance of power. This balance temporarily rested with the Republican party.

In one aspect the era closed as it began: with Rhode Islanders returning home from battle. In April 1898 the Spanish-American War began. The state raised several military units for this bout with Spain, but only the crewmen of the U.S.S. *Vulcan,* a repair ship, saw combat in this brief conflict. All of the state's 1,780 volunteers were mustered out of service by April 1899 as Rhode Island prepared to greet the new century.

THE SOCIAL.

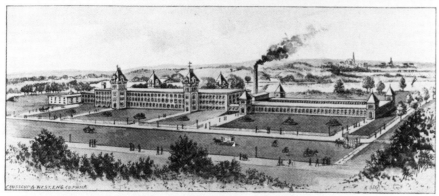

THE NOURSE.

THE GLOBE.

Henry Lippitt, grandson of Charles Lippitt, a founder of the West Warwick mill village that bears this old Rhode Island name, grew to manhood surrounded by successful cotton textile entrepreneurs. His first venture as a mill owner came in 1846 when he and several partners acquired Tiffany Mill in Danielson, Connecticut. In 1854 Henry and his brother Robert purchased an interest in the Social cotton mill in Woonsocket. After Robert's death Henry enlarged his holdings by purchasing Globe Mill in 1876 from the heirs of pioneer Woonsocket industrialist George C. Ballou. Seven years later Lippitt opened the smaller Nourse Mill a short distance from the Social Mill. When these engravings were done in 1890, the three factories employed a total of 1,450 workers at 137,776 spindles, producing twills, sateens, and both fancy and plain cotton goods.

In addition to these mills, Lippitt owned the Silver Spring Bleaching and Dying Company in Providence, the Lippitt Woolen Mill, and the Providence commission (or sales) firm of H. Lippitt and Company. With such economic clout, it is small wonder that Henry Lippitt became Republican governor of Rhode Island from 1875 to 1877 or that his son and business successor Charles Warren Lippitt held the same office from 1895 to 1897. Composite engraving by Grosscup and West in Robert Grieve and John P. Fernald, The Cotton Centennial, 1790–1890 (1891)

The Gorham Manufacturing Company, established in 1818, was one of Providence's five industrial wonders of the Gilded Age. By 1889 it outgrew its bulging Steeple Street complex and moved to a spacious thirty-acre site several hundred feet west of the junction of Elmwood and Reservoir avenues. Here it once employed nearly two thousand workers, many of them highly skilled craftsmen who gained for Gorham a worldwide reputation for excellence in the production of statues and memorials, architectural bronze work, and silver flatware and holloware such as that shown here. In the Gorham plant were crafted the Columbus Monument (1893) gracing nearby Columbus Square; the Independent Man (1899) atop the State House; the Bajnotti Fountain (1901) in City Hall Park; Bruno (1924), the bear guarding Brown's Marvel Gym; and the statues of Oliver Hazard Perry (1928) and Nathanael Greene (1930) in front of the state capitol.

Gorham, which became a division of Textron in 1967, is still in operation, but in 1986 this last survivor of nineteenth-century Providence's "big five" industrial concerns moved from the city to facilities in Johnston and Smithfield. Photograph from Wilfred H. Munro, Picturesque Rhode Island (1881)

121

This somewhat idyllic photo of Westerly's White Rock Mill and its employees was taken sometime in the late nineteenth century. The mill was often cited as a very fine example of ornamental brickwork because of its crenellated (notched) tower, pilasters (support columns), and stone windowsills. It was built in 1849, but subsequent additions give it a Victorian character. By the time this picture was taken, the mill was producing lightweight cotton cloth and material used in making fine sheets. It had also become part of the Knight textile empire. Photo from Martha and Murray Zimiles, Early American Mills *(1973), courtesy of the Westerly Public Library*

This 1877 balloon view of Central Falls shows the dense concentration of mills along the Blackstone River (right) and the equally congested housing stock nearby. Central Falls had recently been set off from Smithfield and was the extreme southeast corner of the newly created town of Lincoln. At this time most of the inhabitants were of English, Irish, or French Canadian stock. In 1895, for political and other reasons, Central Falls was constituted a separate municipality with a city form of government. Its scant 1.32-square-mile area and its high concentration of people have made this Rhode Island's most densely populated community ever since. Lithograph courtesy of RIHS (Rhi x3 1372)

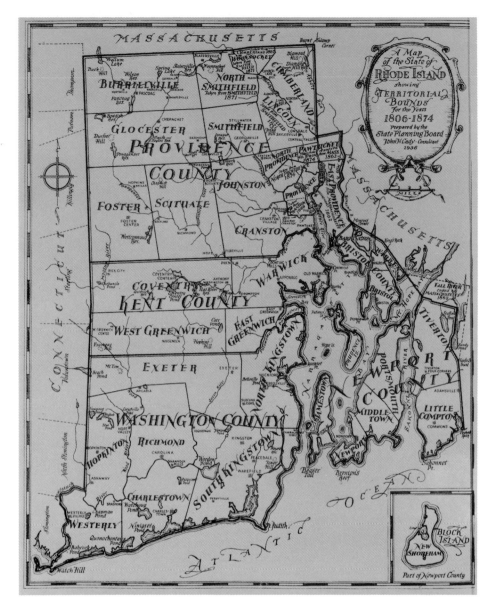

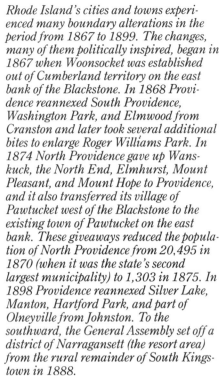

Rhode Island's cities and towns experienced many boundary alterations in the period from 1867 to 1899. The changes, many of them politically inspired, began in 1867 when Woonsocket was established out of Cumberland territory on the east bank of the Blackstone. In 1868 Providence reannexed South Providence, Washington Park, and Elmwood from Cranston and later took several additional bites to enlarge Roger Williams Park. In 1874 North Providence gave up Wanskuck, the North End, Elmhurst, Mount Pleasant, and Mount Hope to Providence, and it also transferred its village of Pawtucket west of the Blackstone to the existing town of Pawtucket on the east bank. These giveaways reduced the population of North Providence from 20,495 in 1870 (when it was the state's second largest municipality) to 1,303 in 1875. In 1898 Providence reannexed Silver Lake, Manton, Hartford Park, and part of Olneyville from Johnston. To the southward, the General Assembly set off a district of Narragansett (the resort area) from the rural remainder of South Kingstown in 1888.

Perhaps the most notable change occurred in the town of old Smithfield, whose boundaries had remained intact since 1731. Then the state's second largest town in area, in 1871 it gave its northernmost mill villages to Woonsocket and was divided into three municipalities—Lincoln (which until 1895 included Central Falls), North Smithfield, and Smithfield. Map by John Hutchins Cady, Rhode Island Boundaries, 1636–1936 *(1936)*

Wood River forms the boundary line between Hopkinton and Richmond. During the late nineteenth century its banks and those of its branches were lined with numerous gristmills and sawmills and several small factories. Hopkinton's largest village along this river was Hope Valley, site of the well-respected Nichols and Langworthy steam-engine factory and home of Hopkinton's only newspaper, the Wood River Advertiser. In 1874 the Wood River Branch Railroad was completed, connecting the village with the Providence-to-New York railroad at a place first called Richmond Switch and now known as Wood River Junction. This five-mile branch line, over which trains traveled several times daily, brought increased prosperity to Hope Valley as well as to the nearby river villages of Locustville and Wyoming. Photo from the Gladys Segar Collection, courtesy of RIHS

123

When these photos of quarrying were taken in the 1870s, the town of Westerly had seven working granite quarries producing stone that was nationally known and sold for its beauty and its strength. Orlando Smith uncovered the first quarry in 1845 on Rhodes Hill; a second, on adjoining land, was opened by George Ledward in 1866. Thereafter, the Civil War-generated demand for monumental stone transformed the industry into Westerly's second largest employer (over three hundred workers in 1875) and the supplier of mausoleums and numerous pieces of statuary for the late war's battlefields, especially Gettysburg. In these photos, workmen put the finishing touches on a monument which did much to spread the fame of Westerly's quarries and stone cutters, the twenty-three-foot-high figure of the ''Antietam Soldier,'' completed in 1876; and a finished thirty-eight-ton granite shaft is hauled down Quarry Hill to the railroad station, with six pair of oxen to pull and three pair to brake the load. Westerly's last granite quarry closed in 1969. *Photos from Ralph Bolton Cooney,* Westerly's Oldest Witness *(1950)*

*The village of Pascoag, on the Clear River
in the geographic center of the town of
Burrillville (1885 population, 5,126), was
a prosperous rural community when this
sketch was made in the mid-1880s. At that
time the hamlet contained the Clear River
Woolen Mills of James O. Inman and
Fisk, Sayles, and Company, both
producers of fine cashmere woolens. The
meetinghouse of the state's first Freewill
Baptist Church, formed in 1812, is to the
right in this view. The cattle in the
foreground indicate the pastoral setting
from which many Rhode Island mill villages like Pascoag sprang in response to the
Industrial Revolution. Engraved sketch
from Welcome A. Greene,* The Providence
Plantations for 250 Years *(1886)*

Despite the advent of the railroad, many towns and villages in rural Rhode Island continued to depend on the stagecoach for mail and transportation until late in the nineteenth century. Shown here are (top) the Providence to Hartford stage at Hopkins Mills in Foster, ca. 1880, and *(bottom) a stagecoach and a buggy in front of the Centredale Hotel on the Putnam Pike in 1873. Photos from* Foster, 1781–1981: A Bicentennial Celebration *(1981) and Frank C. Angell,* Annals of Centredale in the Town of North Providence, 1636–1909 *(1909)*

This is a late nineteenth-century view of Oaklawn Community Baptist Church (built in 1879) and, behind it, the old Quaker Meeting House (1729, demolished in 1956), displaying a huge flag. Cranston was a town of about five thousand inhabitants and Oaklawn was still known as Searle's Corners—a farm hamlet consisting of a church and eight houses—when Job Wilbur and Francis Turner platted their land in 1872 to encourage development. The location of the site on the Providence-to-Hartford railroad prompted their optimism. Wilbur named his plat Oak Lawn and convinced railroad officials to use this designation for their train stop in this Cranston village.

The Baptists acquired the early eight-eenth-century Quaker house of worship in 1864, after that once-flourishing sect declined. Four years later Roby Wilbur, Job's wife, originated the idea of a May breakfast, a springtime event for which Oaklawn and its church are now famous.

During the late nineteenth century the village developed in a picturesque and orderly fashion, in accordance with the plans of Wilbur and Turner, and during the first half of the twentieth century it changed little. From the 1960s onward, however, suburban sprawl, new plats, and the construction of Interstate Route 295 have dramatically altered Oaklawn's rural flavor. *Gladys Brayton Collection, courtesy of the Cranston Historical Society*

Rhode Island's small rural towns had an influence in state government vastly disproportionate to their population (and a dozen of these communities actually declined in population during the Gilded Age). Since the constitution of 1843 gave each municipality, regardless of size, an equal vote in the state Senate, a combination of the smallest rural towns was able to control that body and stymie whatever legislation it found unacceptable. By preference and for profit the old-stock voters of these same communities voted Republican; and in league with urban Yankees, recent Protestant immigrants (Swedes, English, Scots, and Germans), and Franco-Americans, they gave the Republican party nearly unbroken dominance in state politics until the decade of the 1930s.

The man who first presided over this victorious (and scandal-ridden) political coalition was Henry Bowen Anthony (1815–1884), a longtime editor and publisher of the Providence Journal who served as governor (1849–1851) and United States senator (1859–1884). From the foundation of the GOP in the mid-1850s until his death as an incumbent senator, Anthony was "Mr. Republican" and the mentor of such future potentates as Nelson W. Aldrich and Charles R. Brayton.

Political nativism was one persistent and undistinguished feature of Anthony's long career. From his accession to the editorship of the Providence Journal in 1838, he made war upon the "foreign vagabond" (read "Irish Catholic"), who, he said, "came here uninvited and upon whose departure there is no restraint."

Wielding his acid pen during the Dorr Rebellion, Anthony led the forces of Law and Order and was one of the principal supporters of the real estate voting requirement for the naturalized citizen. He defended that discriminatory restriction against all comers until his death, compiling a record nearly unmatched in the annals of American nativism. Photo courtesy of RIHS (Rhi x3 1060)

Two staunch advocates of political reform, Charles E. Gorman (1844–1917) and Edwin D. McGuinness (1856–1901), led the rise of the local Irish-American community to a position of power and influence in opposition to the rural-based Republican machine of Henry Bowen Anthony and his successors. Gorman (shown here) became the first Catholic admitted to the Rhode Island bar (1865), the first to win election to the General Assembly (1870, from Wanskuck in North Providence prior to that district's annexation by Providence), and the first to serve on the Providence City Council (1875). In the aftermath of the Democratic party's electoral victories in 1887 (its first such win since 1853), Gorman became speaker of the House.

That same election saw McGuinness, Gorman's protégé, elected secretary of state, becoming Rhode Island's first Catholic general officer. In 1888 McGuinness turned to Providence politics, serving as alderman until 1893, when he made the first of two unsuccessful bids for mayor.

Victorious on his third try, in 1895 he became the city's first Irish Catholic chief executive, and he won reelection by a large majority the following year. McGuinness's two mayoral terms were characterized by governmental reform, efficiency, and a relentless campaign against public utilities that victimized or disregarded the consumer, such as the Union Street Railroad Company and the New York, New Haven, and Hartford Railroad. Photo from Thomas W. Bicknell, The History of the State of Rhode Island and Providence Plantations (1920)

Mahlon Van Horne, like Charles Gorman and Edwin McGuinness, was also a pathbreaker. This college-educated black, a native of New Jersey, arrived in Newport in 1868 to assume the ministry of Union Congregational Church. By 1873 he had begun a productive nineteen-year tenure as a member of the Newport School Committee. Then, in 1885, he was elected as a Republican to three successive one-year terms in the state House of Representatives, the first black to hold a seat in the Rhode Island legislature. In 1897 President McKinley appointed him U. S. consul in the Danish West Indies, where during the ensuing war with Spain Van Horne was instrumental in preventing the Spanish fleet from purchasing much-needed coal for its naval operations off Cuba. •

Three other blacks soon followed Van Horne into the state House of Representatives: Democrat Joseph Banks (1888) and Republicans John Jenkins (1888-1889) and Joseph H. Monroe (1894-1896). Then occurred a seventy-one-year hiatus before the next Rhode Island black secured election to the General Assembly. Photo courtesy of Rhode Island Black Heritage Society

Also influential in state politics during the late nineteenth century, and standing, too, in sharp contrast to Henry Bowen Anthony, were Elizabeth Buffum Chace (1806-1899) and her colleague Paulina Wright Davis (1813-1876), wife of one-term Rhode Island congressman Thomas Davis, for whom Davis Park in Providence is named.

After the early deaths of her first five children (she had five who survived to adulthood), Mrs. Chace (left) had immersed herself in the antislavery movement and made her Valley Falls home a station of the "Underground Railroad." In the aftermath of the Civil War she became a crusader for women's rights—a logical extension of her belief in human equality. On December 11, 1868, she and Mrs. Davis (right) formed the Rhode Island Woman Suffrage Association at a convention held in Roger Williams Hall on Weybosset Street in Providence. Shortly thereafter, Davis became the first historian of the national women's rights movement.

Mrs. Chace served as president of the Rhode Island suffrage group from 1870 until her death. She also espoused prison reform, successfully advocated a state school for orphans, induced the Providence City Council to require women matrons in all police stations, and worked with Sarah Doyle for the admission of women to Brown University. When she died in 1899 at age ninety-three, her funeral services were conducted by Anna Garlin Spencer, another prominent co-worker in the suffrage cause. Mrs. Spencer, a nationally prominent social reformer, was then minister of Providence's Bell Street Chapel. Photogravures from Lillie Buffum Chace Wyman and Arthur Crawford Wyman, Elizabeth Buffum Chace, 1806–1899: Her Life and Its Environment (1914)

From the mid-1860s until the century's end, French Canada provided the largest single source of migration to Rhode Island. During the Civil War many of the Quebec peasantry (called habitants) were recruited by local textile mill owners to ease the manpower shortage created by the enlistment or draft of Yankee and Irish workers. With this stimulus, immigration from French Canada snowballed to impressive proportions in the decades following the conflict. By the census of 1875 the state had 13,698 residents with parents born in French Canada. By 1895, 45,122 Rhode Islanders had at least one parent of French Canadian birth.

The French influx was directed mainly towards the textile mills of the Blackstone and Pawtuxet valleys. Woonsocket received the greatest number, but mill villages to the west of the city in North Smithfield and Burrillville and those to the south, such as Manville and Albion, were also inundated, as were Central Falls, the Darlington section of Pawtucket, and the villages of Marieville and Centredale in North Providence. The mills in West Elmwood and Olneyville-Manton attracted the habitant to Providence, and thousands more migrated to the villages along the Pawtuxet in Coventry and present-day West Warwick, where Arctic became a Franco-American stronghold. In the East Bay area, however, only Warren attracted sufficient numbers for the creation of a national parish.

The early French Canadians were slow to acculturate and clung to their language, their religion, and their association with Quebec. After acquiring citizenship, they generally voted Republican, partly because of their cultural antagonism toward Irish-American Democrats and partly because of an economic community of interest with their Yankee Republican employers. In this 1890s photo a Woonsocket group awaits the start of the traditional June 24 parade of St. Jean Baptiste, patron of French Canada. Photo courtesy of RIHS (Rhi x3 1234)

For the rural habitant transplanted in a new, urban environment, the national parish became a source not only of religious but also of cultural survival. Here the immigrant could maintain his French language, his Quebec heritage, and his Catholic faith. From 1872 through 1937 the French Canadians established twenty-three national parishes in Rhode Island. For most of that long span of years, Father Charles Dauray (shown here) was the spiritual leader of the Franco-American Catholic community.

Dauray came to the state in 1872 as a young priest from Quebec on a vacation necessitated by ill health and overwork. Urged by Bishop Hendricken to remain and to serve as the founding pastor of Notre Dame parish in Central Falls, Dauray accepted the challenge and built Rhode Island's first Catholic church completed and occupied by French Canadians. The wood-frame structure was dedicated on October 2, 1875. Immediately after this success Dauray was assigned to Precious Blood Church in Woonsocket, established in 1872 as the state's first French national parish. Dauray remained at this mother church of the FrancoAmericans until his death in 1931, earning the title of monsignor for building the parish into a model Franco-American religious community. During the 1920s Monsignor Dauray mediated between French extremists (the Sentinel-lists), who favored parish autonomy, and the Irish-dominated diocesan chancery, who wished to centralize administrative control under the bishop. Photo from Ambrose Kennedy, Quebec to New England: The Life of Monsignor Charles Dauray (1948)

Not all British immigrants came to America on the *Mayflower. During the late nineteenth century Rhode Island experienced a substantial influx of British industrial workers and a significant migration of people from British Canada as well. In the census of 1895, for example, 43,858 Rhode Islanders had at least one parent born in England, a total exceeded only by the Irish (100,545) and the French Canadians (45,122). In addition, 13,081 residents were at least partially of Scottish or Welsh stock, and 12,750 had at least one parent born in English Canada. These British arrivals were most numerous in Providence, Pawtucket, Lincoln, Central Falls, East Providence, Cumberland, Woonsocket, Cranston, and Warwick.*

Some mill owners, especially W. F. and F. C. Sayles, Lincoln's textile magnates, preferred these British craftsmen and recruited them to work at their Saylesville facility and at Lorraine Manufacturing Company in the nearby village of Fairlawn-Lincoln, thereby giving the Moshassuck Valley a strong British flavor. This turn-of-the-century photo shows Saylesville's British immigrants engaged in a spirited soccer match reminiscent of those played in their homeland. Photo courtesy of Walter Marriott from Once in a Hundred Years: A Pictorial History of Lincoln, R. I. *(1971)*

Although the Germans were the largest ethnic group to migrate to the United States, relatively few came to Rhode Island. Most of the state's Germanic population arrived in the three decades from 1865 to 1895 as refugees from Prussian militarism or agricultural dislocation. In the former year the state had 1,626 residents of German stock; by the latter there were 9,258 Rhode Islanders who had at least one German-born parent.

About one in five Germans was Roman Catholic. Though this Catholic element never established a national parish, it did produce a local bishop, the Reverend William Stang of Langbruken and Providence, who became the first bishop of Fall River in 1904. The bulk of the Germans were Protestant, mainly of the Lutheran denomination. Most settled in Providence, but significant colonies existed in Pawtucket, Newport, and Cranston as well.

Providence's Germans resided mainly in the West End—in Olneyville, Manton, Broadway, Elmwood, and West Elmwood. They were usually employed in skilled jobs in such occupations as baking, brewing, cabinetmaking, textiles, and, especially, jewelry and silverware manufacturing. Though they learned English and assimilated rapidly, the Germans maintained several important ethnic associations, such as the "turners" or turnverein *(a gymnastic organization) and various dramatic and choral groups, some of which survive today. Shown here is the Einklang Singing Society in front of German Hall in the Elmwood section of Providence. The building was constructed by a German gymnastics club in 1890. Photo (ca. 1890s) from Raymond E. Sickinger and John K. Primeau,* The Germans in Rhode Island: Pride and Perseverance, 1850–1985 *(1985)*

131

On the heels of the German migration of the late nineteenth century was an exodus from Scandinavia, especially Sweden, prompted by changes in the agricultural system. Most Swedes took up residence on farms in the Midwest, but Rhode Island received a sprinkling from this Scandinavian outpouring as well.

The period from 1875 to 1895 was the peak era for Swedish migration to the state. In the former year Rhode Island had 899 residents of Swedish or Norwegian stock; by 1895 the total had risen to 7,394. Many of these lived along the western and southern periphery of downtown Providence and in the Elmwood section southward into the Auburn and Eden Park neighborhoods of Cranston. The Swedes also established other early colonies in the Pontiac and Natick sections of Warwick and in East Greenwich, Newport, Pawtucket, East Providence, and Cumberland.

Most early-arriving Swedes were employed in the jewelry, base-metals, and textile industries or as carpenters, teamsters, or farm laborers (particularly on Cranston's Budlong Farms). A large number of Swedish women became

domestic servants. The Swedes were staunchly Protestant (Evangelical Lutheran) in religion and predominantly Republican in political affiliation. Like the Germans, they assimilated rapidly, but certain organizations, such as the Order of Vasa, perpetuate their cultural heritage. Also like the Germans, Swedes have a

fondness for song. Shown here in an 1890s photo from J. S. Osterberg's early history of the Swedes in Rhode Island is the Sextetten Norden (Nordic sextet) organized in the mill village of Natick. Photo from J. S. Osterberg, Svenskarna, Rhode Island (1915)

From the 1880s onward, migrants from southern and eastern Europe began their large-scale exodus to America. Providence received a generous share of this so-called "New Immigration." The earliest of this element to arrive were the Azorean Portuguese and the Cape Verdeans, who together totaled 528 in the census of 1875. Both groups were Portuguese by nationality (until 1977) and Roman Catholic in religion, and both were islanders skilled in seafaring and maritime pursuits. Both peoples had made their initial contact with southeastern New England via the whaling industry when they were recruited in their homelands to man the whale ships during long and perilous cruises. Azoreans, however, were white and ethnically Portuguese, whereas Cape Verdeans were of mixed blood, mainly African—a difference which sometimes produced friction between the two groups.

The 1895 state census enumerated 3,525 Rhode Islanders of at least partial Portuguese parentage, including those from "Cape Verde and the Western Islands." Most of the latter (238) resided in Providence. This illustration shows a whale ship and bumboats at the Cape Verdean Island of Brava, whence most of Rhode Island's Cape Verdeans came. Late nineteenth-century painting owned by Nat C. Smith, from Clifford W. Ashley, The Yankee Whaler (1942)

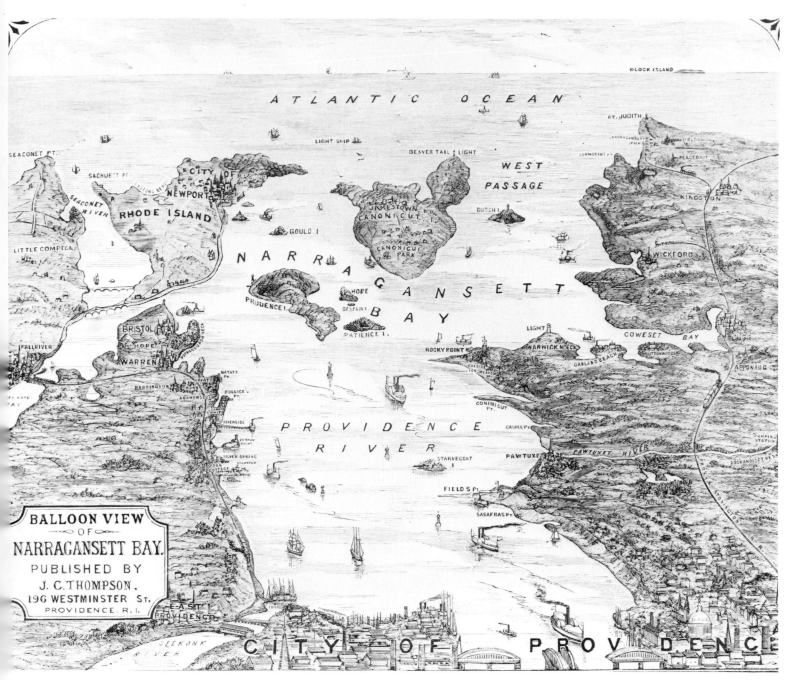

BALLOON VIEW OF NARRAGANSETT BAY.

PUBLISHED BY J. C. THOMPSON. 196 WESTMINSTER ST. PROVIDENCE. R.I.

During the Gilded Age upper Narragansett Bay became the state's playground, as Rhode Islanders flocked in droves to outing and amusement spots like Silver Spring, Crescent Park, Field's Point, Oakland Beach, Buttonwoods, and Rocky Point. Simultaneously, the lower bay and the oceanfront became the playground of the nation's newly rich, although Rhode Islanders were, of course, also in evidence. Block Island, Watch Hill, Narragansett Pier, and, preeminently, Newport attained the status of exclusive resorts.

The importance of the bay as a highway of commerce and a focal point of recreational activity in Rhode Island is suggested by this 1882 balloon view. The panorama shows over thirty bay islands, ranging in size from Aquidneck, or Rhode Island (27,629 acres) to Whale Rock, a flat ledge about a half acre in size. Engraving from J. C. Thompson (pub.), Balloon and Panoramic Views of Narragansett Bay (1882), courtesy of RIHS (Rhi x3 5193)

The balloon view of the bay, striking in many respects, is notable for the prominence it gives to the steamboat. These vessels ranged in size from the 72-foot City of Pawtucket, which plied the waters of the Providence River for a short time in the 1880s, to the luxurious 456-foot Commonwealth of the Fall River Line, a ship that was America's largest inland-water steamboat when it was built in 1908.

The bay steamer best known and most used by Rhode Islanders was the Mount Hope, which cruised the waters of Narragansett Bay for forty-seven years. Built in 1888 at Chelsea, Massachusetts, this 193-foot, 880-ton vessel ran the Providence-Newport-Block Island route for the Newport-Wickford Railroad and Steamboat Company. It was removed from active service in 1934, and two years into its well-deserved retirement the venerable steamer was dismantled. Photo courtesy of RIHS (Rhi x3 468)

One of the bay's most noted nineteenth-century personalities was Ida Lewis, a lighthouse keeper almost as remarkable for her gender as for her heroism. Born in 1842 as Idawalley Zorada Lewis, she was the daughter of Hosea Lewis, keeper of Newport harbor's Lime Rock Light, one of the many lighthouses in the bay. When Hosea became ill in the mid-1850s, his wife and then Ida assumed his duties. Ida made the first of her many rescues at sixteen, and with her fifth lifesaving effort, which involved two soldiers from Fort Adams, she gained great publicity and had this song composed in her honor. Credited with saving eighteen lives during her long career, she received a medal and money from the Life Saving Benevolent Association of New York, and the state legislature repeatedly and officially praised her valuable services. Her fame spread nationally and earned her a personal visit at Lime Rock from President Ulysses Grant. In 1899, on the death of her aged mother, she was formally appointed keeper of the Lime Rock Light. Toward the end of her career, Ida received a gold lifesaving medal from the U.S. government and saw a Newport Fourth of July celebration conducted in her honor. Lime Rock, renamed Ida Lewis Light, is now part of Newport's Ida Lewis Yacht Club. Engraved sheet music cover, courtesy of RIHS (Rhi x3 5720)

During the late nineteenth century Greenwich Cove was regarded as the best fishing ground for scallops on Narragansett Bay. Quahogs and clams were also plentiful in its sheltered waters. This natural bounty gave rise to a community of shellfishermen who lived and worked along the East Greenwich shoreline (top view) in a collection of shanties called Scalloptown. This 1877 sketch from Leslie's Weekly, *a nationally circulated graphic newspaper, shows the interior of a Scalloptown processing house (bottom view) where the popular food was cut and prepared for market.*

Although all the workers in the illustra- tion are white, by the turn of the century Scalloptown had become a black ghetto. In 1902 a settlement house opened there, but it ultimately proved unsuccessful and was closed in 1914.

Today, after many years of decay and neglect, the site of old Scalloptown has been revived by historic restoration, the construction of busy waterfront restaurants and a marina, and such promising business ventures as the Independent Commercial Fishermen's Co-op Association, a leading supplier of littlenecks, cherrystones, and quahogs to the local market. Wood engravings from Leslie's Weekly, *courtesy of RIHS (Rhi x3 5799)*

For Rhode Islanders, the bay and its tributaries were not only highways of commerce but also sources of food and recreation. This photo, taken about 1890, shows men harvesting oysters off the north end of Starve Goat (now Sunshine) Island at the mouth of the Providence River near Field's Point, where the city's notorious sewage treatment plant releases its effluent today.

In this era Narragansett Bay oysters were in demand throughout the region and commanded top prices. As late as 1910 the "oyster-farming" industry employed over a thousand harvesters and produced a crop in excess of fifteen million pounds. Then pollution (from Providence southward), overfishing, poaching, and hurricanes brought rapid decline to this once-thriving enterprise. Photo courtesy of RIHS (Rhi x3 2274)

In the Gilded Age there occurred a popular surge of interest in recreational boating. This trend brought changes to the art of small-boat building, best illustrated by the fortunes of the Herreshoff Yard in Bristol (shown here in this 1890s photo).

Karl Friederich Herreshoff came to Rhode Island from Germany in 1790, worked in John Brown's firm, and later married Brown's daughter. His grandson, John Brown Herreshoff, started the boatyard in 1863, and he was joined by his younger brother, Nathanael Greene Herreshoff ("Captain Nat"), in 1878. The following year the firm incorporated as the Herreshoff Manufacturing Company.

It was Nathanael Greene Herreshoff who began to design the firm's famous racing yachts, beginning with the revolutionary Gloriana, the first craft to use a fin-keeler. From 1893, when the Vigilant defeated

the Valkyrie II for the America's Cup, Herreshoff boats dominated the sport of international yacht racing. The Vigilant (shown here) was followed in turn by the Defender, the Columbia, the Reliance, and the Resolute. These were huge racing machines of up to 144 feet in length, with masts rising as much as 199 feet above the water (too high to sail under the present Mount Hope Bridge) and crews of up to sixty-six men. But these were not the only boats that the firm produced; the Herreshoff Yard built a variety of other craft as well, from little sailing dinghies to cruising sailboats and power yachts. In 1876, workmen there even constructed the very first torpedo boat.

The last of the Herreshoff cup defenders was the Rainbow (built at the Herreshoff Yard but not designed there), which defeated the Endeavour in 1934. The

races in 1937 were won by the Ranger, an American yacht built outside Rhode Island. After World War II the day of the super racing machines had ended; the costs of building them were prohibitive even for syndicates of wealthy sportsmen, and when the cup series resumed in 1958, smaller twelve-meter boats were used.

The Herreshoff Manufacturing Company was sold at auction to R. F. Haffenreffer in 1924, but operations continued until 1946, when the yard was closed. In 1975, after Halsey C. Herreshoff acquired a part of the original site and opened an office in one of the old buildings, a Herreshoff was again designing sailboats and yachts. Photo of boatyard, 1890s, courtesy of RIHS (Rhi x3 160); steel engraving of Vigilant (left) versus Valkyrie II, courtesy of RIHS (Rhi x3 5800)

Newport attained first rank among America's exclusive resorts during the Gilded Age. Fabulously wealthy entrepreneurs, especially those from New York, New Jersey, and Pennsylvania, built private palaces (which they called "cottages" with classic understatement) in view of the ocean. Many of these summer homes, originally occupied for only a few weeks in July and August, were situated along Cliff Walk, a two-mile footpath that follows the contours of the shore. The most prestigious structure on this famed walkway is the Breakers (at the center of this aerial photo), which was designed by Richard Morris Hunt and completed in 1895 as the retreat of New York railroad magnate Cornelius Vanderbilt. This splendid seventy-room mansion, constructed to resemble the palaces of northern Italy, was opened to visitors in 1948 and acquired by the Preservation Society of Newport County in 1972. It is regarded as Rhode Island's most popular tourist attraction. Photo courtesy of the Rhode Island Yearbook Foundation

This ballroom at Rosecliff, the largest in Newport, was the scene of many lavish balls given by Mrs. Herman Oelrichs, born Theresa Fair, the daughter of an Irish immigrant who struck it rich by uncovering Nevada's legendary Comstock Lode. Begun in 1898 on the site of a summer home once owned by famed American historian George Bancroft, Rosecliff was completed in 1900. This forty-room mansion enabled Mrs. Oelrichs to rank with Alva Vanderbilt Belmont and Mrs. Stuyvesant Fish as one of the three great hostesses of Newport society. (Mrs. Fish once held a dinner party on gold plates for the dogs of the elite on the lawn of her Newport estate and then invited Newport society to a reception for a prince—who turned out to be a monkey.)

Mrs. Oelrichs was the wife and benefactor of Herman Oelrichs, the American agent for the German Lloyd steamship line, who died at sea in 1906. After her death in 1926, Rosecliff passed through several changes in ownership before Mr. and Mrs. J. Edgar Monroe donated the house and its contents to the Preservation Society of Newport County. Shortly thereafter, this splendid ballroom became a movie set for The Great Gatsby, starring Robert Redford and Mia Farrow, and The Betsy, starring Laurence Olivier, Katherine Ross, and Robert Duvall. Photo by Richard Cheek from Newport Mansions of the Gilded Age (1982), courtesy of Foremost Publishers and the Preservation Society of Newport County

Marble House has been hailed by architectural historians as perhaps the greatest neoclassical house in America. It was completed in 1892 from designs of Richard Morris Hunt at a then staggering cost to its owners, Mr. and Mrs. William K. Vanderbilt, of eleven million dollars. Built of 500,000 cubic tons of white marble, this classical masterpiece is fronted by four towering Corinthian columns modeled after—but larger than—those of the Temple of the Sun at Heliopolis.

Mr. Vanderbilt, who turned the house over to his energetic and assertive wife Alva upon its completion, spent only two summers here before divorcing her in 1895. In that year Alva sponsored an opulent ball to introduce her daughter Consuelo to international society. This coming-out party achieved its purpose when Consuelo received a proposal of

marriage that very night from the most loftily titled attendee, the duke of Marlborough. Prodded by her mother, Consuelo accepted, achieving what many American heiresses sought during the Gilded Age—entrance into the European nobility.

Alva eventually married Oliver Hazard Perry Belmont, grandson of the famed commodore, and moved across Bellevue Avenue to his estate, Belcourt Castle. Marble House was closed for twelve years, but it was reopened by Alva after Belmont's death. Alva's last years in Rhode

Island were spent in the cause of women's suffrage prior to her move to France, where she died in 1933. Her splendid mansion was purchased for the Preservation Society of Newport County in 1963 with the financial assistance of three-time America's Cup defender Harold S. Vanderbilt, youngest of William and Alva's three children. Photo by Richard Cheek from Newport Mansions of the Gilded Age (1982), courtesy of Foremost Publishers and the Preservation Society of Newport County

In 1899 social critic Thorstein Veblen wrote a scathing critique of America's "robber barons" entitled The Theory of the Leisure Class, *wherein he denounced them for their "conspicuous consumption." Undoubtedly Gilded Age Newport influenced his views. While thousands of immigrant men and women and their young children toiled in hot, poorly ventilated mills just a few miles inland, Newport society had its summer whirl. In the 1890s French visitor Paul Bourget recounted in detail the typical day of a "society lady": After eating a hearty breakfast, she departs her villa for a brisk two-hour carriage ride, attended by a liveried driver. She then changes and journeys to the Casino to watch a tennis match, after which she boards her private yacht for lunch with friends. After relaxing on deck amidst a beautiful ocean vista, she returns to shore to travel by carriage to a polo match. Following this spectacle (depicted here), she returns to her "cottage," changes to formal wear, and departs for dinner and perhaps a ball in one of Newport's summer palaces.*

This 1890 photo (bottom) shows the Casino segment of her daily schedule. Nine years before, in the summer of 1881, Newport's Casino had inaugurated a national all-comers tourney that is regarded as the first national championship of lawn tennis. Henry W. Slocum, champion in 1888 and 1889, later recollected that "no better place could have been selected.... The grounds were picturesque, the accommodations for the players were good, and Newport being, then as now, a fashionable resort, the most beautiful women of the country graced the tournament with their presence." Today the Casino is the site of the International Tennis Hall of Fame.

To add further luster to her reputation, Newport also hosted the first national open golf tournament in the summer of 1895, raising the competitive level of another rich man's game that was the rage at stylish American resorts during the late nineteenth century. Engraving of polo match courtesy of RIHS (Rhi x3 2782); tennis photo from Robert Grieve, The New England Coast *(1891)*

For those not fortunate enough to be driven by private carriage to exclusive Bailey's Beach on Ocean Drive, the trolley was available to take them to Easton's, Atlantic, or the Middletown beaches. This streetcar heads down Bath Road (Memorial Boulevard) shortly after Newport became the first Rhode Island community to use electric trolleys in the spring of 1889. The street railway ran northward along East Main Road to Portsmouth, where a popular amusement spot called Island Park was opened in 1898, and thence across Tiverton's Stone Bridge to Fall River. Photo from Robert Grieve, The New England Coast *(1891)*

The bayside town of Narragansett, established as a special district in 1888 and as a full-fledged municipality in 1901, is famous for the Pier, a summer resort which had its heyday in the late nineteenth century.

The most prominent landmark at the Pier is the Towers, the surviving remnant of the Narragansett Casino (shown top center in this panoramic view). Designed by noted architects McKim, Mead, and White as the recreational center for this fashionable colony, the Casino was completed in 1886. It contained stores, dining rooms, and cafes (shown at right in this 1890 interior view), a billiard room, a

theater, and lounge rooms on several levels, as well as tennis courts on the lawn. The famous New York caterer Louis Sherry was in charge of the restaurant, and the country's finest orchestras played at its Saturday night dances.

Though fire destroyed the Casino in 1900, the Towers were rebuilt in 1910 and continue to stand astride Ocean Road as an imposing memorial to the Pier's reign as one of America's premier seaside resorts. Postcard view of beach and Casino (1890s) courtesy of RIHS (Rhi x3 5755); interior photo courtesy of RIHS (Rhi x3 2325)

In July 1887, just after the completion of Narragansett's famed Casino, three Westerly entrepreneurs obtained a charter to build a "Sea View Rail Road" from the Watch Hill-Westerly area to Narragansett Pier. When this venture failed to get rolling, William Case Clark, Sr., one of the founders of the new Narragansett Pier Electric Light and Power Company, bought out the Westerly incorporators and amended the railroad's charter to build the line northward from the Pier towards East Greenwich. In 1898 Clark began construction along a route that traversed the villages of Saunderstown, Hamilton, and Wickford before reaching East Greenwich on September 15, 1900. At this point the Sea View connected with Marsden Perry's Union Street Railway, which ran to Providence.

The Sea View took Rhode Islanders southward to the beaches and facilitated the transport of South County farm produce to the Providence marketplace. Eventually the line served forty-six listed stops along twenty-two miles of track, including a branch to Wakefield in

competition with the Narragansett Pier Railroad. In September 1920, after two decades of service, the Sea View ceased operation and its rails and rolling stock were sold for scrap. Photo showing the

arrival of the first Sea View trolley at Saunderstown on July 28, 1898, from G. Edward Prentice, Through the Woods and Across the Fields to Narragansett Pier: The Sea View Railroad *(1983)*

During the last third of the nineteenth century, Westerly's Watch Hill also attained prominence as an oceanfront resort. Here large summer hotels rather than palatial private homes were the rule. Shown in this 1880s panorama are (left to right) Ocean House, Plimpton House, Plimpton Annex, Narragansett House, Atlantic House (in rear), Watch Hill House, and Larkin House, with the Larkin Shore Dinner Hall immediately below it. At the extreme right is the steamer Ella out of Norwich, Connecticut.

Named for the fact that a watchtower and a signal station stood here in Revolutionary times, Watch Hill was described in an 1891 guide as commanding a magnificent view of the Atlantic Ocean, Block Island, Fishers Island, the Pawcatuck River, and Little Narragansett Bay. "From the hill or any of the hotels," said the description, "a splendid seaward prospect lies in view, eleven lighthouses and one lightship being in sight." Photo (ca. 1880s) from Ralph Bolton Cooney, Westerly's Oldest Witness *(1950)*

By 1890, when this photo was taken, Block Island (the town of New Shoreham) had also become a fashionable summer resort. Between 1870 and 1872 the federal government made substantial harbor improvements on the island to render it more accessible. In addition to a large stone breakwater, federal funds built a small wall-locked harbor and a larger outer harbor. Also in the early 1870s two lifesaving stations were established, one at the harbor and the other at the west side of the island, while lighthouses continued to be maintained on the north and south ends of New Shoreham. A town historian observed in 1886 that the 1,267 year-round inhabitants were "intelligent and peaceful, and they have never yet had a jail or a resident lawyer on the island." *Photo from Robert Grieve,* The New England Coast *(1891)*

In the Gilded Age, Field's Point, Providence's southernmost extremity, became a famous shore-dinner spot. During the 1880s the point contained meadowland, winding roads, well-kept homes, and the thirty-four-acre Field's Point Farm, designated a public park in 1869 by the General Assembly. Only the presence of the city's smallpox hospital on the north shore detracted from this bucolic setting.

Field's Point Farm was famous at this time as the site of Colonel S. S. Atwell's Clam House. Clambakes had been held on the point since 1860, but Atwell, who presided as bakemaster at the shore dinner hall from 1887 to 1910, raised this traditional New England meal to the status of a feast. For fifty cents the colonel provided chowder, clam cakes, baked fish, oysters picked just offshore, steamers, watermelon, and other side dishes. For an extra quarter he threw in a "good-sized" lobster. Small wonder that many thousands of visitors took one of the Continental Line's steamers on a three-mile, fifteen-minute cruise from downtown Providence to partake of the colonel's culinary delights. The sewage treatment plant, a scrap-metal yard, gas tanks, and the municipal wharf are the principal occupants of the site today. *Painting (ca. 1880), oil on canvas, artist unknown, courtesy of RIHS (Rhi x3 3120); postcard of clambake (ca. 1890s) from the author's collection*

With a commanding view to the west, the elevated shoreline of East Providence became a watering spot for the wealthy as early as the 1840s, when the elegant Vue de L'Eau Hotel was built on a high bluff (the site of present-day Bergin Avenue) overlooking the Providence harbor. The building, owned by George Boyden, burned in the early 1870s, about the time the exclusive Squantum Association staked out its claim to the several acres of choice shoreline which it still occupies. By that time, however, East Providence (which had been annexed from Massachusetts in 1862) had fallen out of favor as a resort for the well-to-do, who then preferred the lower bay region.

In the 1860s the Riverside shoreline began to attract middle-class day excursionists, who could reach the area by the trains of the Providence, Warren, and Bristol Railroad, by steamboat, or eventually by streetcar. Ocean Cottage (1863) was the first shorefront establishment to attract the day-tripper and the short-term guest. Two small summer campgrounds—Cedar Grove and Cape White, consisting of temporary shelters and communal dining facilities—sprang up next, followed in 1869 by Silver Spring (top), a more elaborate facility due east of Starve Goat Island, with a dock, overnight accommodations, and a spacious shore-dinner hall. In 1870 a sizable hotel, the What Cheer House, opened adjacent to Camp White and soon spawned a cottage colony on Bullocks Point (the present site of Narragansett Terrace). These recreational beachheads prompted developer Lysander Flagg in the 1870s to purchase and plat large tracts of land from Cape White south

to Sabin's Point, which he developed into the thriving resort community of Riverside. By 1900 that area of East Providence now known as Riverside consisted of clusters of summer cottages, a dozen hotels,

bathing beaches, and a recreational centerpiece called Crescent Park, and it contained one of the largest concentrations of summer residences on Narragansett Bay. Photo of Silver Spring (ca. 1890) courtesy of PPL

Crescent Park, opened by George Boyden in 1886, quickly became bustling East Providence's premier recreational attraction. By century's end it drew crowds—as many as fifty thousand to seventy-five thousand a day on weekends—from the entire southeastern New England region. Such attendance brought prosperity and further expansion in the form of a dance hall, enlarged dining facilities, a roller coaster, and two carousels. One of these merry-go-rounds (shown here) is now all that survives, but that relic of Crescent Park's heyday is sufficient to give the site continued prominence.

Danish immigrant Charles I. D. Looff (shown at left with his family) was the craftsman who built the surviving carousel in 1895. This nationally renowned artisan lived in Riverside for several years. His son, Charles, Jr., stayed on to operate the carousel and purchased the entire park in

1920, two years after his father's death. The park remained in the hands of the Looff family until 1966, and then it began to experience a marked decline. Eventually it was closed and sold to developers. Fortunately, a strong community effort, spearheaded by the East Providence Carousel Park Commission, saved and restored the sixty-six-figure Looff carousel, which is regarded as the finest surviving example of its type in America. It is now the centerpiece of Carousel Park, a small public area set aside to preserve and display this famous ride.

Not to be outdone, however, is Watch Hill, whose merry-go-round has been in continuous operation for nearly 110 years—a record no other carousel in America can match. Photo (ca. 1900) from Willi Looff Taucher, Looff Photo Memoirs (1982)

145

Rocky Point, the most famous and enduring of the upper bay recreational sites, was also one of the first to be established. William Winslow, captain of the steamboat Argo, *recognized the spot's potential, purchased the point area in 1849, and immediately constructed a wharf to land visitors for picnicking and strolling through the heavily wooded promontory. Eventually natural attractions gave way to such diversions as a carousel, the state's first Ferris wheel, a clam-dinner hall, a bowling alley, and a skating rink. During the 1860s new owner Byron Sprague* added a seventy-five-foot-high observation tower and the Mansion House Hotel. *These and other innovations made Rocky Point the premier amusement center on Narragansett Bay during the Gilded Age. In this lithograph (ca. 1880) the famous* Bay Queen *brings visitors to this Warwick landmark. Though competitors have come and gone, and though its fortunes have waxed and waned with frequent changes in ownership, Rocky Point remains Rhode Island's preeminent attraction of its kind. Lithograph from Robert Grieve,* The New England Coast *(1891)*

Two other Warwick summer resorts, less flamboyant than Rocky Point, were Oakland Beach (top) and Buttonwoods (right), situated side by side on the north shore of Cowesett (Greenwich) Bay. Buttonwoods was the first of these twin attractions to develop, largely as a result of the establishment by Providence Baptists in 1871 of a summer colony where they could relax, play, and worship in a wholesome environment. The growth of this well-kept cottage colony was supervised by their Buttonwoods Beach Association, an organization still in existence. According to an 1891 visitor, the colony's fine beach (shown here) "affords facilities for bathing, boating, and fishing equal to any other place on the bay."

Oakland Beach, a half mile to the east, developed more slowly until the Warwick Railroad reached it in 1874. Then it was transformed into a busy amusement park containing a large hotel (shown here) which burned in 1903.

Residential growth in Oakland Beach was haphazard. As a Warwick architectural survey states, "With the improvement of mass transit facilities,

Oakland Beach experienced a boom. Building was totally unregulated here, in contrast to other cottage resorts like Buttonwoods, and as a result the area eventually attracted lower income families who could not afford houses in more restrictive communities. Oakland Beach was built up with a hodgepodge of structures varying considerably in their

quality of construction and design." Illustration of Buttonwoods (ca. 1886) from Welcome A. Greene, The Providence Plantations for 250 Years (1886); engraved sketch of Oakland Beach (ca. 1890) from Robert Grieve, The New England Coast (1891)

147

The steamboat Vue de L'Eau *(named for the famous mid-nineteenth-century East Providence resort hotel) idles at a Providence dock before departing with its passengers to the upper bay resorts listed on the sign above. Photo (ca. 1890s) courtesy of PPL*

The completion of the Warwick Railroad in 1874 improved access to the Warwick shoreline and spurred its development. When the initial, independent venture failed after two years, the road was acquired by the New York, Providence, and Boston Railroad, which extended the southern terminus southwestward from Oakland Beach to Buttonwoods and reopened the road in 1881. Branching off the main line in Cranston, the railroad ran about a half mile southwest of Pawtuxet village, continued past the old Spring Green Farm of Governor John Brown Francis, and then turned east to run near the shoreline at Conimicut, affording easy access not only to Oakland Beach and Buttonwoods but also to Rocky Point and an exclusive summer colony on Warwick Neck. This route prompted the establishment of both Lakewood, a village laid out between the railroad and Pawtuxet in the 1880s and 1890s, and Duby's Grove, a well-frequented outing spot on the Warwick side of the Pawtuxet River at a site now occupied by the Geigy Chemical Corporation.

By the time this picture was taken at the turn of the century, the Warwick Railroad had been acquired by the Rhode Island Company and its rolling stock ran by using overhead trolley wires instead of steam. A trainman and a conductor pose here at the Buttonwoods terminus of the 8.52-mile line. Photo courtesy of the Wonson Collection

What, in retrospect, has become one of Providence's greatest assets fell into the hands of the city unplanned, unsought, and, by some councilmen, unwanted because of its wild state and its remoteness from the settled neighborhoods. This boon was bequeathed in 1871 by Betsey Williams, whose will gave her 1773 cottage and 103-acre farm to the city for public purposes, provided that a memorial was erected thereon to Betsey's illustrious ancestor, Roger Williams.

Not only did the city construct an impressive monument to its founder near the house, but it also transformed the parcel into a beautiful public park. Three times (in 1873, 1887, and 1892) the General Assembly authorized the annexation of land from Cranston to enlarge the park, which eventually reached a size of 450 acres. In 1891 the legislature created a park commission, headed by Richard H.

Deming, to oversee the facility's development. Under Deming's spirited direction ponds were dredged, roads and bridges built, and several buildings constructed, most notably the beautiful Casino (1897-98, restored in 1982).

From the Gilded Age to the present, Roger Williams Park has been Providence's garden spot and one of the outstanding municipal parks in the country. Its attractions include the Dalrymple Boathouse; a carousel; statuary; ballfields; tennis courts; lakes for boating, skating, and fishing; gardens; floral displays; greenhouses; a bandstand; the Temple to Music; a museum and planetarium; and a first-rate zoo. This turn-of-the-century photo shows the popular children's pony carts with the newly completed Clarke-Dalrymple Boathouse (1897) in the background. Photograph courtesy of RIHS (Rhi x3 5753)

Recreation spots along the upper bay were not the only new diversions for the people of Greater Providence during the Gilded Age, for Providence itself boasted parks, theaters, and a racetrack for the amusement of its people. It was also one of eight cities in America to host a professional major league baseball team. The Providence Grays joined the two-year-old National League in 1878, and the following year they were league champions. This photo of the first-place Grays of 1879 and their rivals, the Boston Red Sox, was taken at their home field, Messer Park, just east of Olneyville near the present site of Bridgham Middle School, where a centennial plaque commemorates their achievement.

Among the stars of this team was nineteen-year-old pitcher John Montgomery "Monte" Ward, who compiled a season record of forty-seven wins and nineteen losses. Ward, a native of Bellefonte, Pennsylvania, was inducted into baseball's Hall of Fame in 1964. At the plate the Grays were led by Paul Hines, who topped the league in batting average (.357), hits, and total bases, and James Henry "Orator Jim" O'Rourke, who posted the league's second highest average at .348. "The Orator," who played most of his career with New York, was also elected to the Hall of Fame.

After three second-place finishes to Chicago, the Grays won the National League crown for the second and final time in 1884, their next-to-last year in the league. Center fielder Paul Hines (.302) was again the batting star, but the team won this title on its phenomenal pitching. Hall of Famer Charles "Old Hoss" Radbourn compiled an all-time major league record of sixty wins and twelve losses, with a 1.38 ERA, while backup hurler Charlie Sweeney (who played only the first half of the season) won seventeen and lost eight, with a 1.55 ERA and nineteen strikeouts in one of his winning efforts (a record broken in 1986 by Roger Clemens).

No local boys starred for the Grays, but a frequent spectator was young Hugh Duffy of Cranston. In 1884 this seventeen-year-old lad was launching his baseball career on the sandlots of Providence and his home town. A decade later, playing outfield for Boston of the National League, Duffy hit a whopping .438, still the unapproachable major league record. During his seventeen years in the majors, Duffy compiled a lifetime batting average of .324. For his exploits he was elected a member of the Hall of Fame, one of the three native Rhode Islanders to achieve this distinction. Photo (ca. 1879) courtesy of RIHS (Rhi x3 847)

149

Because these local spectacles afforded relief from the monotony of the mills or the loneliness of rural life, a nineteenth-century saying affirmed that "everyone loves a parade."

Shown here are relatively typical late nineteenth-century Rhode Island parade scenes: the Veteran Firemen's procession in Pawtucket during the 1890 Cotton Centennial observance (top left); the locally renowned Manville Brass Band (founded in 1882 by Ephrem B. Mandeville) entertaining the residents of its home village in the 1890s (bottom left); the 1899 Fourth of July parade in the village of Hope Valley (top right); and the 1899 Labor Day parade passing over the Court Street Bridge in Woonsocket (bottom right).

Seventeen years earlier a similar Labor Day demonstration had been held in Providence. Local labor historians claim that this August 23, 1882, event, in which a thousand union members strode through the streets, was the first such parade in America. It was followed by a massive outing at Rocky Point, where national labor leader Peter McGuire told his enthusiastic audience that "here in Rhode Island, under the rule of your Spragues and Anthonys, 13,700 children under fourteen years of age have been condemned to work in your cotton and woolen mills." Photo of Pawtucket parade from Robert Grieve and John P. Fernald, The Cotton Centennial (1891); photo of Manville courtesy of Estelle Bacon from Once in a Hundred Years: A Pictorial History of Lincoln (1971); photo of Hope Valley from the Gladys Segar Collection, courtesy of RIHS; photo of Woonsocket from the Lawton Collection, Woonsocket High School

One very important product of industrialization was the growth of a white-collar class. As factories expanded their markets, as businesses became larger and more complex, and as banks and insurance companies proliferated, demand grew for bookkeepers, clerks, stenographers, secretaries, and other office personnel. To meet this demand, a Providence branch of the Bryant and Stratton chain of business colleges was founded in January 1863. It occupied the old Howard Building on Dorrance Street from the time of its inception until 1878, when it moved to the Hoppin Homestead Building on Westminster Street, where this turn-of-the-century photo of a typing class was taken.

The school soon severed its direct connection with the Bryant and Stratton chain, though it retained the name. On July 1, 1878, Theodore B. Stowell became principal and owner, and for a period of over forty years he guided the school's growth and development. In 1925, after absorbing the Rhode Island Commercial School (organized in 1898), Bryant and Stratton built a modern eight-story building (still standing) at Fountain and Union streets. When even this structure became crowded, the college moved to a sprawling East Side campus. In 1971 Bryant College, as the school is called today, left the city for the beautiful, modern 295-acre Tupper campus in Smithfield, off the Douglas Pike. Photo courtesy of RIHS (Rhi x3 4229)

Rhode Island School of Design was founded in Providence in 1877 as an outgrowth of the nation's centennial observance. The prime movers behind its establishment were the members of the Women's Centennial Commission of Rhode Island, especially Mrs. Jesse Metcalf. While in Philadelphia, they became well acquainted with a new educational facility—the design school. This institution, a product of the Industrial Revolution, had first appeared in England and France in the 1850s to satisfy the need of manufacturers for trained persons to give shape and form to the textiles, the apparel, and the other varied products their factories produced, as well as to the buildings that they occupied.

RISD's initial endowment was the $1,675 that remained in the treasury of the Women's Commission after the expenses of Rhode Island's exhibit at Philadelphia had been paid. Until 1893 the school was located in the Hoppin Homestead Building on Westminster Street; then it moved to new quarters on Waterman Street, where this 1895 photo of an art class was taken. This 1893 structure, called Waterman Hall, is still used by RISD, but now the college occupies over thirty additional buildings, most on the East Side. Especially notable is the Museum of Art on Benefit Street, a facility that includes the architecturally significant Pendleton House. Nationally renowned for its excellence in industrial design, architecture, and fine arts, RISD today offers nineteen degree programs to approximately fifty-eight hundred students enrolled in its day, evening, junior, and summer divisions. Photo (1890s) courtesy of the Rhode Island School of Design

The final educational advance of note during the Gilded Age was the construction of this new building and campus for Rhode Island Normal School. This institution for the training of teachers had been established by the General Assembly in 1854. Its first home was at 129 Broad Street in Providence. In 1857 the school moved to Bristol, where it survived until the summer of 1865 before closing. It was reopened in Providence in 1871 and occupied the old high school building on Benefit Street until moving to this campus in 1898.

The college's curriculum was expanded in 1920 when it became RICE—the Rhode Island College of Education. In 1960 its metamorphosis continued when the General Assembly authorized the school to conduct degree programs in arts and sciences as well as teacher education and renamed the institution Rhode Island College.

After RIC's departure from this site in

1958, the structure shown here was occupied by several state agencies, including Family Court. Today it houses the state Department of Education. The other building on this campus is the home of the University of Rhode Island's Extension Division. Postcard view (ca. 1900) courtesy of RIHS (Rhi x3 5756)

In 1884 the long-standing connection between Rhode Island and the United States Navy was cemented when Admiral Stephen B. Luce (right inset) prevailed upon the government to establish a Naval War College, a school at which officers could study the art of naval warfare from a theoretical viewpoint and gain a historical perspective on the elements of global strategy. To house this facility, the navy acquired a Coasters Harbor Island building that had served as the Newport asylum for the poor. From this humble beginning developed one of the world's most prestigious centers of naval education.

As the institution's first president, Admiral Luce recruited a number of able instructors, most notably Captain Alfred Thayer Mahan (left inset). The son of a renowned West Point professor, Mahan (1840-1914) began a productive tour of duty at the Newport facility in the autumn of 1886, serving first as professor and then as president. In 1890 he published the most famous and influential of his numerous historical volumes, The Influence of Seapower upon History, which advocated American expansion on strategic grounds. The country's most famous geopolitician, Mahan served as

president of the American Historical Association in 1902.

Founders Hall (shown here) was the original college building. It was later used as officers' quarters, then as headquarters for the U.S. Naval Training Station, and next as the command post of the Newport Naval Base. In 1974 the building reverted to the War College and now houses the Naval War College Museum. Building sketch (ca. 1885) and Mahan photo courtesy of the Naval War College Museum; Luce photo courtesy of the Newport Historical Society

In 1862 the Morrill Land-Grant College Act authorized the sale of federal lands within the several states (or the sale of scrip for smaller states like Rhode Island, which did not contain such surplus land) to support education in agriculture and the mechanic arts. Following the example of Connecticut, New Jersey, and New Hampshire, Rhode Island chose an established colonial college as its land-grant institution—Brown University. When this well-intentioned but unwise decision proved

unworkable because of the disparity in educational objectives between Brown and successful state universities, the legislature in 1892 established a separate land-grant institution in the rural village of Kingston, a school that it called the Rhode Island College of Agriculture and Mechanic Arts. These photos show the original buildings on the Kingston campus (ca. 1895) with Davis Hall in the right foreground; horticulture students spraying an apple orchard; and one of the college's earliest teams, the 1896 football squad, which played occasional games with secondary-school opponents. Not until 1903 did the Ram eleven take on collegiate foes, and it did so then without success, losing to Massachusetts Agricultural College, Worcester Polytechnic Institute, and the Brown University junior varsity. But

better days were ahead for Ram football teams, which even attained national ranking within their division during the mid-1980s.

On the academic side, the college gained university status in 1951 by implementing a comprehensive graduate program. Twenty years later it became a Sea Grant College with a highly regarded School of Oceanography. Today URI enrolls eleven thousand students in its undergraduate and graduate schools and an additional five thousand persons in its College of Continuing Education. Photos of campus (ca. 1900) and apple orchard, courtesy of PPL; photo of football team from Herman F. Eschenbacher, The University of Rhode Island: A History of Land-Grant Education in Rhode Island (1967)

The opening of Rhode Island Hospital in 1868 has been the single most important health care development in the state's history. The site chosen was one donated by the city of Providence near the old Providence-Cranston line, on land then occupied by the obsolete Marine Hospital. The movement for a modern health services facility had been led by Dr. Usher Parsons and the Providence Medical Association (established in 1848), but it took the generosity of the Ives family—Moses Brown Ives, his son Thomas Poynton Ives, and Moses's brother Robert Hale Ives—to provide the financial base for a successful public fund-raising effort.

With an interior plan formulated by the famous hospital architect Samuel Sloane of Philadelphia and an exterior designed by Alpheus Morse of Providence, the impressive structure opened its doors to the sick on October 1, 1868.

The original building (right center) was demolished in 1956. Today Rhode Island Hospital is dramatically different in physical appearance, but it continues to flourish and to maintain a reputation for medical excellence. Currently the city's largest employer, it is housed in several modern buildings and is in the midst of a massive expansion program in the area of South Providence that it occupies.

During its early years the hospital was the beneficiary of an innovative tax arrangement. In May 1867 the state legislature granted a bank charter to the Rhode Island Hospital Trust Company, an institution created to provide financial assistance to the fledgling hospital. This charter was unique in that Hospital Trust was the first local bank to be granted immunity from state taxation provided it devoted a certain portion of its profits to charitable purposes—specifically, for a time the company was required to pay one-third of its net income over 6 percent to Rhode Island Hospital. William Binney, a Providence lawyer and the organizer of the enterprise, became the bank's first president, serving from 1867 to 1881.

Rhode Island Hospital Trust National Bank—the oldest trust company in New England—is now one of Rhode Island's major banking institutions, and it is in the top one hundred nationwide. Its main offices occupy an entire city block in the heart of Providence's financial district. Postcard view (ca. 1890s) from the author's collection

156

On February 29, 1884, in response to the urging of Dr. Oliver C. Wiggin, a prominent Providence obstetrician, the Providence Lying-In Hospital was incorporated by the General Assembly. Its purpose, as set forth in its bylaws, was "to provide a place for the confinement of women who are without means and suitable abode at the time of childbirth, and of such other women as may wish from any cause to pay a stipulated price for the privilege of being confined in a well-regulated hospital." The facility's first home, from 1885 to 1887, was the General James Estate on Meader Street. The hospital then moved to larger quarters on State Street, where this photo was taken in the 1890s.

Lying-In admitted its first patient on June 16, 1885. During its first year of operation it delivered the babies of thirty-three women, twenty of whom were unmarried. By 1927, the hospital's first full year in its third home on Maude Street, 1,095 babies were born. Today, under a new name—Women and Infants' Hospital—the facility is one of the busiest of its kind in the country. In June 1986 it occupied its fourth site, a thirty-four-million-dollar

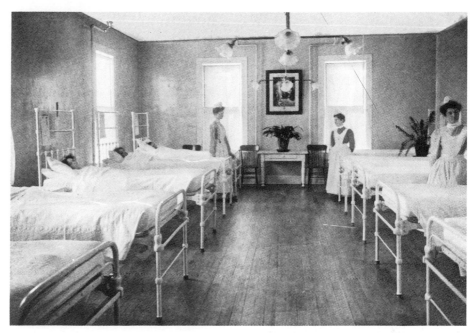

building adjacent to Rhode Island Hospital, thus cementing an affiliation that began in 1903 when Lying-In agreed to receive student nurses from that hospital for obstetrical training. Photo (ca. late 1890s) from Herbert G. Partridge, History of the Providence Lying-In Hospital (1934)

During the final three decades of the nineteenth century, the state government began to assume a major role in social and rehabilitative services to supplement the programs provided by municipalities and private agencies. The site chosen for these new state health and correctional efforts was a rise of land in south central Cranston, just west of the Pawtuxet River, on farmland acquired from Thomas Brayton and William A. Howard. A State Board of Charities and Corrections (created in 1866) supervised the development of a state asylum for the insane (1870), a workhouse and house of correction (1873), an almshouse (1874), the State Prison and Providence County Jail (1878), and the State Reform School, consisting of two departments—the Sockanosset School for Boys (1883) and the Oaklawn School for Girls (1881). In 1890 the Board of Charities and Corrections opened a new and much larger almshouse, a three-and-a-half-story stone building on a bluff overlooking Pontiac Avenue.

The prison (viewed here from the jail

yard) is a massive stone structure designed by the noted Providence architectural firm of Stone and Carpenter. The original prison contained two wings of three-tiered cell blocks flanking an octagonal central administration building. The 250 cells were arranged fronting either east or west for unobstructed sunlight and had corridors on two sides so that each cell was fully accessible to guards. Each floor was formed of a plate of cast-iron ribbed cross wire covered with a coat of cement. The facility (which is still in use) opened under the supervision of Civil War general Nelson Viall, who directed the transfer of criminals as they walked in chains five miles from the old state prison on the Cove in Providence to the new Cranston site. Photo (1880s) courtesy of PPL

This cathedral of the bishops of Providence (shown here in this 1890 engraving) was begun in 1878 by the Irish-born Thomas F. Hendricken, first bishop of the Diocese of Providence. It was constructed near the site of the original church of SS. Peter and Paul, a house of worship built in 1837 that had served as the residence of the bishops of Hartford from 1844 to 1872, when Providence was erected as a separate diocese. Hendricken survived long enough to see the great project of his episcopacy nearly completed. The first service within its walls was his funeral in June 1886. In April 1887 Bishop Matthew Harkins was consecrated there and brought the building to completion during the first year of his administration.

Facing north, the cross-shaped brownstone cathedral features two high square towers, one on either side of the entrance. Among the many notable craftsmen who worked on this Gothic Revival structure was the famous church architect Patrick C. Keeley.

Today the cathedral overlooks a large new European-style square, complete with fountain, and from its site on Weybosset Hill one can peer directly eastward into the downtown Providence business district. A new chancery building, which bounds Cathedral Square on the west, contains offices and the historical archives of the diocese. *Engraving (ca. 1890) from Robert Grieve and John P. Fernald,* The Cotton Centennial *(1891)*

The outbreak of the Spanish-American
War in April 1898 revived Rhode Island's
long dormant martial ardor. According to
the computations of Governor Elisha
Dyer, the state furnished a total of 1,780
volunteers. Rhode Island raised several
military units—the First Regiment, Rhode
Island U.S. Volunteer Infantry; Light
Batteries A and B, First Rhode Island
Volunteer Artillery; the Rhode Island
Naval Militia; a contingent of hospital
corpsmen; and twenty-five crewmen of the
U.S.S. Vulcan, a repair ship. None of these
saw combat in this brief conflict except the
Vulcan crew.

Shown here are the members of Light
Battery B, mustering in at the Quonset
Point training field on June 28, 1898
(lower left); the signal corps of the Rhode
Island U.S. Naval Volunteers on Block
Island in the summer of 1898, vainly
watching for a Spanish ship; and the re-
turn of the colors to Governor Elisha Dyer
by the First Regiment, U.S. Volunteer
Infantry, at the Dexter Training Grounds
on April 1, 1899. This unit got as close to
Cuba as Camp Fornance, South Carolina.
Photos from Elisha Dyer (comp.) Rhode
Island in the War with Spain (1900)

Easily Rhode Island's most impressive public building of this or any era is the State House. When it was finished, Providence became Rhode Island's only capital. Prior to 1854 the city had shared this honor with the other county seats—Newport, East Greenwich, South Kingstown, and Bristol. From 1854 until the ratification of the eleventh amendment to the state constitution in 1900, Providence and Newport were co-capitals.

The history of Rhode Island's State House as recorded in the Rhode Island Manual reads as follows:

"In 1890 the General Assembly created a commission to obtain plans for a new State House, and on September 16, 1895, ground was broken for the construction of the building from the designs of Charles Follen McKim of the New York architectural firm of McKim, Mead & White. The cornerstone was laid October 15, 1896, while Charles Warren Lippitt was governor, and in December 1900, the secretary of state and his staff were the first to occupy offices. Early in 1901 other state officers and the General Assembly followed. On June 11, 1904, the new capitol building, terrace, approaches and grounds were officially turned over to the state by the architects and builders. The building, power house, connecting tunnel, furnishings and decorations cost $3,018,416.33, an astronomical figure for that day.

"Approximately 327,000 cubic feet of white Georgia marble, 1,309 tons of iron floor beams and 15,000,000 bricks were used in its construction. It boasts the second largest of the four famous unsupported marble domes in the world—the others being St. Peter's in Rome, the Taj Mahal in India and the Minnesota State Capitol. Standing atop the dome, 235 feet above the terrace, and 313 feet above mean high water mark, is the statue of the Independent Man. The building is 333 feet long and is 180 feet wide through the central vestibule section." Photo (ca. 1905) courtesy of PPL

BOOM, BUST, AND WAR, 1900-1945

Industrial Rhode Island moved into the twentieth century with a full head of steam, and its booming economy attracted a seemingly endless stream of immigrants, most of whom came from southern and eastern Europe. But the state was not a melting pot despite its many ethnics, for each group retained its own cultural identity, at least for a generation or two. Perhaps it could be said that Rhode Island (especially its northeastern quadrant) was more like a mosaic of diverse peoples—or even a stew, with everybody in one pot contributing to the whole, but with each ingredient maintaining its own flavor and identity.

The earliest arrivals among these so-called new immigrants were the Portuguese. Islanders—whites from the Azores and blacks from Cape Verde—were initially recruited by the whaling industry during the 1850s and 1860s. At voyage's end they settled in such port towns as Providence, Warren, Bristol, and Newport, where they became the pioneers and the beacons who inspired a more massive Portuguese migration to southeastern New England in the period from the 1890s onward. Then, as one historian has phrased it, "the loom replaced the harpoon" as the tool of the typical Portuguese immigrant.

The federal Bureau of Immigration kept detailed statistics from 1898 to 1932 on the ethnicity and destination of all aliens arriving in the ports of the United States. During this thirty-four-year span, those Portuguese designating Rhode Island as their destination numbered approximately 20,000. Included in this figure, especially after 1911, were immigrants from the mainland ("continentals"), many of whom settled in and around the Cumberland village of Valley Falls.

The largest group in the New Immigration was the Italians. From 1898 to 1932 federal tabulations listed 54,973 Italians migrating to Rhode Island. Of these, 51,919 were from the south of Italy (mostly rural peasants called *contadini*), and 3,054 from the more urbanized and culturally distinct north.

An international steamship company, the Fabre Line out of Marseilles, France, chose Providence as its American terminus in 1911. Because the Fabre steamships made calls in Italy, Portugal, and the Azores enroute to Providence, the migration of Italians and Portuguese to Rhode Island was facilitated. The line's local presence also accounted for the great number of returnees among both groups. From 1908 to 1932, the period for which return statistics have been compiled, over 13,000 Italians and 7,000

Portuguese were listed as "emigrant aliens departing" from the Port of Providence. No other local ethnics had such high rates of return.

Notwithstanding this loss, however, those of Italian ancestry are a strong presence in contemporary Rhode Island, especially in Providence (Federal Hill, Silver Lake, and the North End) and the adjacent communities of Cranston, Johnston, and North Providence. Other important Italian-American settlements were made in Woonsocket, Pawtucket, Barrington, Warren, Bristol, Westerly, and the Natick section of West Warwick. The 1980 census listed over 185,000 Rhode Islanders of Italian descent.

The Portuguese-Americans have also remained prominent in the state's cultural life. Most of the 90,000 Rhode Islanders of Portuguese ancestry counted in the 1980 census reside in the state's eastern sector—the Blackstone Valley, the Fox Point neighborhood of Providence, East Providence, Bristol County, Tiverton, Little Compton, and the three Aquidneck Island towns of Portsmouth, Middletown, and Newport. In the West Bay, Portuguese colonies have developed in the South Elmwood section of Cranston, West Warwick, and, most recently, in the Washington Park neighborhood of Providence.

Third in size among the new immigrant groups (42,713 in 1980) were the Poles, who settled mainly in Central Falls, Pawtucket, Warren, West Warwick, and the Olneyville, Manton, Valley, and West River sections of Providence. In 1902 these deeply religious people established St. Adalbert's Roman Catholic Church on Ridge Street, Providence, the mother church of Rhode Island's Polish community. Old World neighbors of the Poles, though for a time culturally estranged from them, were the Lithuanians. From 1898 to 1932, 893 members of this ethnic group arrived in Rhode Island, most of these taking up their first residence on Smith Hill, where they established St. Casimir's national parish in 1919. Another small group to settle in Rhode Island (2,050 from 1898 to 1932) were the Ukrainians. A colony of these Slavic-language eastern Europeans—some Orthodox in religion, others affiliated with the Church of Rome—made its home in Woonsocket during the decade prior to World War I.

Also from eastern Europe, especially Russia and Russian Poland, came the Jews. Intermittent campaigns of persecution called pogroms started their exodus in the early 1880s, but Jewish migration peaked in the years from 1900 to the outbreak of World War I. Most of these refugees settled in the South Providence, Smith Hill, and North End neighborhoods of the capital city, but congregations were also formed in Woonsocket, Pawtucket, Cranston, and Newport, where the famed Touro Synagogue was reopened for worship in 1883. An in-depth 1963 survey of the Greater Providence Jewish community counted 19,695 people of Jewish ancestry in the city and its adjacent municipalities, a figure that has remained fairly constant for the past two decades. Statewide, 27,000 Rhode Islanders claimed Jewish ancestry in the 1980 census. This Jewish community—consisting of Orthodox, Conservative, and Reform elements—is characterized by a low birth rate, a high level of educational achievement, and rapid upward socioeconomic mobility.

Other locally important and identifiable new immigrant groups are the Armenians, the Greeks, and the Syrian-Lebanese. From 1898 to 1932, 6,375 Armenian refugees from Turkish persecution came to Rhode Island. Most settled in Providence, in such areas as the North End, Federal Hill, Olneyville, and, especially, Smith Hill. During the same period 4,201 Greeks arrived, implanting their rich heritage and Orthodox religion primarily in three communities—Providence, Pawtucket, and Newport.

Finally came Christian Arabs (Orthodox, Protestants, and Melkites and Maronites affiliated with Rome) fleeing Moslem persecution and Turkish misrule. The 2,434 Arab-speaking people who arrived during the first three decades of the century settled in Providence, Pawtucket, Central Falls, and Woonsocket.

The New Immigration altered Rhode Island's religious profile. By 1905 the state census revealed that 50.81 percent of all Rhode Islanders claimed allegiance to the Roman Catholic faith. Protestants (at 46.72 percent) had finally lost their numerical ascendancy. In the state elections of 1906, James H. Higgins, an Irish Democrat, was chosen the state's first Roman Catholic governor.

But the influx of these Catholic newcomers was a mixed blessing, for ethnocultural antagonism developed, especially between the dominant Irish Catholics and the large Franco-American and Italian-American Catholic communities. Fortunately, serious conflicts were prevented, in large measure because of the creation of national parishes, the importation of ethnic religious orders, and the sensitive, tolerant, firm, and prudent leadership of Bishop Matthew Harkins (1887–1921), one the era's most able Catholic prelates, known locally as "the Bishop of the Poor."

Apart from its strenuous industrial endeavors and its increasing ethnic diversity, the most notable aspect of early twentieth-century Rhode Island was its turbulent politics. Until the election of 1932, in the depths of the Great Depression, the Republican party was dominant. It owed its ascendancy to many factors, not the least of which was the state's political system established by the constitution of 1843. That document, carefully drafted by the Law and Order

McCLURE'S MAGAZINE

VOL. XXIV   FEBRUARY, 1905   No. 4

RHODE ISLAND: A STATE FOR SALE

WHAT SENATOR ALDRICH REPRESENTS—A BUSINESS MAN'S
GOVERNMENT FOUNDED UPON THE CORRUPTION
OF THE PEOPLE THEMSELVES

BY

LINCOLN STEFFENS

AUTHOR OF "THE SHAME OF THE CITIES"

ILLUSTRATED WITH PORTRAITS

HE political condition of Rhode Island is notorious, acknowledged, and it is shameful. But Rhode Islanders are ashamed of it. There is the shining truth about this state. Not many American communities are so aware of their political degradation, none has a healthier body of conservative discontent ; and the common sense of this good-will, unorganized and impotent though it is, makes the Rhode Islander resent the interest of his neighbors. "Our evils are *our* troubles," he says ; "they don't concern the rest of you. Why should we be singled out ? We are no worse than others. We are better than some ; we want to set things right, but can't. Conditions are peculiar."

This is all wrong. The evils of Rhode Island concern every man, woman, and child in our land. For example :

The United States Senate is coming more and more to be the actual head of the United States government. In the Senate there is a small ring (called the Steering Committee) which is coming more and more to be the head of the United States Senate. The head

of this committee is Senator Nelson W. Aldrich, who has been described as "the boss of the United States," "the power behind the power behind the throne," "the general manager of the United States." The fitness of these titles is a question of national politics, and all I know to the point in that field is what everybody knows : that Senator Aldrich, a very rich man and father-in-law of young Mr. Rockefeller, is supposed to represent "Sugar," "Standard Oil," "New York," and, more broadly, "Wall Street " ; our leading legislative authority on protective tariff, he speaks for privileged business ; the chairman of the Senate finance committee, he stands for high finance. These facts and suppositions, taken together with the praises I have heard of him in Wall Street and the comfortable faith he seems to inspire in business men all over the country, suggest that we have in Senator Aldrich the commercial ideal of political character, and — if not the head — at least the political representative of the head of that System which is coming more and more to take the place of the passing paper government of the United States.

What sort of a man is Senator Aldrich ? What school of politics did he attend, what

---

coalition of upper-class Whigs and rural Democrats that vanquished Thomas Dorr, was designed to prevent the old-stock industrialist and the Yankee farmer from succumbing to the numerically superior urban proletariat, especially those of foreign birth and Catholic faith. When the Republican party formed during the 1850s in response to the slavery issue, it revived the Law and Order coalition of the preceding decade and adopted its nativistic posture, and it determined to use and preserve that party's constitutional checks upon the power of the urban working class.

Included in those checks were (1) a malapportioned Senate which gave a legislative veto to the small rural towns; (2) a cumbersome amendment process to frustrate reform; (3) the absence of procedures for the calling of a constitutional convention; (4) the absence (until 1889) of a secret ballot; (5) a General Assembly that dominated both the legislatively elected Supreme Court and the weak, vetoless (until 1909) governorship; and (6) a real estate voting requirement for the naturalized citizen. This last-mentioned check was eliminated by the Bourn Amendment (VII) in 1888, but it was replaced by a $134 property-tax-paying qualification for voting in city council elections. This requirement had the practical effect of preventing those at the lower socio-economic levels, usually Catholic immigrants, from exercising control over the affairs of the cities in which they resided. This was true because the mayors, for whom all electors could vote, had very limited powers, while the councils, for whom only property owners could vote, were dominant, controlling both the purse and the patronage.

The famous political reformer James Quayle Dealey of Brown University contended in 1909 that "the political effect of this [voting] limitation is to place the control of municipal government in the hands of the Republicans. The general vote which elects the mayor is usually Democratic in the five cities, but the property vote is strongly Republican. As the mayor has small powers in government, control over municipal affairs rests with the Republican organization. This limitation on municipal suffrage is a standing grievance on the part of Democratic, reform, and radical organizations and is pointed at as the only survival in the United States of the old-fashioned, colonial property qualifications." Nearly 60 percent of those who could vote for mayor were disfranchised in council elections.

As if constitutional checks were not sufficient, General Charles Brayton, legendary boss of the Republican party, for good measure engineered the enactment in 1901 of a statute designed to emasculate any Democrat who might back into the governor's chair by virtue of a split in Republican ranks. With a few limited exceptions, this "Brayton Act" placed the ultimate appointive power of state government in the hands of the Senate. In the aftermath of its passage a governor could effectively appoint only his private secretary and a handful of insignificant state officials.

By 1920 the Senate—the possessor of state appointive and budgetary power—was more malapportioned than ever. For example, West Greenwich, population 367, had the same voice as Providence, population 237,595! And the twenty smallest towns, with an aggregate population of 41,660, outvoted Providence twenty to one, although the capital city had over 39 percent of Rhode Island's total population. The Senate, said Democratic congressman George F. O'Shaunessy (1911–1919), was "a strong power exercised by the abandoned farms of Rhode Island."

The Progressive Era (ca. 1898–1917) was an age of national reform—political, economic, and social—but Rhode Island's reactionary constitutional system survived the period relatively intact. Boss Brayton and Nelson Aldrich proved more than a match for Lucius Garvin, James Higgins, Charles E. Gorman, Robert H. I. Goddard, Theodore Francis Green, Amasa Eaton, and other supporters of governmental reform. The Brayton-Aldrich combine even survived a national exposé by noted muckraker Lincoln Steffens, who in 1905 described Rhode Island as "A State for Sale."

The Progressive Movement was eclipsed by American involvement in World War I. In Rhode Island pro-Allied sentiment ran high, conditioned in part by the Anglophilic *Providence Journal,* whose editorials repeatedly urged intervention to halt alleged German aggression. When war finally came in April 1917, the state contributed 28,817 troops, of whom 612 died. Many of these succumbed not to German gas or bullets but to the Spanish influenza, a dread virus that was carried home from the battle-front by returning soldiers. This deadly infection took 941 lives in Providence alone during 1918.

With the return of peace in Europe, Rhode Island's political wars resumed. The stormy decades of the 1920s and 1930s witnessed a major transition from Republican to Democratic control in state government. Economic unrest stemming from such factors as the decline of the textile industry, the crash of 1929, the ensuing Great Depression, and the local rise of organized labor coupled with the development of cultural antagonisms between native and foreign stock to weaken the allegiance of Franco-Americans and Italian-Americans to the Republican party. Simultaneously, vigorous efforts by the Irish-led Democratic party to woo ethnics, key constitutional reforms such as the removal of the property-tax requirement for voting at council elections (by Amendment XX in 1928), the shift in control of the

As Steffens noted, Rhode Island produced the nation's most powerful and influential lawmaker of the early twentieth century, a probusiness U. S. senator who was referred to as "the General Manager of the United States." This solon, Nelson W. Aldrich (1841–1915), came to Providence from a farm in Foster while he was in his mid-teens. Within eight years after he was hired as a bookkeeper in a wholesale grocery firm, he had risen to the position of partner. Aldrich was elected to the Providence Common Council in 1869 and quickly attained the council presidency (1871–1873). In 1875 he was chosen state representative, and again he rose rapidly to the top, assuming the office of speaker in 1876.

During Aldrich's meteoric climb he attracted the attention of Republican party

bosses Henry Anthony and Charles Brayton and became their ally. Anthony engineered Aldrich's nomination and election to Congress in 1878. With the death of U.S. Senator Ambrose Burnside in 1881, the ambitious Aldrich was chosen by the General Assembly to be Anthony's Senate colleague, beginning a thirty-year career during which he became the ally of powerful business interests and an expert on tariff and banking laws. He was the leading proponent of a high protective tariff and a successful promoter of a central banking system. With U.S. senators then chosen by the state legislature, his tenure was rendered secure by a malapportioned General Assembly controlled by members from the small country towns, who were in turn controlled by "Boss" Brayton. Aldrich's contacts contributed to the marriage of his daughter Abby to John D. Rockefeller, Jr. Among their six children was Nelson Aldrich Rockefeller, governor of New York and vice president of the United States. Photo courtesy of RIHS (Rhi x3 5713).

Dr. Lucius F. C. Garvin (1841–1922) ranks among Rhode Island's most tenacious reformers. Tennessee-born to transplanted New England parents, Garvin came north to college just before the Civil War. He served with a Massachusetts unit in that conflict and entered Harvard Medical School shortly after his return to civilian life. In 1867 Dr. Garvin began a fifty-five-year practice in the Cumberland village of Lonsdale. Though he continued his medical duties without interruption, he soon turned his attention to Rhode Island's political and economic ills. In 1883 he entered the state legislature, joining with Charles Gorman, Edwin McGuinness, and Hugh Carroll in the Equal Rights Movement—an effort to remove the real estate voting requirement for naturalized citizens and to apportion the state legislature fairly. He also urged

numerous reforms to improve the health and safety of the workplace. From 1885 onward he wrote many articles for a weekly workers' newspaper called The People.

After an unsuccessful bid for the governorship as the Democratic nominee in 1901, Garvin won election over his favored Republican opponents in 1902 and 1903. As governor, however, he found himself hamstrung in his appointments by the recently enacted Brayton Law, which placed the ultimate appointive power in the hands of the rural-dominated Republican Senate. Beaten in his bids for reelection in 1904 and 1905, Garvin remained active in reform circles, advocating prolabor legislation in numerous speeches and public essays. He regained elective office in 1920 as a state senator from Cumberland, despite the Republican landslide of that year, but died while campaigning for re-election in 1922 at the age of eighty-one. Always the physician, Garvin made house calls to his patients until the day of his death. Photo from Rhode Island Manual (1903).

national Democratic party from rural to urban leadership, the 1928 presidential candidacy of Irish-Catholic Democrat Al Smith, and the social programs of Franklin D. Roosevelt's New Deal combined to pull the newer immigrant groups towards the Democratic fold by the mid-1930s.

At this juncture Democratic leaders—especially Governor Theodore Francis Green, Thomas P. McCoy of Pawtucket, and Lieutenant Governor Robert Emmet Quinn—staged a governmental reorganization known as the Bloodless Revolution of 1935. This bizarre coup, made possible by a controversial scheme that gave Democrats control of the state Senate, resulted in the repeal of the Brayton Act, the reorganization of state government by the replacement of the commission system with the present departmental structure, and the dismissal of the entire five-member Republican Supreme Court.

Soon after this takeover, Democratic factionalism became intense; promised reforms such as the calling of an open constitutional convention went unfulfilled; and a scandalous "Race Track War" at Narragansett Park erupted between Governor Quinn and racetrack owner Walter O'Hara. These local embarrassments were compounded by a national recession in 1937 that brought temporary disillusionment with the Democratic New Deal. The state elections of 1938, therefore, returned the Republicans briefly to power.

Though the GOP enacted a state merit system law in 1939, its well-intentioned governor, William Vanderbilt, became ensnared in a wiretap controversy during his overzealous attempt to implicate Pawtucket's Mayor McCoy in vote fraud, and in 1940 the Democratic tide rolled in once more—this time for a long stay. U.S. District Attorney J. Howard McGrath, who had made political hay with Vanderbilt's federally illegal wiretap, won the governorship and took a giant step upward in a political career that would include several high national offices. Congressmen Aime J. Forand and John E. Fogarty also launched long and successful tenures in that 1940 campaign, as did Dennis J. Roberts, who became mayor of Providence under a new charter that strengthened the powers of that city's chief executive. For the Democrats, happy days were here for the first time since the early 1850s!

Scarcely had the state's political wars subsided when the global conflict of World War II disrupted Rhode Island life. In the three and a half years following Pearl Harbor, many of Rhode Island's sons and daughters fought and died in the great struggle against the Axis powers. An examination of war casualty lists reveals that this was the state's most costly conflict. More men and women served (92,027)

and more died (2,157) than in any other war.

Yet the losses only seemed to spur the citizenry on to greater efforts. Spirited parades were held in Providence and other communities at intervals during the war years, war-bond drives were oversubscribed, and those able-bodied workers that remained at home turned out many articles of war, including boots, knives, parachutes, gauges, and, especially, the Liberty ships and combat cargo vessels that were constructed at the Walsh-Kaiser Shipyard on Field's Point by a work force that numbered twenty-one thousand in early 1945. Civilian workers at Quonset Point Naval Air Station, adjacent Davisville, Charlestown Naval Air Station, and the Newport naval base all performed a variety of tasks to aid the war effort.

During the four and a half decades from the turn of the century to the end of World War II, Rhode Islanders increasingly found escape from work, war, and politics in the worlds of entertainment and sport. Vaudeville, the silent screen, and then "talkies" successively developed wide popular appeal, and Providence (birthplace of George M. Cohan) became a center of the performing and visual arts. Its splendid theaters—Fay's (1912), the Strand (1915), the Majestic (1917), the Albee (1919), Loew's State (1928), and the Metropolitan (1932)—all date from this era. And theatergoers, before or after the show, could visit such bustling department stores as Diamond's, Cherry and Webb, the Boston Store, Gladding's, Shepard's, and the Outlet. Of these big six, all then at their peak, Shepard's and the Outlet were the giants, and their spirited rivalry spilled over from retailing to radio. On June 2, 1922, Shepard's inaugurated Rhode Island's first radio station, WEAN; three months later the Outlet beamed back with WJAR, the embryo of what would become an Outlet broadcasting empire.

In sports, baseball was still king. Minor league teams, usually dubbed the Providence Grays, were formed occasionally and even won championships. Most notable were the International League titlists of 1914, who included a pitcher named Babe Ruth. In the new sport of professional football, Providence boasted its Steam Roller eleven, the National Football League kingpins in 1928. In college football Brown fielded several nationally prominent teams, including the famous Iron Men of 1926 and the 1915 squad that played in the very first Rose Bowl game.

In the 1920s a crosstown athletic rivalry developed between venerable Brown and the new Catholic men's college founded in 1919 by Bishop Matthew Harkins. On June 7, 1924, the Bruins and Providence College played the longest collegiate baseball game on record, a twenty-inning contest in which future Pawtucket mayor Charlie Reynolds went the route in the Friars' 1 to 0 victory.

By the turn of the century, Irish-Americans had seized control of the organizational structure of the state's Democratic party and were persistently advocating economic and social reforms on behalf of the working class, as well as constitutional reforms that would lessen rural influence in state affairs and give lower-class ethnics (themselves included) political control over the cities in which they resided.

Attorney James H. Higgins (shown here), who had succeeded the colorful and dynamic John J. Fitzgerald as mayor of Pawtucket in 1903, won election in 1906 and again in 1907 as Rhode Island's first Irish Catholic governor. Though his efforts at reform were stymied by a Senate con-

trolled by rural Republicans, in one celebrated triumph the feisty Irishman succeeded in ousting Boss Brayton from his unofficial State House office.

Galway-born Democrat George O'Shaunessy (1868–1934) became another local Irish Catholic pathbreaker, securing election four times to the U.S. House of Representatives (1911–1919). In 1913 the Irish began their unbroken sixty-year grip on the Providence mayoralty with the victory of Joseph Gainer.

During the second decade of the present century, Irish Democrats belatedly began their efforts to woo French and Italian voters away from their customary Republican allegiance by advancing such ethnic leaders as Alberic Archambault of West Warwick and Luigi De Pasquale of Providence to high positions within the Democratic hierarchy. Photo from Rhode Island Manual (1907).

The intense rivalry between Irish-Americans and Franco-Americans was highlighted when the Republicans nominated the experienced and popular Aram J. Pothier in the 1908 race for governor to succeed the departing Higgins. Pothier had served successively as state representative (1887–1888), mayor of Woonsocket (1894–1895), lieutenant governor (1897–1898), and member of the state board of education (1907-1909) prior to receiving the GOP gubernatorial endorsement. In November 1908 he won election to the first of his several terms as governor.

The repeated candidacies of this success-

ful banker-industrialist helped the Republicans to maintain their hold on the Franco-American vote. Pothier was reelected in 1909, 1910, 1911, and 1912

(the latter victory for the state's first two-year gubernatorial term). Coming out of retirement to reclaim the wavering political allegiance of the Franco-Americans, he was elected again in 1924 and reelected in 1926. On February 28, 1928, Pothier died in office, having served a total of nine years and two months as governor—the longest of any Rhode Island chief executive since the adoption of the state constitution of 1843. Photo from Marie-Louise Bonier, Débuts de la Colonie Franco-Américaine de Woonsocket, R.I. (1920)

In professional hockey the Rhode Island Reds came to the newly constructed Rhode Island Auditorium in 1926, and from 1930 to 1938, to the delight of local sports fans, the Reds won the Canadian-American Hockey League championship four times. In 1930 America's Cup competition first came to Rhode Island waters as *Enterprise* beat *Shamrock V* off Newport four races to none. Finally, the state got a major thoroughbred racetrack to host "the sport of kings": largely through the exertions of textile magnate Walter E. O'Hara, Narragansett Park opened on the Pawtucket-East Providence line (site of the old What Cheer Airport) on August 1, 1934.

Other highlights of the 1900–1945 era included the establishment of Providence as the sole state capital (1900); the founding of several colleges—Barrington (1900), Johnson and Wales (1914), Providence (1919), and Roger Williams (1919; reorganized in 1948); the creation of the town of West Warwick (1913); the long incumbency of the popular Franco-American Republican governor Aram Pothier (1909–1915 and 1925–1928); the passage of a state women's suffrage law (1917); the distinguished tenure of internationally renowned Dr. Charles V. Chapin as Providence's director of public health (1882–1932); the construction of the Scituate Reservoir (1915–1929); the opening at Hillsgrove of the nation's first state-run airport (1931); the construction of the Providence skyline, especially the Industrial (now Fleet) Bank Building (1928); the completion of the Mount Hope and Jamestown bridges (1929 and 1940); and the opening of the Quonset naval base (1941). On the debit side, one must note the sinking of the steamer *Larchmont* (out of Providence) in Block Island Sound on February 11, 1907, with a loss of 111 lives, and the 1938 hurricane—the state's worst natural disaster—whose 120-mile-per-hour winds and tidal waves caused over a hundred million dollars in damage and took the lives of 311 Rhode Islanders, most in the Westerly-Charlestown area.

In August 1945 war ended. Two months later John O. Pastore, son of Italian immigrants, took his oath as governor of Rhode Island when J. Howard McGrath resigned to accept an appointment from Harry Truman to be the solicitor general of the United States. By year's end the work force at the Walsh-Kaiser Shipyard had been nearly disbanded, veterans were home seeking jobs, and the state's declining textile industry, granted a temporary reprieve by the necessities of war, looked towards a bleak future. An eventful era had passed. But prosperity for Rhode Islanders was no longer on the doorstep or even round the corner. It was somewhere far down a hilly and uncharted road.

Educational advances were a prelude to women's achievements in politics and reform. In 1891 Brown admitted women to university exams, and the following year it gave them the right to receive both graduate and undergraduate degrees. In 1897 Sarah Doyle, a Providence high school teacher and founder of the Rhode Island Women's Club in 1886, allied with Brown president Elisha Benjamin Andrews to establish a separate women's college at that Ivy League institution (where she later became the first woman to receive an honorary degree). Much of the endowment and early support for the new school was provided by the Society for the Collegiate Education of Women, which was founded by Doyle in 1896 and operated under her direction until 1919.

Among the first students to matriculate at Brown's Women's College (later called Pembroke) was Mary Emma Woolley (class of '94), who taught at Wellesley College and then, in 1901, began a thirty-six-year tenure as president of Mount Holyoke College. While Woolley was an instructor at Wellesley, the presidency of that prestigious women's college was assumed by Caroline Hazard, a member of the famous South County clan. The versatile Hazard—a historian, poet, educator, musician, and family chronicler—is depicted here during her 1899-1910 presidential tenure.

In the area of vocational education, Katharine Gibbs in 1911 founded a school in Providence for training business secretaries. From an initial two-room facility, this enterprise has expanded to seven highly-regarded Gibbs schools located in major northeastern cities from Boston to Philadelphia. Photo courtesy of RIHS (Rhi x3 1678)

Nearly all the reforms associated with the Progressive Era bypassed Rhode Island. One reform that finally succeeded after more than fifty years of local effort was women's suffrage. The battle, begun in Providence in 1868 by Paulina Wright Davis, Elizabeth Buffum Chace, and Anna Garlin Spencer, was won on January 6, 1920, when the state Senate (voting 38 to 1) and the House (89 to 3) ratified the Twentieth Amendment to the federal Constitution. The wide margins were deceptive, however, for the Assembly yielded only when it appeared that nationwide approval of women's suffrage was unavoidable.

In this photo, happy suffragettes gather around Republican governor R. Livingston Beeckman as he signs the ratification resolution. Included in the picture is Sara M. Algeo of Providence, the historian of the Rhode Island suffrage movement, and the aging Sarah Doyle.

The Democrats lost no time in recruiting women candidates. In 1920 they ran Elizabeth Upham Yates for lieutenant governor and Helen I. Binning for secretary of state, and in 1922 and 1924 they nominated Susan Sharp Adams for the latter office. All four efforts were unsuccesful, and so the Democrats waited until 1982 to endorse another woman for the state ticket. With both major parties nominating women for secretary of state that year, Providence Republican Susan Farmer prevailed to become Rhode Island's first female general officer.

Despite their early failure to gain statewide elective office, women did register an important breakthrough in 1922 when Mrs. Isabelle Florence Ahearn O'Neill became Rhode Island's first female legislator. Born in Woonsocket, she was educated at such diverse schools as Harvard College, the Boston School of Oratory, and Hemmingway Gymnasium. When she was elected in the Flynn campaign of 1922 as a Democratic representative from the Broadway district of Providence, she was a teacher of elocution and physical education. Mrs. O'Neill served four terms as a member of the House education committee and two terms as state senator prior to retiring undefeated from elective office in 1935. She died in 1975 at the age of ninety-four. Photo from Sara M. Algeo, The Story of a Sub-Pioneer (1925)

No sooner did women gain the vote than they joined the campaign (waged since 1888 by Irish Democratic politicians) to remove the property qualification for voting in council elections, a qualification that worked to the political disadvantage of the numerically significant lower-class ethnics residing in Rhode Island's six cities—Providence (incorporated in 1832), Newport (1853), Pawtucket (1886), Woonsocket (1888), Central Falls (1895), and Cranston (1910). This discriminatory restriction, instituted in 1888 by the Bourn Amendment (Article VII) to the state constitution, imposed a $134-property-tax-paying qualification for voting in city council elections. Since the cities' mayors, for whom all electors could vote, had very limited powers, while the councils, for whom only property owners could vote, were dominant, controlling both the purse and the patronage, the requirement had the practical effect of preventing those at the lower socioeconomic levels—usually immigrants—from exercising control over the affairs of the cities in which

they resided.

Eventually the women, the ethnics, and the Democrats pressured the GOP into framing a provision to eliminate the property qualification. The new measure

became Article of Amendment XX to the state constitution when it was overwhelmingly ratified in 1928. *Photo from Sara M. Algeo,* The Story of a Sub-Pioneer *(1925)*

This photo of Providence's Crawford Street Bridge shows the many modes of transportation in common use at the dawn of the century: horse-drawn carriages and wagons, autos, trucks, the steamboat Warwick, *an electric trolley, and a railroad boxcar (partially visible at extreme right). The towered building (upper left) is Infantry Hall. Photo (ca. 1912) courtesy of RIHS (Rhi x3 1906).*

As the twentieth century dawned, a new invention—the automobile—appeared with increasing frequency on the roads of Rhode Island, and for a time some local entrepreneurs engaged in the manufacture of these "horseless carriages." The auto was destined to exert a greater impact on Rhode Island's cities than any other mechanical innovation, increasing the mobility of the population, accelerating the move to outlying neighborhoods and then to suburbia, forcing a widening and upgrading of streets (yet still congesting them), giving birth to the service station and a host of related facilities and businesses, altering innumerable house lots with garages and driveways, polluting the atmosphere, littering the landscape with its remnants, bringing injury and premature death to thousands, and even affecting public morals. In 1904 the state legislature exerted the first public control over automobiles when it provided for the registration of motor vehicles and the licensing of their drivers.

At first, autos were regarded as either experimental or the toys of the rich. In wealthy Newport they proliferated, and for

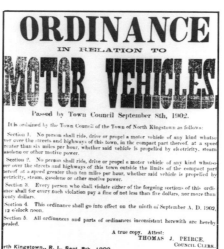

a time auto racing became the rage of the well-to-do. Some of the nation's first races were staged on the beaches of Newport and Middletown, such as the event shown in this 1909 photo of Second Beach. Newport socialite Maud Howe Elliott (daughter of the famed reformer Julia Ward Howe) described these auto contests as follows:

The spectators arrived on bicycles and in horse-drawn vehicles as well as chugging, jerking motors. In the early days you were not considered a motorist if you did not wear a duster, huge goggles, and a great veil swathed around your head, neck and shoulders. These accoutrements were really needed, as the automobiles had no windshields, and the roads of the period were inches deep in dust.... The automobiles, queer-looking contraptions run by steam, gasoline and electricity, all ready to explode, catch fire or break down, whirled across Second Beach. Timid ladies sought refuge in the sand dunes from these monsters going ten—twenty—miles an hour.

North Kingstown took a less indulgent view of the auto, as indicated by this 1902 ordinance that limited the speed in Wickford and other "compact" areas to six miles per hour. Photo of Second Beach courtesy of the Newport Historical Society; broadside courtesy of RIHS (Rhi x3 5744).

Just before America's entrance into World War I, a group of East Greenwich businessmen offered to finance aviation pioneer Edson F. Gallaudet if he would move his aircraft production facilities from Norwich, Connecticut, to their town. Gallaudet accepted, and the state's only aircraft plant began its brief but colorful career. Employing up to eight hundred workers at its ten-acre site on Greenwich Cove, the Gallaudet Corporation assembled Curtis flying boats and De Haviland 4s and built some experimental and advanced-design seaplanes, all-metal bombers and pursuit planes, and ship-based observation planes.

Shown here is Lieutenant E. F. Stone,

navy test pilot, standing in the cockpit of a Gallaudet D-4 seaplane that he flew at 127 miles per hour over Narragansett Bay in 1918. Tragically, this same model claimed

the lives of two other pilots. In June 1918 pioneer Rhode Island aviator and stunt flier Jack McGee of Pawtucket died in the test flight of a D-4, and five weeks later Lieutenant Arthur F. Souther was also killed while testing the plane.

Gallaudet relinquished direction of the company in 1921. Eventually he was replaced by Major Reuben H. Fleet, who moved the operation to Buffalo in 1924 (later it was relocated to San Diego). The Gallaudet plant converted to the manufacture of accessories for the textile industry and operated until it was leveled by the hurricane of 1938. Its site is now a marina. Photo of D-4 courtesy of RIHS (Rhi x3 5684)

The Port of Providence handled a large number of coastal steamers that furnished passenger and freight service to various Atlantic ports. In addition to the Merchants and Miners Transportation Company, other large coastal steamship lines using the port included the Colonial Navigation Company (established 1910), the Winsor Line to Philadelphia, the New Haven Steamship Line to New York (owned by the New York, New Haven, and Hartford Railroad), and the Joy Line, which first contested the New Haven's attempt to establish a monopoly of the Providence-to-New York traffic but was eventually acquired by the voracious railroad in 1905.

The fortunes of the Joy Line were dealt a serious blow on February 11, 1907, when its steamer, the Larchmont (shown here), left Providence, bound for New York City, at 7:00 p.m. in a blinding blizzard. In Block Island Sound, about three miles from Watch Hill, the 250-foot-long side-wheeler collided with the coal schooner Harry Knowlton, 129 feet in length but fully laden. The impact tore a gaping hole in the Larchmont's port side, and the icy sea came pouring through. Within thirty minutes the vessel began her plunge to the bottom.

Because accurate records were not kept, estimates of the death toll vary widely. According to the authoritative history of the Joy Line, 128 passengers and crew departed from Providence, and of these only 17 survived. Other estimates, however, set the toll as high as 192. Some of those who perished were washed ashore on the frozen beaches of Block Island (shown here), where they were carted away for funerals and burial. The General Assembly did not exaggerate when its resolutions

of sympathy declared the Larchmont disaster "a calamity unparalleled in the history of the navigation of the waters in the vicinity of Rhode Island." The Joy Line itself was the disaster's other casualty.

It was dissolved eight months later. Photo of Larchmont courtesy of PPL; photo of victims by H. Ladd Walford, courtesy of RIHS (Rhi x3 5741)

The old Union Street Railroad Company, Providence's first mass transit monopoly, had been acquired by Marsden Perry and Nelson Aldrich, but in 1902 they transferred their city and interurban transportation interests to the Rhode Island Company, a corporation controlled by the Philadelphia-based United Gas Improvement Company. Then, in 1904, financier J. P. Morgan of the New Haven Railroad told its president, Charles S. Mellen, to buy up every trolley line, every steamship company, and every railroad in New England that he could lay his hands on. Mellen attempted to comply with this bold directive, and in 1906 the New Haven acquired a monopoly of Rhode Island mass transit, including the Rhode Island Company.

After nearly a decade of unprofitable operation, the company began to founder badly. Wartime inflation, tax increases, labor demands, and competition from jitneys and autos took their toll. In addition, a federal antitrust decision in 1914 forced the New Haven to divest itself of the Rhode Island Company. Under the management of federally appointed trustees, the streetcar firm slid into bankruptcy by 1919. A business reorganization followed, and on July 9, 1921, a new corporation, the United Electric Railway (UER), assumed control of the Providence-based urban mass transit system. A year later, on July 3, 1922, the UER introduced its first bus into service.

This new company, operating both trolleys and buses, survived until 1952, and then it, too, experienced reorganization as the United Transit Company. The UTC was in turn absorbed by the Rhode Island Public Transit Authority (RIPTA) on July 1, 1966, thus ending (for now, at least) this complex tale of transit company transfers.

During the early years of the century, interurban electric trolleys radiated from Providence like spokes on a wheel, giving relatively remote rural villages like Chepachet quick access to the big city. Even before the impact of the auto, it was these interurban carriers that began the movement towards suburbia. This photo shows the first electric trolley arriving at Chepachet in July 1914 en route to a northern terminus in Burrillville. Passenger service was short-lived, however, giving way to the auto and the bus in 1924. Photo from Glocester: The Way Up Country (1976).

The New Haven Railroad of J. P. Morgan
and Charles S. Mellen not only opened the
century by establishing a monopoly over
local rail, steamboat, streetcar, and
interurban transit, it also tried to block a
potential rival—the Canadian Grand
Trunk Railroad—from making Providence, an ice-free port, the major Atlantic
terminus of a railroad network that could
tap the trade and produce of Canada, including its grain-rich western provinces.

Grand Trunk president Charles M.
Hays proposed to build a railway branching from the Central Vermont Line (a
Grand Trunk subsidiary) at Palmer,
Massachusetts, and running seventy-five
miles southeastward through the Blackstone Valley into Providence. With the
assistance of Providence lawyer-lobbyist
John S. Murdock, Hays got a state charter
for a Southern New England Railway in
April 1910 over the objections of Charles
Mellen. He then began construction and
laid out the roadbed into Providence.
Unfortunately for Rhode Island's future as
the eastern terminus of a major transcon-
tinental railroad, Hays went to the bottom
with the Titanic in 1912, prompting one
writer to speak of "the railroad that
perished at sea." Mellen was later indicted

by a federal grand jury (but not convicted)
for his role in pressuring the Grand Trunk
to halt construction. The death of Hays,
the intervention of World War I, the
takeover of the line by the Canadian
government, the rise of auto and truck use
in the 1920s, and the onset of the Great
Depression combined to put a lid on the
Grand Trunk. The scheme was completely
abandoned by 1930.

The proposed roadbed of this grand and
promising venture is visible in certain sites
today. Two abutments are still to be seen on
Cranston Street at Pavilion Avenue (the
line was designed to skirt the city, entering
at Silver Lake, then crossing Cranston
Street and Reservoir, Elmwood, and
Allens avenues to reach deep water at
Ernest Street). This photo shows a cut for
the road being made by steam-powered
drills near the Lincoln village of Quinnville. Photo (ca. 1912) courtesy of William
Davis from Once in a Hundred Years: A
Pictorial History of Lincoln, R.I. (1971)

Italian and Portuguese arrivals are shown
at Providence's State Pier No. 1 in
December 1913 after debarking from the
Venezia, a ship of the Fabre Line. Because
the Fabre steamships made calls in Italy
and Portugal en route from Marseilles,
many immigrants from those countries
came directly to Providence, though others,
especially Italians, traveled to the city after
landing in New York.

The two groups are today a strong
presence in the state. Portuguese-
Americans are especially numerous in the
Fox Point and Washington Park
neighborhoods of Providence and in such
areas as Pawtucket, Valley Falls, the South
Elmwood section of Cranston, West War-
wick, and the entire East Bay region from
East Providence through Bristol and
Portsmouth to Tiverton and Little
Compton. The Italians are Greater Provi-
dence's dominant ethnic group, being more
numerous than any other in Providence,
North Providence, Johnston, and Cran-
ston. Large Italian-American concentra-
tions exist also in such scattered areas as
Woonsocket, Scituate, Warren, Barrington,
Bristol, Warwick, West Warwick, and
Westerly. Photo from the author's
collection

The Fabre Line—which sent its first vessel, the Madonna, to Providence in May 1911—maintained service to that city until July 1934. Incoming liners left Marseilles and made pickups at Naples and Palermo in Italy, Lisbon in Portugal, and the Azores before discharging their passengers at State Pier No. 1 (shown here), where the federal government had established an immigrant landing station. After leaving Providence, the Fabre steamships visited ports in North Africa and the Near East, as well as cities in Italy and Portugal, before making their return to southern France. Photo (1925) courtesy of RIHS (Rhi L866 922).

Numerically significant Jewish migration to Rhode Island dates from 1881, when the Russian government began to persecute its Jewish citizens. Refugees from Russian pogroms established settlements in South Providence, Smith Hill, and the North End in Providence, as well as in Newport, Pawtucket, and Woonsocket. The largest influx occurred in the decade prior to World War I. A postwar revival of Jewish immigration was cut short, first by discriminatory immigration quotas and then by a worldwide economic depression.

The Jewish people of Rhode Island are distinguished by strong ties to their religion, a high level of educational attainment, rapid upward socioeconomic mobility, and a strong presence in the professions and white-collar occupations. One of their number, Frank Licht, served as governor of Rhode Island from 1969 to 1973.

An in-depth 1963 survey of the Greater Providence Jewish community counted 19,695 people of Jewish ancestry in the city and its adjacent municipalities and approximately 7,000 more in the outlying areas of the state. These figures have remained fairly constant for the past two decades.

Of all Rhode Island's ethnic groups, the Jews have most closely recounted their local history. Professor Sidney Goldstein, a Brown sociologist, not only conducted the detailed 1963 survey but also published Jewish Americans: Three Generations in a Jewish Community (1968), a case study based upon the Providence Hebrew experience. Dr. Seebert Goldowsky was the longtime editor of Rhode Island Jewish Historical Notes, the only local ethnic

journal of its kind. An inspiration to both these scholars was David C. Adelman, a founder of the Rhode Island Jewish Historical Society and the first editor of the Notes.

One of the best known of the early Jewish neighborhoods was in the old Randall Square area of Providence, bounded by Charles Street, Chalkstone Avenue,

Douglas Avenue, and Orms Street. Much of this section has since been claimed by interstates and urban renewal. In this 1903 photo a Jewish peddler passes the shop of baker Hyman Yaffee at 175 Chalkstone Avenue in the heart of the section once called "Jewtown." Courtesy of RIHS (Rhi x3 1164)

An important and sizable migration of
Polish people to Rhode Island occurred
during the first quarter of the twentieth
century, and then again after World
War II, when many displaced Polish
refugees were brought to America by the
Polish-American clergy and other
humanitarians. Polish immigrants settled
mainly in the Olneyville, Manton, and
Valley sections of Providence and in
Pawtucket, Central Falls, Woonsocket,
West Warwick, Coventry, and Warren,
where they took jobs in the base-metals and
textile industries. The highest number of
Polish-born Rhode Islanders—8,696—was
reported in the census of 1930.

The majority of Polish-Americans are
Roman Catholic. There are five Polish
Roman Catholic parishes in Rhode Island
today, reflecting the major areas of Polish
settlement: St. Adalbert's in Providence,
the oldest, established in 1902 on Ridge
Street, Federal Hill (and now on Atwells
Avenue); St. Joseph's in Central Falls,
presently the largest; Our Lady of Czestow-
chowa in Coventry; St. Casimir's in
Warren; and St. Stanislaus Kostka in
Woonsocket. St. Hedwig's, founded in
Providence's North End in 1916, was
destroyed in 1961 and its congregation
scattered by the forces of urban renewal.
St. Joseph's in Hope Valley has a very large
congregation of more recent Polish
arrivals, although it is technically not an
ethnic parish.

In the late nineteenth century a religious
schism developed over a variety of local
issues, and this led certain Polish Catholic
congregations to establish churches separate
from Rome, wherein each maintained a
high degree of local control. There are two
of these Polish National Catholic parishes
in Rhode Island: Holy Cross in Central
Falls and the Church of our Savior in
Woonsocket.

The old-world neighbors of the Poles,
though for a time culturally estranged,
were the Lithuanians. In the period from
1898 to 1932, 893 members of this ethnic
group settled in Rhode Island, nearly all of
these taking up residence in Smith Hill in
Providence. After worshiping for a time
with the Polish or in Catholic territorial
parishes, they dedicated their own church—
St. Casimir's on Smith Street—in May
1921.

Both Lithuanians and Poles maintained
a lively interest in the independence of
their homelands. Towards the end of
World War I, when it became obvious that
an armistice would lead to the restoration
of a free Poland, there was unrestrained
jubilation in the local Polish community,
expressed by a joyous parade through the
streets of Central Falls in late October
1918. During the dramatic program at

Pulaski Hall that followed, these three
young women displayed various aspects of
their Polish-American heritage. The girl
at the left represents Poland with its famed
eagle and the motto "Youth, give me
wings"; the middle figure wears Polish folk
dress; and the girl at the right symbolizes
America. Photo courtesy of Wanda
Moskwa

During the three decades from 1899 to 1932, Rhode Island received 2,050 immigrants from the Ukraine, an agricultural area in east central Europe presently a part of the Soviet Union. Undoubtedly other Ukrainians had come prior to 1899, but since nationality rather than ethnic group was then the means of designation, these earlier arrivals were listed as Russians or Austrians. The peak year of immigration was 1913, when 337 migrants from the Ukraine entered Rhode Island. The principal source of this influx was the western Ukrainian region of Galicia.

The causes for the migration to the United States in the pre-World War I era were many. The leading student of Ukrainian-American history, Wasyl Halich, contends that Russian political and cultural oppression was the primary factor, but even those Ukrainians from East Galicia and Ruthenia who were under Austrian rule prior to 1918 were quite discontented with their lack of national identity. Other motives for the migration of this Slavic group were economic—the promise of high wages and steady employment in America contrasted with poor conditions at home, where farms were too small, taxes too high, and industry too limited. Social and cultural discrimination by Russians or by Polish and Hungarian officials within the Austrian Empire were also sources of discontent.

Although the immigrants came from an agricultural background, many gravitated toward urban areas where they could find immediate employment as unskilled laborers. Woonsocket and Providence were the state's two havens for Ukrainian settlement, with the much larger concentration in the Woonsocket area.

In religion, the majority of the Galician immigrants were Ukrainian Orthodox, though there were many Uniate Catholics (affiliated with Rome) as well. The latter were attached to the Ruthenian rite, in which priests were allowed to marry by virtue of an agreement with the pope in 1595. Today Rhode Island contains one Ukrainian Orthodox church and one Ukrainian Catholic church of the Ruthenian rite—both in Woonsocket, both dedicated to St. Michael, and both located on the same Woonsocket street. In 1955 St. John's Church was built on Public Street in Providence as a Ukrainian Orthodox mission, but a decline in its Elmwood neighborhood caused it to close in the late 1970s. Ukrainian parishes, whether Orthodox or Uniate, serve as cultural as well as religious centers for most of the four thousand Rhode Islanders of Ukrainian ancestry. This 1919 photo shows Father Basil Turula with Heritage School children and the First Communion class of St. Michael's Ukrainian Catholic parish, over which he presided as pastor from 1911 to 1920. Photo by Tenczar Studio, courtesy of Ivanne Hanushevsky.

The major Greek migration to Rhode Island began in the 1890s and continued until the mid-1920s, when it was curtailed by the National Origins Quota Acts. The search for economic opportunity was the main motive prompting the Greek exodus, as overpopulation and the depressed state of agriculture brought hardship to the rural peasantry. From 1898 to 1932 the records indicate that 4,201 Greek arrivals listed Rhode Island as their destination. A sizable number of these migrants returned permanently to their homeland, however, to fight in the Balkan Wars (1910-1914) and World War I.

The oldest and largest Greek settlement in Rhode Island was in Providence, on Smith Hill and in the residential areas bordering on the southern and western fringes of downtown. This community dates from the late 1890s. Most of these early immigrants were employed as either mill workers, foundrymen, or merchant seamen. Before long some enterprising members of the community established themselves as small businessmen in the restaurant, confectionery, and baking

trades. In 1905 these devout Providence Greeks founded a religious society, incorporated as the Church of the Annunciation in 1911. The congregation's first house of worship (formerly a Baptist church) was on Smith Street. When this facility became overcrowded, a new house of worship was constructed at 264 Pine Street. Shown here are this church's opening services, conducted by the Reverend Peter Mihailides on March 25, 1921, the one hundredth anniversary of Greek independence from the Turkish Empire. Father Mihailides (left center) served this parish with distinction until his death in 1955. The out-migration of the Providence Greek community to Cranston and Warwick in the 1950s and 1960s prompted the much-debated relocation of the Church of the Annunciation from Pine Street to its present site on Oaklawn Avenue in Cranston in 1968.

The second oldest Greek community in the state developed in Pawtucket and Central Falls, where its members worked in the local textile mills. In 1912 they built Assumption Greek Orthodox Church on

George Street in Pawtucket. This facility served the spiritual needs of the Blackstone Valley Greeks until 1961, when urban renewal forced its relocation to Wolcott Street. A schism in this church during the mid-1950s (now partially healed) resulted in the establishment of a small independent Greek church on Broadway in Pawtucket. Especially notable among the Greek Americans of this Blackstone Valley community are the Haseotes family, who established the highly successful chain of convenience stores which they called Cumberland Farms.

The youngest and smallest local Greek community is in Newport. Most of its original members were fishermen engaged in lobstering. By 1910 this community had 132 Greek-born residents, and as this number increased, a congregation was formed. After worshiping at various sites, they acquired their present church on Thames Street, which they dedicated to St. Spyridon. Photo (1921) from Church of the Annunciation: 75th Anniversary Celebration (1980) courtesy of Greg Demetrekas

Armenian immigrants had much in common with their Irish, Jewish, and Syrian-Lebanese neighbors. All of these groups fled to America to escape repression in their native land. For Armenia the transgressor was the Turkish Empire, which staged two brutal, large-scale massacres of the Armenian people in 1894 and 1915. To escape this persecution, many Armenians fled to other countries, including the United States. From 1898 to 1932, 6,375 Armenian refugees came to Rhode Island. Most settled in Providence, in such areas as the North End, Federal Hill, the West End, Olneyville, and, especially, Smith Hill. These immigrants found work in the city's factories or became grocers, dry-goods merchants, or produce peddlers. Their second- and third-generation offspring have shown strong upward socioeconomic mobility, and many are now found in the professional class. A good number of Armenians now reside in the suburbs, especially Cranston and Warwick.

Helping to maintain the cultural heritage of the Armenian people are the three Armenian religious congregations in Providence: Saints Sahag and Mesrob, on Jefferson Street overlooking the junction of Routes I-95 and 146; St. Vartanantz, on Broadway; and the Armenian Euphrates Evangelical (Congregational) Church, between Franklin and Fenner streets.

Local Armenians have erected this impressive memorial in the North Burial Ground to the million and a half of their people who perished in the Turkish genocide. Annually, on April 24, they commemorate that tragedy. Photo (April 27, 1981) courtesy of PJC

179

In the last decade of the nineteenth century, an Arab migration to America from the troubled Middle East began. Its source was Lebanon and Syria at the eastern end of the Mediterranean. Nearly 1,600 "Syrian" migrants from this area came to Rhode Island in the period 1898-1914, and another 1,000 settled in Fall River. By 1932, 2,434 had listed Rhode Island as their destination. This Arab migration was caused by overpopulation, primitive methods of agriculture, high taxation, lack of industrial development, religious discrimination by the Moslems, and the oppressive political restrictions within the Turkish Empire. Today the Rhode Island descendants of these early immigrants number about 4,000.

Although the general areas from which these migrants came are predominantly Moslem in religion, nearly all those who made the trek to America were Christians, some Orthodox and others affiliated with the Church of Rome. Based upon their form of religious worship, the Lebanese Catholic immigrants fall into two main groups—the Maronites and the Melkites.

Around the turn of the century a number of Maronite exiles came to Providence and settled in the Federal Hill area. The men found work as peddlers, laborers,

and, eventually, grocers and shopkeepers. Before long, because of the language barrier and because of a strong attachment to their ancient liturgical traditions, these Lebanese petitioned Bishop Matthew Harkins for their own national church. Responding with characteristic sympathy, Harkins established St. George's Maronite parish in a remodeled tenement house on America Street in May 1911.

According to one source, Melkite immigrants from the area around Damascus and Aleppo first arrived in Providence in 1902. After a brief stay they moved to Pawtucket, Central Falls, and Woonsocket in the Blackstone Valley. Their familiarity with silk manufacture (which was carried on extensively in the valley) and the French language (widely spoken in the valley, as it had been in their native Middle East) prompted their relocation.

To preserve their Melkite religious and cultural tradition, these Pawtucket and Central Falls Arabs requested their own national parish. Granting their request, Bishop Harkins dedicated this house of worship to St. Basil in October 1910. In 1921 the Reverend Timothy Jock, the Central Falls church's second pastor, established the first parochial school in any

American Melkite parish, an institution in which the Arabic language was studied daily, and in 1931 Jock founded a Melkite mission church (St. Elias) to serve the Syrian community of Woonsocket.

Two other groups within the local Arab-speaking community, distinguished by religion, are the parishioners of St. Mary's Antiochian Orthodox Church on High Street, Pawtucket, and those of St. Ephraim's Old Syrian (Assyrian) Church on Washington Street, Central Falls.

St. Mary's, whose parishioners arrived from Aleppo, Damascus, and Marrah, is in communion with the Greek church but takes its spiritual direction from the patriarch of Antioch and uses an Arabic liturgy. This congregation formed its religious society in 1910.

St. Ephraim's was founded by immigrants from Mosul and eastern Turkey, many of whom suffered with the Armenians in the Turkish massacres of 1894 and 1915. These immigrants established a religious education society in 1905 but did not open their church until 1926, about six years after this photo of their parish picnic was taken at Cullian's Farm in Berkeley. Photo (1920) courtesy of Eleanor A. Doumato

While some aliens—especially the British and the Germans—found skilled jobs in Rhode Island industry, the peasant migrants from Poland, Armenia, Portugal, the Ukraine, and Italy were not so fortunate. Many immigrant families, including their young children, endured great hardships to make ends meet in the aftermath of their arrival. This photo was taken by Lewis Hine, whose terse caption tells its story: "Overcrowded home of workers in cotton mill, Olneyville, Providence (R.I.). Eight persons live in these three small rooms, three of them are boarders; inner bedrooms are 9 x 8 feet, the largest room, 12 x 12 feet. Polish people. Property owned by the mill. Rent $4.50 a month." Photo (ca. 1910) courtesy of the Library of Congress

Of all the groups who composed the so-called New Immigration, the Italians have exerted the greatest impact upon modern Rhode Island, both because of their large number and because of their rapid rate of upward socioeconomic mobility. In 1932 some of these successful Italian-American businessmen and professionals, led by Judge Antonio Capotosto, formed the Aurora Civic Association on Broadway in Providence. In the words of Capotosto, the club "was formed exclusively by gentlemen.... The individual we desire is motivated by honest principles in life and genuinely strives to improve his family, himself, and the society in which he lives."

An indication of the upwardly mobile nature of the local Italian community can be derived from a mere recitation of the names and positions of those charter members of the Aurora Club (nearly all of whom were foreign stock) shown in this early photo. Sitting, left to right, are Gustavo Galassi, stone and tile manufacturer; Edmund Mauro, architect; Professor Alfonso DeSalvio, head of the Italian Department at Brown University; Judge Antonio A. Capotosto, justice of the Rhode Island Supreme Court; Vincent Sorrentino, president of Uncas Manufacturing Company; and John H. DiStefano, attorney. Standing, left to right, are Raphael Vicario, attorney; Felix Mirando, president of Imperial Knife; Joseph Mercurio, produce wholesaler; Louis Jackvony, attorney and later Rhode Island attorney general; and Raffaele Tortolani, jewelry manufacturer. Photo courtesy of Giulio Del Signore from Paul R. Campbell and Patrick T. Conley, The Aurora Club of Rhode Island: A Fifty-Year History (1982)

Matthew Harkins presided over the Diocese of Providence for more than one-third of its first century (1887-1921). This dignified prelate was renowned for his administrative ability, for his tact in handling immigrant assimiliation, for the establishment of ethnic parishes, for his efforts in the field of education (especially the founding of Providence College), and, perhaps above all, for the manner in which he extended the social and charitable apostolate of the Catholic Church.

This "bishop of the poor," as he was sometimes called, found two diocesan social agencies when he came to Providence from the Boston archdiocese in 1887. When he died, there were more than twenty such agencies, including Hospice St. Antoine, St. Joseph's Hospital, St. Vincent de Paul Infant Asylum, St. Francis Orphanage, Carter Day Nursery, St. Margaret's and St. Maria's homes for working girls, St. Raphael's Industrial Home and School, St. Clare's Home, and the House of the Good Shepherd. They were his legacy to the poor and the socially deprived. Thanks to Harkins, the Diocese of Providence provided more social services than the state itself in the years prior to the New Deal. In fact, Harkins administered so effectively that a visiting European priest in 1921 informed his superiors that "Providence is the pearl among the dioceses of the United States." Photo courtesy of the Providence College Archives

Founded in 1917 by Bishop Matthew Harkins and the Dominican Fathers of the Province of St. Joseph, Providence College today is primarily a four-year college of the liberal arts and sciences, with an undergraduate enrollment of approximately thirty-four hundred men and women. The college now conducts a school of continuing education, a summer school, and a graduate school offering advanced degrees in religious studies, business, biology, education, and history. Being the only college in the nation operated by the Dominican Fathers, it stresses scholastic philosophy and the theology of St. Thomas Aquinas in its undergraduate curriculum, though it is open to students of all creeds.

The college's ninety-two-acre campus in the Elmhurst section of Providence presently contains thirty buildings, the most notable of which are Harkins Hall (the administration building); Martin and Dominic halls, former nineteenth-century Italian villa-style residences that are listed on the National Register; the Phillips Memorial Library; and a new Dominican priory. Its "lower campus" is the former Charles V. Chapin Hospital.

The original purpose of the college—to provide higher education with a Christian perspective to aspiring young men from Greater Providence's Catholic immigrant community—is captured in this photo. This is the dedication mass offered at the doors of Harkins Hall on May 25, 1919. Photo (1919) courtesy of the Providence College Archives

Two of the state's most distinguished secondary schools are St. George's School in Middletown and Portsmouth Priory in the neighboring town of Portsmouth. St. George's is Episcopalian, the Priory Roman Catholic, but the schools otherwise have many similarities: both occupy beautiful campuses on the island of Aquidneck, both are nationally recognized college preparatory schools, both are considered exclusive, and both were founded by the same man—John Diman.

Father Diman (1863–1949), as he was called in his later years, was the Massachusetts-born son of the Reverend J. Lewis Diman, a Congregational minister, and the grandson of Byron Diman, a Bristol whaler and merchant who served as Rhode Island's governor in 1846–47. John Diman's association with Rhode Island began when his father became a professor of history at Brown University. Deviating from his father's religion during his college years, Diman became an Episcopal deacon, assigned to the parish of St. Columba in Middletown. In 1896 he founded St. George's in Newport and in 1901 moved it to its present site, and for nearly twenty years he guided the school's early growth and development. But Diman had intended to establish a school where boys of modest means could get a first-rate education, and this aim did not materialize at St. George's, which instead attracted an elite clientele.

In 1912, therefore, he founded and endowed an industrial training school in Fall River to teach vocational skills to the sons of mill workers. This facility, later incorporated into the public school system, survives today as the highly regarded Diman Vocational School.

After resigning from the headmaster's position at St. George's, the restless Diman traveled to Europe, where he worked with the Red Cross in World War I, and then enrolled in a Roman Catholic seminary for priests. After his 1921 ordination he entered the religious order of St. Benedict, which commissioned him to organize a school on land that it had acquired on the north end of Aquidneck Island. The result of this assignment was the founding of Portsmouth Priory in 1926. Father Diman presided as prior of this Benedictine school until 1940 and as headmaster until 1942, when he gave up his administrative duties to teach. He died on March 17, 1949. Photo (1940s) by Edward Thayer Munroe, courtesy of Portsmouth Priory

The buildup of local support for the Allied cause long preceded both Wilson's call to arms in April 1917 and even the German declaration of unrestricted submarine warfare on January 31, 1917. German blunders such as the invasion of neutral Belgium, acts of sabotage in the United States, the execution of nurse Edith Cavill, and the sinkings of the Gulflight, the Arabic, the Sussex, and (especially) the Lusitania, coupled with effective British propaganda, helped to turn the tide of public opinion towards England. Important also was the forging of powerful economic ties between American bankers, investors, and industrialists and the Allied nations, for whom our businessmen floated bonds and to whom they gave loans and extended credit for the purchase of war materiel.

Small wonder that the public responded so enthusiastically to Wilson's 1916 call for "preparedness." In Providence 52,542 persons (by Journal editor John Rathom's count) marched in the city's great six-and-a-half-hour Preparedness Parade of June 3, 1916. The marchers, led by Grand Marshal G. Edward Buxton, passed in review at City Hall, where this "living flag" composed of 1,560 school children

sang patriotic songs. A guard of honor consisting of more than 200 Civil War veterans served as the border of the flag. Photo (1916) courtesy of RIHS (Rhi x3 355)

Despite Rhode Island's large Irish-American population, the state responded enthusiastically to President Wilson's April 1917 call to rescue England and France from alleged German aggression, or, as the high-minded president phrased it, "to make the world safe for democracy." Local sentiment for intervention on behalf of the Allied powers was conditioned in part by the Anglophilic Providence Journal, *whose dynamic and outspoken Australian-born editor, John R. Rathom, has been accused by some of being* an English agent.

As in the Civil War and the Spanish-American War, the Dexter Training Grounds became a site for the drilling and assembling of troops. In this World War I military scene, however, there is one significant addition. On the skyline to the left of the photo is the Cranston Street Armory, built in the design of a late Victorian castellated fortress in 1907–8 (M. J. Houlihan, contractor; W. R. Walker and Son, architects). Photo (July 25, 1917) courtesy of RIHS (Rhi x3 2874)

In 1911 Admiral Stephen Luce, founder of the Naval War College, wrote in a national journal that "Naragansett Bay...is the greatest strategical point of naval rendezvous north of the Cape of Virginia." He added prophetically that the bay "seems to have been intended by nature for a permanent naval base of the first order." In this photo, taken just after the outbreak of World War I, Luce's vision is realized; navy recruits drill on Coasters Harbor Island, with the War College and Naval Training Station buildings in the background. Today Newport remains the navy's premier educational center, though the size of its home fleet has been greatly diminished. Photo courtesy of the Naval War College Museum

Prior to the era of the talking movie the most exciting form of popular theatrical entertainment was vaudeville, and the most exciting of all vaudevillians was George M. Cohan. Born in Providence on July 3, 1878, to variety performers Jerry and Nellie (Costigan) Cohan, George joined his sister Josie and their parents on stage well before he reached his teens. In the 1890s the four Cohans left the local circuit for Broadway, where Cohan went on to become the most successful theatrical producer in America, as well as a notable actor and playwright and one of the best-known songwriters of his time.

In the course of his fifty-five years in show business, Cohan composed more than five hundred songs. During World War I his patriotic music—including "Over There," "You're a Grand Old Flag," and "Yankee Doodle Boy"—lifted the country's morale, earned him national renown, and won accolades from President Wilson. In 1940 Congress belatedly awarded Cohan a gold medal for writing "Over There," calling the piece the unofficial anthem of World War I. Montage of Cohan and his patriotic music, courtesy of RIHS (Rhi x3 5750)

Your Song—My Song—Our Boys' Song
OVER THERE

With Both English and French Text as sung by
ENRICO CARUSO

PHOTO © 1918
LIFE PUB. CO.

WORDS AND MUSIC BY
GEORGE M. COHAN

POPULAR EDITION
LEO. FEIST INC. NEW YORK
HERMAN DAREWSKI MUSIC PUBLISHING CO. LONDON ENG.

On February 12, 1919, just three months and a day after the armistice and at a time when Wilson was in Paris hammering out the final draft of his League of Nations covenant, the Rhode Island doughboys paraded triumphantly through a victory arch on Exchange Place (shown here) to the cheers of a grateful and admiring citizenry.

During the war those on the home front had responded vigorously to four Liberty-loan campaigns, contributed to several Red Cross drives, and sponsored relief programs for such war-ravaged groups as French orphans, Jewish noncombatants, and Armenian and Syrian refugees. They also worked in Rhode Island's many factories producing war materiel and they planted victory gardens like this plot in Lincoln behind Albion School (top).

On the fighting front the state contributed 28,817 troops, of whom 612 died. Many of those fatalities succumbed not to German gas or bullets but to the Spanish influenza, a dread virus that was carried from the battlefront to Rhode Island by returning soldiers. This deadly infection took 941 lives in Providence during 1918. Most of its victims were in the prime of life—twenty to forty years of age—and in a sense they were remote casualties of the war. Photo of Exchange Place courtesy of PPL; photo of victory garden courtesy of Margaret Scallin from Once in a Hundred Years: A Pictorial History of Lincoln, R.I. (1971)

In 1921 Rhode Island textile mill owners attempted to combat the postwar deflation by imposing a 22½ percent wage cut on their employees. Used to such wage manipulation in previous deflationary periods, the workers acquiesced. In 1922, however, as economic conditions worsened, the owners poured salt on the workers' wounds when they decreed an additional 20 percent wage cut and increased the weekly hours of work from forty-eight to fifty-four. Such harsh measures caused rebellion, and angry operatives struck the mills in the Blackstone and Pawtuxet valleys. When violence threatened, Yankee Republican leaders pressured Franco-American governor Emery J. San Souci to call out the National Guard. An ensuing skirmish between these citizen soldiers and Pawtucket demonstrators left one mill hand dead and fourteen wounded.

Despite such use of force the workers remained adamant, and they continued so though employers sought and secured antilabor injunctions and evicted strikers from their company housing. By late 1922 the Amalgamated Textile Workers Union operating in the Pawtuxet Valley and the AF of L-affiliated United Textile Workers in the Blackstone Valley had averted the second cut and had actually regained some of the first wage reduction. On the workers' demand for a forty-eight-hour week, however, management remained unyielding. A forty-eight-hour bill was sponsored in the General Assembly by the minority Democrats, but the Republicans defeated it, despite massive popular demonstrations in its favor. Not until 1936, after the Democrats had seized power in the state, did the legislature pass a forty-eight-hour law.

The Republican administration's use of the National Guard against the workers, together with the GOP's opposition to the forty-eight-hour bill, prompted a large-scale defection from Republican ranks by Franco-American workers, a rift in the old political and economic alliance between the Yankee Republican mill owners and their Franco-American work force that the Irish were quick to exploit. In November 1922 Democrat William S. Flynn won the governorship with Woonsocket firebrand Felix Toupin as his victorious running mate. Photo montage of Journal headlines (February 21, 1922) and the striker's funeral at St. Patrick's Church in Valley Falls from Paul Buhle et al., A History of Rhode Island Working People *(1983)*

Headlines from the Evening Bulletin *and the* Providence Journal *on February 21, 1922. Casket of Joas Assuncao is carried from St. Patrick's Church, Valley Falls.*

The Great Textile Strike of 1934 has been called by one knowledgeable historian "the most dramatic single illustration of the tragic long-term decline of the textile industry, the economic base supporting much of Rhode Island's working class since the middle of the nineteenth century." In ten years—1923 to 1933—the number of cotton textile wage earners in the state had shrunk from 33,933 to 13,077. Despite the efforts of Roosevelt's NRA, the textile industry remained in distress, and worker complaints of wage cuts, plant shutdowns, and sudden layoffs led to rising militancy. At this juncture the rapidly growing United Textile Workers Union called upon its members nationwide to strike.

On September 3, 1934, the scheduled walkout began to affect mills throughout Rhode Island. By the second week of the strike, tensions between workers and owners erupted into open conflict in the Social District of Woonsocket and the Lincoln village of Saylesville. On September 10 rioting and physical destruction of property reached such levels that Democratic governor Theodore Francis Green mobilized the National Guard and made a request (unanswered) for federal troops. The Journal headline on September 12 told the tragic story: "Guardsmen fire in Saylesville; pickets, sympathizers, and hoodlums run wild in Woonsocket, destroy property in Social district; six shot" (one of whom died). This photo shows the National Guard gassing Saylesville demonstrators. Fortunately the rioting ended swiftly on September 13 and order was restored. Ten days later, after President Roosevelt appointed a national fact-finding commission to address textile workers' grievances, the UTW called off the strike.

On October 2 the Democrats renominated Green for governor, and one month later he won by a plurality greater than the one that had elected him in 1932. In 1922 the use of National Guardsmen had severely hurt the GOP; twelve years later the deployment of similar force in a labor uprising had no detrimental effect upon the Democrats. This anomaly may be explained by several factors: workers were well aware of Green's prolabor sentiments and the labor planks in the 1934 Democratic platform; the governor acted only when violence had become otherwise uncontrollable; and he managed to convince most workers that the rioting and destruction of property were the handiwork of Communist agitators. Somehow Green succeeded in projecting a dual image, both as a protector of public order and as a long-time friend of the working class. The latter image, at least, was reinforced by a litany of social legislation enacted by Green and his party once they gained control of state government via the Bloodless Revolution of January 1935. Photo from Paul Buhle et al., A History of Rhode Island Working People (1983)

Child labor was a long-standing abuse in industrial Rhode Island. Many of Samuel Slater's first employees ranged in age from seven to twelve; according to an 1830 enumeration, 55 percent of the state's mill workers were children. Whole families toiled in Rhode Island's textile plants, pooling their income in an attempt (often vain) to escape to a better life. As employees, children were harshly treated and subject to corporal punishment by their overseers. Many were injured or mutilated by the incessantly moving, voracious machinery at which they worked.

A 1910 census revealed that only 48 percent of Rhode Island children attended school on a systematic basis. Most of the rest, like these cardroom hands in a Lonsdale mill, toiled up to fifty-four hours straight time in buildings that were poorly ventilated and subject to extremes in temperature. Not until 1938, with the passage of the federal Fair Labor Standards Act, was this abuse of child

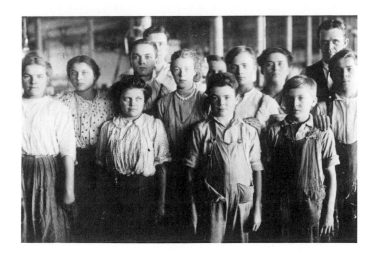

labor finally eliminated.

This photo is one of thousands taken by Lewis W. Hine (1874–1940), a noted documentary photographer who recorded New England immigrant life in the pre-World War I era as part of his work for

the National Child Labor Committee. Hine photographed in dozens of mill towns, concentrating on those where child labor and slum conditions were prevalent. Photo by Lewis Hine (ca. 1910) courtesy of RIHS (Rhi x3 5745)

Women have always been a major component of Rhode Island's industrial work force. In the state census of 1905, women made up 28 percent of all those over thirteen years of age who were gainfully employed, and they were mainstays of the two principal areas of manufacturing endeavor, textiles and jewelry. Of the 22,349 cotton mill operatives, 12,249 were female. By custom (rather than law) they worked a forty-eight-hour week, straight time. Woman workers, such as these dutiful operatives at Pawtucket's Royal Weaving Company, were then

regarded as a relatively docile labor force.

By 1920, however, women got the vote and were soon affected by the revolution in manners and morals that occurred during the Roaring Twenties. When the textile mill owners attempted to shift the economic burden of the postwar recession to their female employees by lengthening their work week to fifty-four hours, the women rebelled and zealously embraced the union movement. A few even turned to socialism as a panacea for society's economic ills. Here Ann Burlak, a youthful organizer for the militant National

Textile Workers Union, addresses a throng of workers at a Pawtucket rally on July 12, 1931, in the depths of the Great Depression. At this time she was free on bail, having been charged with throwing pepper into the eyes of a Central Falls policeman during a labor demonstration. Known as the Red Flame—for the color of her hair and the coloring of her economic philosophy—Ann Burlak symbolized the changing role of women in the workplace. Photo of Royal Weaving Company (ca. 1900) courtesy of RIHS (Rhi x3 487); photo of Ann Burlak courtesy of PJC

This author's choice for the Rhode Island male athlete most proficient in his chosen sport is Napoleon Lajoie (right). "The Big Frenchman," as Lajoie was called, was born in Woonsocket in 1875, the son of French-Canadian immigrants. His baseball accomplishments made him a national sports attraction for a generation and the idol of Franco-American youth. Beginning his professional career in Fall River in 1896, he soon ascended to the major leagues, where he immediately became a star. Over a twenty-year span, during which he played second base for three major league teams, Lajoie compiled a lifetime batting average of .339. He led his league in batting three times, his .422 average in 1901 being the second highest in modern major league history. An excellent fielder and a swift runner, he also proved his managerial ability as player-manager of the Cleveland Indians from 1905 to 1909. Lajoie was elected to the Baseball Hall of Fame in 1937, its second year of existence, having been preceded in this honor by only five baseball immortals.

Lajoie is one of three Rhode Island natives inducted into the Hall of Fame. He was joined by Hugh Duffy (1866-1954) of Cranston, whose 1894 season average of .438 is still the major league record, and Charles "Gabby" Hartnett (1900–1972) of Woonsocket and Millville, Massachusetts, who made his debut with the Chicago Cubs in 1922 and played with them for a nineteen-year span that included four World Series. A fine defensive player and an excellent hitter, Gabby led National League catchers seven times in fielding percentage and six times in home runs. A fourth Hall of Famer, Frank Frisch ("the Fordham Flash"), retired to South County prior to his death in 1973. Photo courtesy of RIHS (Rhi x3 5751)

In the fall of 1926 Rhode Island sports fans thrilled to the exploits of the Iron Men. This was the nickname given to the great Brown football team of that year, a team that shut out Yale and Dartmouth on successive Saturdays without a single substitution and then shut out Harvard two games later with no replacements until the final two minutes of play.

During the 1926 season this Tuss McLaughry-coached team rolled up 223 points while holding the opposition to 36. The only blemish on Brown's 9-0-1 record was a 10-10 tie with Colgate in the season's finale. For their efforts the Iron Men were voted (with Navy) the mythical cochampions of the East. Photo (1926) courtesy of RIHS (Rhi x3 4638)

While Brown was creating a legend on the college football scene, a professional football team in Providence also entered the record books. Founded by Journal sports editor Charles B. Coppen in 1916, the Providence Steam Roller played regional teams at Melrose and Kinsley parks before moving to Peter Laudati's Cyclodrome stadium on North Main Street in 1925. In that year the team went big-time when general manager Coppen, treasurer James E. Dooley, and secretary Peter Laudati entered the Steam Roller (shown at left) in the National Professional Football League. In its first NFL season the Steam Roller beat the formidable Chicago Bears (shown at right) by a score of 9 to 6. Coached by Jim Conzelman, a Helms Hall of Famer, the team won the national championship in 1928, compiling an 8-1-2 record that included victories over the New York Giants, the New York (football) Yankees, and the Detroit Wolverines, and a tie with the Green Bay Packers.

The Steam Roller team fielded several local players who became civic leaders in later years. Halfback Jack Cronin was longtime coach at LaSalle Academy (1927-1972) and director of the Providence Recreation Department; lineman Orland Smith became a highly respected physician; and diminutive quarterback Curley Oden from Brown served for twenty-five years as chief investigator for the state Department of Attorney General.

The Steam Roller abandoned major league football in 1931 but continued as a sandlot team until 1948. Photo (1925) courtesy of RIHS (Rhi x3 1737)

One of Rhode Island's most notable amateur athletes of the early twentieth century was Ellison Myers "Tarzan" Brown (1914-1975), from the South County village of Alton. Of Narragansett Indian stock, Brown first attracted attention for his running feats at the annual Indian powwows. Local track coach and promoter Thomas "Tippy" Salimeno responded to stories of Tarzan's amazing long-distance running prowess by taking the tall Indian youth under his tutelage. Brown not only won his first AAU-sanctioned race—a ten miler in and around Central Falls—but also set a record for that event. In 1936, after numerous victories in regional distance events, he was chosen a member of the U.S. Olympic team. His performance in Berlin, however, was a disappointment, as he ran far back in the field of world-class marathoners.

Upon returning to America, Brown vowed to erase public memory of his Olympic off day. He promptly entered seven marathon races in close succession and won them all. Two of these races—one in New York, the other in New Hampshire—were run within twenty-four hours of each other, making Tarzan's feat one of the most memorable in the annals of distance running. In 1939 he won the famed Boston Marathon in a record time of 2 hours, 28 minutes, 51 seconds, eclipsing the existing Olympic and world records in that grueling event. With the Olympics canceled by war and no more worlds to conquer, Brown hung up his running shoes and retired by the age of thirty.

In addition to Tarzan Brown, Rhode Island has produced several other track and field Olympians: Norman Taber (1912), an American record holder in the mile run; John Collier (1928), bronze medalist in the high jump; Bob Bennett (1948), bronze medalist in the hammer throw; and Janet Moreau (1952), a gold-medal winner in the women's 400-meter relay.

Though not an Olympian, Leslie Pawson of Pawtucket was Brown's great rival in the marathon. Pawson had three victories in the Boston Marathon to his credit, including a record-breaking effort of 2 hours, 31 minutes, 1 second in 1933—his first Boston triumph. Photo (1933) courtesy of the Westerly Sun

191

Glenna Collett Vare (at left in this photo) is this author's choice for Rhode Island's greatest female athlete. This Providence native began her illustrious golfing career in 1917 at East Providence's Metacomet Country Club when she was fourteen years of age (and already proficient in tennis, diving, and swimming). By 1922 she had won her first U.S. Women's Golf Championship at White Sulphur Springs, Virginia. In 1924—at the height of America's Golden Age of Sports—she played sixty matches and won an incredible fifty-nine. After winning four more U.S. championships and sharing the national limelight with golf immortal Bobby Jones, she married Edwin Vare, a wealthy Philadelphian, in 1931, gave birth to two children, took up trapshooting and such noncompetitive pursuits as needlepoint, and played less tournament golf. Her competitive drive and her love for this sport, however, prompted a brief but historic comeback. In 1935 she dueled youthful hometown favorite Patty Berg (right) at the U.S. championships in Minneapolis. On the thirty-fourth hole of play Glenna dropped a long putt to clinch her sixth national championship—more than any other golfer before or since.

In 1985 Mrs. Vare teed off in her sixty-second straight Point Judith Invitational Tourney, carrying a respectable handicap of fifteen. Each year the Ladies' Professional Golfing Association awards the Vare Trophy to the touring player with the lowest scoring average, a continuing testimony to this living legend of women's golf. Photo (1935) courtesy of Wide World Photos

In 1930, as the United States prepared to defend the America's Cup for the fourteenth time, the New York Yacht Club shifted the race site to the waters off Rhode Island, with Newport as the land base. Four racing sloops had been recently built, two of them—the Enterprise and the Weetamoe—by the Herreshoffs. These boats battled in the trials against the Resolute, the successful 1920 defender, and the Vanitie. By early September the Enterprise and the Weetamoe had forged ahead of the pack, with the former a little better on the windward legs and the latter (named for the squaw sachem of the Pocassets) slightly faster while reaching or running.

Eventually Enterprise got the nod, and in a series of four straight races, commencing on September 13, the Bristol boat decisively defeated Sir Thomas Lipton's Shamrock V. Then, according to a local newspaper account, "the crowds of visitors that had thronged Thames Street all summer left, and Newport's hectic season was over." Photo of Enterprise vs. Shamrock V (1930) from Harold S. Vanderbilt, Enterprise: The Story of the Defense of the America's Cup in 1930 (1931)

In a May 18, 1934, special election, approximately 75,000 of the state's 300,000 eligible voters gave their approval by a 4-to-1 margin to a statewide statute legalizing pari-mutuel betting on horse racing. Immediately thereafter Walter O'Hara (inset), a business whiz who started his money-making endeavors as a newsboy and a child laborer in a Fall River textile mill, formed the Narragansett Racing Association. Using 1,825 laborers, on June 2 the association began the whirlwind construction of a first-class track on the grounds of the What Cheer Airport, which straddled the Pawtucket-East Providence boundary line.

By August 1, 1934, a scant seventy-four days after the racing referendum, the facility was completed, and Narragansett Park opened its betting windows to a crowd of nearly 38,000 (the opening-day handle was in excess of $350,000). The new track—which included a large grandstand, a railroad spur, and twenty-two stables to accommodate 1,002 horses—attracted national media attention. The Baltimore Sun, the journal of the then famous H. L. Mencken, hailed the $1.2 million facility as "the showplace of the North; one of the finest tracks in the country."

During its early years "Gansett" (shown here) furnished the state with ample tax revenues (about 11 percent of the state's tax yield in the mid-1930s) while attracting some of the nation's leading horses and jockeys. Its most famous episode occurred on September 19, 1942, when Alsab beat Triple Crown winner Whirlaway before a record crowd in one of the most famous match races in the annals of American sport.

On September 29 of the previous year Rhode Island had acquired a second track when the Burrillville Racing Association opened a rival facility in Pascoag on the site of the former Burrillville Trotting Park. This latter operation moved to Lincoln in July 1947.

During the 1970s both Narragansett Park and Lincoln Downs fell upon hard times as diminished public interest in thoroughbred racing led to lower handles. Competition from dog racing and legalized lotteries, a decline in each track's physical plant, and their consequent inability to attract the better horses, also contributed to their demise. Lincoln discontinued horse racing in August 1976 and became a dog track in June of the following year; once-beautiful Narragansett Park conducted its last race on September 4, 1978, and is now being transformed into an industrial and commercial complex. Photo of O'Hara courtesy of the Rhode Island Yearbook Foundation; photo of Narragansett Park (ca. 1940) courtesy of PPL

Vanity Fair was the state's most ambitious amusement park of the early twentieth century. It stood on the East Providence side of the bay opposite Kirwin's Beach. As conceived, it would have been more grandiose than Rocky Point or Crescent Park, and it was closer than either to such centers of population as Providence, Pawtucket, and Central Falls. Its plan was not the usual loose organization of attractions along a midway but a formal axial arrangement of buildings fronting a lagoon and terminating in a spectacular ride called Shoot the Chutes (shown here). The promotion plans called for forty acres of such diverse entertainment as rides, circus acts, and Wild West shows. Thus completed, the park would have been an early twentieth-century version of Disneyland.

When it opened in 1907, however, Vanity Fair was more modest than its original plans envisioned, largely because of nearby residents' objections, and its gate receipts also fell far short of its promoters' expectations. By 1908 further construction

ceased; by 1910 the operation filed for bankruptcy; and by 1912 the park had closed for good. The Standard Oil Corporation of New York (Socony) purchased the

site in 1915 and proceeded to convert it into a tank farm and oil-import facility, a use it still serves today. Postcard view (1908) courtesy of RIHS (Rhi x3 5746)

The early twentieth century marked the heyday of one of the state's most popular recreation sites—Rhodes-on-the-Pawtuxet. In the 1870s bakemaster Thomas Rhodes had opened a boat-rental and clambake pavilion on his ancestral property along the Pawtuxet River. As the spot grew increasingly popular, his three sons (incorporating as the Rhodes Brothers in 1898) enlarged and diversified the facilities available to the public, building a casino for dancing to the music of the Edward Fay orchestra and then constructing a new boathouse. This expansion encouraged the formation of several canoe clubs, and by 1914 a local newspaper observed that "next to the Charles River in

Boston, it is quite probable that there are more canoes on the Pawtuxet River than any other American river of comparable size."

A February 1915 fire destroyed the old dance hall, but by midsummer the present casino had been constructed and had opened as the "Palais du Dance" with ten thousand revelers in attendance. In the years following, especially during the big-band era between the world wars, Rhodes was Rhode Island's most popular ballroom, attracting the orchestras of Glenn Miller, Paul Whiteman, Guy Lombardo, and many other well-known musical performers. Arthur, the last of the Rhodes Brothers, held his inaugural ball

there in 1925 when he became mayor of Cranston.

Canoeing declined in the 1930s, and following World War II interest in ballroom dancing also diminished. In 1960 Rhodes heirs sold the facility to the Palestine Temple (Shriners), which has rented the casino since that time for political fund-raisers, antique shows, and special entertainment events, including big-band performances. Unfortunately all the auxiliary buildings on the site, such as the boathouses shown here, have been destroyed by fire or vandals. Postcard view (1915) courtesy of RIHS (Rhi x3 2743)

Kirwin's Beach, Providence, R. I.

The Washington Park Yacht Club, Edgewood Beach, and Kirwin's Beach were located side by side just to the south of Field's Point at the Providence-Cranston city line. The Metropolitan Park Commission, a state environmental agency created in 1904, acquired the Edgewood Beach Reservation in 1909 by the power of eminent domain, condemning land belonging to Rhode Island Hospital and formerly used for a quarantine station. It promptly graded the site and filled in the marshy areas with sand.

These facilities were bordered on the south by a small strip of beachfront land and some bathhouses operated by John Kirwin. Steamers for Crescent Park and Riverside left Kirwin's dock at frequent intervals during the summer months.

As this postcard shows, these city beaches drew large crowds—as many as fifteen thousand people a day, according to the 1910 report of the Metropolitan Park Commission. By the early 1920s, however, expansion of the port and pollution of the bay had spelled doom for these recreational attractions. Postcard by Charles Seddon, courtesy of RIHS (Rhi x3 4607)

Despite its dense population and urban-industrial character, many areas of early twentieth-century Rhode Island retained their distinctly rural flavor. One-room schoolhouses, like Middletown's Peabody School (top left) and Little Compton's Number 9 school on Long Highway (bottom left), dotted the rural landscape, and Protestant fundamentalists like the members of Exeter's Liberty Baptist Church (top center) dominated rural religious life.

Farming was the major occupation of these areas; hunting and fishing were the principal year-round diversions. Here (bottom right) a group of Foster residents pose prior to a fox hunt, and (top right) a solitary farmer mows his field in the Limerock section of Lincoln near the site of the famous limestone quarries, which have been worked continuously by the Harris and Dexter families since the 1640s. Photo of Peabody School interior (1902) courtesy of Priscilla B. Peckham from Samuel Greene Arnold, An Historical Sketch of Middletown, R.I. (1876, rev. ed. 1976); photo of Number 9 school (1907) from George E. Stretch (ed.), Three Centuries: Little Compton Tercentennial, 1675–1975 (1975); photo of Liberty Baptist Church (1912) from Florence P. Simister, A Short History of Exeter, Rhode Island (1978); photo of fox hunt (1910) from Foster, 1781–1981 (1981); photo of Limerock farmer (ca. 1920) from Once in a Hundred Years: A Pictorial History of Lincoln, R.I., 1871–1971 (1971)

The influx of Catholic immigrants to the urban areas of the state aroused nativist resentment, and during the 1920s that hostility found expression through the agency of the Ku Klux Klan. The first Klan had been a purely Southern, antiblack phenomenon of the Reconstruction era. The second Klan, dating from 1915, was not only anti-Negro but also against foreigners, Catholics, and Jews, and it was national in scope. Klan activity appeared in the state in 1923, peaked in the following year, and then gradually died away in the early thirties.

In Rhode Island the Klan was mainly a rural phenomenon demonstrating the resentment and antagonism that agrarian, Republican, Protestant, old-stock Rhode Islanders felt toward the increasingly numerous and influential urban ethnics. Cross burnings and camp meetings—such as the 1927 Georgiaville gathering shown here—occurred in many small outlying towns. But Providence did not escape the contagion; Klan rallies were held also in Washington Park, and in January 1925 a thousand people attended a public dinner-dance held by the Providence County Klanton at Rhodes-on-the-Pawtuxet.

The most spectacular incident involving the local Klan was its infiltration of the Providence First Light Infantry Regiment. According to a Providence Journal exposé and a subsequent legislative investigation, nearly two hundred officers and men of this state militia group were Klan members, and recruiting for both organizations was carried on simultaneously. Photo (1927) courtesy of PJC

In Rhode Island, with its large foreign-stock population, the forces of Prohibition were weak, for that movement was mainly a rural, old-stock American crusade. Yet the battle between "drys" and "wets" was another aspect of the rural-vs-urban antagonism that plagued the state in the early half of the century. In 1919 the Eighteenth Amendment was adopted, but no thanks to Rhode Island; not only did the General Assembly vote against ratification (one of just two state legislatures to do so), but it also instructed the attorney general to challenge Prohibition's legality.

Such protests were unavailing, and so the police, sometimes reluctantly, cracked down on bootleggers (as the violators of Prohibition were called). Because of Rhode Island's geographical position, enforcement of Prohibition was doubly difficult. Illegal booze could arrive not only overland but also by sea, in the ships that came to be called the "rum fleet." This large flotilla of speedboats and schooners made nightly runs into the scores of estuaries and coves along the bay, delivering their cargoes to accomplices who either stored them in secret warehouses or sped the whiskey, rum, and gin to speakeasies in Newport, Providence, and the Blackstone Valley in their Packard twin-six touring cars. As in pre-Revolutionary days and in today's drug trade, such smuggling was widespread. Here the U.S. Coast Guard destroyer Beale bears down upon a rum-running sloop that had picked up an illegal cargo from a foreign vessel off the Rhode Island coast but outside U.S. territorial waters.

Eventually the nation came to see the wisdom of Rhode Island's position. On December 12, 1933, Prohibition was repealed by the adoption of the Twenty-first Amendment. In the local referendum on May 1, 1933, which preceded Rhode Island's ratification of that constitutional change, the electorate overwhelmingly rejected the Prohibition experiment by a vote of 150,289 to 20,926. Photo courtesy of the National Archives.

City Hospital (shown here), built at the urging of Providence superintendent of health Charles V. Chapin (inset) to care for those with contagious diseases, opened in 1910. It eventually consisted of several buildings situated on twenty-five acres of land and had a two-hundred-bed capacity. A leading scholarly study by Dr. Charles Winslow, entitled The Conquest of Epidemic Disease, *asserts that Chapin developed the Providence City Hospital as "the first institution on this side of the water [the Atlantic] to apply the new conception that germ diseases were not air-borne but spread by contact." The hospital became a model for similar institutions across the United States. Appropriately, the facility was renamed for Chapin upon his retirement.*

In 1966, after fifty-six years of municipal service, the operation of the historic hospital was temporarily assumed by the state. Eventually, in December 1974, the site was acquired by Providence College, which remodeled Chapin Hospital extensively and made it the school's "lower campus."

During his long tenure as superintendent of health (1884–1932), Charles Chapin was Providence's premier public official, and his work in epidemiology and public health won international acclaim. In his famous study Sources and Modes of Infection *(1910), Chapin vigorously attacked outmoded medical and sanitary theories, among them the ideas that filth causes disease, that diseases are indiscriminately transmitted through the air,*

and that disinfection is a cure-all for sanitary evils. He concluded instead that the ordinary infectious diseases of temperate climates are spread principally through contact between persons.

Chapin served as president of the American Public Health Association (1926–27) and as the first president of the American Epidemiological Society (1927). His biographer, James H. Cassedy, says of Chapin that "he, probably more than anyone else, brought about a change in the image of the American health officer from that of political hack and chaser of smells to that of professional scientist." Photo of City Hospital (ca. 1915) courtesy of PPL; photo of Chapin courtesy of RIHS (Rhi x3 2393)

VALLEY VILLAGE OF ASHLAND
Mill sold at auction but houses are retained as quarters for construction crew. Its site is to be buried deep under water

Journal photos

The construction of the Scituate Reservoir was one of Rhode Island's most significant public works projects. The enterprise was begun in 1915 under the direction of Providence mayor Joseph H. Gainer and a seven-member commission known as the Water Supply Board, with Frank E. Winsor its chief engineer. The main reservoir was formed by damming the north branch of the Pawtuxet River at the village of Kent, which was inundated along with the hamlets of Ashland (shown here), South Scituate, Richmond Village, and Wilbur Hollow—a sacrifice of 375 homes. The Ashland dwellings served as quarters for the construction crews before the village, like a modern Atlantis, was buried beneath the waters. Ponagansett, another small settlement within the watershed, was abandoned. In addition to several dams and dikes, the project involved the building of a large aqueduct, a filtration plant, five supplementary reservoirs, and several pumping stations. It was completed in 1929.

Today the Scituate watershed covers 92.8 square miles, of which Providence owns 23.93—an area larger than the city itself. The reservoir system, with a capacity of more than 41 billion gallons, provides Greater Providence with water nationally recognized for its purity and quality. Photo of the inundated village of Ashland from the author's collection; photo of the building of the Kent Dam courtesy of RIHS (Rhi x3 5752)

The Providence business community's final burst of exuberance prior to grim years of depression was the Industrial Trust Building (now Fleet Bank Building), still Providence's highest structure. This impressive skyscraper, towering 420 feet above the street, was the pet project of Industrial's president Florriman M. Howe and chairman of the board Samuel M. Nicholson (of file company fame). These men wanted a headquarters befitting a bank that had become the state's largest by a series of mergers and acquisitions that included the absorption of the old Providence Bank (established 1791).

When completed in 1928, the Art Deco "set-back" skyscraper became the tallest in New England, far outstripping the highest buildings in Boston. This photo was taken from the vantage point of Union Station shortly after the high-rise structure was completed. Photo courtesy of PPL

The Mount Hope Bridge, completed in 1929, linked Bristol and Portsmouth, replacing a ferry that had operated between these two towns since 1698. Its main span of 1,200 feet made it the eighth largest suspension bridge in the world at the time of its construction. The 6,130-foot-long structure was also considered a masterpiece of engineering design and received the 1930 award of the American Institute of Steel Construction as the most beautiful bridge of its class. Originally the Mount Hope Bridge was privately maintained, but in 1955 a state-created authority assumed ownership.

In 1940 a second major bridge was erected, partially funded by a federal Public Works Administration (PWA) grant. This was the Jamestown Bridge, whose 646-foot main span connected North Kingstown and Jamestown across the bay's west passage. Whereas the Mount Hope Bridge has recently been refurbished, the obsolete Jamestown structure (total length 6,982 feet) is being replaced by a modern bridge.

Shown in this 1929 photo are workmen engaged in the stringing of cable along the Mount Hope Bridge's center span. Photo by Avery Lord, courtesy of RIHS (Rhi L866 694)

The Warwick village of Hillsgrove was named for Providence industrialist Thomas J. Hill, who founded the Rhode Island Malleable Iron Works in this section of Warwick in 1867 and had a railroad station located near the site of his foundry. From World War I onward, meadows to the southeast of Hillsgrove depot were used as an airplane landing field. As aviation technology improved to make commercial air freight and passenger service practical, several private airfields were established in Greater Providence, but metropolitan area businessmen were convinced that only a publicly owned and operated facility would attract major airlines to Rhode Island, and because of their urging the state decided to build a public airport. Warwick sought the facility and won what some residents now feel is a dubious prize.

With the Gaspee Point and Gaspee Plateau areas bypassed in favor of the inland but more spacious Hillsgrove, construction began in 1929. The Rhode Island State Airport, the first state-owned facility of its kind in the nation, was

opened and dedicated on September 26, 1931. On the following day two air shows were held there before a total of 150,000 spectators—reputedly the largest crowd to attend any public event in Rhode Island up to that time.

Shown in this 1940 composite postcard view is the original terminal and administration building (1932), now a National Register structure and the site of the U.S. Weather Service, and Hangar No. 1 (1938, altered 1953). Both buildings are located on Occupasstuxet (Airport) Road. Postcard view courtesy of RIHS (Rhi x3 5743)

A public works effort less striking than a bridge or a reservoir, but far more comprehensive, was the building program undertaken by the state government during the 1930s at the Howard complex in Cranston, the Dr. U. E. Zambarano Memorial Hospital in Burrillville, the Dr. Joseph H. Ladd Center in Exeter, and the veterans' home in Bristol.

The newly ascendant Democratic party demonstrated a zeal for social reform. Under the leadership of Governors Theodore Francis Green and Robert E. Quinn, a heavy outlay of federal Public Works Administration funds and state revenues was spent to expand and modernize the state's social institutions. In the years 1935–1938 eighteen buildings were constructed for the State Hospital for Mental Diseases (now the Institute of Mental Health), including these handsome Georgian Revival dormitories. In addition, three new buildings were erected for the State Infirmary and three for the Socka-nosset School for wayward boys. The appearance of Howard was dramatically altered by these new facilities, which not only furnished appropriate physical accommodations (at least temporarily) for patients, inmates, doctors, and attendants but also provided jobs for thousands during these years of economic depression.

Modern structures also rose at the Exeter State School for the Feeble-Minded (renamed in 1958 for Dr. Joseph H. Ladd, director from its founding in 1908 until his retirement in 1956) and at the Wallum

Lake tuberculosis sanitarium (renamed Zambarano Hospital in 1955 to honor Dr. Ubaldo E. Zambarano, noted specialist in tubercular disease). A joint federal-state effort—a "little New Deal"—transformed the state government's social role in the critical decade of the 1930s.

As remarkable as the health and welfare building boom were the legislative programs designed by the Democrats to assist the sick and underprivileged. Included among these programs was the first state health insurance law in America, enacted in 1942. Together, according to Howard medical superintendent Dr. Henry A. Jones, these efforts brought an end to "the dark days of social welfare" in Rhode Island. Photo by Warren Jagger from Cranston, Rhode Island, Statewide Historical Preservation Report (1980)

In the 1920s, with Brayton gone as a deterrent to reform, Democrats in the General Assembly pressed more vigorously for constitutional change that would give Providence and the other five cities their fair share of seats in the General Assembly. The Senate was so malapportioned that by 1915 Providence, with a population of 247,660, and West Greenwich, with 509, were equally represented. Another major constitutional grievance of the Democrats was the property-tax-paying requirement for voting in city council elections.

A highlight of the turbulent twenties, and one of the most bizarre episodes in the history of any state legislature, was the stinkbombing of the Senate in June 1924. At that stormy session the Democratic minority, led by Robert Quinn and Lieutenant Governor Felix Toupin, the presiding officer, staged a marathon filibuster to force weary Republicans to pass a constitutional convention bill that had already cleared the Democratic House. The strategy of Toupin (right) was to wear some of the elderly Republicans down and then call for a vote on the question when they snoozed or strayed.

In the forty-second hour of the filibuster, as the vigilant Democrats awaited the success of this scheme, Republican party

managers authorized some thugs imported from Boston to detonate a bromine gas bomb under Toupin's rostrum. As the fiery Woonsocket politician keeled over unconscious, senators scrambled for the doors. Within hours most of the Republican majority was transported across the state line into Massachusetts, where

Toupin's summons could not reach them. There they stayed (Sundays excepted) until a new Republican administration assumed office in January 1925.

Ironically, the defeat of the Democrats in the 1924 state elections was due in part to the fact that the Providence Journal wrongly accused them of the bombing. The newspaper had particular reason to discredit the Democrats that year, inasmuch as Jesse H. Metcalf, brother of the Journal's president, was the GOP candidate for U.S. Senate in the fall election against incumbent governor William S. Flynn. The paper's strategy worked.

This photo was taken in Rutland, Massachusetts, during the GOP senators' exile. In it six Republican lawmakers listen to the chaos of the Democratic National Convention of 1924, wherein urban ethnics led by Al Smith and agrarians backing William G. McAdoo created a deadlock not resolved until a compromise nominee was chosen on the 103rd ballot. Shown (left to right) are Senators Cole (Warren), with Peckham (Middletown) and Weaver (Richmond) over his shoulder; Sherman (Portsmouth); Littlefield (New Shoreham); and Evers (Cranston). Photo from David Patten, Rhode Island Story (1954)

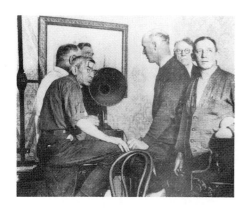

To stem the defection of Franco-Americans from the Republican party, Aram Pothier was summoned from retirement to battle Felix Toupin in the 1924 governor's race. With the Democrats unjustly blamed for the stinkbomb incident, Pothier and the GOP won a decisive victory. The turmoil that convulsed the state legislature in its 1924 session prompted the victorious Republicans who gained control of that body in the fall elections of 1924 to institute checks against the potential for such disruptions in the future.

When the new legislative session opened in January 1925, the Republicans promptly sponsored a bill creating a Department of State Police. Rising violence in labor disputes and the need to enforce a statewide auto code were also

motivating factors in the establishment of this first uniformed statewide law-enforcement agency.

Shortly after passage of the state police statute on April 2, 1925, Governor Pothier appointed Everitte St. John Chaffee of Providence as the department's first superintendent. Chaffee, a military man who had compiled a distinguished World War I record as an officer of the 26th "Yankee" Division, was given comprehensive administrative authority over the new agency, a power that all subsequent state police colonels have wielded.

Chaffee personally selected the first troopers, most of whom had military experience, and established a training camp for them at his twenty-acre summer home in South Kingstown. Within hours of setting up the camp, the department suffered its first fatality when trooper John Weber of Newport was killed in a motorcycle accident on Post Road. Weber was to be a member of the first state police motorcycle patrol, shown here. Photo (June 1925) from William F. Powers, In the Service of the State: The Rhode Island State Police, 1925–1975 (1975)

For the people of Rhode Island, the presidential campaign of 1928, pitting Democrat Al Smith against Republican Herbert Hoover, was among the most exciting ever. Smith, called by his biographers "the Hero of the Cities," appealed to the Catholic ethnic vote, and his candidacy hastened the conversion of local Italians and French Canadians to the Democratic party. When he beat Hoover statewide by a plurality of 1,451, the New York governor became the first Democratic presidential candidate to poll a majority of the state's popular vote since Franklin Pierce turned the trick in 1852.

In what the Providence Journal described as "the most stirring political campaign since the Civil War," Smith (center, with arm outstretched) had barnstormed the state in October, creating pandemonium. According to one newspaper account, "fire engines screeched, band instruments blared, torpedoes tossed by youngsters exploded, tickertape floated in a sinuous maze from the windows of all buildings, automobile horns blasted, shrill whistles and locomotives screamed, confetti and shredded newspapers descended in blinding drifts, and an airplane marked with words of welcome swooped an aerial salute as the governor's procession passed slowly along." Photo by H. Raymond Ball of Smith in northern Rhode Island, courtesy of RIHS (Rhi x3 5747)

Shown here with President Franklin D. Roosevelt is Democratic governor Theodore Francis Green (1867-1966). Green had backed Roosevelt's candidacy in 1932 when many local politicos had remained in the Al Smith camp. In that year Green was elected governor over incumbent Norman S. Case, a victory that came on his third try for the office after a long period of reformist activity in the politics of Providence and the state. A Yankee patrician who had taught Roman law at Brown, Green had served in the Spanish-American War and practiced law prior to winning a House seat from Providence in the Good Government campaign of 1906. After losing the governor's race in 1912 to popular Franco-American Aram Pothier, he became a charter member and then chairman of the prestigious Providence City Plan Commission.

During his two terms as governor, Green worked with fellow Democrats to bring a "little New Deal" to Rhode Island. He supported sizable job-relief programs, far-ranging labor legislation, and impor-

tant public works projects. On constitutional reform, however, he dropped the ball, and he sided with the public utility interests against Thomas McCoy and other local advocates of municipal ownership of gas and electric companies. In 1937 Green went to the U.S. Senate, where he gained three major distinctions during his twenty-four-year tenure: he brought the navy to Quonset Point, a coup resulting mainly from his early support of FDR; he chaired the Senate Foreign Relations Committee (1957-1959); and he became the oldest person ever to serve in the Congress of the United States.

Even closer to FDR than Green was Thomas Gardiner ("Tommy the Cork") Corcoran (1900-1981), a leading draftsman and lobbyist for much of the

legislation now labeled the New Deal. Recommended by his Harvard Law School professor Felix Frankfurter, Corcoran joined the New Deal "Brain Trust" and drafted such landmark laws as those creating the Securities and Exchange Commission, the Federal Housing Administration, the Tennessee Valley Authority, and the Fair Labor Standards Board. Corcoran, a Pawtucket-born son of an Irish immigrant, often entertained Roosevelt with Irish ballads as well as drafting some of the president's political speeches. For forty years after his retirement from government employ in 1940, Corcoran was one of Washington's most prominent and successful lawyer-lobbyists. Photo courtesy of Theodore Francis Green II

Thomas P. McCoy, "the Prince of Pawtucket," is regarded as Rhode Island's closest facsimile to a genuine machine politician. But he was much more than just a powerful political boss. During the 1920s McCoy compiled a distinguished record as a Democratic representative in the General Assembly. There he supported legislation beneficial to working-class ethnics and advocated reorganizing and streamlining state government and strengthening the office of governor. A populist, McCoy also urged other important constitutional reforms to increase public participation in the political process. In 1930 he ran unsuccessfully for lieutenant governor as Theodore Francis Green's Democratic running mate.

After the Democrats gained control of the Pawtucket city government in 1933, McCoy quickly established himself as city boss. Those who acted contrary to his will or attempted to limit his authority quickly found themselves without an official position from which to act.

Motivated by a desire for the governorship, during the mid-1930s McCoy made frequent sorties from his power base in Pawtucket against the state leaders of his own party. Each time he was soundly repulsed. Although he was an architect of the Bloodless Revolution of 1935 and, briefly, state budget director, his Democratic rivals were not willing to trust him with the reigns of state government, for they believed that if the Pawtucket chieftain were given the opportunity to control state patronage—a necessary factor in forging a statewide machine—their own positions would be in jeopardy.

By the late 1930s the influential Providence Journal had begun to view McCoy's bossism with disdain, and from then until his death in office in August 1945, the newspaper relentlessly pursued a campaign of vituperation to destroy him politically. The Journal was often joined in this endeavor by the Pawtucket Times.

With his public reputation tainted by frequent (and often valid) charges of election frauds, McCoy abandoned his statewide aspirations after 1940. Instead he contented himself with local power, insisting only that he be given his fair share of state patronage and that legislation that he demanded for Pawtucket be accepted by the state organization.

McCoy did much good for his native Pawtucket despite his unsavory tactics. His debt-refunding program, although carried

to an excess in later years, leveled off the city's annual debt-service payments and enabled the boss to lower the tax rate, a boon to both homeowners and businesses. Quick to perceive the benefits of Roosevelt's New Deal programs, McCoy sought and received millions of federal dollars for a host of city projects that served the dual

purpose of putting men to work and adding to the municipality's capital stock. These federally subsidized projects and the resulting patronage also helped McCoy strengthen his already powerful political machine. Photo (ca. 1940) courtesy of PJC

In the fall of 1937 Narragansett Park became the focal point of the bitter Democratic party factionalism that had vexed state politics since the Bloodless Revolution of January 1935 brought that hungry party to power. Flamboyant Walter E. O'Hara had made huge donations to both major political organizations and employed numerous state legislators and party regulars in lucrative part-time posts at the track. He repeatedly lobbied for more racing dates and sought to limit the state's take of the betting handle. Intensely partisan but highly principled, Robert E. Quinn (inset) resented what he viewed as O'Hara's baneful influence on state government. When Quinn succeeded Green as governor in January 1937, the stage was set for a showdown between these two extremely combative Irishmen.

Former newsboy O'Hara had acquired two newspapers (the Pawtucket Star and Peter Gerry's Providence Tribune), which he merged in 1937 to create the Star Tribune. When Quinn intensified state surveillance of the track's operation (with the enthusiastic backing of the moralistic Sevellon Brown's Providence Journal), O'Hara declared war on Quinn in the pages of the Star Tribune and strength-

ened his relationship with Mayor Thomas McCoy and House leader Harry Curvin, two of Quinn's intraparty rivals.

The smoldering resentments ignited on September 2, 1937, when O'Hara's guards beat up and forcibly ejected Journal reporter John Aborn from the track. Quinn ordered his supporters on the State Racing Commission to investigate O'Hara's long train of abuses and rescind his right to operate Narragansett Park. When the commission promptly complied, McCoy used his influence with the new state Supreme Court (he had secured the appointments of Francis Condon of Central Falls and Chief Justice Edmund Flynn) to have the racing commission's ruling quashed. Quinn countered by directing the commission to cancel Gansett's fall racing dates, but once again the high court blocked the move. Meanwhile O'Hara let loose a barrage of libelous charges against the governor.

"Battling Bob" Quinn refused to be deterred. First he filed a criminal libel action against O'Hara, and then, on October 16, 1937, one day after the second Supreme Court ruling and two days before the park was scheduled to open, he issued a proclamation declaring that the track and its environs were in a state of insurrection

justifying the establishment of martial law. Several hundred armed national guardsmen, such as those pictured here, joined with state police to cancel the fall meet. McCoy and Curvin, who doubled as Pawtucket's public safety director, dispatched the Pawtucket police, who wisely backed off.

Quinn won the battle, but the national embarrassment to Rhode Island caused by the "Race Track War" contributed to his defeat in 1938, when he ran ten thousand votes behind the remainder of the Democratic ticket. O'Hara suffered greater wounds: he was ousted as president and manager of the racing association by its stockholders; his newspaper went into receivership (after which the Journal acquired and destroyed much of the Star Tribune's equipment); and he was indicted for illegal use of corporate funds (though the charges were later dropped). In February 1941 O'Hara died on Route 44 in a spectacular head-on auto crash, ending his turbulent career. Photo of Quinn courtesy of the Providence College Archives; photo of National Guard troops from Zechariah Chafee, Jr., State House versus Pent House: Legal Aspects of the Race Track Row (1937)

Newport millionaire William H. Vanderbilt—an avid horseman and the eldest son of Alfred Gwynne Vanderbilt, who had perished with the Lusitania—rode to the rescue of the recently deposed Republican party in the 1938 election.

Helping Vanderbilt's candidacy was the nationwide recession of 1937, which shook public confidence in the New Deal, and the scandalous Race Track War, which severely hurt the image of Governor Quinn and the local Democratic party. Seizing the opportunity to regain power, the GOP nominated the honest, willing, prestigious, and politically naive Vanderbilt to battle Quinn. The socialite prevailed (167,003 to 129,603), leading a Republican landslide at every level, with one notable exception—the Pawtucket mayoralty, where Thomas McCoy actually increased his 1936 margin of victory. In fact, the boss polled

more ballots in some city districts than there were registered voters! Later, at a communion breakfast, while a state criminal probe of this phenomenon was under way, McCoy wryly explained the secret of his political survival: "We're politically sophisticated in Pawtucket. Elsewhere they use arithmetic to count votes; here we use algebra."

The righteous "boy governor" (he was thirty-six when elected) was determined to bring McCoy to justice. Though he secured the enactment of a state merit system law in 1939, Vanderbilt became ensnared in a wiretap controversy during his overzealous attempt to implicate McCoy in vote fraud, and in 1940 the Democratic tide rolled in once more—this time for a long stay. United States District Attorney J. Howard McGrath, who had made political hay with Vanderbilt's federally illegal wiretap,

won the governorship and took a giant step upward in a political career that would include several high national offices. Congressmen Aime J. Forand and John E. Fogarty also launched long and successful tenures in that 1940 campaign, as did Dennis J. Roberts, who became mayor of Providence under a new charter that strengthened the powers of that city's chief executive. For the Democrats, happy days were here for the first time since the early 1850s.

Meanwhile, a disillusioned, embarrassed, and bitter Vanderbilt rode off into the sunset, seldom returning to Rhode Island after his 1940 electoral defeat. Photo (1930s), by Avery Lord, of Vanderbilt driving his coach "Venture" on Oakland Farm, his Portsmouth estate, courtesy of RIHS (Rhi L866 339)

With the inauguration of Franklin D. Roosevelt in March 1933, voluntarism gave way to unprecedented peacetime involvement by the federal government in the economic order. The keystone of Roosevelt's early New Deal in the urban Northeast was the National Industrial Recovery Act of June 16, 1933, a measure designed to revive business activity and to reduce unemployment. It was based on the principle of industrial self-regulation through codes of fair competition framed jointly by the managers and workers of each industry in cooperation with the government.

Stressing a federal role in economic planning, this collectivistic approach was supervised by the National Recovery Administration (NRA). General Hugh S. Johnson, appointed by FDR as NRA director, embraced the blue eagle as the agency's symbol and sought to mobilize the workers behind the recovery effort by staging parades and demonstrations throughout the nation. The fact that the act guaranteed to labor the right "to organize and bargain collectively through representatives of their own choosing" heightened working-class enthusiasm.

On October 2, 1933, a massive six-and-a-half-hour NRA parade was held in Providence, where more than seventy thousand participants registered their faith in the Roosevelt program, vowing "We Do Our Part." Among the marchers were these children from the Candace Street School. Less than two years later a sick chicken brought the blue eagle to earth when the U.S. Supreme Court, in the case of Schechter Poultry v. United States, declared the NIRA unconstitutional for its excessive delegation of legislative power to the president. Photo (1933) courtesy of PJC

The depression that began with the great stock market crash of October 1929 reached its depths in 1932–33. President Hoover's relief policy, to which local Republicans subscribed, consisted of a decentralized approach whereby the federal government would merely provide direction to a voluntary effort by agencies operating on a self-help basis. The president's object was to "preserve the principles of individual and local responsibility."

Providence tried private voluntarism with the establishment of the Providence Emergency Unemployment Committee (PEUC) by local business leaders in the fall of 1930. This group quickly initiated a "buy-an-apple-and-help-the-unemployed" campaign that put apple vendors on the city's streets by Thanksgiving. After a year of valiant effort, however, the PEUC and its successor, the Providence Central Relief Committee, found that they could not cope with the city's massive unemployment, hunger, and destitution, though such private efforts continued nonetheless, especially those of the Catholic diocese and its St. Vincent de Paul societies.

Since Hoover's solution of private voluntarism was hopelessly inadequate, Providence, Pawtucket, and other hard-hit cities assumed the primary burden of relief. Providence mayor James Dunne and Edward P. Reidy, his competent director of the Department of Public Aid, proposed borrowing in anticipation of taxes to fund both direct grants to the needy and a city work-relief project providing jobs at parks, reservoirs, City Hall, Dexter Asylum, and other public facilities. Supplemented by loans from the state and, after 1933, by New Deal recovery programs, this approach would be followed for the duration of the depression.

In Pawtucket, Thomas McCoy combated the economic downturn by creatively manipulating municipal finances. Inheriting a burdensome debt from the Republicans, McCoy made significant progress in reducing it during his initial years as city auditor. He also refunded the debt as it matured in an attempt to defer payment until the economy recovered. This tactic allowed him to lower taxes dramatically and thus strengthen his popular appeal. During McCoy's tenure as city boss, Pawtucket constructed numerous federally subsidized projects, including a new and imposing city hall (above), a water filtration plant, a new high school (West, now Shea), and a stadium that now bears his name. Postcard view (ca. 1940) courtesy of RIHS (Rhi x3 5742)

As the New Deal evolved, reform of the socioeconomic system came to share the spotlight with relief and recovery efforts. The foremost reform statute was the Social Security Act of August 1935, which levied a tax for old-age and survivor's insurance, authorized money grants to the states to help them meet the cost of old-age pensions, provided funds to the state for the care of the handicapped and for deprived children, and established a cooperative federal-state system of unemployment compensation.

On January 3, 1938, the first jobless applicants were able to file claims under the Social Security Act. Statewide, 9,144 registered on that day and 13,043 more were given appointments to file on future dates. The longest unemployment line was this one at Providence's Cranston Street Armory, where 4,002 registrants were enrolled on opening day. Despite the myriad New Deal efforts, only war would restore employment to predepression levels. Photo(1938) courtesy of PJC

While still experiencing the Great Depression, and on the heels of the recession of 1937—both national catastrophes—Rhode Island suffered a more localized disaster, the great hurricane of 1938. This huge tropical storm, with winds in excess of 120 miles per hour, raced up the Atlantic coast with such forward speed (up to an incredible 70 miles per hour) that it caught the population by surprise. It hit Rhode Island at high tide on the afternoon of September 21. In downtown Providence a tidal wave flooded the business district to a depth of more than thirteen feet above mean high water, or seven feet above street level. Thousands of those starting home during the five o'clock rush hour stepped out into a storm that was at its peak. People were drowned in their attempt to escape the hurricane's fury, as autos were submerged by murky waters raging through the streets as if in search of victims. Others died or were injured when hit by falling trees, walls, signs, or chimneys, or by glass or other flying debris.

Hardest hit by wind and tidal wave were the residents of Rhode Island's coastal communities. Fortunately the state's summer colonies had been vacated, but year-round residents of the shore incurred a heavy loss of life. Physical destruction was without parallel in the state's history, as these photos indicate. Annawamscutt Beach in West Barrington (top) looked like a woodyard, as debris from demolished homes on the east shore mingled with the wreckage of houses carried across Narragansett Bay and deposited on the Barrington beach. The awesome power of the waves is indicated by the devastation of Narragansett Pier's famed Ocean Road (center). Here the fieldstone seawall was reduced to rubble, and the drive itself was broken up and swept onto the lawns that lined the waterfront. In Misquamicut (bottom) three stunned survivors sit amid the ruins of the Pleasant View Hotel. Not as lucky were the 311 other Rhode Islanders who perished in this monster storm. Photos from the Providence Journal Company, The Great Hurricane and Tidal Wave: Rhode Island, September 21, 1938 (1938)

Long-simmering World War II erupted on September 1, 1939, when Germany invaded Poland. As in the months following the outbreak of the First World War, Allied demands for American goods gave an impetus to the local economy. Eventually (though perhaps not inevitably), the United States was drawn into the conflict, and as in World War I, the state responded with enthusiasm.

The war's death statistics reveal that this was Rhode Island's most costly conflict: more of its men and women served (92,027) and more died (2,157) than in any other war. Yet the losses seemed only to spur the citizenry on to greater efforts. On the home front most Rhode Islanders cheerfully complied with rationing, and self-sacrifice became a way of life. War bond campaigns were oversubscribed; civilian defense programs swelled with volunteers. The state was well organized, and thousands gave regular hours to airplane spotting, air raid drills, fire protection, evacuation drills, emergency medical and police assistance, and the salvage of needed commodities. Many women who were not part of the regular work force joined war-related volunteer agencies such as the USO and the Red Cross, the latter of which prepared tons of surgical dressings and other medical supplies. Shown here are Providence Red Cross volunteers packing their handiwork for shipment to the boys overseas. Photo from Paul F. Gleeson, Rhode Island: The Development of a Democracy (1957)

Largely through the efforts of United States Senator Theodore Francis Green, the federal government decided to locate major naval installations on Narragansett Bay in the North Kingstown hamlet of Davisville and at nearby Quonset Point, a small peninsula which contained both a summer resort and a training camp for the Rhode Island National Guard.

On May 25, 1939, President Franklin D. Roosevelt signed a bill appropriating one million dollars for the purchase of this North Kingstown land. By July 12, 1941, the Quonset Naval Air Station was commissioned. In the interim eleven thousand civilian laborers dramatically transformed the area: peat bogs, some as deep as thirty feet and four hundred feet long, were removed; nearly forty-five thousand cubic feet of ledge rock was dynamited to provide room for the spur-track railroad; millions of square feet of asphalt were laid over the once grassy landscape; and some twenty million cubic yards of fill were taken from Narragansett Bay to add two-hundred man-made acres to the air station area.

The Naval Air Station and the adjoining base at Davisville, which serves as the home of the Atlantic Seabees (the Naval Construction Batallion), have had a remarkable impact on North Kingstown, on Rhode Island, and on the nation. Here in 1941 the famous Quonset hut (top right) was developed. Then, during the years of World War II, antisubmarine warfare patrols flew constantly from Quonset and its auxiliary station at Charlestown; pilots and crews were trained for carrier operations; and seven days a week, around the clock, the Overhaul and Repair Department's navy-civilian team worked to "Keep 'em Flying."

In the years following the war Quonset played a major role in the operational development of carrier-based jet aviation, and it was at Quonset that the navy's first all-jet fighter squadron was formed and trained.

In its final years, before closing in 1974, Quonset served as the home of sub-hunting ships and aircraft and as a base of operations for the navy's Antarctic exploration. Throughout the station's entire lifetime, Quonset's O & R Department, manned by a civilian work force, played a vital role in keeping the Atlantic Fleet's aircraft and ordnance in ready condition.

Largely because of the bases at Quonset Point and Davisville, the navy became Rhode Island's largest single employer. These installations had a particularly dramatic effect on the economic and physical growth of North Kingstown: whereas that community had gained only 1,697 inhabitants in the century and a half from 1790 to 1940, during the decade of the forties it increased its population by 10,206. This leap from 4,604 to 14,810 residents was a 221.7 percent increase, by far the highest growth rate in the state for that ten-year period.

Shown (top left) is a Grumman JF-1 Duck making the first wheel landing at the new base on December 23, 1940, and a ubiquitous Quonset hut, designed by a four-man engineering team headed by Otto Brandenberger. Today seventeen surviving huts located at various sites around Rhode Island have been placed on the National Register of Historic Buildings. Photo of plane courtesy of Sean Milligan; photo of Quonset hut courtesy of RIHS (Rhi x3 5740)

Though 92,027 Rhode Islanders either enlisted or were drafted into military service, a substantial work force remained behind. To utilize this resource, the federal government's Maritime Commission selected Providence in early 1942 as the site for a shipyard. Vice Admiral Howard Vickery decided that the Providence facility should have six ways and that it should be developed by the Rheem Manufacturing Company, a firm experienced in making water heaters and cartridge cases (but not ships).

When Rheem proved unequal to this formidable task, the company was relieved of control in February 1943 and replaced by a new combine, the Walsh-Kaiser Company. In this partnership the Walsh Construction Company, experienced in building such public works as the Grand Coulee Dam (but not ships), controlled the Providence operation.

Thirty ships, most of them Liberty-class, had already been launched when the production of larger combat-cargo vessels was urged by Vickery in the spring of 1944. From that point until early August 1945, thirty-two of these armed cargo carriers were built under Walsh-Kaiser's direction by a local work force that reached more than twenty-one thousand. By the time of the final launching, however, fewer than forty-eight hundred workers remained on the payroll, and with the coming of peace they also were rapidly dismissed. The facility was eventually sold to a private developer in 1949.

This photo shows the Rheem shipyard in operation with the launching of the William Coddington in late November 1942, a Liberty-class ship named in honor of Newport's founder. Photo by the U.S. Maritime Commission, courtesy of the Newport Historical Society

Five weeks after the William Coddington traveled down the ways, the war production facilities at Field's Point became the site of Rhode Island's most costly single fire loss in history. Just after two o'clock on the afternoon of December 31, 1942, workers at the Rheem Shipyard's fabrication plant noticed smoke billowing from the pump house at the east wall of the huge 640-foot-long building. In the plant at the time were several hundred workers cutting steel plates used in the construction of Liberty ships. The 156,000-square-foot multistory structure had been sheathed in plywood because of the unavailability of sheet metal.

Flames vaulted the east wall, and within minutes the fire was out of control. Workers in the plant literally ran for their

lives. Compounding the problem was the fact that sprinkler equipment that had arrived at the plant five months earlier had not been installed. By three o'clock more than thirty pieces of fire equipment from Providence and nearby Cranston were battling the enormous blaze. Thick black smoke rising from the plant could be seen as far as Fall River. In Providence members of twelve auxiliary fire companies were summoned to stand by.

Almost within an hour all that remained of the building was its steel framework. The loss was later estimated at a staggering $1.7 million, including valuable production equipment. Miraculously, no one was seriously injured. Photo (December 31, 1942) courtesy of PJC

In 1869 the U.S. Navy began its permanent presence in Rhode Island by establishing a torpedo station on Goat Island in Newport harbor. From the mid-1870s onward, torpedo boats built by the Herreshoffs of Bristol were stationed there. During World War I the facility became the nation's largest producer of torpedoes and was very actively involved in the war effort. Such work could, of course, be dangerous; in 1917 sixteen workers died there in explosions or accidents.

This interior view of a torpedo assembly line shows some of the thirteen thousand people employed during the 1940s in the production of these lethal navy weapons. The station's mainly civilian work force manufactured nearly 80 percent of the torpedoes used by the U.S. Navy in World War II. Today Goat Island, connected to the mainland by a causeway, is the site of the Sheraton Islander Hotel, a marina, and luxury condominiums. Photo (ca. 1943) courtesy of the Naval War College Museum

On the afternoon of May 5, 1945, a German submarine, the U-853, lurking just four miles south of Point Judith, found a victim. The Black Point, a 5,353-ton collier en route from New York to Boston with a load of soft coal, was blasted to the bottom of Rhode Island Sound by the U-boat's well-aimed torpedo. Twelve of the American vessel's forty-six crewmen were lost in this presumably safe coastal waterway.

Within two hours of the attack, several U.S. Navy and Coast Guard vessels converged on the area. A deadly cat-and-mouse game commenced at 7:30 p.m., with the USS Atherton and the USS Moberly stalking the sub. Depth charges were dropped intermittently until the early morning hours of May 6, when ships searching the area found an oil slick and debris rising to the surface. At dawn the location of the sub was pinpointed in a stationary position 130 feet down. Additional attacks (shown in this navy photo) were ordered until underwater instruments revealed that the U-boat had been destroyed. About twenty-four hours after the U-853 had sunk the Black Point, a navy diver spotted the doomed sub lying on the bottom of the sound, seven and a half miles west of Block Island, with her side and hull split and her fifty-five-man crew entombed therein.

Not since the American Revolution had a warship stirred such commotion in Rhode Island waters. But there was an aspect of irony and futility to the episode, for the U-853 and its 24-year-old commander, Helmut Froemsdorf, struck the Black Point only twenty-eight hours before Germany surrendered to Allied forces at Rheims, France, ending the war in Europe. In fact, on May 4 the German admiralty had ordered all its warships to cease hostilities and return to port. The U-853's first kill became its last; and for Rhode Island the shooting war, so belatedly begun, was quickly over. National Archives photo (May 6, 1945) from Walter K. Schroder, Defenses of Narragansett Bay in World War II (1980)

215

Woonsocket-born J. Howard McGrath
(1904–1966) was undoubtedly Rhode
Island's most versatile politician of this or
any era. A protégé of U.S. Senator Peter
Gerry, McGrath served successively as
Democratic state chairman and U.S.
district attorney in the 1930s and as Rhode
Island's governor during the war years
(1941–1945). In 1945 President Harry
Truman (shown here with McGrath)
appointed him U.S. solicitor general, and
in 1946 J. Howard won election as U.S.
senator. The following year Truman
conferred upon the Rhode Islander the
national chairmanship of the Democratic
party. In 1949 McGrath gave up his
Senate seat to become the U.S. attorney
general. After resigning this post in 1952,
he returned to private business and the
successful practice of law. In 1960
McGrath lost a comeback bid in a heated
three-way Democratic senatorial primary
to newcomer Claiborne Pell, the eventual
winner. Photo courtesy of PJC

THE ERA OF TRANSITION, 1946-1986

In the postwar years Rhode Island experienced the second phase in the decline of its industrial base. Temporarily buoyed by wartime production, Rhode Island's textile industry resumed its demise at an ever-accelerating pace, due largely to antiquated manufacturing facilities, high energy and transportation costs, and the abundance of cheap labor in the South. In 1919 the textile industry employed almost 75,000 workers, accounting for more than half the manufacturing jobs in the state. By 1985 only 11,236 of Rhode Island's 122,000 manufacturing jobs—fewer than 11 percent—were in textile production.

The exodus of the textile industry after the war paralleled the flight of another sort that would have far-reaching impact on the future of the state. The lure of suburbia after 1950 produced a massive outpouring of "new" middle-class ethnics fed up with cramped housing, deteriorating social services, and rising crime rates. Their flight was facilitated by dramatic improvements in the local interstate transportation network and easy home mortgages offered by various federal agencies. In the census of 1950 Providence boasted a population of 248,674. Two decades later that number had dwindled to 179,116, the largest proportionate out-migration from any major city in the United States. One neighborhood, South Providence, lost 40 percent of its available housing units by 1980. The erosion of the tax base, the concentration of the poor and elderly in the inner cities, and the corresponding decline of Providence as a retail center placed enormous burdens on the capital city's government in its efforts to stem the tide of deterioration and decay.

The movement out of Providence included educational institutions as well. Providence-Barrington Bible College left Capitol Hill in the early 1960s, shortening its name to fit its new Barrington home. (It has since closed.) Roger Williams grew from a two-year college based at the Providence YMCA to a four-year institution (1967) and then moved to Bristol in 1969. Two years later Bryant (established in 1863) departed its sprawling East Side campus for a beautiful site in Smithfield. A state junior college (now CCRI) was opened in September 1964 and took up residence in the former Brown and Sharpe complex on Promenade Street, but it, too, left Providence, opening its Knight campus in Warwick in 1972 and its Flanagan campus in Lincoln in 1976. The state normal school, however, remained in the city, moving in 1958 from its cramped quarters between

Hayes and Promenade streets to a 125-acre campus in Providence's Mount Pleasant section. Two years later the General Assembly gave the teachers' college an expanded role and a new name—Rhode Island College.

Rising labor and energy costs, a higher than average state corporate income tax, and outdated facilities resulted in the removal from Providence of the four remaining "big five" firms of the Gilded Age. In 1949 American Screw closed its doors and departed for Willimantic, Connecticut. Ten years later Nicholson File relocated to Indiana. Brown and Sharpe abandoned its massive Providence plant in 1964 but fortunately remained in Rhode Island, relocating to "Precision Park," North Kingstown. In 1986 Gorham sold its sprawling complex on Mashapaug Pond to private developers.

In many respects, the inner-city's loss was suburbia's gain. The population of Warwick doubled between 1950 and 1980, increasing from 43,028 to 87,123. The city of Cranston experienced a similar though less dramatic influx of inner-city emigrés. Retail facilities were soon established to meet the needs of these growing suburban communities. The 233-acre Garden City development, established in 1947, epitomized the process of suburbanization in Rhode Island. The "city within a city" offered a variety of housing styles, a school, and open space, as well as the state's first suburban shopping center.

The completion of Routes 95 in 1966 and 295 two years later produced even more profound changes in the business and social habits of Rhode Islanders. The intersection of these superhighways just east of Natick offered an ideal location for commercial development. In 1965 this area was selected as the location for Midland (now Rhode Island) Mall, the state's first enclosed, climate-controlled shopping plaza. Completed in 1968, it was joined four years later by the equally impressive Warwick Mall. Convenient access, as well as national chains like Sears and J. C. Penney and large Boston-based anchor retailers such as Filene's and Jordan Marsh, brought shoppers from far beyond the Warwick area. The opening of Lincoln Mall in 1975 at the confluence of Routes 295 and 146 drew shoppers from the region's northern sector. One by one Providence's better-known retailers—W. T. Grant, City Hall Hardware, J. J. Newberry, Shepard's, and, finally, the Outlet Company—closed their doors. By the early 1970s the state's several downtown areas were pockmarked with empty storefronts and abandoned theaters. Concern grew among city officials that something must be done to reverse a trend that was afflicting Providence, Pawtucket, Woonsocket, and other older northeastern cities.

Rhode Island's urban centers developed an approach to address the challenges of suburbanization.

It combined urban renewal through clearance of substandard housing with the ofttimes conflicting but equally strong commitment to preserve the community's rich architectural heritage. Threatened demolition of Newport's historic William Hunter House in 1945 resulted in the formation of the Preservation Society of Newport County. Three years later the society assumed care of the lavish Vanderbilt mansion The Breakers. By 1980 the society operated six Bellevue Avenue mansions, which were toured by more than three-quarters of a million visitors. Other Newport preservation efforts included Operation Clapboard, founded in 1963, and the Newport Restoration Foundation, established five years later by multimillionaire tobacco heiress Doris Duke. These efforts were, in most cases, complemented by the work of the Redevelopment Agency of Newport, which in 1962 implemented a multiyear revitalization plan that transformed Thames Street, Long Wharf, and Brick Market. A new thoroughfare—America's Cup Avenue—was constructed to connect Connell Highway with Memorial Boulevard. The derelict torpedo station on Goat Island was cleared to make way for a marina, an apartment complex, and a luxury Sheraton hotel.

In the capital city the efforts of a reorganized City Plan Commission were strengthened by the establishment of the Providence Redevelopment Agency in 1948. Deteriorating housing on lower College Hill, along with growing concern over Brown University's encroachment on residential housing, provided the impetus for the creation of the Providence Preservation Society in 1956. Working in concert with the City Plan Commission, in 1959 the PPS prepared a pathbreaking report entitled *College Hill: Demonstration Study of Historic Area Renewal* that sparked the restoration of Benefit Street and its immediate environs. Success was due in part to aesthetic-minded private investors, especially Mrs. Malcolm G. Chace, Jr., who acquired and restored for resale about forty houses on College Hill. Many of these structures are now visited in the Preservation Society's walking tours.

The Plan Commission itself produced a master blueprint for downtown renewal in 1960. The first of the commission's imaginative recommendations to be implemented was the construction of a pedestrian shopping mall on Westminster Street from Dorrance to Aborn. The project was begun in 1964 and completed a year later. The master plan's goal of "strengthening the city's retail core" via a shopping mall, however, has not been fully realized, nor have extensive renovations to the area in 1979 revived the commercial prominence the strip enjoyed earlier in the century.

The pace of renewal and revitalization quickened

Rhode Island's most famous political figure of the postwar era was John O. Pastore, a Providence native who rose from humble surroundings on Federal Hill to become one of the nation's most influential and respected United States senators. The son of Italian immigrants, Pastore is cited by famous political scientist Samuel Lubell in his book The Future of American Politics *as the individual who epitomized the rise of the Italian-American to a position of political power and influence. As the first governor and the first U.S. senator of Italo-American stock, Pastore was enormously popular with Rhode Island's Italian community, but he also won the respect and support of a much larger constituency.*

Pastore began the practice of law in Providence in 1932 and launched his career in politics shortly afterward, securing election as Democratic state representative from Providence in 1934. After one legislative term, he served a six-year stint as assistant attorney general and was also a member of the 1939 Providence Charter Revision Commission.

His big break came when party chieftains J. Howard McGrath and Dennis Roberts selected him over fellow Italian-American Christopher DelSesto as Democratic nominee for lieutenant governor in 1944. Victorious in that election, he succeeded to the governorship on October 6, 1945, when McGrath resigned to become Harry Truman's solicitor general. After two

convincing triumphs in gubernatorial elections, Pastore ran for the U.S. Senate in 1950, defeating his Republican opponent by nearly seventy thousand votes. He assumed office (again as McGrath's successor) on December 19, 1950, and served with distinction for the next twenty-six years. Among his many important senatorial posts were the chairmanship of the Communications Subcommittee of the Senate Commerce Committee, where he was often referred to as "the conscience of the television industry," and the chairmanship of the Joint Committee on Atomic Energy. Photo of Pastore delivering the keynote speech of the 1964 Democratic National Convention, courtesy of Providence College Archives

throughout the 1960s. Weybosset Hill, Randall Square, and Lippitt Hill began their remarkable transformation into modern residential and commercial centers. Massive amounts of Model Cities money and, later, Community Development funds were funneled into Rhode Island's urban centers in a partially successful effort to halt urban blight.

The state did not fare as well in meeting the challenge of nature's unpredictable onslaughts. On August 31, 1954, Hurricane Carol slammed Rhode Island with gusts reaching 115 miles per hour. Southern coastal areas were particularly hard-hit. Almost 3,800 homes were destroyed and nineteen lives lost. The downtown area of Providence was inundated, with water rising thirteen feet above mean high water level—slightly less than a foot below the 1938 record. In all, estimated property damage exceeded $90 million.

Less than a year later, on August 19, 1955, Hurricane Diane brought the worst flooding in the state's history. More than six inches of rain wreaked havoc in the Blackstone Valley as all the dams on the Blackstone and Mill rivers were breached. Flood waters cut Woonsocket in half, leaving stores and homes under tons of mud. Losses here reached $170 million. Fears of recurrent deluges prompted Rhode Island voters to approve funding for the construction of a flood-control system in Woonsocket and a hurricane barrier across the Providence River. Completed in 1966, the Fox Point barrier has yet to be put to a stringent test, since the next major hurricane to hit the state—Hurricane Gloria, on July 27, 1985—arrived at low tide.

A natural disaster of another sort occurred on February 6, 1978, when the state was visited by the worst snowstorm in its recorded history. The heavy snowfall caught unsuspecting motorists during the afternoon rush hours, resulting in an unprecedented traffic jam on Route 95. Providence streets were utter chaos as thousands abandoned their cars. Snowfall estimates varied from sixteen inches along the southeastern coast to a reported fifty-five inches in the Manville section of Lincoln. Troops were airlifted from southern bases to help local Army and Air National Guard units dig the state out. Only on February 13—a full week after it all began—was commuter traffic allowed into downtown Providence. The Blizzard of '78 claimed twenty-one lives and resulted in $110 million lost in gross product and wages.

Although it had helped to rescue Rhode Island from nature's devastation in 1978, the United States military had been the principal cause of an economic disaster five years earlier. Between 1945 and 1973 the navy was the state's largest civilian employer, and the arrival in Newport of the Cruiser-Destroyer Force

of the United States Atlantic Fleet in 1952 had produced a major influx of naval personnel. But the military bubble burst in 1973 with the Nixon administration's decision to relocate the destroyer force to southern ports. It was by far the most severe economic jolt to the state since the crash of 1929. The support facilities at Quonset were closed and Davisville was cut back drastically, with a resulting loss of sixteen thousand civilian jobs. During 1973 and 1974 more than twenty thousand navy personnel left the state. Middletown suffered a 41 percent decline in population. Ironically, Department of Defense officials in 1982 began to show renewed interest in returning portions of the Atlantic Fleet to Newport. State and local officials understandably viewed the news with a wary eye.

In the political realm, Rhode Island continued the trend established by the Democratic revolution of the New Deal years. Of the ten chief executives to hold office since 1946, seven have been Democrats. Rhode Island's major ethnic groups were well represented, with the Italian-Americans contributing four governors and the Irish three. John H. Chafee was the only "Yankee" Republican elected during this period.

Republican party dominance of small towns in Rhode Island began to erode with the large-scale influx of urban ethnics and the application of the "one man, one vote" princple to state legislatures, upheld by a 1964 U.S. Supreme Court mandate. Prior to that time the apportionment of the Rhode Island Senate gave small rural Republican towns an undue influence in state affairs—a key factor in Rhode Island's political history for more than a century. After a 1965 redistricting statute was enacted, the fifty-member state Senate, like the one-hundred-member House, became overwhelmingly Democratic. A special election in 1983, however, resulted in the election of twenty-one Republicans to the upper chamber, the highest number by far since the reapportionment of the mid-1960s.

During the post-World War II era, more Rhode Island politicians attained national prominence than in any comparable period. Theodore Francis Green, who went to the U.S. Senate in 1937, became chairman of the Senate Foreign Relations Committee in 1957 at the age of eighty-nine. John O. Pastore also rose to political heights, becoming governor in 1945 and moving to the U.S. Senate five years later. These political accomplishments earned Pastore the distinction of being the first person of Italian ancestry to serve in the U.S. Senate and the first Italian-American to be elected governor of any state. Most remember his oratorial talents, highlighted perhaps by his masterful keynote address before the Democratic National Convention in 1964. After more than a quarter century of service to his state and his nation,

On August 31, 1954, the state received an unwelcome visitor. Her name was Carol. Without adequate warning once again, Rhode Island was ill-prepared for the hurricane's onslaught. As in 1938, the storm, which reached its peak intensity at 11:37 a.m., hit at high tide and was accompanied by tidal waves. Again downtown Providence was flooded, with waters reaching thirteen feet above mean high water, just nine-tenths of a foot below the 1938 mark; and again records and merchandise were destroyed in flooded stores and basements. Thousands of autos were inundated; trees were felled; electric and telephone service was disrupted for days; and the harbor was battered by wind and waves. The Hillsgrove weather station reported sustained winds of 90 miles per hour just before noon, with gusts reaching 115 miles per hour. The hurricane claimed nineteen lives statewide.

As shown in this photo, taken at the storm's height, boats at Galilee were driven ashore and a truck was carried out to sea. The Coast Guard boathouse is visible above the partly submerged truck on the Jerusalem side of the harbor.

Another tropical storm—Hurricane Edna—hit the state less than two weeks later, with heavy rains and gale-force winds but no tidal wave, though flooding in the Blackstone Valley was severe when the Blackstone River overflowed its banks. Photo courtesy of PJC

Less than a year after the ravages of Hurricane Carol, a tropical storm called Diane visited Rhode Island. This hurricane of August 19, 1955, differed from the state's other devastating gales in that its damage was done not mainly by winds or ocean-borne waves but by rain and swollen rivers. The Blackstone Valley bore the brunt of Diane's devastation.

The 6.13 inches of rain dumped upon Rhode Island by the storm caused the worst flood in the state's history. Rampaging waters cut Woonsocket in half when they breached all of the dams on the Blackstone and Mill rivers. Flood crest reached fifteen feet above the Blackstone's normal flow to put Woonsocket's Social District under eight feet of water and tons of mud. Fortunately, ample warning and quick action by state and local agencies kept the storm's death toll to two. Here the Blackstone's waters tear away mill walls along both banks in the village of Manville. Atlantic Mills and the Royal Electric Company are the victims.

With the troublesome trio of Carol, Edna, and Diane fresh in mind, the state, in concert with the federal government, took major steps to minimize future hurricane losses. A system of dams and flood-control gates (shown here) were installed along the Blackstone in the flood-devastated area of Woonsocket, and after much delay a hurricane barrier was constructed (1961–1966) in the Providence River at Fox Point to prevent such disastrous flooding of downtown as had occurred in 1815, 1938, and 1954. Photo of flood courtesy of PPL; photo of Woonsocket dam from Marion I. Wright and Robert J. Sullivan, The Rhode Island Atlas (1982)

221

including the chairmanship of the Joint Committee on Atomic Energy, Pastore retired in December 1976.

Claiborne Pell, Green's successor in the Senate, has served with distinction for more than two and a half decades, during which time he has become nationally known for his sponsorship of higher education grants to low-income students and his support of the humanities and oceanography. He is now the chairman of the Senate Foreign Relations Committee. In the House, John E. Fogarty (1941–1967) became recognized as "Mr. Public Health," and Aime J. Forand (1937–1939, 1941–1961) won acclaim as "the Father of Medicare." Forand's successor in the First Congressional District, Fernand St Germain (1961–   ), has established a national reputation for expertise in the area of commercial banking legislation.

The most successful and enduring Republican of the era has been John H. Chafee. After three terms as governor (1963–1969), Chafee served as secretary of the navy (1969–1972) in the Nixon administration. Following an unsuccessful U.S. Senate campaign against Pell, Chafee made a second bid for the Senate in 1976 and won. In 1982 he was reelected by a narrow margin, and he now plays an influential role on Capitol Hill.

The highest-ranking federal appointee from Rhode Island in recent years has been G. William Miller, former board chairman of Textron, Inc., the state's leading conglomerate. Miller served the Carter administration first as chairman of the Federal Reserve Board (1978) and then as secretary of the treasury (1979–1981).

J. Howard McGrath was undoubtedly the state's most versatile politician. After spending the war years as Rhode Island's governor, he was appointed U.S. solicitor general by his close political ally Harry S. Truman. In 1946 McGrath was elected to the U.S. Senate. The following year Truman named him Democratic national chairman. McGrath quickly proved his worth by overseeing the surprising upset of presidential hopeful Thomas E. Dewey in 1948. In the following year the ambitious Rhode Islander gave up his Senate seat to become U.S. attorney general. After resigning this post in 1952, he returned to private business and the successful practice of law.

On the local stage, Democrat Dennis J. Roberts enjoyed a highly successful political career that included a ten-year reign as mayor of Providence (1941–1951) followed by four terms as governor (1951–1959). Another Providence mayor, Republican Vincent A. Cianci, Jr., shocked politicos in 1974 when he began a productive yet controversial nine-year tenure by unseating incumbent mayor Joseph A. Doorley in a heated campaign marked by bitter infighting among the city's Democrats. In the

Democratic primary that same year, Edward Beard, a housepainter-turned-politician, pulled off an equally surprising upset by defeating incumbent congressman Robert O. Tiernan, a legislator well connected with Democratic congressional leaders.

In recent years women and minorities have exerted an increasingly powerful influence in local and state politics. Republican Claudine Schneider ousted Ed Beard in 1980 to become the first woman ever elected to Congress from the state. Two years later another Republican, Susan Farmer, won her bid to become Rhode Island's first female general officer. Then, in 1984, Republican Arlene Violet, a former Sister of Mercy, became the first woman in America elected to the office of state attorney general. Presently the GOP has Leila Mahoney as its state chairman—another first.

Blacks have also begun to flex their political muscle in Rhode Island's urban centers. Providence's new fifteen-member city council now includes three blacks, and in 1982 south side voters elected the state's first black senator. Newport councilman Paul Gaines became that city's first black mayor in 1980.

Over half the state's municipalities have adopted a home-rule charter since that option was made available to them by constitutional amendment in 1951. Under its provisions two cities (Newport and East Providence) and several towns have embraced the manager form of government. In the smaller communities the famous New England town meeting still persists, whereby the town's eligible voters assemble to directly approve the municipal budget, set the tax levy, and decide other local measures.

In 1964 a state constitutional convention was held to revise or replace Rhode Island's basic law. Chaired by Dennis J. Roberts, the convention deliberated for more than four years, and although it produced a worthwhile product, it was one that the electorate rejected in April 1968 by a 4-to-1 margin. A limited convention in 1973 was more successful. Of the constitutional amendments it proposed, five were approved by the state's voters, including one that repealed the long-standing ban on lotteries and another that provided for a popular referendum at least once every decade on whether or not to convene a constitutional convention. That reform, sponsored by convention secretary Patrick T. Conley, led directly to the call of the 1986 convention, a body that has streamlined the state's basic law and added seven substantive amendments to the state constitution.

Latest census figures indicate that during the 1970s only two states—Rhode Island and New York—suffered a loss in population. However, the Ocean State's .4 percent decline (from 949,723 in 1970 to 947,154 in 1980) was due in large measure to the removal of the cruiser-destroyer group in 1974 and

Another visitor to Rhode Island during the 1940s and 1950s was even more devastating in its toll on human life and health than the violent hurricane. It was the scourge of polio, or infantile paralysis, a disease that terrified the children of the mid-twentieth century as much as small-pox, cholera, and yellow fever had produced fear among the nineteenth-century citizenry. During the epidemic years of 1953 and 1955, many youngsters had nightmares of being confined by polio to respirators called iron lungs.

But in 1955, when polio claimed 421 victims in Rhode Island (giving the state the third highest polio rate in the nation), a miracle preventative was being prepared for general use. On March 28, 1953, Dr. Jonas Salk of the University of Pittsburgh had announced the development of a polio vaccine. Two years later, on April 13, 1955, Salk inoculated the first person to receive the vaccine after its approval by the National Institute of Health, a federal agency created and endowed in large measure through the efforts of Rhode Island congressman John E. Fogarty. Immediately thereafter, the first shipment

of vaccine arrived at Hillsgrove airport (shown here), and health officials began a massive statewide inoculation program for schoolchildren in the first four elementary grades. In 1956 only nine cases were reported statewide, and in 1957 Rhode Island recorded a polio-free year.

Then, as the summer of 1960 began, laxness among the general public led to a revival of the disease. During that year over a hundred new cases were reported statewide. This resurgence led the Provi-

dence Journal to conduct a series of free polio clinics that immunized tens of thousands of Rhode Islanders. Navy captain Edward A. Anderson of Quonset provided paramedics and helped develop a new hypo-spray jet injector to speed the process and make it less alarming, especially for the very young. This second bout with the dread disease proved decisive, and polio became a dim but terrifying memory. Photo (1955) courtesy of PJC

Rhode Island's twenty-one hospitals (including five run under the auspices of the state or federal governments) furnish quality health care to a state population that ranks behind Florida as the second oldest in the nation. Notable among these health care facilities are Emma Pendleton Bradley Hospital in East Providence, which became the nation's first children's neuropsychiatric hospital when it opened in 1931; Roger Williams General Hospital in Providence, a clinical cancer research center of the National Cancer Institute; St. Joseph's Hospital, a center for neuro-surgery whose Providence and North

Providence units combined give it a licensed capacity of 496 beds, the state's second largest total; and Kent County Memorial Hospital (opened in 1951), one of the state's fastest-growing health care facilities.

The most significant health services development, however, has been the recent expansion of Rhode Island Hospital into a comprehensive medical center linked with the Brown University School of Medicine (established in 1973) and Women and Infants Hospital (founded in 1884 as Providence Lying-In Hospital). This photo reveals the scope of the medical complex's

recent growth: left to right, the new Women and Infants' Hospital, which opened in June 1986; the twelve-story Rhode Island Hospital Ambulatory Patient Center, which opened in May 1973; the spire of the hospital's last surviving nineteenth-century building; and the ten-story main building, facing on Eddy Street, which opened in December 1955. With a campus consisting of twenty-five buildings sited on forty acres, the medical center presently serves as Providence's largest employer. Photo from Gay Street looking northeast (August 1986), by the author

223

Exerting a major impact upon the Rhode Island landscape were the interstate highways, I-95 and I-195. In 1947 a consultant's report, entitled Expressway System for Metropolitan Providence, *observed that the city's obsolete radial-concentric street pattern was one of the worst in the nation. It recommended a north-south freeway from the Massachusetts line to the Pawtuxet River to replace U.S. Route 1. The report envisioned that the proposed road would be primarily an urban expressway facilitating the movement of local traffic. As federal plans for a national system of interregional highways took shape in 1956 with the passage of the Federal Highway Act, this proposed road became a portion of I-95.*

Despite grandiose plans, construction was slow in starting. In the years from 1946 to 1955, Rhode Island ranked forty-seventh among the forty-eight states in highway spending per vehicle. Finally, in 1955, a portion of the system was begun, extending from Beacon Avenue in South Providence to the George M. Cohan Boulevard and including a Providence River bridge (shown here under construction near Wickenden and South Main streets). This section, which eventually became a part of I-195, was opened in 1956. Photo (1956) from Paul F. Gleeson, Rhode Island: The Development of a Democracy *(1958), courtesy of the Rhode Island Department of Public Works*

the loss of its attendant naval personnel. During the 1970s the tidal wave of out-migration from the cities ebbed, a development undoubtedly aided by the construction of many federally financed urban housing complexes for low-income and elderly tenants. The growth of Rhode Island's suburban communities slowed almost to a halt. Warwick's population increased by a meager 4 percent, and Cranston actually experienced a 3 percent loss of inhabitants.

Rural towns, conversely, experienced rapid growth during the 1970s. Charlestown, Glocester, Narragansett, Scituate, and West Greenwich all recorded increases in population of 40 percent or more. In 1980 Central Falls remained the state's most densely populated municipality, while New Shoreham (Block Island), with fewer than 54 residents per square mile, was the most sparsely settled.

Demographically, the relaxation of federal immigration quotas by the Immigration and Nationality Act of 1965 has permitted a new influx of foreign-born residents, especially Portuguese, Hispanics, and Southeast Asians. Nearly 65 percent of all Rhode Islanders claim Roman Catholicism as their religion—the highest percentage of any state in the nation. In 1980 Rhode Island women outnumbered men by almost forty-five thousand.

Despite the removal of the navy from Quonset in 1973, the state still relies heavily on the defense industry to fuel its economy. Nearly six thousand local residents are employed by the Electric Boat Division of the General Dynamics Corporation, a new Quonset tenant.

Manufacturing in the state is presently dominated by the growing metals and machinery industry, which employs well over 30 percent of the industrial work force. This sector includes primary metals (iron and steel foundries, forges, and smelting and refining plants), fabricated metals (valves, fittings, screws, pipe, hardware, bolts, nails, cutlery, wire, tin cans, tubes, containers, and hand tools), machinery (machine tools and business machines), and electrical equipment (motors, generators, appliances, and wiring devices). Next in significance is jewelry and silverware (Providence is still the costume jewelry capital of the country), followed by textiles (yarn, thread, and fabric mills, dyeing and finishing plants, and lace mills) and rubber products. Rising industries are electronics, instrumentation, chemicals, plastics, and transportation equipment.

The greatest expansion in the state's labor force has taken place in tertiary occupations, especially government service, wholesale and retail trade, transportation, finance and insurance, private education, health care, business and repair services, and the professions. In 1985, for example, health service providers employed more people than the state's entire jewelry industry (36,479 vs. 23,100). The tourist and convention business is now a major economic influence, with Newport, the South County beaches, and Providence the prime sites.

Until the early 1980s, Rhode Island's economy was drifting aimlessly. High energy costs and corporate taxes, the perception of state government as prolabor, foreign competition, and the fact that Rhode Island factory workers are among the lowest paid in the country were frequently cited as prime causes for the state's ailing economy. A 1983 study by a national accounting firm, in cooperation with the Conference of State Manufacturers' Associations, concluded that of the forty-eight contiguous states, Rhode Island ranked second to the bottom in "attractiveness of business climate."

To remedy this condition, business, labor, and government joined forces to improve the state's economic image. The law authorizing unemployment benefits to strikers was repealed, the workers' compensation system was revamped, business taxes were cut, and job training programs were expanded. Though factory jobs have declined as a percentage of the total work force (34 percent in 1978 to 28 percent in 1985), factory production has increased; and the tremendous economic boom in nearby Boston is now beginning to exert a beneficial impact on Providence and the Blackstone Valley. By late 1986 the state achieved the second lowest unemployment rate in America.

On their 350th birthday, Rhode Islanders can also point to many other promising conditions: a rejuvenated capital city boasting revitalized historic districts; a great natural resource, Narragansett Bay, educational and cultural institutions; and a building boom in both commercial and residential construction.

The massive Capital Center Project, begun in 1982, gives the state an impressive focal point. Already it has resulted in the relocation of existing railroad tracks to the base of Capitol Hill and the completion of a modern railroad terminal. Soon to follow will be river and harbor improvements, a major highway interchange, the construction of numerous buildings for office and residential use, and the redevelopment of the adjacent Promenade Center.

The renaissance in Newport, fueled by that city's growing reputation as a tourist mecca, should continue (despite the loss of the America's Cup in 1983), and Rhode Island's rural communities should remain attractive sites for further residential development. Realtors estimate, for example, that property values in South County and the Blackstone Valley were rising at the rate of 2 percent a month through 1985 and 1986.

Despite its recent changes and challenges, Rhode Island still maintains its character as an urban-industrial state with considerable ethnocultural and physical diversity. By vigorous and successful programs of historic preservation and environmental protection, present-day Rhode Islanders are seeking to preserve the best of their heritage while striving to improve the quality of life for Rhode Islanders of future generations.

The construction of the main trunk of I-95 through Providence was delayed by a political dispute over methods of financing the state's share of the expenses. Most Democrats advocated construction on a pay-as-you-go basis, whereas Republicans and business leaders such as Royal Little, a leading highway promoter, favored a resort to borrowing to speed up the program. Under GOP governor Christopher DelSesto, the project picked up momentum. In May 1960 the voters approved three separate referenda authorizing $98 million in borrowing for road and highway projects. By the end of 1961 most of the land condemnation for I-95 had been completed in Providence, and construction was underway on several segments of the superhighway. By July 1964 the Providence downtown loop, with its six overpasses, was ready at a cost of $11.7

million. In October of that year the section from Thurbers Avenue to Elmwood Avenue was officially opened shortly after President Lyndon Johnson had traveled over it during a visit to Providence. The final city segment to be completed was that from downtown to the Pawtucket line.

Whereas relatively few people were relocated as the road plowed through South Providence (the south side of Byfield Street and Detroit Avenue were the notable exceptions), I-95 cut a wide swath through a residential area of Smith Hill and through densely populated neighborhoods in Pawtucket, especially Woodlawn, causing much destruction of residential housing stock and family relocation. Shown here under construction is the I-95 bridge over the Seekonk, just south of downtown Pawtucket. Photo (May 1963) courtesy of PJC

In 1928 thirty-two-year-old Royal Little, nephew of Arthur D. Little, founder of the famous consulting firm, made his first business contact with Providence. Little's company, Special Yarns Corporation, a Boston firm that specialized in the dyeing and processing of synthetic yarns, merged with the Franklin Rayon Dyeing Company of Crary Street. According to Little's entertaining autobiography, How to Lose $100,000,000 and Other Valuable Advice, "Franklin Rayon Corporation was the name of the new company formed when Special Yarns and Franklin Rayon Dyeing were merged. As a result of this transaction Special Yarns Corporation really was the predecessor for what became Textron."

After other acquisitions, including that of a parachute-manufacturing firm, Little adopted the Textron name in 1943 "to connote textile products made from synthetics." For the next decade this firm bought up numerous obsolete New England textile mills. Little's management plan prescribed modern machinery and total reorganization of each mill according to a scientific time-study analysis. Simultaneously Textron expanded into the South. Then the company began the liquidation of its archaic New England

factories, using the proceeds and the tax losses to diversify its holdings and acquire nontextile concerns. This diversification move, begun in 1953, resulted in the acquisition of a number of unrelated firms, including Bell Helicopter, Homelite

chain saws, and Schaeffer pens, and such local firms as Bostitch (1966), Gorham (1967), and Speidel (1964). By 1980 the Textron conglomerate, with headquarters at 40 Westminster Street, Providence, generated $3.4 billion in sales and employed over three thousand Rhode Islanders.

Little, who retired in 1962, has established several trusts that provide substantial annual sums for local charitable and educational purposes. One of Little's proteges, G. William Miller, not only became chairman of Textron's board but also ascended to the chairmanship of the Federal Reserve Board in 1978 before serving as secretary of the treasury in the Carter administration from 1979 to 1981.

In the 1980s two other Rhode Island firms joined Textron in the famous Fortune 500 listing of America's largest companies: Providence-based Nortek, a holding company similar to Textron, directed by Ralph Papitto, and Hasbro Industries, a Pawtucket and Central Falls concern operated by members of the Hassenfeld family, which has emerged as one of the world's premier manufacturers of children's toys. Photo (1966) from The Royal Little Story

The construction of the interstate highways encouraged factories and businesses to follow the workers to suburbia. Other influences such as obsolete plants, cramped quarters, increasing vandalism, and rising property taxes contributed to the exodus. Brown and Sharpe, Nicholson File, A. T. Cross, Trifari, B. A. Ballou,

Builders Iron Foundry (BIF), Davol, Allendale Insurance, and Gorham have been among the largest firms to relocate from the central city to suburban sites, while large national corporations such as Raytheon, Kaiser Aluminum, Peterson-Puritan, and Amperex have chosen suburban or rural locations upon their

arrival in Rhode Island. Shown here in a park like setting is the modern building of Allendale Insurance Company of Johnston, a firm with Providence origins that is the oldest and largest company in the Factory Mutual System. Photo (ca. 1980) courtesy of Allendale Mutual Insurance Company

This photo of Woonsocket's derelict Hamlet cotton textile mill symbolizes the fate of Rhode Island's textile industry. At its peak in 1923, textile production employed about 60 percent of the state's total manufacturing work force (approximately 80,000 out of 135,000 industrial workers). At that time jobs in manufacturing and construction, the so-called secondary industries, accounted for nearly three out of every five Rhode Islanders who were gainfully employed.

By 1985 employment in the manufacture of textile-mill products, apparel, and other finished cloths had declined in the state to only 14,768 (in that year the Amalgamated Clothing and Textile Workers, Rhode Island's major textile union, sold its Providence meeting hall to the author and moved its headquarters to Connecticut). Meanwhile, jobs in the so-called tertiary industries—trade, transportation, communications, utilities, finance, insurance, real estate, and services (especially in the areas of health, education, and recreation)—employed 219,048 of the state's workers, compared with a total manufacturing job force of 121,946. Clearly, the last three generations have wrought a dramatic transformation in the economy of Rhode Island. Photo (ca. 1939) by Joseph McCarthy, courtesy of PPL

In the years since the closing of Quonset Point Naval Air Station in March 1974, the state government has made a persistent attempt to attract industrial and commercial firms to the site, emphasizing Quonset's proximity to sea, air, rail, and interstate road transport. In August 1974 Governor Philip Noel signed a lease bringing the first industrial tenant to the former navy base. That firm, the Electric Boat Division of General Dynamics, has since become Rhode Island's largest private employer and a major producer of components for America's fleet of nuclear submarines. Photo of welders at Electric Boat (ca. 1980), courtesy of PJC

Rhode Island's fisheries are a small but still significant component of the state's economy. Shellfishing accounts for over 60 percent of the industry's total yield, with East Greenwich the center of this bay-related activity. Since oysters, scallops, crabs, and lobsters have all become scarce because of pollution, natural predators, violent storms, and other factors, quahogs and clams are the main shellfish harvested. The Narragansett Marine Laboratory, established in 1937 at URI, conducts continuing research on the problems confronting the state's fisheries, while a vigorous private organization, Save the Bay, is now engaged in an increasingly effective campaign to restore the bay to its early, productive condition.

Finfishing, based primarily in Newport and the Narragansett village of Galilee, supplies the state's fishing industry with one-third of its income. The most significant venture in this sector of the maritime economy was the establishment in 1948 of the Point Judith Fishermen's Cooperative Association. This fisherman-owned enterprise specializes in the direct delivery of fresh fish and frozen fillet to East Coast markets. Since 1950 the association has operated a fish-processing plant at Galilee that converts low-grade fish into animal feed.

Although fishing, like farming, is no longer the mainstay of Rhode Island's economy that it was in bygone times, it still affords a living to some, attests to the state's diversity, and offers a picturesque and interesting glimpse of the Ocean State's maritime heritage. An example of the latter is this photo of Roman Catholic bishop Louis E. Gelineau conferring his annual blessing on the fishing fleet at Galilee. *Photo (1986) by Ernest A. Myette, courtesy of the* Providence Visitor

Sportfishing is another aspect of Rhode Island's affair with the sea. Several big-game tournaments are based in Galilee, Newport, and Block Island, including the U.S. Atlantic Tuna Tournament, the Rhode Island Tuna Tournament, the Point Judith Masters Invitational, the Snug Harbor Shark Tourney, the Block Island Bluefish Tournament, and the Block Island Striper Tournament.

The giant bluefin tuna, swordfish, and white marlin usually migrate to Rhode Island waters in the late summer and early autumn; but as spectacular as these fish are for the big-game fishermen, the striped bass is the prime target for most Rhode Island anglers who surfcast or do their fishing just offshore in smaller boats. Bluefish, cod, pollock, and mackerel are also local favorites.

The granddaddy of all local fishing competitions is the Point Judith-based U.S. Atlantic Tuna Tournament, begun in the early 1940s. Shown here is part of that tourney's record-breaking catch in 1962, when 19,247½ pounds of the giant bluefin were boated. The average weight of each catch that year was 535 pounds; the largest, 690 pounds. *Photo (1962) courtesy of PPL*

Newport Bridge (above) is Narragansett Bay's most spectacular man-made sight. At the time of its dedication in June 1969, its main span of sixteen hundred feet ranked it as the longest suspension bridge in New England. This imposing structure, 2.13 miles in total length, connects Jamestown (lower right) with Newport (upper left) across the bay's east passage. Its opening brought about the demise of the Jamestown ferry, whose last trip to Newport (left) retired the oldest continuous ferry service in the nation. Photo of bridge courtesy of PPL; photo of ferry courtesy of the Rhode Island Development Council.

Mainland Rhode Island has approximately forty linear miles of Atlantic coastline extending from Watch Hill in Westerly to Point Judith in Narragansett (Block Island Sound) and along the south shore of Little Compton (Rhode Island Sound). Narragansett Bay, with nearly four hundred miles of irregular coastline, extends inland for twenty-eight miles and varies in width from three miles in the north to twelve miles at the entrance. Its major saltwater estuaries are Mount Hope Bay, Greenwich Cove, and the Sakonnet and Providence rivers. Marinas, docks, and other boating facilities have proliferated along this extensive shoreline. One of the biggest and best refuges for Rhode Island's pleasure boats is Wickford harbor, shown in this aerial view. In addition to its spectacular water scenes, Wickford also boasts a galaxy of historic houses. This North Kingstown village, established in 1637 by Roger Williams and Richard Smith as an Indian trading post, is one of the oldest, most picturesque, and best-preserved communities in the state. Photo (ca. 1960) courtesy of PPL

One of the most important results of the navy's 1974 cutback was that it declared as excess much of its property on the islands of Narragansett Bay. Acres of fortifications, storage depots, and training facilities were thereby transferred to state ownership under a federal regulation that allowed Rhode Island to acquire these "excessed lands" free of charge if it dedicated them to public recreational use.

These circumstances prompted the state to create a Bay Island Park System in 1975. This important and innovative plan, which also acquired land from private owners, called for establishing a far-flung park comprising the north and south ends of Prudence Island, Patience Island, Hope Island, and Dutch Island, together with sizable waterfront parcels in the lower bay at Beavertail and Fort Wetherill on Jamestown and Brenton

Point and Fort Adams in Newport.

By the early 1980s the state had completed most of the bureaucratic details for transferring land from the federal government, and a group called the Nature Conservancy had facilitated the purchase by the state of Patience Island and the northern part of Prudence Island. The major problem of public access to the island portions of the park has been addressed by the Bay Queen (shown here), built and operated by the Blount Marine Company of Warren. This excursion vessel conducts regular cruises to the bay islands.

One of the fortified areas included in the new park system, Fort Wetherill, is located on the southern end of Jamestown near the Dumplings Rocks. This World War II photo shows the fort (bottom) as the western terminus of an antisubmarine net across the east passage to the Newport shore

(top). Photo of Bay Queen courtesy of Blount Marine Company; photo of Fort Wetherill, courtesy of the National Archives, from Walter K. Schroder, Defenses of Narragansett Bay in World War II (1980)

231

Despite the demise of Quonset Point and the cutback in the Naval Construction Batallion at Davisville, the U.S. Navy maintains a very significant presence in Rhode Island. In Newport this presence includes about thirty different navy and Department of Defense commands and activities. These have kept the navy the largest employer in Newport County and second only to state government as Rhode Island's major employer. In 1985 thirty-nine hundred civilians were on the Newport navy payroll.

Although a small fleet of vessels is now berthed at Aquidneck Island and the important Naval Underwater Systems Center is located there, by far the most important naval commands pertain to education. The renowned Naval War College, the diverse Naval Education and Training Center, the Surface Warfare Officers School, and the Naval Justice School (which specializes in military law) firmly establish Newport as the center of U.S. naval education and make young officers, such as these, familiar sights on the streets of the City by the Sea. Photo by Hartley Alley

The R/V Trident, a deep-water research vessel of the University of Rhode Island's School of Oceanography, symbolizes modern Rhode Island's connection with the sea. This ship (a former army maintenance and supply vessel) and its more modern successor, the Endeavor, have made every ocean in the world an affiliated laboratory for the university's marine scientists.

The famed URI graduate school of oceanography, situated on a 165-acre campus at South Ferry in Narrangansett, was founded in 1961 as an outgrowth of the efforts of Dr. Charles J. Fish. Still under the able direction of John A. Knauss, its original dean, the school has developed into a facility with a truly global reputation. In 1971, with the assistance of Rhode Island senator Claiborne Pell, URI

became a pioneer sea-grant college eligible for significant amounts of federal funding through Pell's innovative Sea Grant College Act. Currently the school operates its scientific programs with an $18.2 million annual budget that includes nearly $15 million in federal research grants. Photo (ca. 1967) courtesy of the Rhode Island Yearbook Foundation

Lou Pieri's Rhode Island Reds (shown at the old Auditorium on North Main Street in Providence during the 1971 Calder Cup playoffs) was one of Rhode Island's few professional sports teams of this era. The Reds began operation in 1926 and were owned until the 1937–38 season by Rhode Island Auditorium, Inc. During that period the franchise was leased to James E. Dooley of Steam Roller and Narragansett Race Track fame. Pieri, who had been rink manager during the Auditorium's early years, took over the squad in 1938. Upon his death in 1967 the Reds descended to Pieri's son, who sold the franchise to George Sage, the Bonanza Bus magnate.

During the team's half century of operation, the Reds gained a postseason playoff berth twenty-five times and captured the Calder Cup, symbolic of the playoff championship, four times, their final win

coming in the 1955–56 season. The league in which the Reds played carried three names—Canadian-American, International, and American. It was the principal hockey loop below the National Hockey League, so many topflight players (but few locals) performed on Auditorium ice.

When the Providence Civic Center opened during the 1972–73 season, the Reds acquired a new and spacious home which they could not fill. Sage surrendered the franchise in 1976, and Providence hockey enthusiasts Thomas O'Halloran and former congressman Bob Tiernan made a last-ditch effort to save the city's lone professional team. Unfortunately their Reds finished dead last in the 1976–77 season, and the oldest continuous minor league hockey franchise in the nation folded.

Although the state no longer boasts a professional hockey team, the sport is now

more popular than ever before. Brown University and Providence College are national collegiate powers. The Friars in 1985 were runners-up in the NCAA championship tourney and are often ranked among the top ten college teams. From the 1960s onward, the proliferation of indoor hockey rinks has produced a bevy of outstanding local players, including Bob Carpenter, the National Hockey League's number-one draft pick in 1983.

Rhode Island's high school hockey program is the strongest area of schoolboy athletic competition in the state. Throughout the 1980s Mount St. Charles Academy in Woonsocket (where Carpenter played) has been the nation's number-one-ranked high school hockey team, and LaSalle Academy and Hendricken High School also rate well in national schoolboy hockey polls. Photo (April 26, 1971) courtesy of PJC

233

In collegiate sports, much of the modern era belonged to Providence College basketball. When Coach Joe Mullaney came to the small Dominican school in 1955, he inherited a squad with a mediocre 9-12 record. Mullaney immediately produced a winning team (14-8), and he went on to register only one losing season during his initial fourteen-year tenure. Mullaney's 271-94 overall record earned him several head coaching positions in the professional ranks before his return to Providence in 1981. Dave Gavitt, who became Mullaney's successor in 1969, compiled an equally impressive record, for which he was designated head coach of the 1980 U.S. Olympic team.

During the Mullaney-Gavitt era (1955–1979), tiny Providence College was often a nationally ranked basketball power. The Friars won two titles in the National Invitational Tournament (1961 and 1963) and were selected for several NCAA tourneys. Their 1972–73 team, starring two hometown boys—Ernie DiGregorio of North Providence and Marvin Barnes of South Providence (shown here)—won the NCAA Eastern Regionals. This squad is regarded as PC's all-time best. Other Friar luminaries who thrilled local basketball fans included Johnny Egan, Lenny Wilkens, Vin Ernst, Ray Flynn, Bill Blair, Jimmy Walker, Jim Hadnot, John Thompson, Jim Benedict, Mike Riordan, Kevin Stacom, Fran Costello, and Providence's own Joe Hassett and Andy Clary, now a respected local clergyman. Several of these PC greats also enjoyed successful careers in the National Basketball Association, and Flynn went on to become mayor of Boston.

When the fortunes of the basketball Friars declined in the early 1980s in the face of Big East competition, Providence College hockey and, especially, cross-country grabbed the spotlight. For a decade in the 1970s and early 1980s, Friar runners dominated New England long-distance running events and were consistently among the best in the nation. This dominance was due primarily to a steady stream of Irish imports, some of whom took up permanent residence in Rhode Island. The most notable performer among this wave of talented runners was John Treacy, the 1984 Olympic silver medalist for Ireland in the marathon. Photo (1973) courtesy of the Providence College Archives

234

McCoy Stadium in Pawtucket was a depression-era project begun and completed by Mayor Thomas P. McCoy despite strong criticism from political opponents and the misgivings of his associates. The structure, built at a cost of $1.2 million on the swampy site of Hammond Pond, was dedicated in July 1942, and it was named for its sponsor after his death in 1945. From 1942 to 1949 it was home to the Pawtucket Slaters of the Class A New England League, and in 1966 and 1967 it was the ballpark of the Pawtucket Indians.

Then, in 1973, the Boston Red Sox made Pawtucket the home of their Triple-A International League farm team, the Pawtucket Red Sox. Since that time the "Pawsox," under owner Ben Mondor, have provided Rhode Islanders with quality professional baseball, and Pawtucket has been a steppingstone for such future major league stars as strikeout king Roger Clemens and American League batting champions Jim Rice, Fred Lynn, and Wade Boggs. In 1981 McCoy Stadium entered the record books as the site of professional baseball's longest game ever—a thirty-three inning interrupted contest in which Pawtucket beat Rochester, 3 to 2. Photo (ca. 1985) courtesy of Pawtucket Red Sox and Lou Schwecheimer

The state's most renowned sports attraction is the International Tennis Hall of Fame and Tennis Museum at the Newport Casino. James H. Van Alen, president of the Casino since 1951 and head of the museum since 1957, was the tennis devotee most responsible for this shrine to the greats of the court. It was at Newport's famed Casino that Richard D. Sears—the hall's first inductee—won the first national lawn tennis championship in 1881. "Now," says Van Alen, "a lover of tennis can come to Newport and see the finest of the past and present in tennis—major competition on the actual courts used by our first champion, and a museum commemorating the greats from Sears himself to the present." Presently the Virginia Slims tourney for women and the Volvo Hall of Fame classic for men attract the best professionals to the Newport Casino's hallowed grass courts on an annual basis. Photo courtesy of PPL

Hispanic (or Spanish-speaking) residents of Rhode Island are one of the more recent additions to the state's ethnically diverse population and its most rapidly growing ethnocultural group. In 1960, shortly after an initial migration from Castro's Cuba, the state had only a handful of Spanish-speaking inhabitants. By 1970 the number had grown to 6,961, and in the 1980 census it stood at 19,707. The present Hispanic population of the state probably exceeds 35,000, according to knowledgeable sources, because of several factors: the 1980 count was understated; Hispanics have a high birth rate; and a steady flow of immigrants has continued through the present decade. Providence contains approximately half the Hispanic population, but large numbers also live in Pawtucket and Central Falls. Despite local population gains, however, Hispanics are not as numerically significant in Providence and the Blackstone Valley as they are in many other northeastern industrial centers.

Rhode Island's Hispanics are not a homogeneous lot. Some are white, some predominantly black; others are of mixed blood, including a few of American Indian ancestry. Some, such as the Puerto Ricans, came here as U.S. citizens, but most arrived as aliens. Some came from South America and countries as remote as Argentina and Peru; others hail from Central America and Mexico; still others ventured to the state from the Caribbean islands, especially Puerto Rico, Cuba, and Santo Domingo. Some came directly from their homeland, while others journeyed to Rhode Island's urban areas from the slums of larger municipalities such as New York City and Newark. In fact, the Latin "community" is not one united group at all, but rather a loose confederation of recently arrived Spanish-speaking migrants from about a dozen and a half separate (and sometimes antagonistic) Latin American nations.

Because most Spanish-speaking people are nominally Roman Catholic, Bishop Russell J. McVinney established a Latin American apostolate in 1970 under the direction of Father Raymond L. Tetreault to meet their spiritual and cultural needs. The old Irish parish of St. Michael's in South Providence conducts Spanish-language masses and provides other

services to these newcomers, most of whom live in the city's south side. In Central Falls, where many Colombians reside, Holy Trinity Church performs a similar spiritual and cultural function.

The continuing connection of Colombians with their homeland, while a cultural stimulus, has had one undesirable effect: because of a few immigrants, some of them illegal aliens, Central Falls has gained widespread notoriety as a center of illicit drug trafficking. The national media has in fact recently accorded Rhode Island's smallest city the dubious title of "Cocaine Capital of the North." Generally, however, Rhode Island's Hispanics are law-abiding and exhibit a strong work ethic of long hours and second jobs in their drive for upward socioeconomic mobility. Photo courtesy of PJC

Southeast Asians, victims of the political and military upheavals in that area of the globe, are Rhode Island's newest immigrants, arriving in the state from 1975 onward. Like the Hispanics, they are diverse in their old-world backgrounds. According to 1983 estimates, about 300 are Vietnamese, 2,300 are Hmong, 2,500 are Khmer from Cambodia, and 600 are Laotian. The Vietnamese, who are either Catholic or Buddhist, enjoy the highest socioeconomic standing among the Southeast Asians and are spread geographically throughout the state. Those who are Catholic (owing to the labors of missionary priests in French Indochina) attend services conducted for them at St. Michael's Church in South Providence.

The Hmong are tribal, hill-country people from northern Laos who have settled mostly on the south side of Providence. The size of their community gives Providence the largest colony of Hmong refugees east of the Mississippi. Most of these migrants came to Providence from Thai refugee camps, bringing with them few or no material possessions. During the Vietnam War the Hmong had been dependable U.S. allies, serving as a secret army that helped to check Communist troop movements in Laos.

The Khmer are Cambodian refugees from the bloody purge of Western culture visited upon their homeland by the Communist Khmer Rouge led by Pol Pot. Their principal Rhode Island area of settlement has been Providence, especially Smith Hill, South Providence, Elmwood, and the West End. Most Khmer are devout Buddhists.

The fourth major Southeast Asian group to find refuge in Rhode Island are Laotians who fled the repression of the Communist Pathet Lao. Also Buddhists, the six-hundred member Laotian community is divided between Providence (250) and Woonsocket (350), where this photo shows a Laotian family pausing in prayer before festivities begin at their South Main Street home. The food around the centerpiece is a symbolic offering to ancestors.

Regardless of their religion or national origin, Southeast Asian refugees have impressed social workers and resettlement officials as very industrious and extremely family-oriented. One characteristic that bodes well for the future of these new immigrants is their strong interest in education. More than 250 Southeast Asian students were enrolled during the 1985–86 academic year at the University of Rhode Island alone, and many others are taking courses at the state's community college.

Between 1983 and 1986 the state's Southeast Asian population doubled, reaching over 12,000, according to leaders of the local resettlement effort. Photo (ca. 1985) courtesy of Louise Lind

Although the Narragansett Indians were detribalized in 1880 and sold the last 922 acres of their reservation to the state for five thousand dollars, their nondenominational church in Charlestown (established in 1741) remained in use, and many mixed-blood descendants of the Narragansetts continued to observe Indian traditions and festivals. Then, in 1934, the Narragansetts incorporated and reorganized under an elected chief and a tribal council.

Prompted by the national Native American rights movement of the 1960s and 1970s, the Narragansetts filed suit in federal court to regain 3,200 acres of land allegedly taken from them in violation of a 1790 federal statute. Following lengthy negotiations, an out-of-court settlement was signed in 1978 that provided for the return of over 1,800 acres of ancestral lands in Charlestown to the Narragansett Tribe of Indians, Inc. This vindication brought a resurgence in cultural activity, and the annual powwows, such as the one depicted (left), took on new meaning and significance. In 1985, however, the Indians received a setback when the federal government rejected a Narragansett request to grant reservation status to their tribal domain. Photo of annual Narragansett Indian powwow in Charlestown (1980) courtesy of George H. Utter and the Westerly Sun

During the 1930s and 1940s, the decades of depression and war, the status of Newport as a summer resort had waned. In 1957, however, national attention again focused on this historic city when President Dwight D. Eisenhower selected Newport as the site for his summer White House. Here Ike and Mamie are shown at the Newport Naval Base en route to Fort Adams, where they resided in a Victorian mansion that has since been named Eisenhower House in honor of its distinguished occupant.

In 1961 Eisenhower's successor, John F. Kennedy, also chose Newport for his summer White House, which he established at Hammersmith Farm, an Ocean Drive estate belonging to the Auchincloss family. Kennedy's wife, the former Jacqueline Bouvier, was a member of this famous clan, and JFK had married her in Newport in 1953 at historic St. Mary's Roman Catholic Church on Spring Street.

Presidential selection of Newport by both a Republican and a Democrat as the place to spend the summer was a bipartisan endorsement that did much to reestablish the Ocean State's reputation as a desirable resort area. Photo (ca. 1957) courtesy of PPL

The most successful and durable Republican of the era has been John H. Chafee. After a stint in the legislature, part of it as minority leader, and three terms as governor (1963–1969), Chafee served as secretary of the navy (1969–1972) in the Nixon administration. Though unsuccessful in his 1972 campaign against incumbent senator Claiborne Pell, Chafee won a seat in the U.S. Senate on his second try in 1976. He was reelected by a narrow margin in 1982.

This photo of Chafee meeting the press shows him in a most appropriate pose, for the Warwick Republican has effectively employed the media and the techniques of modern public relations to overcome strong Democratic grass-roots organizational advantages. In his skillful use (critics say manipulation) of the media and public opinion, Chafee became the first of Rhode Island's new-style politicians. Photo (ca. 1965) courtesy of PPL

Though Rhode Island women received the vote in 1920, it has been only in the last decade that they have exerted a powerful influence in local and state politics. In 1980 Claudine Schneider became the first woman ever elected to Congress from Rhode Island; two years later Susan Farmer (right) was elected secretary of state, thus becoming the Ocean State's first female general officer. Meanwhile, from 1975 to 1984, Lila M. Sapinsley efficiently presided as minority leader of the state Senate. The most spectacular breakthrough of all, however, occurred in 1984, when former Sister of Mercy Arlene Violet, on her second try, became Rhode Island's (and America's) first female attorney general, attracting nationwide recognition in the process. Significantly, all four of this political vanguard are members of the GOP, a party that recorded another political breakthrough when it selected a woman—Leila Mahoney (left)—as its state chairman in 1986. Ironically, both Farmer and Violet were defeated in the 1986 general election.

On the Democratic side, the most notable female achiever thus far is Florence Kerins Murray of Newport, who became, successively, the first woman associate justice of the Superior Court (1956), that court's first female presiding justice (1978), and the first woman to sit on the Rhode Island Supreme Court (1979). In the 1986 election another Newporter, Kathleen Connell, also achieved political distinction when she won the race for secretary of state, becoming the first Democratic woman to gain general office in Rhode Island. Photo (1986) courtesy of the Republican State Central Committee

Modern Rhode Island has produced several writers of widely recognized ability. The scholarly output of the Brown University faculty has, of course, been enormous, but popular authors have also been significant. One of these is Howard Phillips Lovecraft (1890–1937). Relatively obscure during his lifetime, Lovecraft has recently emerged as a major figure in the field of occult and horror fiction, with some critics even dubbing this Providence native "the Edgar Allan Poe of the twentieth century."

One measure of literary attainment in modern America has been the Pulitzer Prize, a coveted award presented annually by Columbia University. A number of Rhode Island writers have earned this distinguished prize, including Newport's Maud Howe Elliott (1917) for coauthoring a biography of her famed mother, Julia Ward Howe; Oliver La Farge (1929), also of Newport, for Laughing Boy, his novel of southwestern Indian life; Leonard Bacon of Peace Dale (1941) for his poetry; Providence Journal writers George W. Potter (1944) for his distinguished editorials and Jack White (1974) for his investigative reporting of the Nixon scandals; and, most widely read of all among this prize-wining contingent, Edwin O'Connor.

Born in Providence in 1918, O'Connor (shown here) spent his early life in Woonsocket, attended its public schools and La Salle Academy, and finished his education at the University of Notre Dame. After graduation in 1939, he worked in several cities as a radio announcer, served as a coastguardsman in World War II, and then settled in Boston to work as a

EDWIN O'CONNOR   *Fabian Bachrach*

writer-producer for the Yankee radio network. Before long he left radio to become a free-lance writer. In 1946 he sold his first piece to the Atlantic Monthly, *and a year later he published his first short story. While he continued to write short stories and articles, O'Connor became best known as the author of several important novels, including* The Last Hurrah *(1956), a classic tale of Irish-American political life;* The Edge of Sadness *(1961), for which he received the Pulitzer Prize in 1962; and* All in the Family *(1966). He died in 1968.*

Among the state's other major literati are S. J. Perelman, a prolific and highly regarded humorist, raised on Providence's Smith Hill; Edward McSorley, author of Our Own Kind *(1948), a Book-of-the-Month Club novel about Irish-American life in South Providence; Faith McNulty of Wakefield, author of* The Burning Bed *(1980), upon which a major TV film concerning wife abuse was based; and Providence-born David Plante, author of a trilogy about local Franco-American life. Photo by Fabian Bachrach*

In the period from World War II to the present, Rhode Island provided Broadway, Hollywood, and the national news media with several notable personalities. Providence's contribution has been the most impressive. Nelson Eddy (1901–1967), the son of a toolmaker from Hartford Park, and Elmwood's Ruth Hussey (born Ruth Carol O'Rourke in 1914) gained fame for their acting ability. Fred Friendly, president of CBS News from 1964 to 1966 and a highly regarded authority on issues relating to the media, was born in 1915 as Fred Wachenheimer, the son of an East Side jeweler. Renowned jazz trumpeter Robert L. "Bobby" Hackett (1915–1976), the son of a North End blacksmith, began his career at He Gong "Charlie" Tow's famous Port Arthur Restaurant on Weybosset Street; composer-pianist Frankie Carle, whose compositions include "Autumn Leaves," grew up in Eagle Park; and rock star Jeffrey Osborne is also a Providence native.

Pawtucket has produced two well-known news commentators, Irving R. Levine of NBC (who also had connections with South Providence and Hope High School) and David Hartman, host of "Good Morning America." Comedienne Ruth Buzzi hails from Westerly, actor James Woods from Warwick, and actor Van Johnson from Newport. Woonsocket has furnished the entertainment field with Metropolitan Opera star Eileen Farrell, the first inductee into that city's Hall of Fame, and Eddie Dowling (born Nelson Gaucher in 1889), who used his mother Bridget's maiden name of Dowling during

a brilliant Broadway career as actor, composer, producer, and Pulitzer Prize-winning playwright. Though not native Rhode Islanders, sportscaster Chris Schenkel and TV actor Ted Knight (1923–1986) are among the notables who have launched their careers in the Ocean State.

On the local scene, Providence's Trinity Square Repertory Company has been guided to national prominence by its

director, Adrian Hall. In 1981 Trinity won the coveted Tony award for its sustained contribution to American theater arts.

In this 1955 photo, taken at the annual Woonsocket Mardi Gras festival, Eddie Dowling (right) poses with another notable Woonsocket native, Leo "Gabby" Hartnett (left), a member of baseball's Hall of Fame. Photo by Andrew P. Palmer, courtesy of the Woonsocket Call

The broadcast media has had an enormous impact on modern Rhode Island, shaping public opinion, providing entertainment, and informing Rhode Islanders about the world around them. It all began on June 2, 1922, when Shepard's department store sponsored the state's first radio station (WEAN). Three months later, on September 6, the Outlet Company beamed back with WJAR, the embryo of what has become the Providence-based Outlet Broadcasting empire. Mowry Lowe—the best known of the pioneer announcers—has written a brief history of the early years of radio in Rhode Island.

Television made its debut after World War II. The first station—WJAR-TV, Channel 10—began operating on July 10, 1949, with an NBC and ABC affiliation; a second—WPRO-TV (later WPRI), Channel 12—commenced its telecasts on March 27, 1955, as a member of the CBS network; and a third major station—WTEV (later WLNE), Channel 6—was established on January 1, 1963, to serve both Providence and New Bedford audiences. A state educational station, Channel 36, originally based at Rhode Island College, began programming on June 5, 1967.

The influence of the electronic media on any state is subtle but pervasive. Media personalities often capture the attention of the listening or viewing public, some for brief periods, a few for a generation or more, becoming local institutions as well known as any governor. The most durable media personalities have been Harry McKenna, WEAN's dean of news commentators, and WPRO's Bud Toevs, talk-show hosts Sherm Strickhouser and Jack Comley, and all-purpose radio and TV celebrity Tony DiBiasio. Television anchorpersons have come and gone with remarkable frequency, but Dave Layman and Ann Conway (TV-6), Doug White and Patrice Wood (TV-10), and Walter Cryan (TV-12) have shown remarkable longevity. Mort Blender and John Sweeney

were also longtime local favorites. The most hardy of the weathermen have been Hank Bouchard, Art Lake, and John Ghiorse. Memorable sportscasters include multitalented Warren Walden, Chris Clark (voice of the PC Friars), and Mike Gorman. The grand old men among radio disc jockeys have been Chuck Stevens and Carl Henry, both dating from the early years of rock and roll. But the most venerable and popular media personality of all is Walter L. "Salty" Brine of WPRO-AM.

Salty (right) made his debut in the early 1940s, and his ratings remain consistently high. Even more than many other media personalities, he has been heavily involved in charitable and civic projects. This 1976

photo was taken when he officially greeted the Freedom Train during its bicentennial visit. Another member of the reception committee was Vincent A. "Buddy" Cianci (center), then in his first term as mayor of Providence. The controversial Cianci, after more than nine eventful, memorable, and productive years in office, was forced to resign in 1984 following an assault charge arising out of a family dispute. Always resilient, the former mayor became a radio talk-show host in 1985 and promptly boosted his WHJJ program to the top of the ratings, rivaling Salty himself in popularity. (At left in this picture is the author, who has yet to make his media debut.) Photo (1976) by Louis Notarianni, from the author's collection

First-rate summer entertainment has been a Rhode Island tradition for more than a century. In the modern era, producer George Wein's Newport jazz and folk festivals and Tommy Brent's live stage productions at Matunuck's Theatre-by-the-Sea have gained national recognition. Though well attended by Rhode Islanders, these attractions have drawn a major portion of their audiences from out of state.

Another and locally more popular source of entertainment is the Warwick Musical Theatre. From its first show on June 24, 1955, starring Judy Tyler (of the "Howdy Doody Show") in the musical Annie Get Your Gun, to 1986's "something for everyone" schedule of one-nighters, the Warwick Musical Theatre has been the place for Rhode Islanders to be entertained during the summer months.

The theater had its inception when Burton "Buster" Bonoff, Ben Segal, and an enthusiastic and supportive board of directors visualized the cow pasture on Quaker Lane as becoming a Rhode Island landmark for quality entertainment. They transformed the grounds into a 2,200-seat theater-in-the-round, with no seat more than twenty rows from the stage. The intimacy of a central stage with a minimum of scenery was readily accepted by the public, some of whom included their front-row season seats in their wills, bequeathing them to favorite relatives.

Broadway's hit musicals, such as Show Boat, Gentlemen Prefer Blondes, Carousel, and South Pacific, were the nucleus of each season, with a repertory company rehearsing one show during the day and presenting another in the evening (shown here is a cast rehearsal in the old tent for the musical Can-Can). The "no-name" format was broken in 1958 when Howard Keel appeared in Carousel, and the star system was born. The first one-man spectacular was "An Evening with Danny Kaye" in 1961.

In 1967 the Warwick Musical Theatre became a hardtop, and a mezzanine brought its capacity to the present 3,328. The theater's green, yellow, and white tents, although colorful and pleasing to the eye, had a lifespan of only four years.

When Broadway failed to produce hit musicals in abundance, the theater compensated by booking Las Vegas headliners for week-long stays. The roster of stars who have appeared includes some of the brightest performers of stage, movies, and television. Show business legends— Jack Benny, George Burns, Perry Como, Sammy Davis, Jr., Johnny Carson, Bob Hope, Liberace (whose fifteen years of appearances are the theater's record)— have performed to standing-room-only audiences. Some of today's top stars were opening acts at Warwick for more famous performers: Wayne Newton was on the bill with Jack Benny; George Carlin and Joan Rivers warmed up the audience for John Davidson; the Oak Ridge Boys preceded Mel Tillis; and Neil Sedaka started his comeback with the Carpenters, then returned the following year as the head-liner. In recent years the theater has moved toward scheduling shorter engage-ments, a trend culminating in its 1986 series of one-nighters. Photo courtesy of the Warwick Musical Theatre

In the years following World War II, a scarcity of new housing (resulting from depression and war), an abundance of newly-married couples, an expansion of the highway system, and easy mortgage terms offered by the Federal Housing Administration (FHA) and the Veterans' Administration (VA), combined to generate an enormous home construction boom in suburbia. Most of the building occurred in contractors' developments that occupied a substantial land area. Plats like Governor Francis Farms, Dean Estates, Oak Hill, Garden Hills, Saylesville Highlands, Brentwood, and Kent Heights became symbols of this new suburban lifestyle. These plats differed from their urban predecessors in two key ways: rather than forming rectangular blocks, most were laid out along new, gently curving streets; and they were usually developed by builders who constructed on speculation rather than on order for individual clients.

The most famous and ambitious of the new suburban developments was Garden City, a 233-acre Cranston community established by Nazarene Meloccarro in an area off Reservoir Avenue near the site of a former coal mine. Garden City offered home buyers not only easy access to Providence but also a variety of architectural styles to choose from, unlike some plats that endlessly replicated the single-level ranch house. The development was also unusual in being a totally planned community, one that included a cluster of apartment buildings, a school whose site was donated to the city by the developer, and the Garden City Shopping Center, the state's first suburban mall.

The migrants to Garden City came mainly from Providence and the older area of eastern Cranston. Generally they were middle-class families with school-age children, drawn by the suburban ideal of private home ownership, respectability, and open space. In 1986 Garden City experienced a revitalization when its new owner, the Massachusetts-based Flatley Company, began a projected $15 million renovation. Photo (1965) courtesy of the Cranston Historical Society

This street-level view of a typical suburban dwelling features the dominant architectural style in postwar suburbia—the ranch. During this era Warwick attracted more new suburbanites than any Rhode Island community, growing from a 1940 population of 28,757 (the state's sixth largest total) to a count of 87,123 in 1980. At that time Warwick ranked only behind Providence, which had supplied it with many of its new inhabitants. Photo (ca. 1960) courtesy of Rhode Island Historical Preservation Commission

In 1950 Providence, Pawtucket, Woonsocket, and Newport, in that order, were Rhode Island's most important retail trade centers. By 1982 suburbanization had propelled Warwick into the number one position as it outstripped Providence by a margin of $663 million to $600 million in the value of retail sales. Warwick's rapid rise was hastened by the construction of two major shopping malls during the late 1960s at the junction of Interstate Routes 95 and 295 (shown in this aerial view).

The Rhode Island (originally Midland) Mall, consisting of 490,000 square feet, was constructed between 1965 and 1968; Warwick Mall (in the upper part of the photo), consisting of 1,045,000 square feet, was begun in 1968 and opened in 1972.

Three years later the merchants of Pawtucket and Woonsocket were also confronted with new retailing competition when the 447,000-square-foot Lincoln Mall opened on the Washington Highway

near the intersection of Route 146 and Interstate Route 295.

In the 1980s Providence has staged a comeback, leading the state with over 1,500,000 square feet of new commercial development, though most of this has been office space rather than retail stores. Photo (1976) by Earl H. Goodison, from Rhode Island Historical Preservation Commission, Warwick (1981)

The postwar suburban exodus affected not only homes, factories, and stores but Providence educational institutions as well. Providence-Barrington Bible College moved from Smith Hill to the Peck estate in Barrington before closing in 1985; Bryant moved from the East Side to Smithfield in 1971; the state junior college left the Promenade industrial area for Warwick in 1972; Rhode Island College went from downtown to a spacious 125-acre campus on the Providence-North Providence line in 1958; and the ever-expanding Johnson and Wales branched out into Warwick, Cranston, Scituate, and Seekonk, Massachusetts. But no urban school chose a site more picturesque than Roger Williams College.

The seal of Roger Williams bears the inscription "Incorporated 1956," but the college's origins go back to the fall of 1919, when Boston's prestigious Northeastern University opened a business-administration extension school in the Providence YMCA. To this an evening law school was added the following year. After graduating a number of competent students (including John O. Pastore), the state's only law school closed in 1933, and a wartime decline in students prompted the shutdown of the business school in 1942. At that point the YMCA combined this business program with its own technical institute to form the Providence Institute of Engineering and Finance, a school that offered certificates rather than college degrees. Then, in 1948, the institute applied for and received designation as Rhode Island's

first junior college. In 1956 Roger Williams severed its legal connection with the Y and assumed its present identity, though it continued to occupy space in the YMCA and adjacent industrial buildings.

In July 1963 Dr. Ralph E. Gauvey, an Ohioan, became president of Roger Williams, and while emphasizing that his institution existed primarily "to provide an opportunity for students of average or unrealized potentiality," he led the fledgling college through a period of impressive growth and development. Highlights of Gauvey's regime were the transformation of Roger Williams to four-year college status in 1967 and the acquisition of this 63-acre campus in Bristol over-

looking Mount Hope Bay. The new facility opened in 1969, in part through the generosity of Dr. and Mrs. Marshall N. Fulton (she the former Mary Howe De Wolf).

Today Roger Williams has twenty-four hundred day students and fourteen hundred evening students, many of whom attend the extension division at La Salle Academy in Providence. Among its wide range of courses, the programs in architecture and the administration of justice have brought the college local distinction. Postcard view (ca. 1970) courtesy of RIHS

The Newport College—Salve Regina is a Catholic coeducational college of arts and sciences conducted under the auspices of the Sisters of Mercy. Since it first opened its doors to fifty women students in 1947, enrollment has climbed to seventeen hundred men and women, and the campus has expanded from this one original building—Ochre Court (1888-89), the famous Ogden Goelet mansion designed by Richard Morris Hunt—to eighteen buildings on fifty-five acres of Newport's beautiful and historic seacoast. The college sits on Cliff Walk off Bellevue Avenue, a street famous for its nineteenth-century mansions. The curriculum presently provides opportunities for over twenty areas of concentration leading to associate's, bachelor's, and master's degrees. Photo (ca. 1973) by Edward Tenczar, courtesy of the Rhode Island Yearbook Foundation

In September 1964 the Community College of Rhode Island began its existence as Rhode Island Junior College in classrooms fashioned from the offices of the old Brown and Sharpe Manufacturing Company on Promenade Street in Providence. In September 1972 the school moved to this "megastructure" designed by Howard H. Juster and built by the Dimeo Construction Company in Warwick on a farm donated to the state for educational use by Webster Knight. One architectural historian has described this innovative building as "probably the most significant contemporary structure in Rhode Island. Dramatically situated on a hilltop, it is admirably scaled to the highways it overlooks and from which its monumental appearance can be appreciated."

A second campus was opened in Lincoln in September 1976 and named in honor of Dr. William F. Flanagan, the able edu-

cator who guided the development of CCRI during its crucial formative years. From an original student body of 325, the junior college has expanded to enroll more than 12,000 full- and part-time students annually. Photo by Robert O. Jones from the Rhode Island Historical Preservation Commission, Warwick (1981)

With farmland totaling 62,466 acres in 1982 (approximately 10 percent of Rhode Island's land area), farm organizations and activities are still much in evidence throughout this highly urban state. Meeting halls for the Patrons of Husbandry (the Grange) exist in several rural villages, 4-H clubs are very active, the federal Farmers' Home Administration maintains an office in West Warwick, and two large agricultural fairs—Rocky Hill in East Greenwich and the Washington County Fair in Richmond—draw hundreds of participants and thousands of spectators each summer. Photo of an ox-pulling contest at the Washington County Fair (1974) by Charles Thibeault, courtesy of George H. Utter and the Westerly Sun

According to a 1980 state census of agriculture, Rhode Island had 470 farms, including those agricultural units designated as nurseries (133), sawmills (29), and Christmas-tree farms (120). This figure constrasted with a 1940 figure of 3,014 and an 1880 tally of 6,216 farms. The units that remain operative have survived in competition with other land uses, and their survival has depended upon both their adjustment to the surrounding urban landscape and favorable tax valuations of agricultural land by local governments. Nearly all the state's remaining farms are commercial enterprises; the early general family farm has virtually disappeared.

The present basic sources of farm income, ranked in order, are (1) dairy farming; (2) crops, especially hay, potatoes, and apples; and (3) nursery and greenhouse products. Middletown and Portsmouth are the towns with the largest percentage of intensively cultivated agricultural land, and only Pawtucket and Central Falls have none.

In 1985, agriculture, forestry, fisheries, and mining together employed only 2,986 Rhode Islanders—less than 1 percent of the total work force. Yet agriculture has a value beyond its ability to produce food or provide employment. Farmland recharges the water table, provides a buffer against noise, supports greater populations of small-game animals than forest cover alone can do, and adds to the aesthetic quality of the landscape.

An increasing awareness of the value of the state's farms prompted the General Assembly to pass the Farmland Preservation Act in 1981. This farsighted measure allows the state to buy development rights to agricultural land "so as to maintain farming, productive open spaces, and ground water recharge areas." To administer the program, the act established an eleven-member Agricultural Land Preservation Commission charged with conserving "land suitable for food production," which it termed an "extremely scarce and valuable resource." Photo of East Greenwich dairy farm (ca. 1970s) from Marion I. Wright and Robert J. Sullivan, The Rhode Island Atlas (1982)

On February 6, 1978, Rhode Island began one of its major bouts with the forces of nature. That was the day on which the Great Blizzard began. In the state's annals it will be as memorable as the hurricanes of 1815, 1938, and 1954.

The snow began about 10:30 a.m. Monday and continued through the night and the daylight hours of the following day. By the time the storm finally subsided about 10:00 p.m. on Tuesday, the state had been buried under a mantle of snow that varied in depth from ten inches on Block Island and fourteen inches in Newport to an incredible fifty-five inches in Manville. The intensity and duration of the storm—labeled afterwards by meteorologists as a "winter hurricane"—were not accurately predicted, and thus it caught most people by surprise.

Providence was the municipality most affected by the blizzard's impact. The city was rendered immobile under thirty-five inches of snow. As workers fled for home, they found the on-ramps and the inter-

states themselves unplowed, and so their backed-up traffic clogged not only I-95 and I-195 but the streets of downtown and the major city thoroughfares as well. This compounded the difficulty of plowing, and some streets remained impassable for as long as a week. This photo of commuters from Lincoln debarking from a RIPTA bus at Hay and Dyer streets in downtown Providence was taken on Monday, February 13, seven days after the blizzard's onset.

Since the state and the city were brought to a standstill and twenty-one snow-related deaths were recorded, Rhode Island was designated a federal disaster area, allowing the dispatch of army and National Guard units with heavy equipment to aid in the dig-out. With auto traffic virtually halted, the Great Blizzard proved to have at least one salutary effect: temporarily, at least, face-to-face pedestrian encounters overcame the impersonality of the fast-paced mode of travel foisted upon us by the automobile. *Photo courtesy of PJC*

With a higher percentage of its structures on the National Register than any other state, Rhode Island is a national leader in the field of historic preservation. Several small communities, especially Bristol and the North Kingstown village of Wickford, have an impressive number of historic buildings, but Providence and Newport abound with such structures.

Taking inspiration and direction from the pioneering efforts of architects Norman M. Isham (1864–1943) and John Hutchins Cady (1881–1967), the Providence Preservation Society (PPS) was organized in 1956 to salvage historic College Hill architecture for private residential use. John Nicholas Brown became the society's first chairman of the board, and Mrs. William Slater Allen its dynamic president.

Working in concert with the City Plan Commission, the PPS prepared a pathbreaking report, College Hill: Demonstration Study of Historic Area Renewal (1959; revised edition, 1967), that sparked the restoration of Benefit Street and its surrounding area. Success was due in part to aesthetically oriented private investors, especially Mrs. Malcolm G. Chace, Jr., who acquired and restored for resale about forty houses on College Hill.

Newport, whose architecture is even more spectacular than Providence's, has been equally vigorous. In 1945 the Preservation Society of Newport County was formed to save the Hunter House on Washington Street, and it thereafter turned its efforts toward restoring the aura of Gilded Age Newport by acquiring and refurbishing such splendid mansions as The Breakers, The Elms, Rosecliff, Kingscote, Marble House, and Chateau-sur-Mer. A group of preservation-minded Newporters led by Nadine Pepys founded Operation Clapboard in 1963 to save the city's older houses, especially those in the historic Point district. Rather than acquire ownership of these structures, Operation Clapboard established a small revolving fund to take options on them until a suitable buyer could be found.

Most ambitious of all preservation efforts has been the Newport Restoration Foundation, established in 1968 under the direction of heiress Doris Duke to preserve and refurbish the eighteenth- and early nineteenth-century domestic architecture of Newport. This nonprofit agency has salvaged and restored nearly a hundred houses, which have then been leased to private individuals. One such structure is the King's Arms Tavern (1698) on Cross Street, shown in this sequence before, during, and after restoration.

In 1968 the Rhode Island Historical Preservation Commission was created to enable the state to partake in the recently established federal preservation program. This state agency was placed under the able and zealous direction of Antoinette F. Downing, who had made her debut as an architectural historian and preservationist in 1937 by publishing a Carnegie-financed study entitled Early Homes of Rhode Island. Later she coauthored the Architectural Heritage of Newport, Rhode Island, 1640–1915 (1952; rev. ed. 1967). Her efforts in Providence, and statewide since 1968, have been recognized by her selection as trustee of the National Trust for Historic Preservation and as fellow of the Rhode Island Historical Society. Photos by Robert Foley, courtesy of the Rhode Island Yearbook Foundation

Rhode Island boasts two major heritage observances conducted on an annual basis—Gaspee Days and the Bristol Fourth of July parade. By far the newer is Gaspee Days, initiated in 1966 by David Stackhouse and others to commemorate the June 1772 burning of the infamous British customs ship *Gaspee* on Namquit Point. Run by a dedicated group of volunteers who style themselves the Gaspee Days Committee, the observance is centered in the village of Pawtuxet and usually extends for a two-week period in late May and early June.

Across the bay in Bristol occurs the granddaddy of all American patriotic celebrations, the Bristol Fourth of July parade, which has been held in almost unbroken succession since 1786. With nearly the entire town of twenty thousand residents mobilizing to stage this mammoth event, the parade attracts heritage groups from throughout the region as well as a hundred thousand spectators or more. This photo from a Bristol parade in the 1970s shows an antique auto entered by Channel 6 television—a consistent supporter of public heritage projects, including this 350th anniversary history. In the early 1980s WLNE-TV 6 broadcast two three-hour Bristol parades live and in their entirety, adding greatly to the impact of this historic and nationally renowned observance. Photo by Hartley Alley

A state symbol and Providence's most famous piece of statuary is the Gorham-cast Independent Man. As one historian puts it, the Man recalls "the individualism, autonomy, democratic localism, self-reliance, and entrepreneurial leadership which characterized Rhode Island during the colonial and early national periods."

On August 9, 1975, the Independent Man was lifted from his lofty perch atop the State House for repairs and a new coat of gold leaf. His regilding was undertaken by the state as a bicentennial project, one which attracted great public attention. The refurbished figure was then placed on display in November 1975 at Warwick Mall (shown here with the statue, left to right, are Marty Byrne, a state labor leader who supervised the Man's descent as organized labor's contribution to the statewide observance; Lieutenant Governor J. Joseph Garrahy; William Dugan, director of public buildings; and Dr. Patrick Conley, Rhode Island Bicentennial Commission chairman). At this site the Man drew thousands of admirers, prompting a lawsuit by owners of other malls that forced his return to the State House (though a full-size replica now marks the spot of the Man's bicentennial visit). After greeting visitors for several months in the rotunda, the eleven-foot statue was returned (with difficulty) to the capitol's dome by helicopter on July 20, 1976, in a spectacle that attracted thousands of viewers.

Rhode Island was very active in celebrating the bicentennial observance, earning national recognition for the scope and variety of its events. The state commission (ri76) was headquartered in the Old State House on Benefit Street, from which it arranged hundreds of historical commemorations and ethnic heritage events throughout the state. The commission supplied the seed money to lure the Tall Ships to Newport in June 1976 and staged a mammoth Rhode Island Independence Day parade in May 1976—reputedly the largest demonstration of its kind since World War II—that drew more than eighty thousand viewers to downtown Providence. In 1976 the commission coordinated the local arrival of the Bicentennial Wagon Train and the much-heralded Freedom Train. Further, it published about two dozen books and pamphlets concerning Rhode Island's Revolutionary experience, sponsored numerous historical reenactments and commemorations, and awarded funds to many private agencies, municipalities, militia groups, and heritage-oriented organizations to assist them in observing the bicentennial. In sum, Rhode Island was as much of a leader in the observance of the bicentennial of American independence as it was in the movement to gain that independence two hundred years before. Photo (November 1975) by Louis Notarianni, from the author's collection

In 1986 both the state and the city of Providence celebrated their 350th anniversaries. Neighborhood festivals, fireworks, laser shows, concerts, and appearances by world-famous entertainers marked the observance. As in 1976, when the bicentennial of independence was celebrated, a visit to Newport by the Tall Ships was a highlight of the celebration, consistent with Rhode Island's maritime tradition. Shown at anchor in Newport on June 27 are three of these famous sail training vessels: Venezuela's Simon Bolivar, left, tied up near Mexico's Cuauhtemoc, outboard, and the Sagres II from Portugal, inboard.

Unlike 1976, however, the 350th birthday bash was all "bread and circuses," a PR-man's creation on both the state and city levels. Notable and regrettable was the lack of permanent or long-range heritage projects: there were few historical publications, no special preservation efforts, no scholarly research or production, and no enduring cultural programs. When the sound and light waves generated by the major events dissipated in space and time, only memories remained. Photo by Andy Dickerman, courtesy of PJC

RHODE ISLAND CONSTITUTIONAL CONVENTION

19 86
GET THE FACTS ✦ KNOW THE ISSUES

Shall the action of the Constitutional Convention in amending the Constitution in the following manner be ratified and approved?

1 REWRITE OF THE PRESENT CONSTITUTION
☐ YES Shall the Constitution of 1843 and the 44 amendments ratified since
☐ NO then be adopted as rewritten, in proper order, with annulled sections removed? Shall the Constitutional Convention publish the Constitution in proper form, including new amendments, if they are approved by the voters? (Resolution 86-00042 B)

2 JUDICIAL SELECTION AND DISCIPLINE
☐ YES Shall a non-partisan, independent commission be established to
☐ NO nominate judges for appointment by the general assembly in the case of supreme court vacancies and for appointment by the governor in the case of vacancies in other courts? Shall the commission have authority to discipline or remove all judges? Shall judges appointed hereafter be required to retire at 72 years of age? Shall the duty of the supreme court to give advisory opinions be abolished? (Resolution 86-00080 A)

3 LEGISLATIVE PAY AND MILEAGE
☐ YES Shall the daily pay of general assembly members be established at a
☐ NO sum equal to the average weekly wage of Rhode Island manufacturing workers, divided by a four-day legislative week (about $76), the speaker receiving twice that amount; and shall mileage compensation be equal to the rate paid U.S. government employees, such pay and mileage to be limited to 60 days per year? (Resolution 86-00094 B)

4 FOUR-YEAR TERMS AND RECALL
☐ YES Beginning in 1988, shall the governor, lieutenant governor, secretary
☐ NO of state, attorney general, general treasurer and members of the general assembly be elected to four-year terms and be subject to recall by voters? (Resolution 86-00028 A)

5 VOTER INITIATIVE
☐ YES Shall voters be empowered to petition certain laws and/or constitu-
☐ NO tional amendments onto the ballot for voter approval or rejection? Shall future constitutional convention candidates be elected on a non-partisan basis? (Resolutions 86-00001 B, 86-00136)

6 ETHICS IN GOVERNMENT
☐ YES Shall more specific impeachment standards be established? Shall an
☐ NO ethics commission be established with authority to adopt a code of ethics and to discipline or remove public officials and employees found in violation of that code? Shall the general assembly adopt limits on campaign contributions and shall the general assembly enact a voluntary system of public campaign financing, coupled with limitations on total campaign spending by participating candidates? (Resolutions 86-00047 A, 86-00060 A, 8G-00145 A)

7 BUDGET POWERS AND EXECUTIVE SUCCESSION
☐ YES Shall the governor be constitutionally empowered to present an
☐ NO annual budget? Shall the speaker of the house become governor if both the governor and lieutenant governor die or are unable to serve? (Resolutions 86-00222, 86-00246)

8 RIGHTS OF THE PEOPLE
☐ YES Shall free speech, due process and equal protection clauses be added
☐ NO to the Constitution? Shall the state or those doing business with the state be prohibited from discriminating against persons solely on the basis of race, gender or handicap? Shall victims of crime have constitutionally endowed rights, including the right to compensation from perpetrators? Shall individual rights protected by the state constitution stand independent of the U.S. Constitution? (Resolutions 86-00033, 86-00032, 86-00140, 86-00002 B, 86-00171)

9 SHORE USE AND ENVIRONMENTAL PROTECTION
☐ YES Shall rights of fishery and privileges of the shore be described and
☐ NO shall the powers of the state and local government to protect those rights and the environment be enlarged? Shall the regulation of land and waters for these purposes not be deemed a public use of private property? (Resolutions 86-00003, 86-00004A)

10 FELON OFFICE HOLDING AND VOTING
☐ YES Shall felons' voting rights, removed upon conviction, be restored
☐ NO upon completion of sentence and probation or parole? Shall felons and certain misdemeanants be banned from holding office for three years after completion of sentence and probation or parole? (Resolutions 86-00149 A, 86-00025 B)

11 LIBRARIES
☐ YES Shall it be a duty of the general assembly to promote public libraries
☐ NO and library services? (Resolution 86-00098)

12 BAIL
☐ YES Shall the courts be authorized to deny bail to persons accused of the
☐ NO unlawful sale or distribution of controlled substances punishable by a sentence of ten years or more? (Resolution 86-00153 B)

13 HOME RULE
☐ YES Shall cities and towns with charters have more authority over local
☐ NO affairs, within the limits of the General Laws, including the power to tax and borrow with local voter approval (unless overridden by a three-fifths vote in the general assembly); to protect public health, safety, morals and the environment; to regulate local businesses and local planning and development? Shall new or increased tax exemptions pertaining to cities and towns be subject to local voter approval? Shall cities and towns be reimbursed for certain state-mandated programs? Shall charter adoption and amendment procedures be simplified? (Resolution 86-00196 B)

14 PARAMOUNT RIGHT TO LIFE/ABORTION
☐ YES To the extent permitted by the U.S. Constitution, shall all persons,
☐ NO including their unborn offspring, without regard to age, health, function, or condition of dependency, be endowed with an inalienable and paramount right to life; and to the extent permitted by the U.S. Constitution, shall abortion be prohibited, except that justified medical procedures to prevent the death of a pregnant woman shall be permitted? Shall the use of government monies to fund abortions be prohibited by the Constitution? (Resolution 86-00212 A)

VOTE
ON THE CONSTITUTIONAL QUESTIONS
TUESDAY, NOVEMBER 4th

As of 1986, the 143-year-old state constitution had been amended forty-four times, with suffrage requirments the most altered area. Although the amendment procedure was once very cumbersome, a change in the basic law can now be ratified by a majority of the whole membership of each house of the legislature, together with a majority of those electors voting thereon at a general election. This simpler process was accomplished in 1973 by Article of Amendment XLII, one of five changes successfully proposed by the limited constitutional convention of that year. In addition, Article XLII, sponsored by convention secretary Patrick T. Conley, professor of history and law at Providence College, provided a mechanism for allowing the voters to convene constitutional conven-

tions on a regular basis at least once every twelve years. This amendment was described editorially by the Providence Journal as "the most significant substantive alteration ever made in the state constitution."

The unlimited convention of 1986, which had the power to restructure Rhode Island's government, is Amendment XLII's direct legacy. That convention, chaired by Keven McKenna, made fourteen proposals (shown here) to the electorate in a November 1986 referendum. The most significant of these recommendations were a so-called "neutral rewrite" to delete annulled sections of the constitution and integrate the amendments into the main body of the document without substantive change; the establishment of a commission

on judicial selection and discipline; a proposal to increase legislators' pay; four-year terms for general officers and members of the General Assembly; voter initiative; a strengthening of the state bill of rights; greater home-rule powers for municipalities; and a very controversial provision prohibiting the use of government money to fund abortion and declaring the paramount right to life of all persons, including the unborn, to the extent permitted by the U.S. Constitution.

On November 4, 1986, Question 1 (the neutral rewrite) and Questions 6, 7, 8, 9, 10, 11, and 12 were approved by the electorate, while the others failed to pass. Broadside from the author's collection

The most ambitious and exciting plan for Providence's future is the Capital Center Project, a development that has been suggested in bits and pieces for decades—ever since the city engineers of the Gilded Age proposed a relocation of the railroad tracks northward to the base of Capitol Hill. The complete project now envisions not only the railroad relocation but also an office park and residential structures on the site of the present municipal parking lot, a civic-center highway interchange, a commerce and visitors' center in the old Union Station, and a possible convention center north of the Bonanza Bus Terminal.

In February 1982 a giant step towards the realization of the scheme was taken when Mayor Vincent A. Cianci, Jr., and the U.S. secretary of transportation signed a federal-state-city agreement to relocate the tracks. Simultaneously the Federal Railroad Administration released $32.5 million to fund the track-shift costs. Soon after, the Providence-Worcester Railroad began dismantling the "Chinese Wall" of elevated railroad tracks in the Canal Street-Memorial Square area.

The total project cost was estimated by planners in 1980 as $67 million, with the projected date of completion optimistically set for the late 1980s. The target date still appears realistic, but the cost of this massive undertaking may be three times original expectations because of rising prices and such addenda to the plan as the relocation of the Moshassuck and Woonasquatucket rivers. A Capital Center Commission was created at the outset to oversee this huge and promising enterprise.

This June 1986 aerial view of the development is diagonally bisected by the Woonasquatucket River. In the upper center, above I-95, is the incomplete Francis Street connector to downtown, which passes over the newly relocated main-line tracks. At the junction of Route 95 and the Woonasquatucket can be seen the beginnings of the Capital Center interchange; to the upper left is the new Union Station.

At the lower left center is the old Brown and Sharpe industrial complex, which private promoters, led by Anthony Guerra, have chosen as the site of a $120 million commercial development called The Foundry, to be anchored by a 300-room Sheraton Promenade Hotel. Clearly, Providence is again on the move! Photo (1986) by Andy Dickerman, courtesy of PJC

Dedicated in June 1986, the new Union Station is the keystone of Providence's Capital Center and that project's first building. It has allowed the elevated tracks separating downtown from the State House to be dismantled. According to one architectural historian, "Its size and limestone finish give it the monumental quality a train station deserves. The dome, colonnade and clock tower lend it the visual interest and presence that establish it as a major public structure."

In this frontal view of the new station, its dome is harmonized with those of the State House, which looms behind it. Photo (1986) by the author

This July 1986 photo of the Providence skyline was taken from the new Union Station plaza. Since the author's publication of a Providence pictorial history in 1982, two high-rise office buildings have been constructed. The buildings shown in this photo (left to right, with the dates of their completion) are the Old Stone tower (1986, extreme left, background); the Hospital Trust Building (1919); 40 Westminster Street (1969, located behind the Hospital Trust Building); the Hospital Trust Tower (1974); the Turk's Head Building (1913, background); the Fleet Center (1986); the Fleet Bank Building (1928); the Howard Building (1957, enlarged 1959, which appears as two structures because of the addition); City Hall (1878, with French Empire roof); and the Biltmore Plaza (1922). Photo (1986) by the author

Fortunately, the intrepid explorers and determined pioneers whose exploits were recounted at the outset of this volume have their modern-day Rhode Island counterparts. One such contemporary Rhode Islander, Colonel Sherwood C. "Woody" Spring, is the state's first astronaut. Raised in the Eden Park section of Cranston and the Glocester village of Harmony, Woody went from Ponagansett High School to West Point, where he received his degree in general engineering, and then on to the University of Arizona, where he earned his master's degree in aerospace engineering. After tours of duty in Vietnam and Korea and service as a test pilot, Spring was selected as an astronaut in May 1980.

On November 26, 1985, Woody blasted off from the Kennedy Space Center as mission specialist on the twenty-third flight in the space shuttle program. In the course of this flight, on two space walks 219 miles above the earth's surface, he became the first human to test techniques for the construction of a space station. In 1986 Woody returned from Houston to his home state, first to receive honorary degrees and public testimonials and then to be awarded the Rhode Island Star from the Rhode Island National Guard. In presenting Spring with an official citation from the state House of Representatives, speaker Matthew J. Smith captured the feeling of Rhode Islanders when he described the Glocester spaceman as "an authentic American hero." Photo courtesy of PJC

Bayles, Richard M., ed. *History of Newport County, Rhode Island*. New York, 1888.

Bayles, Richard M., ed. *History of Providence County, Rhode Island*. 2 vols. New York, 1891.

Boss, Judith A. *Newport: A Pictorial History*. Norfolk, Va., 1981.

Bridenbaugh, Carl. *Fat Mutton and Liberty of Conscience: Society in Rhode Island, 1636-1690*. Providence, 1974.

Cady, John H. *The Civic and Architectural Development of Providence*. Providence, 1957.

Carroll, Charles. *Rhode Island: Three Centuries of Democracy*. 4 vols. New York, 1932.

Cole, J. R. *History of Washington and Kent Counties, Rhode Island*. New York, 1889.

Coleman, Peter J. *The Transformation of Rhode Island, 1790-1860*. Providence, 1963.

Conley, Patrick T. *Democracy in Decline: Rhode Island's Constitutional Development, 1776-1841*. Providence, 1977.

Conley, Patrick T., and Paul R. Campbell. *Providence: A Pictorial History*. Norfolk, Va., 1982.

Conley, Patrick T., and Matthew J. Smith. *Catholicism in Rhode Island: The Formative Era*. Providence, 1976.

Davis, Hadassah, and Natalie Robinson. *History You Can See: Scenes of Change in Rhode Island, 1790-1910*. Providence, 1986.

Downing, Antoinette F. *Early Homes of Rhode Island*. Richmond, Va., 1937.

Downing, Antoinette F., and Vincent J. Scully, Jr. *The Architectural Heritage of Newport, 1640-1915*. 2nd ed. New York, 1967.

Federal Writers' Project, W.P.A. *Rhode Island: A Guide to the Smallest State*. Boston, 1937.

Field, Edward, ed. *State of Rhode Island and Providence Plantations at the End of the Century*. 3 vols. Boston, 1902.

Gleeson, Paul F. *Rhode Island: The Development of a Democracy*. Providence, 1957.

Greene, Welcome A. *The Providence Plantations for Two Hundred and Fifty Years*. Providence, 1886.

Hale, Stuart O. *Narragansett Bay: A Friend's Perspective*. URI, 1980.

Hedges, James B. *The Browns of Providence Plantations*. 2 vols. Providence, 1952 and 1968.

Hitchcock, Henry R. *Rhode Island Architecture*. New York, 1968.

James, Sydney V. *Colonial Rhode Island*. New York, 1975.

Lemons, J. Stanley, and George H. Kellner. *Rhode Island: The Independent State*. Woodland Hills, Calif., 1982.

Lovejoy, David S. *Rhode Island Politics and the American Revolution, 1760-1776*. Providence, 1958.

Mayer, Kurt B. *Economic Development and Population Growth in Rhode Island*. Providence, 1953.

McLoughlin, William G. *Rhode Island: A History*. New York, 1978.

Polishook, Irwin H. *Rhode Island and the Union, 1774-1795*. Evanston, Ill., 1969.

Providence Journal-Bulletin Almanac. Providence, annually since 1887.

Rhode Island Historical Preservation Commission. Municipal and neighborhood architectural surveys. Providence, irregularly.

Rhode Island History. Providence, quarterly. The journal of the Rhode Island Historical Society.

Rhode Island Publications Society. The Rhode Island Ethnic Heritage Pamphlet Series (1985-   ).

Rhode Island Secretary of State. *Rhode Island Manual*. Providence, biennially since 1867.

Rhode Island Yearbook (1963-1974).

Steinberg, Sheila, and Cathleen McGuigan. *Rhode Island: An Historical Guide*. Providence, 1976.

Wright, Marion I., and Robert J. Sullivan. *The Rhode Island Atlas*. Providence, 1982.

For a complete listing of published works on every phase of Rhode Island history, consult Roger Parks, comp., *Rhode Island: A Bibliography of Its History*. Hanover, N.H., 1983.

APPENDIX I

Population of Rhode Island
From 1708 to 1776

Towns and Divisions of the State	Settled or Incorp'ted	1708	1730	1748	1755	1774	1776
Barrington............	1770	....	....	....	....	601	538
Bristol...............	1747	....	....	1,069	1,080	1,209	1,067
Warren...............	1747	....	....	680	925	979	1,005
BRISTOL COUNTY.....	1747			1,749	2,005	2,789	2,610
Coventry..............	1741	....	....	792	1,178	2,023	2,300
East Greenwich.........	1677	240	1,223	1,044	1,167	1,663	1,664
West Greenwich.........	1741	....	....	766	1,246	1,764	1,653
Warwick..............	1643	480	1,178	1,782	1,911	2,438	2,376
KENT COUNTY........	1750	720	2,401	4,384	5,502	7,888	7,993
Fall River............	1856	....	....	....	....	....	....
Jamestown.............	1678	206	321	420	517	563	322
Little Compton.........	1747	....	....	1,152	1,170	1,232	1,302
Middletown............	1743	....	....	680	778	881	860
Newport..............	1639	2,203	4,640	6,508	6,753	9,209	5,299
New Shoreham.........	1672	208	290	300	378	575	478
Portsmouth...........	1638	628	813	992	1,363	1,512	1,347
Tiverton..............	1747	....	....	1,040	1,325	1,956	2,091
NEWPORT COUNTY....	1703	3,245	6,064	11,092	12,284	15,928	11,699
Burrillville...........	1806	....	....	....	....	....	....
Cranston..............	1754	....	....	....	1,460	1,861	1,701
Cumberland...........	1747	....	....	806	1,083	1,756	1,686
East Providence.........	1862	....	....	....	....	....	....
Foster...............	1781	....	....	....	....	....	....
Glocester.............	1731	....	....	1,202	1,511	2,945	2,832
Johnston..............	1759	....	....	....	....	1,031	1,022
Lincoln...............	1871	....	....	....	....	....	....
North Providence........	1765	....	....	....	....	830	813
North Smithfield.........	1871	....	....	....	....	....	....
Pawtucket............	1862	....	....	....	....	....	....
Scituate..............	1731	....	....	1,232	1,813	3,601	3,289
Smithfield............	1731	....	....	450	1,921	2,888	2,781
Woonsocket..........	1867	....	....	....	....	....	....
TOWNS, PROV. CO......	1703	....	....	3,690	7,788	14,912	14,124
PROVIDENCE CITY....	1636	1,446	3,916	3,452	3,159	4,321	4,355
Charlestown...........	1738	....	....	1,002	1,130	1,821	1,835
Exeter...............	1743	....	....	1,174	1,404	1,864	1,982
Hopkinton............	1757	....	....	....	....	1,808	1,845
North Kingstown........	1674	1,200	2,105	1,935	2,109	2,472	2,761
South Kingstown........	1723	....	1,523	1,978	1,913	2,835	2,779
Richmond.............	1747	....	....	508	829	1,257	1,204
Westerly.............	1669	570	1,926	1,809	2,291	1,812	1,824
WASHINGTON COUNTY	1729	1,770	5,554	8,406	9,676	13,869	14,230
WHOLE STATE........	1636	7,181	17,935	32,773	40,414	59,707	55,011

Population of Rhode Island
From 1782 to 1840

Towns and Divisions of the State	1782	1790	1800	1810	1820	1830	1840
Barrington	534	683	650	604	634	612	549
Bristol	1,032	1,406	1,678	2,693	3,197	3,034	3,490
Warren	905	1,122	1,473	1,775	1,806	1,800	2,437
BRISTOL COUNTY	2,471	3,211	3,801	5,072	5,637	5,446	6,476
Coventry	2,107	2,477	2,423	2,928	3,139	3,851	3,433
East Greenwich	1,609	1,824	1,775	1,530	1,519	1,591	1,509
West Greenwich	1,698	2,054	1,757	1,619	1,927	1,817	1,415
Warwick	2,112	2,493	2,532	3,757	3,643	5,529	6,726
KENT COUNTY	7,526	8,848	8,487	9,834	10,228	12,788	13,083
Fall River	....	....	....	....	....	....	....
Jamestown	344	507	501	504	448	415	365
Little Compton	1,341	1,542	1,577	1,553	1,580	1,378	1,327
Middletown	678	840	913	976	949	915	891
Newport	5,532	6,716	6,739	7,907	7,319	8,010	8,333
New Shoreham	478	682	714	722	955	1,185	1,069
Portsmouth	1,351	1,560	1,684	1,795	1,645	1,727	1,706
Tiverton	1,959	2,453	2,717	2,837	2,875	2,905	3,183
NEWPORT COUNTY	11,683	14,300	14,845	16,294	15,771	16,535	16,874
Burrillville	....	....	....	1,834	2,164	2,196	1,982
Cranston	1,594	1,877	1,644	2,161	2,274	2,652	2,901
Cumberland	1,548	1,964	2,056	2,110	2,653	3,675	5,225
East Providence	....	....	....	....	....	....	....
Foster	1,763	2,268	2,457	2,613	2,900	2,672	2,181
Glocester	2,791	4,025	4,009	2,310	2,504	2,521	2,304
Johnston	996	1,320	1,364	1,516	1,542	2,115	2,477
Lincoln	....	....	....	....	....	....	....
North Providence	698	1,071	1,067	1,758	2,420	3,503	4,207
North Smithfield	....	....	....	....	....	....	....
Pawtucket	....	....	....	....	....	....	....
Scituate	1,635	2,315	2,523	2,568	2,834	3,993	4,090
Smithfield	2,217	3,171	3,120	3,828	4,678	6,857	9,534
Woonsocket	....	....	....	....	....	....	....
TOWNS, PROV. COUNTY	13,242	18,011	18,240	20,698	23,969	30,184	34,901
PROVIDENCE CITY	4,312	6,380	7,614	10,071	11,767	16,836	23,172
Charlestown	1,523	2,022	1,454	1,174	1,160	1,284	923
Exeter	2,058	2,495	2,476	2,256	2,581	2,383	1,776
Hopkinton	1,735	2,462	2,276	1,774	1,821	1,777	1,726
North Kingstown	2,328	2,907	2,794	2,957	3,007	3,036	2,909
South Kingstown	2,675	4,131	3,438	3,560	3,723	3,663	3,717
Richmond	1,094	1,760	1,368	1,330	1,423	1,363	1,361
Westerly	1,744	2,298	2,329	1,911	1,972	1,915	1,912
WASHINGTON COUNTY	13,157	18,075	16,135	14,962	15,687	15,421	14,324
WHOLE STATE	52,391	68,825	69,122	76,931	83,059	97,210	108,830

Population of Rhode Island
From 1850 to 1885

Towns and Divisions of the State	1850	1860	1865	1870	1875	1880	1885
Barrington	795	1,000	1,028	1,111	1,185	1,359	1,394
Bristol	4,616	5,271	4,649	5,302	5,829	6,028	5,737
Warren	3,103	2,636	2,792	3,008	4,005	4,007	4,209
BRISTOL COUNTY	8,514	8,907	8,469	9,421	11,019	11,394	11,340
Coventry	3,620	4,247	3,995	4,349	4,580	4,519	4,806
East Greenwich	2,358	2,882	2,400	2,660	3,120	2,887	2,659
West Greenwich	1,350	1,258	1,228	1,133	1,034	1,018	863
Warwick	7,740	8,916	7,696	10,453	11,614	12,164	13,286
KENT COUNTY	15,068	17,303	15,319	18,595	20,348	20,588	21,614
Fall River	....	3,377	....	....	....	....	....
Jamestown	358	400	349	378	488	459	516
Little Compton	1,462	1,304	1,197	1,166	1,156	1,202	1,055
Middletown	830	1,012	1,019	971	1,074	1,139	1,166
New Shoreham	1,262	1,320	1,308	1,113	1,147	1,203	1,267
Portsmouth	1,833	2,048	2,153	2,003	1,893	1,979	2,008
Tiverton	4,699	1,927	1,973	1,898	2,101	2,505	2,702
TOWNS, NEWPORT CO.	10,444	11,388	7,999	7,529	7,859	8,487	8,714
NEWPORT CITY	9,563	10,508	12,688	12,521	14,028	15,693	19,566
Burrillville	3,538	4,140	4,861	4,674	5,249	5,714	5,126
Cranston	4,311	7,500	9,177	4,822	5,688	5,940	6,005
Cumberland	6,661	8,339	8,216	3,882	5,673	6,445	7,163
East Providence	....	....	2,172	2,668	4,336	5,056	6,816
Foster	1,932	1,935	1,873	1,630	1,543	1,552	1,397
Glocester	2,872	2,427	2,286	2,385	2,098	2,250	1,922
Johnston	2,937	3,440	3,436	4,192	4,999	5,765	7,274
Lincoln	....	....	....	7,889	11,565	13,765	17,229
North Providence	7,680	11,818	14,553	20,495	1,303	1,467	1,478
North Smithfield	....	....	....	3,052	2,797	3,088	3,077
Pawtucket	....	....	5,000	6,619	18,464	19,030	22,906
Scituate	4,582	4,251	3,538	3,846	4,101	3,810	3,606
Smithfield	11,500	13,283	12,315	2,605	2,857	3,085	2,338
Woonsocket	....	....	....	11,527	13,576	16,050	16,199
TOWNS, PROV. COUNTY	46,013	57,133	67,427	80,286	84,249	93,017	102,536
PROVIDENCE CITY	41,513	50,666	54,595	68,904	100,675	104,857	118,070
Charlestown	994	981	1,134	1,119	1,054	1,117	1,042
Exeter	1,634	1,741	1,498	1,462	1,355	1,310	1,086
Hopkinton	2,477	2,738	2,512	2,682	2,760	2,952	2,796
North Kingstown	2,971	3,104	3,166	3,568	3,505	3,949	3,894
South Kingstown	3,807	4,717	4,513	4,493	4,240	5,114	5,549
Richmond	1,784	1,964	1,830	2,064	1,739	1,949	1,744
Westerly	2,763	3,470	3,815	4,709	5,408	6,104	6,333
WASHINGTON COUNTY	16,430	18,715	18,468	20,097	20,061	22,495	22,444
WHOLE STATE	147,545	174,620	184,965	217,353	258,239	276,531	304,284

Population of Rhode Island
From 1890 to 1920

Towns and Cities of the State	1890	1895	1900	1905	1910	1915	1920
Barrington	1,461	1,668	1,135	1,923	2,452	2,982	3,897
Bristol	5,478	6,730	6,901	7,512	8,565	10,302	11,375
Warren	4,489	3,826	5,108	5,613	6,585	7,241	7,841
BRISTOL COUNTY	11,428	12,224	13,144	15,048	17,602	20,525	23,113
Coventry	5,068	5,065	5,279	5,698	5,848	5,669	5,670
East Greenwich	3,127	3,096	2,775	3,218	3,420	3,604	3,290
West Greenwich	798	721	606	474	481	509	367
Warwick	17,761	21,168	21,316	24,773	26,629	13,302	13,481
West Warwick	....	....	....	....	....	15,782	15,461
KENT COUNTY	26,754	30,050	29,976	34,163	36,378	38,866	38,269
Jamestown	707	813	1,498	1,337	1,175	1,518	1,633
Little Compton	1,128	1,112	1,132	1,232	1,276	1,382	1,389
Middletown	1,154	1,413	1,457	1,581	1,708	1,992	2,094
Newport	19,457	21,537	22,034	25,039	27,149	30,472	30,255
New Shoreham	1,320	1,300	1,396	1,273	1,314	1,414	1,038
Portsmouth	1,949	1,833	2,105	2,371	2,681	2,678	2,590
Tiverton	2,837	2,964	2,977	3,240	4,032	4,409	3,894
NEWPORT COUNTY	28,552	30,972	32,599	36,073	39,335	43,865	42,893
Burrillville	5,494	5,674	6,317	7,425	7,878	8,086	8,606
Central Falls	....	15,828	18,167	19,446	22,754	23,708	24,174
Cranston	8,099	10,575	13,343	17,570	21,107	26,940	29,407
Cumberland	8,090	8,507	8,925	9,378	10,107	9,929	10,077
East Providence	8,422	10,170	12,138	13,750	15,808	18,584	21,793
Foster	1,252	1,190	1,151	1,160	1,124	1,076	905
Glocester	2,095	1,633	1,462	1,557	1,404	1,491	1,389
Johnston	9,778	11,203	4,305	4,550	5,935	6,693	6,855
Lincoln	20,355	8,350	8,937	9,222	9,825	10,149	9,543
North Providence	2,084	2,437	3,016	3,816	5,407	6,780	7,697
North Smithfield	3,173	2,826	2,422	2,496	2,699	2,805	3,200
Pawtucket	27,633	32,577	39,231	43,381	51,622	55,335	64,248
Providence	132,146	145,472	175,597	198,635	224,326	247,660	237,595
Scituate	3,174	3,529	3,361	3,207	3,493	3,342	3,006
Smithfield	2,500	2,337	2,107	2,267	2,739	3,284	3,199
Woonsocket	20,830	24,468	28,204	32,196	38,125	40,075	43,496
PROVIDENCE COUNTY	255,125	286,776	328,683	370,056	424,353	465,937	475,190
Charlestown	915	984	975	959	1,037	901	759
Exeter	964	917	841	789	778	904	1,033
Hopkinton	2,864	2,713	2,602	2,453	2,324	2,496	2,316
Narragansett	1,408	1,250	1,523	1,469	1,250	1,431	993
North Kingstown	4,193	4,417	4,194	4,046	4,048	3,931	3,397
South Kingstown	4,823	5,163	4,972	5,224	5,176	5,497	5,181
Richmond	1,669	1,656	1,506	1,421	1,633	1,458	1,301
Westerly	6,813	7,636	7,541	8,381	8,696	10,175	9,952
WASHINGTON COUNTY	23,649	24,736	24,154	24,742	24,942	26,793	24,932
WHOLE STATE	345,508	384,758	428,556	480,082	542,610	595,986	604,397

Population of Rhode Island
From 1925 to 1965

Towns and Cities of the State	1925	1930	1936	1940	1950	1960	1965
Barrington	4,938	5,162	5,501	6,231	8,246	13,826	16,390
Bristol	12,707	11,953	10,885	11,159	12,320	14,570	15,716
Warren	7,997	7,974	7,389	8,158	8,513	8,750	9,749
BRISTOL COUNTY	25,642	25,089	23,775	25,548	29,079	37,146	41,855
Coventry	6,379	6,430	6,907	6,998	9,869	15,432	19,577
East Greenwich	4,157	3,666	3,518	3,842	4,923	6,100	8,228
West Greenwich	407	402	400	526	847	1,169	1,499
Warwick	18,273	23,196	27,072	28,757	43,028	68,504	77,637
West Warwick	18,215	17,696	17,397	18,188	19,096	21,414	21,915
KENT COUNTY	47,431	51,390	55,294	58,311	77,763	112,619	128,856
Jamestown	1,773	1,599	1,897	1,744	2,068	2,267	2,567
Little Compton	1,383	1,382	1,589	1,492	1,556	1,702	2,040
Middletown	2,245	2,499	3,007	3,379	7,382	12,675	19,562
Newport	27,757	27,612	29,202	30,532	37,564	47,049	35,901
¹New Shoreham	1,070	1,029	1,044	848	732	486	....
Portsmouth	2,798	2,969	3,603	3,683	6,578	8,251	10,664
Tiverton	4,539	4,578	5,118	5,018	5,659	9,461	10,966
NEWPORT COUNTY	41,565	41,668	45,460	46,696	61,539	81,891	81,700
Burrillville	9,413	7,677	7,335	8,185	8,774	9,119	9,682
Central Falls	25,403	25,898	23,996	25,248	23,550	19,858	18,677
Cranston	34,471	42,911	44,533	47,085	55,060	66,766	71,913
Cumberland	10,238	10,304	10,160	10,625	12,842	18,792	23,839
East Providence	26,088	29,995	30,113	32,165	35,871	41,955	44,828
Foster	1,069	946	1,167	1,237	1,630	2,097	2,479
Glocester	1,630	1,693	1,901	2,099	2,682	3,397	4,142
Johnston	8,668	9,357	9,768	10,672	12,725	17,160	19,547
Lincoln	10,581	10,421	10,453	10,577	11,270	13,551	14,600
North Providence	9,055	11,104	11,770	12,156	13,927	18,220	21,206
North Smithfield	3,571	3,945	3,764	4,196	5,726	7,632	8,716
Pawtucket	69,760	77,149	72,820	75,797	81,436	81,001	77,538
Providence	267,918	252,981	243,006	253,504	248,674	207,498	187,061
Scituate	3,348	2,292	2,729	2,838	3,905	5,210	6,180
Smithfield	3,948	3,967	4,566	4,611	6,690	9,442	12,031
Woonsocket	49,681	49,376	46,822	49,303	50,211	47,080	46,678
PROVIDENCE COUNTY	534,842	540,016	524,903	550,298	574,973	568,778	569,117
Charlestown	1,124	1,118	1,260	1,199	1,598	1,966	2,586
Exeter	1,182	1,314	1,617	1,790	1,870	2,298	2,987
Hopkinton	2,737	2,823	3,277	3,230	3,676	4,174	4,674
Narragansett	1,357	1,258	1,593	1,560	2,288	3,444	5,043
New Shoreham	....	....	....	....	....	....	527
North Kingstown	4,399	4,279	4,767	4,604	14,810	18,977	23,013
South Kingstown	6,085	6,010	6,100	7,282	10,148	11,942	14,405
Richmond	1,719	1,535	1,667	1,629	1,772	1,986	2,235
Westerly	11,177	10,997	10,999	11,199	12,380	14,267	15,711
WASHINGTON COUNTY	29,780	29,334	31,280	32,493	48,542	59,054	71,181
WHOLE STATE	679,260	687,497	680,712	713,346	791,896	859,488	892,709

¹Now part of Washington County (chap. 84, P.L. 1963).

Population of Rhode Island
From 1970 to 1980

Towns and Cities of the State	1970	1980	Percent Change 1970-80
Barrington	17,554	16,174	− 7.8
Bristol	17,860	20,128	+ 12.7
Warren	10,523	10,640	+ 1.1
BRISTOL COUNTY	45,937	46,942	+ 2.2
Coventry	22,947	27,065	+ 17.9
East Greenwich	9,577	10,211	+ 6.6
West Greenwich	1,841	2,738	+ 48.0
Warwick	83,694	87,123	+ 4.0
West Warwick	24,323	27,026	+ 11.1
KENT COUNTY	142,382	154,163	+ 8.4
Jamestown	2,911	4,040	+ 38.7
Little Compton	2,385	3,085	+ 29.3
Middletown	29,290	17,216	− 41.2
Newport	34,562	29,259	− 15.3
Portsmouth	12,521	14,257	+ 13.8
Tiverton	12,559	13,526	+ 7.7
NEWPORT COUNTY	94,228	81,383	− 13.6
Burrillville	10,087	13,164	+ 30.5
Central Falls	18,716	16,995	− 9.2
Cranston	74,287	71,992	− 3.0
Cumberland	26,605	27,069	+ 1.7
East Providence	48,207	50,980	+ 5.7
Foster	2,626	3,370	+ 28.3
Glocester	5,160	7,550	+ 46.3
Johnston	22,037	24,907	+ 13.0
Lincoln	16,182	16,949	+ 4.7
North Providence	24,337	29,188	+ 19.9
North Smithfield	9,349	9,972	+ 6.6
Pawtucket	76,984	71,204	− 7.5
Providence	179,116	156,804	− 12.4
Scituate	7,489	8,405	+ 12.2
Smithfield	13,468	16,886	+ 25.3
Woonsocket	46,820	45,914	− 1.9
PROVIDENCE COUNTY	581,470	571,349	− 1.7
Charlestown	2,863	4,800	+ 67.6
Exeter	3,245	4,453	+ 37.2
Hopkinton	5,392	6,406	+ 18.8
Narragansett	7,138	12,088	+ 69.3
New Shoreham	489	620	+ 26.7
North Kingstown	29,793	21,938	− 26.3
South Kingstown	16,913	20,414	+ 20.7
Richmond	2,625	4,018	+ 53.0
Westerly	17,248	18,580	+ 7.7
WASHINGTON COUNTY	85,706	93,317	+ 8.9
WHOLE STATE	949,723	947,154	− 0.4

Source: Federal and state censuses

County and Municipal Creation and Development
Towns and Cities, Original Names, Boundaries, Size

Counties and Towns	Date of Incorporation	From what taken, original names, changes of boundaries, etc.
BRISTOL COUNTY	Feb. 17, 1746/47	Incorporated with same county limits as at present. Originally the county consisted of two towns, Bristol and Warren; Indian name, Sowams. Afterwards, June 1770, Warren was divided and the town of Barrington was incorporated. (See Bristol.) Area, 24.91 square miles.
Barrington	Nov. 18, 1717	Taken from Swansea and incorporated as a town by Massachusetts, Nov. 18, 1717; transferred to Rhode Island by royal decree, May 28, 1746; parts of Swansea and Rehoboth were added to Barrington on the north and east by the new boundary line and its name was changed to Warren, Jan. 27, 1746/47, in honor of Sir Peter Warren, admiral in the British navy. Barrington was taken from Warren and incorporated June 16, 1770. Home rule charter, chap. 34, P.L. 1959. Area, 8.46 square miles.
Bristol	Oct. 28, 1681	Incorporated by Plymouth Colony, Oct. 28, 1681. By royal decree, dated May 28, 1746, the eastern boundary was settled and the jurisdiction of the colony established over the territory embraced in the towns of Bristol, Barrington, Tiverton, Little Compton, and Cumberland. A portion of Bristol annexed to Warren, May 30, 1873. Named for Bristol, England. Area, including Hog Island, 9.89 square miles.
Warren	Jan. 27, 1746/47	See Bristol. The territory of the town of Warren at this date included the present town of Barrington and a portion of the towns of Swansea and Rehoboth in Massachusetts. In 1770 Warren was divided, and one of the original names (Barrington) was given to the new town. Named for Sir Peter Warren, admiral in the British navy. Area, 6.56 square miles.
KENT COUNTY	June 11, 1750	Taken from Providence County. Incorporated with the same county limits as at present and same towns, except West Warwick, which was taken from Warwick in 1913. Area, 174.85 square miles.
Coventry	Aug. 21, 1741	Taken from Warwick. Area, 62.87 square miles.
East Greenwich	Oct. 31, 1677	Incorporated as the town of East Greenwich. Name changed to Dedford, June 23, 1686. The original name restored in 1689. The town divided in 1741. Area, 16.07 square miles.
Warwick	Original Town	First settled January 1642/43. Named for earl of Warwick, who signed the Patent of Providence Plantations, March 14, 1643/44. The first action of the inhabitants as a town was on August 8, 1647. Indian name, Shawomet. Act dividing town approved by the governor March 14, 1913, with Representative Dist. Nos. 1 and 2 of old town remaining as Warwick and Representative Dists. 3, 4, and 5 of old town becoming West Warwick. Incorporated as a city by chap. 1852, P.L. 1931, and the charter accepted April 21, 1931. Home rule charter, chap. 150, P.L. 1960. Area, including Greene Island, 36.26 square miles.

Towns and Cities, Original Names, Boundaries, Size

Counties and Towns	Date of Incorporation	From what taken, original names, changes of boundaries, etc.
West Greenwich	April 6, 1741	Taken from East Greenwich. Area, 51.47 square miles.
West Warwick	March 14, 1913	Taken from Warwick and consists of Representative Dists. 3, 4, and 5 of old town. Area, 8.18 square miles.
NEWPORT COUNTY	June 22, 1703	Originally incorporated as Rhode Island County; June 16, 1729, incorporated as Newport County, and included Newport, Portsmouth, Jamestown, and New Shoreham. Area, 108.36 square miles.
Fall River	Oct. 6, 1856	Taken from Tiverton. Ceded to Massachusetts in the settlement of the boundary question, March 1, 1862. See Pawtucket and East Providence.
Jamestown	Oct. 30, 1678	Named in honor of King James II. Indian name, Quononoqutt (Conanicut). Area, including Dutch and Gould islands, 9.76 square miles.
Little Compton	Jan. 27, 1746/47	One of the five towns received from Massachusetts pursuant to royal decree, May 28, 1746 (see Bristol). Annexed to Newport County, Feb. 17, 1746/47. Indian name, Seaconnet. Incorporated by Plymouth Colony in 1682. Area, 21.94 square miles.
Middletown	June 16, 1743	Town in the "middle" of the island. Taken from Newport. Home rule charter, chap. 52, P.L. 1969. Area, 13.45 square miles.
Newport	Original Town	Settled in 1639. Line between Newport and Portsmouth established Sept. 14, 1640. Incorporated as a city June 1, 1784. City charter repealed March 27, 1787. City incorporated the second time May 6, 1853, and the charter accepted May 20, 1853. Home rule charter, chap. 3234, P.L. 1953. Area, including Rose, Goat, and Coaster's Harbor islands, 7.94 square miles.
Portsmouth	Original Town	Settled in 1638. Indian name, Pocasset. "At a quarter meeting of the first of ye 5th month, 1639, it is agreed upon to call this town Portsmouth." At the "Generall Courte" at "Nieuport," 12th of first month, 1640, the name of Portsmouth was confirmed. Area, including Prudence, Patience, Hope, and Dyer islands, 23.84 square miles.
Tiverton	Jan. 27, 1746/47	One of the five towns received from Massachusetts by royal decree. See Bristol, Warren, etc. Indian name, Pocasset. Incorporated by Province of Massachusetts, 1694. Annexed to Newport County, February 17, 1746/47. Area, 31.43 square miles.
PROVIDENCE CO.	June 22, 1703	Originally incorporated as the County of Providence Plantations, and included the present territory of Providence, Kent, and Washington counties, excepting the present towns of Cumberland, Pawtucket, and East Providence. The name was changed to Providence County, June 16, 1729. See Kent and Washington counties. Area, 432.46 square miles.
Burrillville	Oct. 29, 1806	Taken from Glocester. The town was first authorized to meet to elect officers November 17, 1806. Named for Hon. James Burrill. Area, 57.59 square miles.
Central Falls	Feb. 21, 1895	Taken from Lincoln and incorporated as a city. Act of incorporation accepted February 27, 1895, by a vote of 1,531 for to 794 against. The new city government was organized on the eighteenth day of March 1895. Home rule charter, chap. 3239, P.L. 1953. Area, 1.32 square miles.

Towns and Cities, Original Names, Boundaries, Size

Counties and Towns	Date of Incorporation	From what taken, original names, changes of boundaries, etc.
Cranston	June 14, 1754	Taken from Providence. Probably named for Samuel Cranston, who was governor of Rhode Island from March 1698 to April 27, 1727, when he died. Portions reunited to Providence, June 10, 1868, and March 28, 1873. Incorporated as a city March 10, 1910. The new city government was organized May 2, 1910, the first election having been held April 19, 1910. Home rule charter approved by referendum, November 6, 1962; validating act, chap. 183, P.L. 1963. Area, 28.20 square miles.
Cumberland	Jan. 27, 1746/47	One of the five towns received from Massachusetts by royal decree. See Bristol, Warren, etc. Until incorporated in Rhode Island, it was known as Attleboro Gore. Named in honor of William, duke of Cumberland. Annexed to Providence County, February 17, 1746/47. A portion of Cumberland was incorporated as the town of Woonsocket, January 31, 1867. Area, 28.64 square miles.
East Providence	March 1, 1862	The westerly part of Rehoboth, Massachusetts, was incorporated as Seekonk, February 26, 1812. The westerly part of Seekonk was annexed to Rhode Island, incorporated as a town, and named East Providence in the settlement of the boundary question in 1862. See Pawtucket and Fall River. Incorporated as a city by chap. 33, P.L. 1957, and chap. 8, P.L. 1958. The first city administration was sworn in December 1, 1958. Home rule charter, chap. 33, P.L. 1957. Area, 13.85 square miles.
Foster	Aug. 24, 1781	Taken from Scituate. Named probably for Hon. Theodore Foster. Area, 52.15 square miles.
Glocester	Feb. 20, 1730/31	Taken from Providence. At this date an act was passed "for erecting and incorporating the outlands of the town of Providence into three towns." These towns were Scituate, Glocester, and Smithfield. Said to be named for Frederick Lewis, duke of Glocester and son of King George II. Area, 56.51 square miles.
Johnston	March 6, 1759	Taken from Providence and named in honor of Augustus Johnston, Esq., the attorney general of the colony at that time. A portion reannexed to Providence, June 1, 1898, and April 16, 1919. Home rule charter, chap. 187, P.L. 1963. Area, 25.09 square miles.
Lincoln	March 8, 1871	Taken from Smithfield and named in honor of Abraham Lincoln. Home rule charter, chap. 38, P.L. 1959. Area, 19.36 square miles.
North Providence	June 13, 1765	Taken from Providence. A small portion reunited to Providence, June 29, 1767, and March 28, 1873. The town was divided March 27, 1874; a portion was annexed to the city of Providence, making the tenth ward in that city, and a portion was annexed to the town of Pawtucket. The act went into effect May 1, 1874. Area, 5.90 square miles.
North Smithfield	March 8, 1871	Taken from Smithfield and incorporated as the town of Slater. Name changed to North Smithfield, March 24, 1871. Home rule charter, chap. 11, P.L. 1969. Area, 25.38 square miles.
Pawtucket	March 1, 1862	Name of Indian origin. Taken from Seekonk, Mass., and incorporated as the town of Pawtucket, Mass., Feb. 29, 1828. The whole town of Pawtucket, except a small portion lying easterly of Seven and Ten Mile rivers, was

Towns and Cities, Original Names, Boundaries, Size

Counties and Towns	Date of Incorporation	From what taken, original names, changes of boundaries, etc.
		annexed with East Providence to Rhode Island (see East Providence). A portion of the town of North Providence annexed to Pawtucket, May 1, 1874. Incorporated as a city March 27, 1885; act of incorporation accepted April 1, 1885, by a vote of 1,450 for to 721 against. The new city government was organized on the first Monday of January 1886. Home rule charter, chap. 3238, P.L. 1953. Area, 8.68 square miles.
Providence	Original Town	Settled in 1636. Named Providence by Roger Williams "in gratitude to his supreme deliverer." Originally comprised the whole of present-day Providence County west of the Blackstone River. City incorporated by act passed Nov. 5, 1831, which act went into operation on the first Monday in June 1832. Portions of the town of Cranston were reannexed to Providence, June 10, 1868, Mar. 28, 1873, and July 1, 1892. Portions of North Providence were reannexed June 29, 1767, Mar. 28, 1873, and May 1, 1874. A portion of the town of Johnston was reannexed June 1, 1898, and April 16, 1919. Home rule charter, chap. 37, P.L. 1981. Area, 18.91 square miles.
Scituate	Feb. 20, 1730/31	Taken from Providence. See Glocester. Named for Scituate, Mass. Area, 55.28 square miles.
Smithfield	Feb. 20, 1730/31	Taken from Providence. See Glocester. The town was divided March 8, 1871, a portion being annexed to Woonsocket and the remainder divided into three towns. See Lincoln and North Smithfield. Area, 27.60 square miles.
Woonsocket	Jan. 31, 1867	Name of Indian origin. Taken from Cumberland. A portion of Smithfield was annexed to Woonsocket, March 8, 1871. Incorporated as a city June 13, 1888. Home rule charter, chap. 3235, P.L. 1953. Area, 8.00 square miles.
WASHINGTON CO.	June 16, 1729	Originally called the Narragansett Country. Named King's Province, March 20, 1654. Boundaries established May 21, 1669. Incorporated, June 1729, as King's County, with the three towns of South Kingstown, North Kingstown, and Westerly, and, except for Block Island, same territory as at present. Name changed to Washington County, October 29, 1781. Area, 343.42 square miles.
Charlestown	Aug. 22, 1738	Taken from Westerly. Named "to the honor of King Charles II, who granted us our charter." Area, 38.46 square miles.
Exeter	March 8, 1742/43	Taken from North Kingstown. Area, 59.21 square miles.
Hopkinton	March 19, 1757	Taken from Westerly. Area, 44.08 square miles.
Narragansett	March 28, 1901	Taken from South Kingstown. Incorporated as a district March 22, 1888. Home rule charter, chap. 17, P.L. 1967. Area, 14.42 square miles.

Towns and Cities, Original Names, Boundaries, Size

Counties and Towns	Date of Incorporation	From what taken, original names, changes of boundaries, etc.
North Kingstown	Oct. 28, 1674	First settlement, 1641. Incorporated in 1674 under the name of Kings Towne as the seventh town in the colony. Incorporation reaffirmed in 1679. Name changed to Rochester, June 23, 1686, but restored in 1689. Kingstown divided into North Kingstown and South Kingstown, February 1722/23. The act provided that North Kingstown should be the elder town. Home rule charter, chap. 3437, P.L. 1955. Area, including Cornelius, Fox, and Rabbit islands, 44.15 square miles.
New Shoreham	Nov. 6, 1672	Purchased and occupied April 1661. Admitted to colony as Block Island, May 4, 1664. When incorporated in 1672, name changed to New Shoreham "as signs of our unity and likeness to many parts of our native country." Indian name, Manasses or Manisses. Named Block Island by Adrian Block, the Dutch navigator. Formerly in Newport County; see chap. 84, P.L. 1963. Area, 10.95 square miles.
Richmond	Aug. 18, 1747	Taken from Charlestown. Area, 41.82 square miles.
South Kingstown	Feb. 26, 1722/23	See North Kingstown. Pettaquamscutt settled January 20, 1657/58. Home rule charter, chap. 115, P.L. 1969. Area, 61.17 square miles.
Westerly	May 14, 1669	Original name, Misquamicut. Incorporated in May 1669 under the name of Westerly as the fifth town in the colony. Name of Westerly changed to Haversham, June 23, 1686, but restored in 1689. Home rule charter, chap. 88, P.L. 1969. Area, 29.16 square miles.

In several cases the exact date of the passage of the act of incorporation of towns cannot be ascertained. In such cases the date given is that of the meeting of the General Assembly at which the act was passed.

Sources: *Rhode Island Manual;* John Hutchins Cady, *Rhode Island Boundaries, 1636-1936.*

Rhode Island Governors under the Royal Charter Granted by King Charles II, July 8, 1663

Name of Governor	Years of Service	Political Affiliation
[1]Benedict Arnold	1663-1666	
	1669-1672	
	1677-1678	
William Brenton	1666-1669	
Nicholas Easton	1672-1674	
[2]William Coddington	1674-1676	
	1678-1678	
Walter Clarke	1676-1677	
	1686-1686	
	1696-1698	
[3]John Cranston	1678-1680	
Peleg Sanford	1680-1683	
William Coddington, Jr.	1683-1685	
Henry Bull	1685-1686	
	1690-1690	
John Easton	1690-1695	
[4]Caleb Carr	1695-1695	
[5]Samuel Cranston	1698-1727	
Joseph Jencks	1727-1732	
[6]William Wanton	1732-1733	
[7]John Wanton	1734-1740	
Richard Ward	1740-1743	
[8]William Greene	1743-1745	
	1746-1747	
	1748-1755	
	1757-1758	

[1]Died in office, June 20, 1678.

[2]Died in office, November 1, 1678.

[3]Died in office, March 12, 1680.

[4]Died in office, December 17, 1695.

[5]Died in office, April 26, 1727. His tenure of 29 years was the longest of any Rhode Island governor.

[6]Died in office, December 7, 1733.

[7]Died in office, July 5, 1740.

[8]Died in office, February 22, 1758.

Rhode Island Governors under the Royal Charter Granted by King Charles II, July 8, 1663

Name of Governor	Years of Service	Political Affiliation
Gideon Wanton	1745-1746	
	1747-1748	
Stephen Hopkins	1755-1757	
	1758-1762	
	1763-1765	
	1767-1768	
Samuel Ward	1762-1763	
	1765-1767	
Josias Lyndon	1768-1769	
Joseph Wanton	1769-1775	
Nicholas Cooke	1775-1778	
William Greene, Jr.	1778-1786	
John Collins	1786-1790	Country Party
[9]Arthur Fenner	1790-1805	Country/Democratic-Republican
Isaac Wilbour	1806-1807	Democatic-Republican
James Fenner	1807-1811	Democratic-Republican
	1824-1831	Democrat
William Jones	1811-1817	Federalist
[10]Nehemiah R. Knight	1817-1821	Democratic-Republican
William C. Gibbs	1821-1824	Democratic-Republican
[11]Lemuel H. Arnold	1831-1833	National Republican/Whig
John Brown Francis	1833-1838	Democrat
William Sprague	1838-1839	Whig
Samuel Ward King	1840-1843	Whig
[12]Thomas Wilson Dorr	1842	People's Party

[9]Died in office, October 15, 1805.

[10]Elected United States senator, January 9, 1821, for unexpired term of James Burrill, Jr., deceased.

[11]No election of governor, lieutenant governor, or senators in 1832. Elections were successively ordered for May 16, July 18, Aug. 28, and Nov. 21, 1832, with no candidate receiving the required majority vote. At the January session, 1833, the incumbents were continued in office until the next session.

[12]Elected under the provisions of the People's Constitution, which was subsequently overthrown by the Charter government under Samuel Ward King. Dorr went into exile on June 28, 1842.

Rhode Island Governors under the Constitution of 1843

No.	Name of Governor	Term in Office	Political Affiliation
1	James Fenner	1843-1845	Law and Order
2	Charles Jackson	1845-1846	Liberation
3	Byron Diman	1846-1847	Law and Order
4	Elisha Harris	1847-1849	Law and Order
5	Henry B. Anthony	1849-1851	Law and Order/Whig
6	[1]Philip Allen	1851-1853	Democrat
7	Francis M. Dimond	1853-1854	Democrat
8	William W. Hoppin	1854-1857	Whig/American Party/Republican
9	Elisha Dyer, Sr.	1857-1859	Republican
10	Thomas G. Turner	1859-1860	Republican
11	[2]William Sprague II	1860-1863	Conservative Fusion-Unionist-Republican
12	William C. Cozzens	1863-1863	Republican
13	James Y. Smith	1863-1866	Republican
14	Ambrose E. Burnside	1866-1869	Republican
15	Seth Padelford	1869-1873	Republican
16	Henry Howard	1873-1875	Republican
17	Henry Lippitt	1875-1877	Republican
18	Charles C. Van Zandt	1877-1880	Republican
19	Alfred H. Littlefield	1880-1883	Republican
20	Augustus O. Bourn	1883-1885	Republican
21	George P. Wetmore	1885-1887	Republican
22	[3]John W. Davis	1887-1888	Democrat
23	Royal C. Taft	1888-1889	Republican
24	[4]Herbert W. Ladd	1889-1890	Republican
25	[3]John W. Davis	1890-1891	Democrat
26	[4]Herbert W. Ladd	1891-1892	Republican
27	D. Russell Brown	1892-1895	Republican

[1]Resigned July 20, 1853, having been elected United States senator May 4, 1853. Francis M. Dimond, lieutenant governor, succeeded him.

[2]Governor Sprague resigned March 3, 1863, to accept the office of United States senator, and Lieutenant Governor Arnold having been previously elected to the Senate of the United States to fill the vacancy caused by the resignation of James F. Simmons, William Cozzens became governor by virtue of his office as president of the state Senate. Sprague is often incorrectly listed as a Democratic governor. Actually he was the candidate of Republican moderates and Democrats who feared that the election of Seth Padelford, his extremist opponent in 1860, would jeopardize the continuance of the Union.

[3]John W. Davis served two nonconsecutive terms and is referred to by most historians as the 22nd and 25th governor.

[4]Herbert W. Ladd served two nonconsecutive terms and is referred to as the 24th and 26th governor.

Rhode Island Governors under the Constitution of 1843

No.	Name of Governor	Term in Office	Political Affiliation
28	Charles W. Lippitt	1895-1897	Republican
29	Elisha Dyer, Jr.	1897-1900	Republican
30	⁵William Gregory	1900-1901	Republican
31	Charles D. Kimball	1901-1903	Republican
32	Lucius F. C. Garvin	1903-1905	Democrat
33	George H. Utter	1905-1907	Republican
34	James H. Higgins	1907-1909	Democrat
35	⁶Aram J. Pothier	1909-1915	Republican
36	R. L. Beeckman	1915-1921	Republican
37	Emery J. San Souci	1921-1923	Republican
38	William S. Flynn	1923-1925	Democrat
39	⁷Aram J. Pothier	1925-1928	Republican
40	Norman S. Case	1928-1933	Republican
41	Theodore F. Green	1933-1937	Democrat
42	Robert E. Quinn	1937-1939	Democrat
43	William H. Vanderbilt	1939-1941	Republican
44	⁸J. Howard McGrath	1941-1945	Democrat
45	⁹John O. Pastore	1945-1950	Democrat
46	John S. McKiernan	1950-1951	Democrat
47	Dennis J. Roberts	1951-1959	Democrat
48	Christopher DelSesto	1959-1961	Republican
49	John A. Notte, Jr.	1961-1963	Democrat
50	John H. Chafee	1963-1969	Republican
51	Frank Licht	1969-1973	Democrat
52	Philip W. Noel	1973-1977	Democrat
53	J. Joseph Garrahy	1977-1985	Democrat
54	Edward D. DiPrete	1985-	Republican

⁵William Gregory was reelected governor November 5, 1900, but died December 16, 1901, and Lieutenant Governor Kimball became governor.

⁶Aram J. Pothier served two nonconsecutive terms and is referred to as the 35th and 39th governor.

⁷Governor Pothier died in office on February 3, 1928, and Lieutenant Governor Norman S. Case succeeded to the governorship.

⁸J. Howard McGrath resigned to become U. S. solicitor general, and John O. Pastore was sworn in as governor.

⁹John O. Pastore resigned to beome U. S. senator, and Lieutenant Governor McKiernan was sworn in as governor.

Under the present constitution of 1843:

    The average age of the governors of Rhode Island entering office is 49 years, 9 months.

    The longest nonconsecutive term of office was Aram J. Pothier—9 years, 53 days.

    The longest consecutive terms of office were those of Dennis J. Roberts and J. Joseph Garrahy—8 years.

Source: *Rhode Island Manual* (as revised and corrected by author)

Rhode Island in Presidential Elections

Election		Candidates for President	Vote for Candidates			
			Popular	Majority	Total Vote	Electoral Vote
No.	Year					
1	1789	George Washington, president (69 electoral votes), and John Adams, vice-president (34), in nonpartisan balloting. Rhode Island, having failed to ratify the Constitution, did not participate.				
2	1792	George Washington, president (132), and John Adams, vice-president (77), in nonpartisan balloting. Each of Rhode Island's four electors, chosen by the General Assembly, had 2 votes and cast them for Washington and Adams.				
3	1796	John Adams (Federalist), president (71), in the first partisan election, and Thomas Jefferson (Democratic-Republican), vice-president (68). Each of Rhode Island's four electors, chosen again by the General Assembly, cast 4 votes for Adams and 4 votes for Oliver Ellsworth of Connecticut.				
4	1800	Thomas Jefferson (Dem.-Rep.), president (73), and Aaron Burr (Dem.-Rep.), vice-president (73). Rhode Island's four electors, chosen at large by popular vote for the first time, with Federalist electors polling 1,941 votes and Democratic-Republicans 1,694, cast 4 votes for John Adams (Fed.), 3 votes for Charles C. Pinckney (Fed.), and 1 vote for John Jay (Fed.). In the runoff election between Jefferson and Burr (who had tied in the electoral column), Rhode Island's two U.S. representatives voted consistently for Burr on all 36 House ballots.				
5	1804	Thomas Jefferson (Dem.-Rep.), president (162), and George Clinton (Dem.-Rep.), vice-president, in the first election where separate electoral balloting was required for each office. There are no figures on Rhode Island's popular vote, but it went Democratic-Republican because the state's 4 electoral votes were cast for Jefferson.				

Rhode Island in Presidential Elections

No.	Year	Candidates for President	Popular	Majority	Total Vote	Electoral Vote
6	1808	James Madison (Dem.-Rep.).....	2,692		5,764	
		Charles Cotesworth Pinckney (Fed.)....................	3,072	380		4
7	1812	James Madison (Dem.-Rep.).....	2,084		6.116	
		DeWitt Clinton (Fed.)........	4,032	1,948		4
8	1816	James Monroe (Dem.-Rep.)......	NA	NA		4
		Rufus King (Fed.)............	NA	NA		
9	1820	James Monroe (Dem.-Rep.)......	Unopposed			4
10	1824	John Quincy Adams (Dem.-Rep.).	2,145	1,945	2,345	4
		William H. Crawford (Dem.-Rep.)...............	200			
11	1828	Andrew Jackson (Democrat).....	821		3,575	
		John Quincy Adams (National-Republican)	2,754	1,933		4
12	1832	Andrew Jackson (Dem.).........	2,126			4
		Henry Clay (Nat.-Rep.).......	2,810		5,814	
		William Wirt (Anti-Mason)....	878			
13	1836	Martin Van Buren (Dem.).......	2,966	255	5,677	4
		William Henry Harrison (Whig)	2,711			
14	1840	William Henry Harrison (Whig)..	5,278	1,935		4
		Martin Van Buren (Dem.).....	3,301		8,621	
		James G. Birney (Liberty).....	42			
15	1844	James K. Polk (Dem.)..........	4,867			
		Henry Clay (Whig)...........	7,322	2,348	12,296	4
		James G. Birney (Liberty).....	107			
16	1848	Zachary Taylor (Whig)..........	6,779	2,403		4
		Lewis Cass (Dem.)............	3,646		11,155	
		Martin Van Buren (Free Soil)...	730			
17	1852	Franklin Pierce (Dem.)..........	8,735	465		4
		Winfield Scott (Whig).........	7,626		17,005	
		John P. Hale (Free Soil).......	644			
18	1856	James Buchanan (Dem.).........	6,680			
		John C. Fremont (Rep.).......	11,467	3,112	19,822	4
		Millard Fillmore (Amer.)......	1,675			
19	1860	Abraham Lincoln (Rep.)........	12,244	4,537	19,951	4
		Stephen A. Douglas (Dem.)....	7,707			
20	1864	Abraham Lincoln (Rep.)........	14,343	5,625	23,061	4
		George B. McClellan (Dem.)...	8,718			
21	1868	Ulysses S. Grant (Rep.)..........	12,993	6,445	19,541	4
		Horatio Seymour (Dem.)......	6,548			
22	1872	Ulysses S. Grant (Rep.)..........	13,665	8,336	18,994	4
		Horace Greeley (Lib. and Dem.)	5,329			
23	1876	Rutherford B. Hayes (Rep.)......	15,787	4,947		4
		Samuel J. Tilden (Dem.).......	10,712		26,627	
		Peter Cooper (Greenback).....	68			
		Green C. Smith (Prohib.)......	60			
24	1880	James A. Garfield (Rep.)........	18,195	7,155		4
		Winfield S. Hancock (Dem.)...	10,779		29,235	
		James B. Weaver (Greenback)	236			

Names indented denote unsuccessful candidates.

Rhode Island in Presidential Elections

Election		Candidates for President	Vote for Candidates			
No.	Year	(at least 200 popular votes)	Popular	Majority	Total Vote	Electoral Vote
25	1884	Grover Cleveland (Dem.)........	12,391			
		James G. Blaine (Rep.)........	19,030	5,239		4
		John P. St. John (Prohib.)....	928		32,771	
		Benjamin F. Butler (People's)	422			
26	1888	Benjamin Harrison (Rep.).......	21,969	3,163		4
		Grover Cleveland (Dem.)......	17,530		40,775	
		Clinton B. Fisk (Prohib.)......	1,251			
27	1892	Grover Cleveland (Dem.)........	24,336			
		Benjamin Harrison (Rep.).....	26,975	754		4
		John Bidwell (Prohib.)........	1,654		53,196	
		James B. Weaver (People's)....	228			
28	1896	William McKinley (Rep.)........	37,437	20,089		4
		William J. Bryan (Dem.).......	14,459			
		John M. Palmer (Nat. Dem.)...	1,166		54,785	
		Joshua Levering (Prohib.).....	1,160			
		Charles H. Matchett (Soc. Labor)	588			
29	1900	William McKinley (Rep.)........	33,784	11,020		4
		William J. Bryan (Dem.)......	19,812		56,548	
		John C. Woolley (Pro.).......	1,529			
		Joseph F. Malloney (Soc. Labor)	1,423			
30	1904	Theodore Roosevelt (Rep.)......	41,605	14,554		4
		Alton B. Parker (Dem.).......	24,839			
		Eugene V. Debs (Socialist).....	956		68,656	
		Silas C. Swallow (Pro.)........	768			
		Charles H. Corregan (Soc. Labor)	488			
31	1908	William H. Taft (Rep.)..........	43,942	15,567		4
		William J. Bryan (Dem.)......	24,706			
		Eugene V. Debs (Socialist).....	1,365		73,317	
		Thomas L. Hisgen (Independence)	1,105			
		Eugene Wilder Chafin (Prohib.)	1,016			
32	1912	Woodrow Wilson (Dem.)........	30,412	*2,709		5
		William H. Taft (Rep.)........	27,703			
		Theodore Roosevelt (Prog.)....	16,878			
		Eugene V. Debs (Socialist).....	2,049		77,891	
		Eugene W. Chafin (Prohib.)...	616			
		Arthur E. Reimer (Soc. Labor)	236			
33	1916	Woodrow Wilson (Dem.)........	40,394			5
		Charles E. Hughes (Rep.)......	44,858	1,900		
		Allan L. Benson (Soc.)........	1,914		87,816	
		J. Frank Hanley (Prohib.).....	470			
34	1920	Warren G. Harding (Rep.).......	107,463	46,945		5
		James M. Cox (Dem.)........	55,062			
		Eugene V. Debs (Socialist).....	4,351		167,981	
		William W. Cox (Soc. Labor)..	495			
		Aaron S. Watkins (Prohib.)....	510			
35	1924	Calvin Coolidge (Rep.)..........	125,286	40,457		5
		John W. Davis (Dem.)........	76,606			
		Frank T. Johns (Soc. Labor)...	268		210,115	
		William Z. Foster (Workers)...	289			
		Robert M. LaFollette (Prog.)..	7,628			
36	1928	Herbert Hoover (Rep.)..........	117,522			5
		Alfred E. Smith (Dem.).......	118,973	752		
		Verne L. Reynolds (Soc. Labor)	416		237,194	
		William Z. Foster (Workers)...	283			

*Plurality

Rhode Island in Presidential Elections

Election		Candidates for President	Vote for Candidates			
No.	Year	(at least 200 popular votes)	Popular	Majority	Total Vote	Electoral Vote
37	1932	Franklin D. Roosevelt (Dem.)....	146,604	27,038		4
		Herbert Hoover (Rep.)........	115,266			
		Verne L. Reynolds (Soc. Lab.).	423		266,170	
		William Z. Foster (Com.)......	546			
		Norman Thomas (Soc.).......	3,138			
38	1936	Franklin D. Roosevelt (Dem.)....	165,238	19,298		4
		Alfred M. Landon (Rep.)......	125,031			
		William Lemke (Union).......	19,569		311,178	
		J. W. Aiken (Soc. Labor)......	929			
		Earl R. Browder (Com.).......	411			
39	1940	Franklin D. Roosevelt (Dem.)....	182,182	43,216		4
		Wendell L. Willkie (Rep.).....	138,653		321,148	
		Earl R. Browder (Com.).......	239			
40	1944	Franklin D. Roosevelt (Dem.)....	175,356	51,436		4
		Thomas E. Dewey (Rep.)......	123,487		299,276	
		Claude A. Watson (Nat. Prohib.)	433			
41	1948	Harry S. Truman (Dem.)........	188,736	49,770		4
		Thomas E. Dewey (Rep.).......	135,787			
		Henry A. Wallace (Progress.)....	2,619		327,702	
		Norman Thomas (Soc.)........	429			
42	1952	Dwight D. Eisenhower (Rep.).....	210,935	7,372		4
		Adlai E. Stevenson (Dem.)......	203,293		414,498	
43	1956	Dwight D. Eisenhower (Rep.).....	225,819	64,029		4
		Adlai E. Stevenson (Dem.)......	161,790		387,609	
44	1960	John F. Kennedy (Dem.)........	258,032	110,530		4
		Richard M. Nixon (Rep.)......	147,502		405,534	
45	1964	Lyndon B. Johnson (Dem.)......	315,463	240,848		4
		Barry Goldwater (Rep.).......	74,615		390,078	
46	1968	Richard M. Nixon (Rep.)........	122,359			4
		Hubert H. Humphrey (Dem.)..	246,518	108,098	384,938	
		Fred Halstead (Soc. Wkrs.)....	383			
		George C. Wallace (Wall. Ind.).	15,678			
47	1972	Richard M. Nixon (Rep.)........	220,383	25,009		4
		George S. McGovern (Dem.)...	194,645		415,757	
		Linda Jenness (Soc. Wkrs.)....	729			
48	1976	James E. Carter, Jr. (Dem.)......	227,636	44,688		4
		Gerald R. Ford (Rep.).........	181,249			
		Gus Hall (Com.).............	334		410,584	
		Roger I. McBride (Lib.).......	715			
		Peter Camejo (Soc. Wkrs.)....	462			
49	1980	Ronald W. Reagan (Rep.).......	154,793			4
		James E. Carter (Dem.).......	198,342	43,549		
		John B. Anderson (Ind.)......	59,819		415,967	
		Gus Hall (Com.).............	218			
		Ed Clark (Lib.)..............	2,458			
50	1984	Ronald W. Reagan (Rep.)........	212,080			4
		Walter Mondale (Dem.)	197,106			
		Bob Richard (Am. Ind.)	510	13,671		
		Sonia Johnson (Citizens)	240		410,489	
		David B. Bergland (Lib.)	277			

Sources: Svend Petersen, comp., *A Statistical History of the American Presidential Elections* (1963); *Rhode Island Manual* (as corrected by author)

INDEX

O

Oakland Beach, 118, 133, 147, 148
Oaklawn, 127
Oaklawn Community Baptist Church, 126
O'Connor, Edwin, 239
Oden, Curley, 191
O'Hara, Walter, 166, 168, 193, 206
Oldham, John, 17
Old State House (Providence), 53, 95, 251
Old Stone Tower, 257
Olympic Games, 191, 234
O'Neill, Isabelle Florence Ahern, 169
Operation Clapboard, 218, 249
Order of Vasa, 132
O'Reilly, Bernard, 90, 106, 107
Ormsbee, Elijah, 70
O'Rourke, James Henry ("Orator Jim"), 149
Orthodox churches, 162, 177, 178, 179, 180
Osborne, Jeffrey, 240
O'Shaunessy, George F., 164, 167
Osterberg, J. S., 132
Outlet Department Store, 166, 218, 241
"Over There," 185

P

Pabodie, Betty (Alden), 34
Padelford, Seth, 90, 108
Paper money (1786), 64
Papitto, Ralph, 227
Parsons, Usher, 156
Pascoag, 125, 193
Pastore, John O., 168, 219, 220, 245
Patent of 1644, 19
Patience Island, 231
Pawcatuck River, 10, 81, 142
Pawson, Leslie, 191
Pawtucket, 10, 12, 66–67, 70, 80, 82, 84, 89, 96,
  97, 102, 103, 116, 118, 119, 123, 130, 131, 132,
  150, 162, 166, 167, 168, 170, 172, 174, 175,
  176, 178, 180, 187, 189, 191, 193, 194, 205,
  206, 207, 209, 218, 226, 227, 235, 236, 240,
  244, 247
Pawtucket Falls, 22, 66, 67, 83
Pawtucket Indians, 235
Pawtucket Red Sox, 235
Pawtucket Slaters, 235
Pawtucket Times, 205
Pawtuxet, 19, 22, 96, 111, 148, 250
Pawtuxet River, 22, 97, 118, 130, 148, 157, 194,
  200, 224
Pawtuxet Valley, 69, 82, 97, 114–15, 116, 130,
  187
Peace Dale, 94, 239
Pell, Claiborne, 216, 222, 232, 238
Pembroke College, 120, 169
People, The, 165
People's Constitution, 69, 85, 86
People's Convention, 69, 84
Pepys, Nadine, 249
Pequot tribe, 10, 17, 20, 30
Perelman, S. J., 239
Perry, Christopher, 73, 77
Perry, Matthew C., 77, 95
Perry, Marsden, 63, 142, 163, 173
Perry, Oliver Hazard, 77, 78, 95, 121, 138
Perry, Sarah Wallace (Alexander), 77
Peterson-Puritan Corporation, 227
Pierce, Michael, 20, 28
Pieri, Lou, 233
Pilgrims, 16, 20, 34
Pitman, Joseph T., 109
Plainfield Pike, 80
Plante, David, 239
Plymouth Colony, 10, 16, 18, 20, 21, 25, 28, 29,
  34, 40
Point Judith, 192, 215, 229, 231
Point Judith Fishermen's Cooperative
  Association, 229
Polio (Infantile paralysis), 223

Polish-Americans, 59, 118, 162, 176, 181
Polish National Catholic Church, 176
Polo, 139
Ponagansett, 200, 258
Pontiac, 114, 132
Pontiac Mill, 114
Poppasquash Point, 100
Portsmouth, 19, 23, 24, 25, 55, 57, 82, 91, 140,
  162, 174, 183, 201, 203, 207, 247
Portsmouth Priory, 183
Portugal (Portuguese-Americans), 9, 13, 45,
  46, 118, 132, 161–62, 174–75, 181, 224, 252
Pothier, Aram J., 166, 203, 204
Potter, Elisha R., Jr., 107
Potter, George W., 239
Power, Hope, 46
Power, Nicholas, 44, 46
Precious Blood Church, 130
Prescott, Richard, 55
Prescott Farm (Overing House), 55
Preservation Society of Newport County,
  137–38, 218, 249
Prison (state), 87, 157
Prohibition, 105, 198
Providence, 10, 19, 20, 21, 22, 25, 27, 28, 31, 32,
  39, 42, 43, 46, 47, 48, 49, 50, 51, 52, 53, 54,
  55, 58, 59, 61, 62, 65, 67, 68, 69, 70, 71, 75,
  76, 78, 80, 81, 84, 85, 86, 87, 88, 89, 90, 91,
  93, 95, 96, 102, 105, 106, 108, 109, 110, 113,
  114–16, 117, 118, 119, 121, 123, 126, 128, 129,
  130, 131, 132, 136, 142, 144, 148, 149, 150,
  152, 153, 156, 157, 158, 159, 160, 161, 162,
  163, 164, 165, 166, 167, 168, 169, 170, 171,
  172, 173, 174, 175, 176, 177, 178, 179, 180,
  181, 182, 183, 184, 185, 186, 191, 192, 194,
  195, 198, 199, 200, 203, 204, 207, 208, 209,
  210, 211, 213, 217, 218, 219, 220, 221, 222,
  223, 224, 225, 226, 227, 228, 233, 234, 236,
  239, 240, 243, 244, 245, 246, 248, 249, 251,
  252, 254–57
Providence (ship, formerly *Katy*), 54
Providence and Worcester Railroad, 67, 81, 91,
  95, 102, 254
Providence Athenaeum, 68
Providence-Barrington Bible College (*see*
  Barrington College)
Providence City Council, 128, 129, 164, 222
Providence City Hall, 257
Providence City Hospital (Charles V. Chapin
  Hospital), 199
Providence College, 166, 168, 182, 199, 233,
  234, 253
Providence County, 27, 32, 80, 198
Providence Gas Company, 89
Providence Gazette, 43, 44, 49, 65
Providence Grays, 118, 149, 166
Providence Home for Aged Women, 90
Providence Journal, 90, 106, 107, 128, 164,
  183–84, 187–88, 191, 198, 203, 204, 205, 206,
  223, 239, 253
Providence Marine Corps of Artillery, 90, 91,
  108, 110
Providence Medical Society, 156
Providence Mental Health Center, 93
Providence Preservation Society (PPS), 218,
  249
Providence Public Library, 120
Providence Redevelopment Agency (PRA), 218
Providence Reform School, 90
Providence River, 21, 22, 81, 89, 134, 136, 220,
  221, 224, 231
Providence Steam Engine Company, 91
Providence Steam Roller, 166, 191, 233
Providence Tool Company, 91
Providence Town Meeting, 47
Providence, Warren, and Bristol Railroad, 89,
  145
Prox (ballot), 42
Prudence Island, 231

Public Works Administration (PWA), 201,
  202, 209
Pulitzer prize, 239
Puritans, 17, 28, 62
Putnam Pike, 80, 126

Q

Quakers (Society of Friends), 19, 28, 33, 49,
  60, 65, 68, 107, 127
Quasi-War with France (1798–1800), 73, 77
Quinn, Robert E., 166, 202, 203, 206–07
Quinnville, 174
Quonset hut, 212
Quonset Point, 158–59, 166, 168, 204, 212, 220,
  223, 224, 228, 232

R

Race Track War, 166, 206–07
Radbourn, Charles ("Old Hoss"), 118, 149
Radio, 166, 239, 240–41
Railroads, 67, 80, 81, 82, 89, 95, 96, 123, 127,
  142, 172, 173, 174, 225, 254–55
Rathom, John R., 183–84
Ray, Isaac, 93
Raytheon Corporation, 227
Recollections of Olden Times, 94
Red Cross, 211
Redevelopment Agency of Newport, 218
Redwood, Abraham, 37
Redwood Library, 37, 62
Reeves, David Wallis, 118
Rehoboth (Mass.), 25, 40, 102
Reidy, Edward P., 209
Renunciation of Allegiance (R.I.), 47, 53
Republican party, 90, 105, 108, 116, 118, 120,
  128, 129, 130, 132, 162–67, 168, 169, 170, 187,
  188, 198, 203, 204, 207, 209, 220, 222,
  226, 238
Retail trade, 218, 243, 244
Reynolds, Charles, 166
Rheem Manufacturing Company, 213
Rhode Island Bible Society, 68
Rhode Island College (Rhode Island Normal
  School), 88, 121, 153, 217–18, 241, 245
Rhode Island Company, 148, 173
Rhode Island Gazette, 37
Rhode Island Historical Preservation
  Commission, 249
Rhode Island Historical Society, 63, 71, 76,
  249
Rhode Island Hospital, 120, 156, 157, 195, 223
Rhode Island Hospital Trust Company, 156,
  257
Rhode Island Locomotive Works, 110
Rhode Island (Midland) Mall, 218, 244
Rhode Island Malleable Iron Works, 202
Rhode Island Peace Society, 68
Rhode Island Public Transit Authority
  (RIPTA), 173, 248
Rhode Island Red (hen), 104
Rhode Island Reds (hockey team), 168, 233
Rhode Island School of Design (RISD), 95,
  120, 152
Rhode Island Soldiers' Home (Bristol),
  113, 202
Rhode Island Suffrage Association, 84, 85
Rhode Island Train of Artillery, 57
Rhode Island Women's Suffrage Association,
  129
Rhodes, Elisha H., 111
Rhodes family, 194
Rhodes-on-the-Pawtuxet, 194, 198
Rice, Jim, 235
Rich, Robert (earl of Warwick), 25
Richmond, 123, 203, 246
Richmond Village, 200
Rider, Sidney S., 12
Rights of Colonies Examined, 49
Riordan, Mike, 234

ABOUT THE AUTHOR

Patrick T. Conley holds an A.B. from Providence College, an M.A. and Ph.D. from the University of Notre Dame, and a J.D. from Suffolk University Law School. His previous publications include *Democracy in Decline: Rhode Island's Constitutional Development, 1775-1841, Catholicism in Rhode Island: The Formative Era, Rhode Island Profile, Providence: A Pictorial History, The Irish in Rhode Island,* and more than a dozen scholarly articles for history, law, and political science journals. The youngest person ever elevated to the rank of full professor at Providence College, Dr. Conley also practices law, runs a used and rare book firm, and manages a real estate development business. He has served as chairman of the Cranston Historic District Commission, chairman of the Rhode Island Bicentennial Commission and Foundation (ri76), chairman and founder of the Providence Heritage Commission, chairman and founder of the Rhode Island Publications Society, and general editor of the Rhode Island Ethnic Heritage Pamphlet Series. In 1977 Dr. Conley founded the Rhode Island Heritage Commission as a successor organization to ri76.